The Prince of
Or, Why Constantinople Fe

Lew Wallace

Alpha Editions

This edition published in 2024

ISBN 9789362096746

Design and Setting By

Alpha Editions

www.alphaedis.com

Email - info@alphaedis.com

Contents

BOOK I
THE EARTH AND THE SEA ARE ALWAYS GIVING UP THEIR SECRETS

CHAPTER I.
THE NAMELESS BAY

In the noon of a September day in the year of our dear Lord 1395, a merchant vessel nodded sleepily upon the gentle swells of warm water flowing in upon the Syrian coast. A modern seafarer, looking from the deck of one of the Messagerie steamers now plying the same line of trade, would regard her curiously, thankful to the calm which held her while he slaked his wonder, yet more thankful that he was not of her passage.

She could not have exceeded a hundred tons burthen. At the bow and stern she was decked, and those quarters were fairly raised. Amidship she was low and open, and pierced for twenty oars, ten to a side, all swaying listlessly from the narrow ports in which they were hung. Sometimes they knocked against each other. One sail, square and of a dingy white, drooped from a broad yard-arm, which was itself tilted, and now and then creaked against the yellow mast complainingly, unmindful of the simple tackle designed to keep it in control. A watchman crouched in the meagre shade of a fan-like structure overhanging the bow deck. The roofing and the floor, where exposed, were clean, even bright; in all other parts subject to the weather and the wash there was only the blackness of pitch. The steersman sat on a bench at the stern. Occasionally, from force of habit, he rested a hand upon the rudder-oar to be sure it was yet in reach. With exception of the two, the lookout and the steersman, all on board, officers, oarsmen, and sailors, were asleep—such confidence could a Mediterranean calm inspire in those accustomed to life on the beautiful sea. As if Neptune never became angry there, and blowing his conch, and smiting with his trident, splashed the sky with the yeast of waves! However, in 1395 Neptune had disappeared; like the great god Pan, he was dead.

The next remarkable thing about the ship was the absence of the signs of business usual with merchantmen. There were no barrels, boxes, bales, or packages visible. Nothing indicated a cargo. In her deepest undulations the water-line was not once submerged. The leather shields of the oar-ports were high and dry. Possibly she had passengers aboard. Ah, yes! There under the awning, stretched halfway across the deck dominated by the steersman, was a group of persons all unlike seamen. Pausing to note them, we may find the motive of the voyage.

Four men composed the group. One was lying upon a pallet, asleep yet restless. A black velvet cap had slipped from his head, giving freedom to thick black hair tinged with white. Starting from the temples, a beard with scarce a suggestion of gray swept in dark waves upon the neck and throat, and even invaded the pillow. Between the hair and beard there was a narrow margin of sallow flesh for features somewhat crowded by knots of wrinkle. His body was wrapped in a loose woollen gown of brownish-black. A hand, apparently all bone, rested upon the breast, clutching a fold of the gown. The feet twitched nervously in the loosened thongs of old-fashioned sandals. Glancing at the others of the group, it was plain this sleeper was master and they his slaves. Two of them were stretched on the bare boards at the lower end of the pallet, and they were white. The third was a son of Ethiopia of unmixed blood and gigantic frame. He sat at the left of the couch, cross-legged, and, like the rest, was in a doze; now and then, however, he raised his head, and, without fully opening his eyes, shook a fan of peacock feathers from head to foot over the recumbent figure. The two whites were clad in gowns of coarse linen belted to their waists; while, saving a cincture around his loins, the negro was naked.

There is often much personal revelation to be gleaned from the properties a man carries with him from home. Applying the rule here, by the pallet there was a walking-stick of unusual length, and severely hand-worn a little above the middle. In emergency it might have been used as a weapon. Three bundles loosely wrapped had been cast against a timber of the ship; presumably they contained the plunder of the slaves reduced to the minimum allowance of travel. But the most noticeable item was a leather roll of very ancient appearance, held by a number of broad straps deeply stamped and secured by buckles of a metal blackened like neglected silver.

The attention of a close observer would have been attracted to this parcel, not so much by its antique showing, as by the grip with which its owner clung to it with his right hand. Even in sleep he held it of infinite consequence. It could not have contained coin or any bulky matter. Possibly the man was on some special commission, with his credentials in the old roll. Ay, who was he?

Thus started, the observer would have bent himself to study of the face; and immediately something would have suggested that while the stranger was of this period of the world he did not belong to it. Such were the magicians of the story-loving Al-Raschid. Or he was of the type Rabbinical that sat with Caiphas in judgment upon the gentle Nazarene. Only the centuries could have evolved the apparition. Who was he?

In the course of half an hour the man stirred, raised his head, looked hurriedly at his attendants, then at the parts of the ship in view, then at the steersman still dozing by the rudder; then he sat up, and brought the roll to his lap, whereat the rigor of his expression relaxed. The parcel was safe! And the conditions about him were as they should be!

He next set about undoing the buckles of his treasure. The long fingers were expert; but just when the roll was ready to open he lifted his face, and fixed his eyes upon the section of blue expanse outside the edge of the awning, and dropped into thought. And straightway it was settled that he was not a diplomatist or a statesman or a man of business of any kind. The reflection which occupied him had nothing to do with intrigues or statecraft; its centre was in his heart as the look proved. So, in tender moods, a father gazes upon his child, a husband at the beloved wife, restfully, lovingly.

And that moment the observer, continuing his study, would have forgotten the parcel, the white slaves, the gigantic negro, the self-willed hair and beard of pride—the face alone would have held him. The countenance of the Sphinx has no beauty now; and standing before it, we feel no stir of the admiration always a certificate that what we are beholding is charming out of the common lines; yet we are drawn to it irresistibly, and by a wish vague, foolish—so foolish we would hesitate long before putting it in words to be heard by our best lover—a wish that the monster would tell us all about itself. The feeling awakened by the face of the traveller would have been similar, for it was distinctly Israelitish, with exaggerated eyes set deeply in cavernous hollows—a mobile mask, in fact, concealing a life in some way unlike other lives. Unlike? That was the very attraction. If the man would only speak, what a tale he could unfold!

But he did not speak. Indeed, he seemed to have regarded speech a weakness to be fortified against. Putting the pleasant thought aside, he opened the roll, and with exceeding tenderness of touch brought forth a sheet of vellum dry to brittleness, and yellow as a faded sycamore leaf. There were lines upon it as of a geometrical drawing, and an inscription in strange characters. He bent over the chart, if such it may be called, eagerly, and read it through; then, with a satisfied expression, he folded it back into the cover, rebuckled the straps, and placed the parcel under the pillow. Evidently the business drawing him was proceeding as he would have had it. Next he woke the negro with a touch. The black in salute bent his body forward, and raised his hands palm out, the thumbs at the forehead. Attention singularly intense settled upon his countenance; he appeared to listen with his soul. It was time for speech, yet the master merely pointed to one of the sleepers. The watchful negro caught the idea, and going to the man, aroused him, then resumed his place and posture by the pallet. The action revealed his proportions. He looked as if he could have lifted the gates of Gaza, and borne them easily away; and to the strength there were superadded the grace, suppleness, and softness of motion of a cat. One could not have helped thinking the slave might have all the elements to make him a superior agent in fields of bad as well as good.

The second slave arose, and waited respectfully. It would have been difficult to determine his nationality. He had the lean face, the high nose, sallow complexion, and low stature of an Armenian. His countenance was pleasant and intelligent. In addressing him, the master made signs with hand and finger; and they appeared sufficient, for the servant walked away quickly as if on an errand. A short time, and he came back bringing a companion of the genus sailor, very red-faced, heavily built, stupid, his rolling gait unrelieved by a suggestion of good manners. Taking position before the black-gowned personage, his feet wide apart, the mariner said:

"You sent for me?"

The question was couched in Byzantine Greek.

"Yes," the passenger replied, in the same tongue, though with better accent. "Where are we?"

"But for this calm we should be at Sidon. The lookout reports the mountains in view."

The passenger reflected a moment, then asked, "Resorting to the oars, when can we reach the city?"

"By midnight."

"Very well. Listen now."

The speaker's manner changed; fixing his big eyes upon the sailor's lesser orbs, he continued:

"A few stadia north of Sidon there is what may be called a bay. It is about four miles across. Two little rivers empty into it, one on each side. Near the middle of the bend of the shore there is a well of sweet water, with flow enough to support a few villagers and their camels. Do you know the bay?"

The skipper would have become familiar.

"You are well acquainted with this coast," he said.

"Do you know of such a bay?" the passenger repeated.

"I have heard of it."

"Could you find it at night?"

"I believe so."

"That is enough. Take me into the bay, and land me at midnight. I will not go to the city. Get out all the oars now. At the proper time I will tell you what further I wish. Remember I am to be set ashore at midnight at a place which I will show you."

The directions though few were clear. Having given them, the passenger signed the negro to fan him, and stretched himself upon the pallet; and thenceforth there was no longer a question who was in control. It became the more interesting, however, to know the object of the landing at midnight on the shore of a lonesome unnamed bay.

CHAPTER II
THE MIDNIGHT LANDING

The skipper predicted like a prophet. The ship was in the bay, and it was midnight or nearly so; for certain stars had climbed into certain quarters of the sky, and after their fashion were striking the hour.

The passenger was pleased.

"You have done well," he said to the mariner. "Be silent now, and get close in shore. There are no breakers. Have the small boat ready, and do not let the anchors go."

The calm still prevailed, and the swells of the sea were scarce perceptible. Under the gentlest impulse of the oars the little vessel drifted broadside on until the keel touched the sands. At the same instant the small boat appeared. The skipper reported to the passenger. Going to each of the slaves, the latter signed them to descend. The negro swung himself down like a monkey, and received the baggage, which, besides the bundles already mentioned, consisted of some tools, notably a pick, a shovel, and a stout crowbar. An empty water-skin was also sent down, followed by a basket suggestive of food. Then the passenger, with a foot over the side of the vessel, gave his final directions.

"You will run now," he said to the skipper, who, to his credit, had thus far asked no questions, "down to the city, and lie there to-morrow, and to-morrow night. Attract little notice as possible. It is not necessary to pass the gate. Put out in time to be here at sunrise. I will be waiting for you. Day after to-morrow at sunrise—remember."

"But if you should not be here?" asked the sailor, thinking of extreme probabilities.

"Then wait for me," was the answer.

The passenger, in turn, descended to the boat, and was caught in the arms of the black, and seated carefully as he had been a child. In brief time the party was ashore, and the boat returning to the ship; a little later, the ship withdrew to where the night effectually curtained the deep.

The stay on the shore was long enough to apportion the baggage amongst the slaves. The master then led the way. Crossing the road running from Sidon along the coast to the up-country, they came to the foothills of the mountain, all without habitation.

Later they came upon signs of ancient life in splendor—broken columns, and here and there Corinthian capitals in marble discolored and sunk deeply in sand and mould. The patches of white on them had a ghastly glimmer in the starlight. They were approaching the site of an old city, a suburb probably of Palae-Tyre when she was one of the spectacles of the world, sitting by the sea to rule it regally far and wide.

On further a small stream, one of those emptying into the bay, had ploughed a ravine for itself across the route the party was pursuing. Descending to the water, a halt was made to drink, and fill the water-skin, which the negro took on his shoulder.

On further there was another ancient site strewn with fragments indicative of a cemetery. Hewn stones were frequent, and mixed with them were occasional entablatures and vases from which the ages had not yet entirely worn the fine chiselling. At length an immense uncovered sarcophagus barred the way. The master stopped by it to study the heavens; when he found the north star, he gave the signal to his followers, and moved under the trail of the steadfast beacon.

They came to a rising ground more definitely marked by sarcophagi hewn from the solid rock, and covered by lids of such weight and solidity that a number of them had never been disturbed. Doubtless the dead within were lying as they had been left—but when, and by whom? What disclosures there will be when at last the end is trumpeted in!

On further, but still connected with the once magnificent funeral site, they encountered a wall many feet thick, and short way beyond it, on the mountain's side, there were two arches of a bridge of which all else had been broken down; and these two had never spanned anything more substantial than the air. Strange structure for such a locality! Obviously the highway which once ran over it had begun in the city the better to communicate with the cemetery through which the party had just passed. So much was of easy understanding; but where was the other terminus? At sight of the arches the master drew a long breath of relief. They were the friends for whom he had been searching.

Nevertheless, without stopping, he led down into a hollow on all sides sheltered from view; and there the unloading took place. The tools and bundles were thrown down by a rock, and preparations made for the remainder of the night. The pallet was spread for the master. The basket gave up its contents, and the party refreshed themselves and slept the sleep of the weary.

The secluded bivouac was kept the next day. Only the master went forth in the afternoon. Climbing the mountain, he found the line in continuation of the bridge; a task the two arches serving as a base made comparatively easy. He stood then upon a bench or terrace cumbered with rocks, and so broad that few persons casually looking would have suspected it artificial. Facing fully about from the piers, he walked forward following the terrace which at places was out of line, and piled with debris tumbled from the mountain on the right hand side; in a few minutes that silent guide turned with an easy curve and disappeared in what had yet the appearance hardly distinguishable of an area wrenched with enormous labor from a low cliff of solid brown limestone.

The visitor scanned the place again and again; then he said aloud:

"No one has been here since"—

The sentence was left unfinished.

That he could thus identify the spot, and with such certainty pass upon it in relation to a former period, proved he had been there before.

Rocks, earth, and bushes filled the space. Picking footway through, he examined the face of the cliff then in front of him, lingering longest on the heap of breakage forming a bank over the meeting line of area and hill.

"Yes," he repeated, this time with undisguised satisfaction, "no one has been here since"—

Again the sentence was unfinished.

He ascended the bank next, and removed some of the stones at the top. A carved line in low relief on the face of the rock was directly exposed; seeing it he smiled, and replaced the stones, and descending, went back to the terrace, and thence to the slaves in bivouac.

From one of the packages he had two iron lamps of old Roman style brought out, and supplied with oil and wicks; then, as if everything necessary to his project was done, he took to the pallet. Some goats had come to the place in his absence, but no living creature else.

After nightfall the master woke the slaves, and made final preparation for the venture upon which he had come. The tools he gave to one man, the lamps to another, and the water-skin to the negro. Then he led out of the hollow, and up the mountain to the terrace visited in the afternoon; nor did he pause in the area mentioned as the abrupt terminus of the highway over the skeleton piers. He climbed the bank of stones covering the foot of the cliff up to the precise spot at which his reconnoissance had ended.

Directly the slaves were removing the bank at the top; not a difficult task since they had only to roll the loose stones down a convenient grade. They worked industriously. At length—in half an hour probably—an opening into the cliff was discovered. The cavity, small at first, rapidly enlarged, until it gave assurance of a doorway of immense proportions. When the enlargement sufficed for his admission, the master stayed the work, and passed in. The slaves followed. The interior descent offered a grade corresponding with that of the bank outside—another bank, in fact, of like composition, but more difficult to pass on account of the darkness.

With his foot the leading adventurer felt the way down to a floor; and when his assistants came to him, he took from a pocket in his gown a small case filled with a chemical powder which he poured at his feet; then he produced a flint and steel, and struck them together. Some sparks dropped upon the powder. Instantly a flame arose and filled the place with a ruddy illumination. Lighting the lamps by the flame, the party looked around them, the slaves with simple wonder.

They were in a vault—a burial vault of great antiquity. Either it was an imitation of like chambers in Egypt, or they were imitations of it. The excavation had been done with chisels. The walls were niched, giving them an appearance of panelling, and over each of the niches there had been an inscription in raised letters, now mostly defaced. The floor was a confusion of fragments knocked from sarcophagi, which, massive as they were, had been tilted, overturned, uncovered, mutilated, and robbed. Useless to inquire whose the vandalism. It may have been of Chaldeans of the time of Almanezor, or of the Greeks who marched with Alexander, or of Egyptians who were seldom regardful of the dead of the peoples they overthrew as they were of their own, or of Saracens, thrice conquerors along the Syrian coast, or of Christians. Few of the Crusaders were like St. Louis.

But of all this the master took no notice. With him it was right that the vault should look the wreck it was. Careless of inscriptions, indifferent to carving, his eyes ran rapidly along the foot of the northern wall until they came to a sarcophagus of green marble. Thither he proceeded. He laid his hand upon the half-turned lid, and observing that the back of the great box—if such it may be termed—was against the wall, he said again:

"No one has been here since"—

And again the sentence was left unfinished.

Forthwith he became all energy. The negro brought the crowbar, and, by direction, set it under the edge of the sarcophagus, which he held raised while the master blocked it at the bottom with a stone chip. Another bite, and a larger chip was inserted. Good hold being thus had, a vase was placed for fulcrum; after which, at every downward pressure of the iron, the ponderous coffin swung round a little to the left. Slowly and with labor the movement was continued until the space behind was uncovered.

By this time the lamps had become the dependencies for light. With his in hand, the master stooped and inspected the exposed wall. Involuntarily the slaves bent forward and looked, but saw nothing different from the general surface in that quarter. The master beckoned the negro, and touching a stone not wider than his three fingers, but reddish in hue, and looking like mere chinking lodged in an accidental crevice, signed him to strike it with the end of the bar. Once—twice—the stone refused to stir; with the third blow it was driven in out of sight, and, being followed vigorously, was heard to drop on the other side. The wall thereupon, to the height of the sarcophagus and the width of a broad door, broke, and appeared about to tumble down.

When the dust cleared away, there was a crevice unseen before, and wide enough to admit a hand. The reader must remember there were masons in the old time who amused themselves applying their mathematics to such puzzles. Here obviously the intention had been to screen an entrance to an adjoining chamber, and the key to the design had been the sliver of red granite first displaced.

A little patient use then of hand and bar enabled the workman to take out the first large block of the combination. That the master numbered with chalk, and had carefully set aside. A second block was taken out, numbered, and set aside; finally the screen was demolished, and the way stood open.

CHAPTER III
THE HIDDEN TREASURE

The slaves looked dubiously at the dusty aperture, which held out no invitation to them; the master, however, drew his robe closer about him, and stooping went in, lamp in hand. They then followed.

An ascending passage, low but of ample width, received them. It too had been chiselled from the solid rock. The wheel marks of the cars used in the work were still on the floor. The walls were bare but smoothly dressed. Altogether the interest here lay in expectation of what was to come; and possibly it was that which made the countenance of the master look so grave and absorbed. He certainly was not listening to the discordant echoes roused as he advanced.

The ascent was easy. Twenty-five or thirty steps brought them to the end of the passage.

They then entered a spacious chamber circular and domed. The light of the lamps was not enough to redeem the ceiling from obscurity; yet the master led without pause to a sarcophagus standing under the centre of the dome, and when he was come there everything else was forgotten by him.

The receptacle of the dead thus discovered had been hewn from the rock, and was of unusual proportions. Standing broadside to the entrance, it was the height of an ordinary man, and twice as long as high. The exterior had been polished smoothly as the material would allow; otherwise it was of absolute plainness, looking not unlike a dark brown box. The lid was a slab of the finest white marble carven into a perfect model of Solomon's Temple. While the master surveyed the lid he was visibly affected. He passed the lamp over it slowly, letting the light fall into the courts of the famous building; in like manner he illuminated the corridors, and the tabernacle; and, as he did so, his features trembled and his eyes were suffused. He walked around the exquisite representation several times, pausing now and then to blow away the dust that had in places accumulated upon it. He noticed the effect of the transparent whiteness in the chamber; so in its day the original had lit up the surrounding world. Undoubtedly the model had peculiar hold upon his feelings.

But shaking the weakness off he after a while addressed himself to work. He had the negro thrust the edge of the bar under the lid, and raise it gently. Having thoughtfully provided himself in the antechamber with pieces of stone for the purpose, he placed one of them so as to hold the vantage gained. Slowly, then, by working at the ends alternately, the immense slab was turned upon its centre; slowly the hollow of the coffin was flooded with light; slowly, and with seeming reluctance, it gave up its secrets.

In strong contrast to the plainness of the exterior, the interior of the sarcophagus was lined with plates and panels of gold, on which there were cartoons chased and beaten in, representing ships, and tall trees, doubtless cedars of Lebanon, and masons at work, and two men armed and in royal robes greeting each other with clasped hands; and so beautiful were the cartoons that the eccentric medalleur, Cellini, would have studied them long, if not enviously. Yet he who now peered into the receptacle scarcely glanced at them.

On a stone chair seated was the mummy of a man with a crown upon its head, and over its body, for the most part covering—the linen wrappings, was a robe of threads of gold in ample arrangement. The hands rested on the lap; in one was a sceptre; the other held an inscribed silver tablet. There were rings plain, and rings with jewels in setting, circling the fingers and thumbs; the ears, ankles, even the great toes, were ornamented in like manner. At the feet a sword of the fashion of a cimeter had been laid. The blade was in its scabbard, but the scabbard was a mass of jewels, and the handle a flaming ruby. The belt was webbed with pearls and glistening brilliants. Under the sword were the instruments sacred then and ever since to Master Masons—a square, a gavel, a plummet, and an inscribing compass.

The man had been a king—so much the first glance proclaimed. With him, as with his royal brethren from the tombs along the Nile, death had asserted itself triumphantly over the embalmer. The cheeks were shrivelled and mouldy; across the forehead the skin was drawn tight; the temples were hollows rimmed abruptly with the frontal bones; the eyes, pits partially filled with dried ointments of a bituminous color. The monarch had yielded his life in its full ripeness, for the white hair and beard still adhered in stiffened plaits to the skull, cheeks, and chin. The nose alone was natural; it stood up thin and hooked, like the beak of an eagle.

At sight of the figure thus caparisoned and maintaining its seat in an attitude of calm composure the slaves drew back startled. The negro dropped his iron bar, making the chamber ring with a dissonant clangor.

Around the mummy in careful arrangement were vessels heaped with coins and pearls and precious stones, cut and ready for the goldsmith. Indeed, the whole inner space of the sarcophagus was set with basins and urns, each in itself a work of high art; and if their contents were to be judged by what appeared overflowing them, they all held precious stones of every variety.

The corners had been draped with cloths of gold and cloths embroidered with pearls, some of which were now falling to pieces of their own weight.

We know that kings and queens are but men and women subject to the same passions of common people; that they are generous or sordid according to their natures; that there have been misers amongst them; but this one—did he imagine he could carry his amassments with him out of the world? Had he so loved the gems in his life as to dream he could illumine his tomb with them? If so, O royal idiot!

The master, when an opening had been made sufficiently wide by turning the lid upon the edge of the sarcophagus, took off his sandals, gave a foot to one of his slaves, and swung himself into the interior. The lamp was then given him, and he surveyed the wealth and splendor as the king might never again. And as the king in his day had said with exultation, Lo! it is all mine, the intruder now asserted title.

Unable, had he so wished, to carry the whole collection off, he looked around upon this and upon that, determining where to begin. Conscious he had nothing to fear, and least of all from the owner in the chair, he was slow and deliberate. From his robe he drew a number of bags of coarse hempen cloth, and a broad white napkin. The latter he spread upon the floor, first removing several of the urns to obtain space; then he emptied one of the vessels upon it, and from the sparkling and varicolored heap before him proceeded to make selection.

His judgment was excellent, sure and swift. Not seldom he put the large stones aside, giving preference to color and lustre. Those chosen he dropped into a bag. When the lot was gone through, he returned the rejected to the vessel, placing it back exactly in its place. Then he betook himself to another of the vessels, and then another, until, in course of a couple of hours, he had made choice from the collection, and filled nine bags, and tied them securely.

Greatly relieved, he arose, rubbed the benumbed joints of his limbs awhile, then passed the packages out to the slaves. The occupation had been wearisome and tensive; but it was finished, and he would now retire. He lingered to give a last look at the interior, muttering the sentence again, and leaving it unfinished as before:

"No one has been here since"—

From the face of the king, his eyes fell to the silver tablet in the nerveless hand. Moving close, and holding the lamp in convenient position, he knelt and read the inscription.

I.

"There is but one God, and He was from the beginning, and will be without end.

II.

"In my lifetime, I prepared this vault and tomb to receive my body, and keep it safely; yet it may be visited, for the earth and sea are always giving up their secrets.

III.

"Therefore, O Stranger, first to find me, know thou!

"That in all my days I kept intercourse with Solomon, King of the Jews, wisest of men, and the richest and greatest. As is known, he set about building a house to his Lord God, resolved that there should be nothing like it in the world, nothing so spacious, so enriched, so perfect in proportions, so in all things becoming the glory of his God. In sympathy with him I gave him of the skill of my people, workers in brass, and silver, and gold, and products of the quarries: and in their ships my sailors brought him the yield of mines from the ends of the earth. At last the house was finished; then he sent me the model of the house, and the coins, and cloths of gold and pearl, and the precious stones, and the vessels holding them, and the other things of value here. Ad if, O Stranger, thou dost wonder at the greatness of the gift, know thou that it was but a small part of what remained unto him of like kind, for he was master of the earth, and of everything belonging to it which might be of service to him, even the elements and their subtleties.

IV.

"Nor think, O Stranger, that I have taken the wealth into the tomb with me, imagining it can serve me in the next life. I store it here because I love him who gave it to me, and am jealous of his love; and that is all.

V.

"So thou wilt use the wealth in ways pleasing in the sight of the Lord God of Solomon, my royal friend, take thou of it in welcome. There is no God but his God!

"Thus say I—HIRAM, KING OF TYRE."

"Rest thou thy soul, O wisest of pagan kings," said the master, rising. "Being the first to find thee here, and basing my title to thy wealth on that circumstance, I will use it in a way pleasing in the sight of the Lord God of Solomon. Verily, verily, there is no God but his God!"

This, then, was the business that brought the man to the tomb of the king whose glory was to have been the friend of Solomon. Pondering the idea, we begin to realize how vast the latter's fame was; and it ceases to be matter of wonder that his contemporaries, even the most royal, could have been jealous of his love.

Not only have we the man's business, but it is finished; and judging from the satisfaction discernible on his face as he raised the lamp and turned to depart, the result must have been according to his best hope. He took off his robe, and tossed it to his slaves; then he laid a hand upon the edge of the sarcophagus preparatory to climbing out. At the moment, while giving a last look about him, an emerald, smoothly cut, and of great size, larger indeed than a full-grown pomegranate, caught his eyes in its place loose upon the floor. He turned back, and taking it up, examined it carefully; while thus engaged his glance dropped to the sword almost at his feet. The sparkle of the brilliants, and the fire-flame of the great ruby in the grip, drew him irresistibly, and he stood considering.

Directly he spoke in a low voice:

"No one has been here since"—

He hesitated—glanced hurriedly around to again assure himself it was not possible to be overheard—then finished the sentence:

"No one has been here *since I came a thousand years ago.*"

At the words so strange, so inexplicable upon any theory of nature and common experience, the lamp shook in his hand. Involuntarily he shrank from the admission, though to himself. But recovering, he repeated:

"Since I came a thousand years ago."

Then he added more firmly:

"But the earth and the sea are always giving up their secrets. So saith the good King Hiram; and since I am a witness proving the wisdom of the speech, I at least must believe him. Wherefore it is for me to govern myself as if another will shortly follow me. The saying of the king is an injunction."

With that, he turned the glittering sword over and over admiringly. Loath to let it go, he drew the blade partly from the scabbard, and its clearness had the depth peculiar to the sky between stars at night.

"Is there anything it will not buy," he continued, reflectively. "What king could refuse a sword once Solomon's? I will take it."

Thereupon he passed both the emerald and the sword out to the slaves, whom he presently joined.

The conviction, but a moment before expressed, that another would follow him to the tomb of the venerated Tyrian, was not strong enough to hinder the master from attempting to hide every sign which might aid in the discovery. The negro, under his direction, returned the lid exactly to its former fitting place on the sarcophagus; the emerald and the sword he wrapped in his gown; the bags and the tools were counted and distributed among the slaves for easy carriage. Lamp in hand, he then walked around to see that nothing was left behind. Incidentally he even surveyed the brown walls and the dim dome overhead. Having reached the certainty that everything was in its former state, he waved his hand, and with one long look backward at the model, ghostly beautiful in its shining white transparency, he led the way to the passage of entrance, leaving the king to his solitude and stately sleep, unmindful of the visitation and the despoilment.

Out in the large reception room, he paused again to restore the wall. Beginning with the insignificant key, one by one the stones, each of which, as we have seen, had been numbered by him, were raised and reset. Then handfuls of dust were collected and blown into the slight crevices till they were invisible. The final step was the restoration of the sarcophagus; this done, the gallery leading to the real vault of the king was once more effectually concealed.

"He who follows, come he soon or late, must have more than sharp eyes if he would have audience with Hiram, my royal friend of Tyre," the adventurer said, in his meditative way, feeling at the same time in the folds of his gown for the chart so the object of solicitude on the ship. The roll, the emerald, and the sword were also safe. Signing the slaves to remain where they were, he moved slowly across the chamber, and by aid of his lamp surveyed an aperture there so broad and lofty it was suggestive of a gate rather than a door.

"It is well," he said, smiling. "The hunter of spoils, hereafter as heretofore, will pass this way instead of the other."

The remark was shrewd. Probably nothing had so contributed to the long concealment of the gallery just reclosed the second time in a thousand years as the high doorway, with its invitation to rooms beyond it, all now in iconoclastic confusion.

Rejoining his workmen, he took a knife from the girdle of one of them, and cut a slit in the gurglet large enough to admit the bags of precious stones. The skin was roomy, and received them, though with the loss of much of the water. Having thus disposed of that portion of the plunder to the best advantage both for portage and concealment, he helped swing it securely upon the negro's shoulder, and without other delay led from the chamber to the great outdoors, where the lamps were extinguished.

The pure sweet air, as may be imagined, was welcome to every one. While the slaves stood breathing it in wholesome volumes, the master studied the stars, and saw the night was not so far gone but that, with industry, the sea-shore could be made in time for the ship.

Still pursuing the policy of hiding the road to the tomb much as possible, he waited while the men covered the entrance as before with stones brought up from the bank. A last survey of the face of the rock, minute as the starlight allowed, reassured him that, as to the rest of the world, the treasure might remain with its ancient owner undisturbed for yet another thousand years, if not forever; after which, in a congratulatory mood, he descended the mountain side to the place of bivouac, and thence in good time, and without adventure, arrived at the landing by the sea. There the negro, wading far out, flung the tools into the water.

In the appointed time the galley came down from the city, and, under impulsion of the oars, disappeared with the party up the coast northward.

The negro unrolled the pallet upon the deck, and brought some bread, Smyrna figs, and wine of Prinkipo, and the four ate and drank heartily.

The skipper was then summoned.

"You have done well, my friend," said the master. "Spare not sail or oar now, but make Byzantium without looking into any wayside port. I will increase your pay in proportion as you shorten the time we are out. Look to it—go—and speed you."

Afterward the slaves in turn kept watch while he slept. And though the coming and going of sailors was frequent, not one of them noticed the oil-stained water-skin cast carelessly near the master's pillow, or the negro's shaggy half-cloak, serving as a wrap for the roll, the emerald, and the sword once Solomon's.

The run of the galley from the nameless bay near Sidon was without stop or so much as a headwind. Always the blue sky above the deck, and the blue sea below. In daytime the master passenger would occasionally pause in his walk along the white planks, and, his hand on the gunwale, give a look at some of the landmarks studding the ancient Cycladean Sea, an island here, or a tall promontory of the continent yonder, possibly an Olympian height faintly gray in the vaster distance. His manner at such moments did not indicate a traveller new to the highway. A glance at the points such as business men closely pressed give the hands on the face of a clock to determine the minute of the hour, and he would resume walking. At night he slept right soundly.

From the Dardanelles into the Hellespont; then the Marmora. The captain would have coasted, but the passenger bade him keep in the open. "There is nothing to fear from the weather," he said, "but there is time to be saved."

In an afternoon they sighted the great stones Oxia and Plati; the first, arid and bare as a gray egg, and conical like an irregular pyramid; the other, a plane on top, with verdure and scattering trees. A glance at the map shows them the most westerly group of the Isles of the Princes.

Now Nature is sometimes stupid, sometimes whimsical, doing unaccountable things. One gazing at the other isles of the group from a softly rocking caique out a little way on the sea divines instantly that she meant them for summer retreats, but these two, Oxia and Plati, off by themselves, bleak in winter, apparently always ready for spontaneous combustion in the heated months, for what were they designed? No matter—uses were found for them—fitting uses. Eremites in search of the hardest, grimmest places, selected Oxia, and pecking holes and caves in its sides, shared the abodes thus laboriously won with cormorants, the most gluttonous of birds. In time a rude convent was built near the summit. On the other hand, Plati was converted into a Gehenna for criminals, and in the vats and dungeons with which it was provided, lives were spent weeping for liberty. On this isle, tears and curses; on that, tears and prayers.

At sundown the galley was plying its oars between Oxia and the European shore about where St. Stephano is now situated. The dome of Sta. Sophia was in sight; behind it, in a line to the northwest, arose the tower of Galata. "Home by lamplighting—Blessed be the Virgin!" the mariners said to each other piously. But no! The master passenger sent for the captain.

"I do not care to get into harbor before morning. The night is delicious, and I will try it in the small boat. I was once a rower, and yet have a fancy for the oars. Do thou lay off and on hereabouts. Put two lamps at the masthead that I may know thy vessel when I desire to return. Now get out the boat."

The captain thought his voyager queer of taste; nevertheless he did as told. In a short time the skiff—if the familiar word can be pardoned—put off with the negro and his master, the latter at the oars.

In preparation for the excursion the gurglet half full of water and the sheepskin mantle of the black man were lowered into the little vessel. The boat moved away in the direction of Prinkipo, the mother isle of the group; and as the night deepened, it passed from view.

When out of sight from the galley's deck, the master gave the rowing to the negro, and taking seat by the rudder, changed direction to the southeast; after which he kept on and on, until Plati lay directly in his course.

The southern extremity of Plati makes quite a bold bluff. In a period long gone a stone tower had been constructed there, a lookout and shelter for guardsmen on duty; and there being no earthly chance of escape for prisoners, so securely were they immured, the duty must have been against robbers from the mainland on the east, and from pirates generally. Under the tower there was a climb difficult for most persons in daylight, and from the manoeuvring of the boat, the climb was obviously the object drawing the master. He at length found it, and stepped out on a shelving stone. The gurglet and mantle were passed to him, and soon he and his follower were feeling their way upward.

On the summit, the chief walked once around the tower, now the merest ruin, a tumbledown without form, in places overgrown with sickly vines. Rejoining his attendant, and staying a moment to thoroughly empty the gurglet of water, on his hands and knees he crawled into a passage much obstructed by debris. The negro waited outside.

The master made two trips; the first one, he took the gurglet in; the second, he took the mantle wrapping the sword. At the end, he rubbed his hands in self-congratulation.

"They are safe—the precious stones of Hiram, and the sword of Solomon! Three other stores have I like this one—in India, in Egypt, in Jerusalem— and there is the tomb by Sidon. Oh, I shall not come to want!" and he laughed well pleased.

The descent to the small boat was effected without accident.

Next morning toward sunrise the passengers disembarked at Port St. Peter on the south side of the Golden Horn. A little later the master was resting at home in Byzantium.

Within three days the mysterious person whom we, wanting his proper name and title, have termed the master, had sold his house and household effects. In the night of the seventh day, with his servants, singular in that all of them were deaf and dumb, he went aboard ship, and vanished down the Marmora, going no one but himself knew whither.

The visit to the tomb of the royal friend of Solomon had evidently been to provide for the journey; and that he took precious stones in preference to gold and silver signified a journey indefinite as to time and place.

BOOK II
THE PRINCE OF INDIA

CHAPTER I
A MESSENGER FROM CIPANGO

Just fifty-three years after the journey to the tomb of the Syrian king—more particularly on the fifteenth day of May, fourteen hundred and forty-eight—a man entered one of the stalls of a market in Constantinople—to-day the market would be called a bazaar—and presented a letter to the proprietor.

The Israelite thus honored delayed opening the linen envelope while he surveyed the messenger. The liberty, it must be remarked, was not a usual preliminary in the great city, the cosmopolitanism of which had been long established; that is to say, a face, a figure, or a mode, to gain a second look from one of its denizens, had then, as it has now, to be grossly outlandish. In this instance the owner of the stall indulged a positive stare. He had seen, he thought, representatives of all known nationalities, but never one like the present visitor—never one so pinkish in complexion, and so very bias-eyed—never one who wrapped and re-wrapped himself in a single shawl so entirely, making it answer all the other vestments habitual to men. The latter peculiarity was more conspicuous in consequence of a sack of brown silk hanging loosely from the shoulder, with leaves and flowers done in dazzling embroidery down the front and around the edges. And then the slippers were of silk not less rich with embroidery, while over the bare head a sunshade of bamboo and paper brilliantly painted was carried.

Too well bred to persist in the stare or attempt to satisfy his curiosity by a direct question, the proprietor opened the letter, and began reading it. His neighbors less considerate ran together, and formed a crowd around the stranger, who nevertheless bore the inspection composedly, apparently unconscious of anything to make him such a cynosure.

The paper which the removal of the envelope gave to the stall-keeper's hand excited him the more. The delicacy of its texture, its softness to the touch, its semi-transparency, were unlike anything he had ever seen; it was not only foreign, but very foreign.

The lettering, however, was in Greek plainly done. He noticed first the date; then, his curiosity becoming uncontrollable, and the missive being of but one sheet, his eyes dropped to the place of signature. There was no name there—only a seal—an impression on a surface of yellow wax of the drooping figure of a man bound to a cross.

[Illustration]

At sight of the seal his eyes opened wider. He drew a long breath to quiet a rising feeling, half astonishment, half awe. Retreating to a bench near by, he seated himself, and presently became unmindful of the messenger, of the crowd, of everything, indeed, except the letter and the matters of which it treated.

The demand of the reader for a sight of the paper which could produce such an effect upon a person who was not more than an ordinary dealer in an Eastern market may by this time have become imperious; wherefore it is at once submitted in free translation. Only the date is modernized.

"ISLAND IN THE OVER-SEA. FAR EAST. *May* 15, A.D. 1447.

"Uel, Son of Jahdai.

"Peace to thee and all thine!

"If thou hast kept faithfully the heirlooms of thy progenitors, somewhere in thy house there is now a duplication of the seal which thou wilt find hereto attached; only that one is done in gold. The reference is to prove to thee a matter I am pleased to assert, knowing it will at least put thee upon inquiry—I knew thy father, thy grandfather, and his father, and others of thy family further back than it is wise for me to declare; and I loved them, for they were a virtuous and goodly race, studious to do the will of the Lord God of Israel, and acknowledging no other; therein manifesting the chiefest of human excellences. To which, as more directly personal to thyself, I will add that qualities of men, like qualities in plants, are transmissible, and go they unmixed through many generations, they make a kind. Therefore, at this great distance, and though I have never looked into thy face, or touched thy hand, or heard thy voice, I know thee, and give thee trust confidently. The son of thy father cannot tell the world what he has of me here, or that there is a creature like unto me living, or that he has to do with me in the least; and as the father would gladly undertake my requests, even those I now reveal unto thee, not less willingly will his son undertake them. Refusal would be the first step toward betrayal.

"With this preface, O Son of Jahdai, I write without fear, and freely; imparting, first, that it is now fifty years since I set foot upon the shores of this Island, which, for want of a name likely to be known to thee, I have located and described as 'In the Over-Sea. Far East.' Its people are by nature kindly disposed to strangers, and live simply and affectionately. Though they never heard of the Nazarene whom the world persists in calling the Christ, it is truth to say they better illustrate his teachings, especially in their dealings with each other, than the so-called Christians amongst whom thy lot is cast. Withal, however, I have become weary, the fault being more in myself than in them. Desire for change is the universal law. Only God is the same yesterday, to-day, and to-morrow eternally. So I am resolved to seek once more the land of our fathers and Jerusalem, for which I yet have tears. In her perfection, she was more than beautiful; in her ruin, she is more than sacred.

"In the execution of my design, know thou next, O Son of Jahdai, that I despatch my servant, Syama, intrusting him to deliver this letter. When it is put into thy hand, note the day, and see if it be not exactly one year from this 15 May, the time I have given him to make the journey, which is more by sea than land. Thou mayst then know I am following him, though with stoppages of uncertain duration; it being necessary for me to cross from India to Mecca; thence to Kash-Cush, and down the Nile to Cairo. Nevertheless I hope to greet thee in person within six months after Syama hath given thee this report.

"The sending a courier thus in advance is with a design of which I think it of next importance to inform thee.

"It is my purpose to resume residence in Constantinople; for that, I must have a house. Syama, amongst other duties in my behalf, is charged to purchase and furnish one, and have it ready to receive me when I arrive. The day is long passed since a Khan had attractions for me. Much more agreeable is it to think my own door will open instantly at my knock. In this affair thou canst be of service which shall be both remembered and gratefully recompensed. He hath no experience in the matter of property in thy city; thou hast; it is but natural, therefore, if I pray thou bring it into practice by assisting him in the selection, in perfecting the title, and in all else the project may require doing; remembering only that the tenement be plain and comfortable, not rich; for, alas! the time is not yet when the children of Israel may live conspicuously in the eye of the Christian world.

"Thou wilt find Syama shrewd and of good judgment, older than he seemeth, and quick to render loyalty for my sake. Be advised also that he is deaf and dumb; yet, if in speaking thou turn thy face to him, and use the Greek tongue, he will understand thee by the motion of thy lips, and make answer by signs.

"Finally, be not afraid to accept this commission on account of pecuniary involvement. Syama hath means of procuring all the money he may require, even to extravagance; at the same time he is forbidden to contract a debt, except it be to thee for kindness done, all which he will report to me so I may pay them fitly.

"In all essential things Syama hath full instructions; besides, he is acquainted with my habits and tastes; wherefore I conclude this writing by saying I hope thou wilt render him aid as indicated, and that when I come thou wilt allow me to relate myself to thee as father to son, in all things a help, in nothing a burden.

"Again, O Son of Jahdai, to thee and thine—Peace!"

[Seal.]

The son of Jahdai, at the conclusion of the reading, let his hands fall heavily in his lap, while he plunged into a study which the messenger with his foreign airs could not distract.

Very great distance is one of the sublimities most powerful over the imagination. The letter had come from an Island he had never heard named. An Island in the Over-Sea which doubtless washed the Eastern end of the earth, wherever that might be. And the writer! How did he get there? And what impelled him to go?

A chill shot the thinker's nerves. He suddenly remembered that in his house there was a cupboard in a wall, with two shelves devoted to storage of heirlooms; on the upper shelf lay the *torah* of immemorial usage in his family; the second contained cups of horn and metal, old phylacteries, amulets, and things of vertu in general, and of such addition and multiplication through the ages that he himself could not have made a list of them; in fact, now his attention was aroused, he recalled them a mass of colorless and formless objects which had ceased to have history or value. Amongst them, however, a seal in the form of a medallion in gold recurred to him; but whether the impression upon it was raised or sunken he could not have certainly said; nor could he have told what the device was. His father and grandfather had esteemed it highly, and the story they told him about it divers times when he was a child upon their knees he could repeat quite substantially.

A man committed an indignity to Jesus the pretended *Christ*, who, in punishment, condemned him to linger on the earth until in the fulness of time he should come again; and the man had gone on living through the centuries. Both the father and grandfather affirmed the tale to be true; they had known the unfortunate personally; yet more, they declared he had been an intimate of the family, and had done its members through generations friendlinesses without number; in consequence they had come to consider him one of them in love. They had also said that to their knowledge it was his custom to pray for death regularly as the days came and went. He had repeatedly put himself in its way; yet curiously it passed him by, until he at last reached a conviction he could not die.

Many years had gone since the stall-keeper last heard the tale, and still more might have been counted since the man disappeared, going no one knew whither.

But he was not dead! He was coming again! It was too strange to believe! It could not be! Yet one thing was clear—whatever the messenger might be, or presuming him a villain, whatever the lie he thought to make profitable, appeal could be safely and cheaply made to the seal in the cupboard. As a witness it, too, was deaf and dumb; on its face nevertheless there was revelation and the truth.

Through the momentary numbness of his faculties so much the son of Jahdai saw, and he did not wait. Signing the messenger to follow, he passed into a closet forming part of the stall, and the two being alone, he spoke in Greek.

"Be thou seated here," he said, "and wait till I return."

The messenger smiled and bowed, and took seat; thereupon Uel drew his turban down to his ears, and, letter in hand, started home.

His going was rapid; sometimes he almost ran. Acquaintances met him on the street, but he did not see them; if they spoke to him, he did not hear. Arrived at his own door, he plunged into the house as if a mob were at his heels. Now he was before the cupboard! Little mercy the phylacteries and amulets, the bridle-spanglery of donkeys, the trinketry of women, his ancestresses once famous for beauty or many children—little mercy the motley collection on the second shelf received from his hands. He tossed them here and there, and here and there again, but the search was vain. Ah, good Lord! was the medalet lost? And of all times, then?

The failure made him the more anxious; his hands shook while he essayed the search once more; and he reproached himself. The medal was valuable for its gold, and besides it was a sacred souvenir. Conscience stung him. Over and over he shifted and turned the various properties on the shelf, the last time systematically and with fixed attention. When he stopped to rest, the perspiration stood on his forehead in large drops, and he fairly wrung his hands, crying, "It is not here—it is lost! My God, how shall I know the truth now!"

At this pause it is to be said that the son of Jahdai was wifeless. The young woman whom he had taken as helpmeet in dying had left him a girl baby who, at the time of our writing, was about thirteen years old. Under the necessity thus imposed, he found a venerable daughter of Jerusalem to serve him as housekeeper, and charge herself with care of the child. Now he thought of that person; possibly she knew where the seal was. He turned to seek her, and as he did so, the door of an adjoining room opened, and the child appeared.

He held her very dear, because she had the clear olive complexion of her mother, and the same soft black eyes with which the latter used to smile upon him in such manner that words were never required to assure him of her love. And the little one was bright and affectionate, and had prettinesses in speech, and sang low and contentedly the day long. Often as he took her on his lap and studied her fondly, he was conscious she promised to be gentle and beautiful as the departed one; beyond which it never occurred to him there could be superior excellences.

Distressed as the poor man was, he took the child in his arms, and kissed her on the round cheek, and was putting her down when he saw the medal at her throat, hanging from a string. She told him the housekeeper had given it to her as a plaything. Untied at last—for his impatience was nigh uncontrollable—he hurried with the recovered treasure to a window, to look at the device raised upon it; then, his heart beating rapidly, he made comparison with the impression sunk in the yellow wax at the foot of the letter; he put them side by side—there could be no mistake—the impression on the wax might have been made by the medallion!

Let it not be supposed now that the son of Jahdai did not appreciate the circumstance which had befallen. The idea of a man suffering a doom so strange affected him, while the doom itself, considered as a judgment, was simply awful; but his thought did not stop there—it carried him behind both the man and the doom. Who was He with power by a word, not merely to change the most fixed of the decrees of nature, but, by suspending it entirely, hold an offending wretch alive for a period already encroaching upon the eternal? One less firmly rooted in the faith of his fathers would have stood aghast at the conclusion to which the answer as an argument led—a conclusion admitting no escape once it was reached. The affair in hand, however, despite its speculative side, was real and urgent; and the keeper of the stall, remembering the messenger in half imprisonment, fell to thinking of the practical questions before him; first of which was the treatment he should accord his correspondent's requests.

This did not occupy him long. His father, he reflected, would have received the stranger cordially, and as became one of such close intimacy; so should he. The requests were easy, and carried no pecuniary liability with them; he was merely to aid an inexperienced servant in the purchase of a dwelling-house, the servant having plenty of funds. True, when the master presented himself in person, it would be necessary to determine exactly the footing to be accorded him; but for the present that might be deferred. If, in the connection, the son of Jahdai dwelt briefly upon possible advantages to himself, the person being presumably rich and powerful, it was human, and he is to be excused for it.

The return to the market was less hurried than the going from it. There Uel acted promptly. He took Syama to his house, and put him into the guest-chamber, assuring him it was a pleasure. Yet when night came he slept poorly. The incidents of the day were mixed with much that was unaccountable, breaking the even tenor of his tradesman's life by unwonted perplexities. He had not the will to control his thoughts; they would go back to the excitement of the moment when he believed the medallion lost; and as points run together in the half-awake state on very slender threads, he had a vision of a mysterious old man coming into his house, and in some way taking up and absorbing the life of his child. When the world at last fell away and left him asleep, it was with a dread tapping heavily at his heart.

The purchase which Uel was requested to assist in making proved a light affair. After diligent search through the city, Syama decided to take a two-story house situated in a street running along the foot of the hill to-day crowned by the mosque Sultan Selim, although it was then the site of an unpretentious Christian church. Besides a direct eastern frontage, it was in the divisional margin between the quarters of the Greeks, which were always clean, and those of the Jews, which were always filthy. It was also observed that neither the hill nor the church obstructed the western view from the roof; that is to say, it was so far around the upper curve of the hill that a thistle-down would be carried by a south-east wind over many of the proudest Greek residences and dropped by the Church of the Holy Virgin on Blacherne, or in the imperial garden behind the Church. In addition to these advantages, the son of Jahdai was not unmindful that his own dwelling, a small but comfortable structure also of wood, was just opposite across the street. Everything considered, the probabilities were that Syama's selection would prove satisfactory to his master. The furnishment was a secondary matter.

It is to be added that in course of the business there were two things from which Uel extracted great pleasure; Syama always had money to pay promptly for everything he bought; in the next place, communication with him was astonishingly easy. His eyes made up for the deficiency in hearing; while his signs, gestures, and looks were the perfection of pantomime. Of evenings the child never tired watching him in conversation.

While we go now to bring the Wanderer up, it should not be forgotten that the house, completely furnished, is awaiting him, and he has only to knock at the door, enter, and be at home.

CHAPTER II
THE PILGRIM AT EL KATIF

The bay of Bahrein indents the western shore of the Persian Gulf. Hard by the point on the north at which it begins its inland bend rise the whitewashed, one-story mud-houses of the town El Katif. Belonging to the Arabs, the most unchangeable of peoples, both the town and the bay were known in the period of our story by their present names.

The old town in the old time derived importance chiefly from the road which, leading thence westwardly through Hejr Yemameh, brought up, after many devious stretches across waterless wastes of sand, at El Derayeh, a tented capital of the Bedouins, and there forked, one branch going to Medina, the other to Mecca. In other words, El Katif was to Mecca on the east the gate Jeddo was to it on the west.

When, in annual recurrence, the time for the indispensable Hajj, or Pilgrimage, came, the name of the town was on the lips of men and women beyond the Green Sea, and southwardly along the coast of Oman, and in the villages and dowars back of the coast under the peaks of Akdar, only a little less often than those of the holy cities. Then about the first of July the same peoples as pilgrims from Irak, Afghanistan, India, and beyond those countries even, there being an East and a Far East, and pilgrims from Arabia, crowded together, noisy, quarrelsome, squalid, accordant in but one thing—a determination to make the Hajj lest they might die as Jews or Christians.

The law required the pilgrim to be at Mecca in the month of Ramazan, the time the Prophet himself had become a pilgrim. From El Katif the direct journey might be made in sixty days, allowing an average march of twelve miles. By way of Medina, it could be made to permit the votary to be present and participate in the observances usual on the day of the Mysterious Night of Destiny.

The journey moreover was attended with dangers. Winds, drouth, sand storms beset the way; and there were beasts always hungry, and robbers always watchful. The sun beat upon the hills, curtained the levels with mirage, and in the *fiumuras* kindled invisible fires; so in what the unacclimated breathed and in what they drank of the waters of the land there were diseases and death.

The Prophet having fixed the month of Ramazan for the Hajj, pilgrims accustomed themselves to assemblage at Constantinople, Damascus, Cairo and Bagdad. If they could not avoid the trials of the road, they could lessen them. Borrowing the term caravan as descriptive of the march, they established markets at all convenient places.

This is the accounting for one of the notable features of El Katif from the incoming of June till the caravan extended itself on the road, and finally disappeared in the yellow farness of the Desert. One could not go amiss for purveyors in general. Dealers in horses, donkeys, camels, and dromedaries abounded. The country for miles around appeared like a great stock farm. Herds overran the lean earth. Makers of harness, saddles, box-houdahs, and swinging litters of every variety and price, and contractors of camels, horses, and trains complete did not wait to be solicited; the competition between them was too lively for dignity. Hither and thither shepherds drove fatted sheep in flocks, selling them on the hoof. In shady places sandal merchants and clothiers were established; while sample tents spotted the whole landscape. Hucksters went about with figs, dates, dried meats and bread. In short, pilgrims could be accommodated with every conceivable necessary. They had only to cry out, and the commodity was at hand.

Amongst the thousands who arrived at El Katif in the last of June, 1448, was a man whose presence made him instantly an object of general interest. He came from the south in a galley of eight oars manned by Indian seamen, and lay at anchor three days before landing. His ship bore nothing indicative of nationality except the sailors. She was trim-looking and freshly painted; otherwise there was nothing uncommon in her appearance. She was not for war—that was plain. She floated too lightly to be laden; wherefore those who came to look at her said she could not be in commercial service.

Almost before furling sail, an awning was stretched over her from bow to stern—an awning which from the shore appeared one great shawl of variegated colors. Thereupon the wise in such matters decided the owner was an Indian Prince vastly rich, come, like a good Mohammedan, to approve his faith by pilgrimage.

This opinion the stranger's conduct confirmed. While he did not himself appear ashore, he kept up a busy communication by means of his small boat. For three days, it carried contractors of camels and supplies aboard, and brought them back.

They described him of uncertain age; he might be sixty, he might be seventy-five. While rather under medium height, he was active and perfectly his own master. He sat in the shade of the awning cross-legged. His rug was a marvel of sheeny silk. He talked Arabic, but with an Indian accent. His dress was Indian—a silken shirt, a short jacket, large trousers, and a tremendous white turban on a red tarbousche, held by an aigrette in front that was a dazzle of precious stones such as only a Rajah could own. His attendants were few, but they were gorgeously attired, wore *shintyan* swung in rich belts from their shoulders, and waited before him speechless and in servile posture. One at his back upheld an umbrella of immense spread. He indulged few words, and they were strictly business. He wanted a full outfit for the Hajj; could the contractor furnish him twenty camels of burden, and four swift dromedaries? Two of the latter were to carry a litter for himself; the other two were for his personal attendants, whom he desired furnished with well-shaded *shugdufs*. The camels he would load with provisions. While speaking, he would keep his eyes upon the person addressed with an expression uncomfortably searching. Most extraordinary, however, he did not once ask about prices.

One of the Shaykhs ventured an inquiry.

"How great will his Highness' suite be?"

"Four."

The Shaykh threw up his hands.

"O Allah! Four dromedaries and twenty camels for four men!"

"Abuser of the salt," said the stranger calmly, "hast thou not heard of the paschal charity, and of the fine to the poor? Shall I go empty handed to the most sacred of cities?"

Finally an agent was found who, in concert with associates, undertook to furnish the high votary with all he asked complete.

The morning of the fourth day after his arrival the Indian was pulled ashore, and conducted out of town a short distance to where, on a rising ground, a camp had been set up provisionally for his inspection. There were tents, one for storage of goods and provisions; one for the suite; one for the chief Shaykh, the armed guards, the tent pitchers, and the camel drivers; and a fourth one, larger than the others, for the Prince himself. With the dromedaries, camels, and horses, the camp was accepted; then, as was the custom, the earnest money was paid. By set of sun the baggage was removed from the ship, and its partition into cargoes begun. The Prince of India had no difficulty in hiring all the help he required.

Of the thirty persons who constituted the train ten were armed horsemen, whose appearance was such that, if it were answered by a commensurate performance, the Prince might at his leisure march irrespective of the caravan. Nor was he unmindful in the selection of stores for the journey. Long before the sharp bargainers with whom he dealt were through with him, he had won their best opinion, not less by his liberality than for his sound judgment. They ceased speaking of him sneeringly as the *miyan*. [Footnote: Barbarous Indian]

Soon as the bargain was bound, the stranger's attendants set about the furnishment of the master's tent. Outside they painted it green. The interior they divided into two equal compartments; one for reception, the other for a *maglis* or drawing-room; and besides giving the latter divans and carpets, they draped the ceiling in the most tasteful manner with the shawls which on the ship had served for awning.

At length, everything in the catalogue of preparation having been attended to, it remained only to wait the day of general departure; and for that, as became his greatness, the Prince kept his own quarters, paying no attention to what went on around him. He appeared a man who loved solitude, and was averse to thinking in public.

CHAPTER III
THE YELLOW AIR

[Footnote: The plague is known amongst Arabs as "the Yellow Air."]

One evening the reputed Indian sat by the door of his tent alone. The red afterglow of the day hung in the western sky. Overhead the stars were venturing timidly out. The camels were at rest, some chewing their cuds, others asleep, their necks stretched full length upon the warm earth. The watchmen in a group talked in low voices. Presently the cry of a muezzin, calling to prayer, flew in long, quavering, swelling notes through the hushed air. Others took up the call, clearer or fainter according to the distance; and so was it attuned to the feeling invoked by the conditions of the moment that no effort was required of a listener to think it a refrain from the sky. The watchmen ceased debating, drew a little apart from each other, spread their *abbas* on the ground, and stepping upon them barefooted, their faces turned to where Mecca lay, began the old unchangeable prayer of Islam— *God is God, and Mahomet is His Prophet.*

The pilgrim at the tent door arose, and when his rude employes were absorbed in their devotions, like them, he too prayed, but very differently.

"God of Israel—my God!" he said, in a tone hardly more than speaking to himself. "These about me, my fellow creatures, pray thee in the hope of life, I pray thee in the hope of death. I have come up from the sea, and the end was not there; now I will go into the Desert in search of it. Or if I must live, Lord, give me the happiness there is in serving thee. Thou hast need of instruments of good; let me henceforth be one of them, that by working for thy honor, I may at last enjoy the peace of the blessed—Amen."

Timing his movements with those of the watchmen, he sank to his knees, and repeated the prayer; when they fell forward, their faces to the earth in the *rik'raths* so essential by the Mohammedan code, he did the same. When they were through the service, he went on with it that they might see him. A careful adherence to this conduct gained him in a short time great repute for sanctity, making the pilgrimage enjoyable as well as possible to him.

The evening afterglow faded out, giving the world to night and the quiet it affects; still the melancholy Indian walked before his tent, his hands clasped behind him, his chin in the beard on his breast. Let us presume to follow his reflections.

"Fifty years! A lifetime to all but me. Lord, how heavy is thy hand when thou art in anger!"

He drew a long breath, and groaned.

"Fifty years! That they are gone, let those mourn to whom time is measured in scanty dole."

He became retrospective.

"The going to Cipango was like leaving the world. War had yielded to contentions about religion. I wearied of them also. My curse is to weary of everything. I wonder if the happiness found in the affection of women is more lasting?"

He pursued the thought awhile, finishing with a resolution.

"If the opportunity comes my way, I will try it. I remember yet the mother of my Lael, though I did not understand the measure of the happiness she brought me until she died."

He returned then to the first subject.

"When will men learn that faith is a natural impulse, and pure religion but faith refined of doubt?"

The question was succeeded by a wordless lapse in his mind, the better apparently to prolong the pleasure he found in the idea.

"God help me," he presently resumed, "to bring about an agreement in that definition of religion! There can be no reform or refinement of faith except God be its exclusive subject; and so certainly it leads to lopping off all parasitical worships such as are given to Christ and Mahomet.... Fifty years ago the sects would have tortured me had I mentioned God as a principle broad and holy enough for them to stand upon in compromise of their disputes; they may not be better disposed now, yet I will try them. If I succeed I will not be a vulgar monument builder like Alexander; neither will I divide a doubtful fame with Caesar. My glory will be unique. I will have restored mankind to their true relations with God. I will be their Arbiter in Religion. Then surely"—he lifted his face appealingly as to a person enthroned amidst the stars—"surely thou wilt release me from this too long life.... If I fail"—he clinched his hands—"if I fail, they may exile me, they may imprison me, they may stretch me on the rack, but they cannot kill me."

Then he walked rapidly, his head down, like a man driven. When he stopped it was to say to himself uncertainly:

"I feel weak at heart. Misgivings beset me. Lord, Lord, how long am I to go on thus cheating myself? If thou wilt not pardon me, how can I hope honor from my fellow men? Why should I struggle to serve them?"

Again he clinched his hands.

"Oh, the fools, the fools! Will they never be done? When I went away they were debating, Was Mahomet a Prophet? Was Christ the Messiah? And they are debating yet. What miseries I have seen come of the dispute!"

From this to the end, the monologue was an incoherent discursive medley, now plaintive, now passionate, at times prayerful, then exultant. As he proceeded, he seemed to lose sight of his present aim at doing good in the hope of release from termless life, and become the Jew he was born.

"The orators called in the sword, and they plied each other with it through two hundred years and more. There were highways across Europe blazoned with corpses.... But they were great days. I remember them. remember Manuel's appeal to Gregory. I was present at the Council of Clermont. I heard Urban's speech. I saw Walter, the beggar of Burgundy, a fugitive in Constantinople; but his followers, those who went out with him—where were they? I saw Peter, the eremite and coward, dragged back, a deserter, to the plague-smitten camps of Antioch. I helped vote Godfrey King of Jerusalem, and carried a candle at his coronation. I saw the hosts of Louis VII and Conrad, a million and more, swallowed up in Iconia and the Pisidian mountains. Then, that the persecutors of my race might not have rest, I marched with Saladin to the re-conquest of the Holy City, and heard Philip and Richard answer his challenge. The brave Kurd, pitying the sorrows of men, at last agreed to tolerate Christians in Jerusalem as pilgrims; and there the strife might have ended, but I played upon the ambition of Baldwin, and set Europe in motion again. No fault of mine that the knight stopped at Constantinople as King of the East. Then the second Frederick presumed to make a Christian city of Jerusalem. I resorted to the Turks, and they burned and pillaged it, and captured St. Louis, the purest and best of the crusaders. He died in my arms. Never before had I a tear for man or woman of his faith! Then came Edward I., and with him the struggle as a contest of armies terminated. By decision of the sword, Mahomet *was* the Prophet of God, and Christ but the carpenter's son.... By permission of the Kaliphs, the Christians might visit Jerusalem as pilgrims. A palmer's staff in place of a sword! For shield, a beggar's scrip! But the bishops accepted, and then ushered in an age of fraud, Christian against Christian.... The knoll on which the Byzantine built his church of the Holy Sepulchre is not the Calvary. That the cowled liars call the Sepulchre never held the body of Christ. The tears of the millions of penitents have but watered a monkish deceit.... Fools and blasphemers!

The Via Dolorosa led out of the Damascus gate on the north. The skull-shaped hill beyond that gate is the Golgotha. Who should know it better than I? The Centurion asked for a guide; I walked with him. Hyssop was the only green thing growing upon the mount; nothing but hyssop has grown there since. At the base on the west was a garden, and the Sepulchre was in the garden. From the foot of the cross I looked toward the city, and there was a sea of men extending down to the gate.... I know!—I know!—I and misery know!... When I went out fifty years ago there was an agreement between the ancient combatants; each vied with the other in hating and persecuting the Jew, and there was no limit to the afflictions he endured from them.... Speak thou, O Hebron, city of the patriarchs! By him who sits afar, and by him near unto thee, by the stars this peaceful night, and by the Everlasting who is above the stars, be thou heard a witness testifying! There was a day when thou didst stand open to the children of Israel; for the cave and the dead within it belonged to them. Then Herod built over it, and shut it up, though without excluding the tribes. The Christian followed Herod; yet the Hebrew might pay his way in. After the Christian, the Moslem; and now nor David the King, nor son of his, though they alighted at the doors from chariots, and beat upon them with their crowns and sceptres, could pass in and live.... Kings have come and gone, and generations, and there is a new map from which old names have been dropped. As respects religion, alas! the divisions remain—here a Mohammedan, there a Christian, yonder a Judean.... From my door I study these men, the children of those in life at my going into exile. Their ardor is not diminished. To kiss a stone in which tradition has planted a saying of God, they will defy the terrors of the Desert, heat, thirst, famine, disease, death. I bring them an old idea in a new relation—God, giver of life and power to Son and Prophet—God, alone entitled to worship—God, a principle of Supreme Holiness to which believers can bring their creeds and doctrines for mergence in a treaty of universal brotherhood. Will they accept it? ... Yesterday I saw a Schiah and a Sunite meet, and the old hate darkened their faces as they looked at each other. Between them there is only a feud of Islamites; how much greater is their feud with Christians? How immeasurably greater the feud between Christian and Jew? ... My heart misgives me! Lord! Can it be I am but cherishing a dream?"

At sight of a man approaching through the dusk, he calmed himself.

"Peace to thee, Hadji," said the visitor, halting.

"Is it thou, Shaykh?"

"It is I, my father's son. I have a report to make."

"I was thinking of certain holy things of priceless worth, sayings of the Prophet. Tell me what thou hast?"

The Shaykh saluted him, and returned, "The caravan will depart to-morrow at sunrise."

"Be it so. We are ready. I will designate our place in the movement. Thou art dismissed."

"O Prince! I have more to report."

"More?"

"A vessel came in to-day from Hormuz on the eastern shore, bringing a horde of beggars."

"Bismillah! It was well I hired of thee a herd of camels, and loaded them with food. I shall pay my fine to the poor early."

The Shaykh shook his head.

"That they are beggars is nothing," he said. "Allah is good to all his creatures. The jackals are his, and must be fed. For this perhaps the unfortunates were blown here by the angel that rides the yellow air. Four corpses were landed, and their clothes sold in the camp."

"Thou wouldst say," the Prince rejoined, "that the plague will go with us to the Kaaba. Content thee, Shaykh. Allah will have his way."

"But my men are afraid."

"I will place a drop of sweetened water on their lips, and bring them safe through, though they are dying. Tell them as much."

The Shaykh was departing when the Prince, shrewdly suspecting it was he who feared, called him back.

"How call ye the afternoon prayer, O Shaykh?"

"El Asr."

"What didst thou when it was called?"

"Am I not a believer? I prayed."

"And thou hast heard the Arafat sermon?"

"Even so, O Prince."

"Then, as thou art a believer, and a hadji, O Shaykh, thou and all with thee shalt see the Khatib on his dromedary, and hear him again. Only promise me to stay till his last *Amin*."

"I promise," said the Shaykh, solemnly.

"Go—but remember prayer is the bread of faith."

The Shaykh was comforted, and withdrew.

With the rising of the sun next day the caravan, numbering about three thousand souls, defiled confusedly out of the town. The Prince, who might have been first, of choice fell in behind the rest.

"Why dost thou take this place, O Prince?" asked the Shaykh, who was proud of his company, and their comparative good order.

He received for answer, "The blessings of Allah are with the dying whom the well-to-do and selfish in front have passed unnoticed."

The Shaykh repeated the saying to his men, and they replied: "Ebn-Hanife was a Dervish: so is this Prince—exalted be his name!"

Eulogy could go no further.

CHAPTER IV
EL ZARIBAH

"I will be their Arbiter in Religion," said the Indian Mystic in his monologue.

This is to be accepted as the motive of the scheme the singular man was pursuing in the wastes of Arabia.

It must be taken of course with his other declaration—"There can be no reform or refinement of faith except God be its exclusive subject; and so certainly it leads to lopping off all parasitical worships such as are given to Christ and Mahomet."

Fifty years prior, disgusted with the endless and inconsequential debates and wars between Islam and Christianity, he had betaken himself to Cipango, [Footnote: Supposably Japan.] wherever that might be. There, in a repentant hour, he had conceived the idea of a Universal Religious Brotherhood, with God for its accordant principle; and he was now returned to present and urge the compromise. In more distinct statement, he was making the pilgrimage to ascertain from personal observation if the Mohammedan portion of the world was in a consenting mood. It was not his first visit to Mecca; but the purpose in mind gave the journey a new zest; and, as can be imagined, nothing in the least indicative of the prevalent spirit of the Hajj escaped him. Readers following the narrative should keep this explanation before them.

From El Derayah the noble pilgrim had taken the longer route by way of Medina, where he scrupulously performed the observances decreed for the faithful at the Mosque of the Prophet. Thence he descended with the caravan from Damascus.

Dawn of the sixth of September broke over the rolling plain known as the Valley of El Zaribah, disclosing four tents pitched on an eminence to the right of a road running thence south-west. These tents, connected by ropes, helped perfect an enclosure occupied by horses, donkeys, camels and dromedaries, and their cumbrous equipments. Several armed men kept watch over the camp.

The Valley out to the pink granite hills rimming it round wore a fresh green tint in charming contrast with the tawny-black complexion of the region through which the day's journey had stretched. Water at a shallow depth nourished camel grass in patches, and Theban palms, the latter much scattered and too small to be termed trees. The water, and the nearness of the Holy City—only one day distant—had, in a time long gone, won for El Zaribah its double appointment of meeting place for the caravans and place of the final ceremony of assumption of the costume and vows *El Ihram*.

The Prophet himself had prescribed the ceremony; so the pilgrims in the camp on the eminence, the better to observe it and at the same time get a needful rest, had come up during the night in advance of the caravans. In other words, the Prince of India—the title by which he was now generally known—might, at the opening hour of the day, have been found asleep in the larger of the four tents; the one with the minaret in miniature so handsomely gilded and of such happy effect over the centre pole.

Along the roadsides and on the high grounds of the Valley other tints were visible, while faint columns of smoke arising out of the hollows told of preparations for breakfast. These signified the presence of hucksters, barbers, costume dealers, and traders generally, who, in anticipation of the arrival of the caravans, had come from the city to exercise their callings. Amongst them, worthy of special attention, was a multitude of professional guides, [Footnote: *Mutawif.*] ready for a trifling hire to take charge of uninitiated pilgrims, and lead them regardfully through the numerous ceremonies to which they were going.

Shortly after noon the Prince called in a guide, and several barbers, men with long gowns, green turbans, brass basins, sharp knives, and bright bladed scissors. The assumption of the real pilgrimage by his people was then begun. Each man submitted his head, mustaches, and nails to the experts, and bathed and perfumed himself, and was dusted with musk. Next the whole party put off their old garments, and attired themselves in the two white vestments *El Ihram.*[Footnote: A mantle and skirt of white cloth unsewn.] The change of apparel was for the better. Finally the votaries put on sandals peculiar in that nothing pertaining to them might cover the instep; then they stood up in a row faced toward Mecca, and repeated the ancient formula of dedication of the *Ihram* to the Almighty slowly intoned for them by the guide.

The solemn demeanor of the men during the ceremony, which was tedious and interspersed with prayers and curious recitals, deeply impressed the Prince, who at the end of the scene retired into his tent, with his three mute attendants, and there performed the vows for himself and them. There also they all assumed the indispensable costume. Then, as he well might do, the law permitting him to seek the shade of a house or a tent, he had a rug spread before his door, where, in the fresh white attire, he seated himself, and with a jar of expressed juice of pomegranates at his side made ready to witness the passing of the caravans, the dust of which was reported visible in the east.

Afterwhile the cloud of dust momentarily deepening over in that direction was enlivened by a clash of cymbals and drums, blent with peals of horns, the fine, high music yet cherished by warriors of the Orient. Presently a body of horsemen appeared, their spear points glistening in the sunlight. A glance at them, then his gaze fixed upon a chief in leading.

The sun had been hot all day; the profiles of the low hills were dim with tremulous haze lying scorchingly upon them; the furred hulks of the camels in the enclosure looked as if they were smoking; the sky held nothing living except two kites which sailed the upper air slowly, their broad wings at widest extension; yet the chief persisted in wearing his arms and armor, like the soldiers behind him. Ere long he rode up and halted in front of the Prince, and near by.

His head was covered with a visorless casque, slightly conical, from the edge of which, beginning about the temples, a cape of fine steel rings, buckled under the chin, enveloped the neck and throat, and fell loosely over the neck and shoulders, and part way down the back. A shirt of linked mail, pliable as wool, defended the body and the arms to the elbows; overalls of like material, save that the parts next the saddle were leather, clothed the thighs and legs. As the casque and every other link of the mail were plated with gold, the general effect at a distance was as if the whole suit were gold. A surcoat of light green cloth hung at the back half hiding a small round shield of burnished brass; at the left side there was a cimeter, and in the right hand a lance. The saddle was of the high-seated style yet affected by horsemen of Circassia; at the pommel a bow and well-filled quiver were suspended, and as the stirrups were in fact steel slippers the feet were amply protected by them.

At sight of the martial figure, the Indian, in admiration, arose to a sitting posture. Such, he thought, were the warriors who followed Saladin! And when the stranger, reaching the summit of the eminence, turned out of the road coming apparently to the door of the tent, he involuntarily sprang to his feet ready to do him honor.

The face, then plainly seen, though strong of feature, and thoroughly bronzed, was that of a young man not more than twenty-two or three, dark-eyed, mustached and bearded, and of a serious though pleasant expression. He kept his seat with ease and grace; if he and the broad-chested dark-bay horse were not really one, they were one in spirit; together they wrought the impression which was the origin of *majesty*, a title for kings.

While the Prince was turning this in his mind, the soldier pulled rein, and stopped long enough to glance at him and at the camp; then, turning the horse, he looked the other way, making it apparent he had taken position on the rise to overlook the plain, and observe the coming and dispersion of the caravans.

Another mounted man ascended the hill, armed and armored like the first one, though not so richly, and bearing a standard of dulled yellow silk hanging from a gilded staff. The ground of the standard was filled with inscriptions in red lettering, leaving the golden crescent and star on the point of the staff to speak of nationality. The bearer of the flag dismounted, and at a sign planted it in the ground.

Seeing his Shaykh, the Prince called him:

"Who is the warrior yonder?—He in the golden armor?"

"The Emir El Hajj, [Footnote: Chief officer of the Pilgrimage. The appointment was considered the highest favor in the Sultan's gift.] O Prince."

"He the Emir El Hajj!—And so young?—Oh! a hero of the Serail. The Kislar Aga extolled him one day."

"Thy remark and common report, O excellent Prince, could not journey together on the same camel," said the Shaykh. "In the Khan at Medina I heard his story. There is a famous enemy of the Turks, Iskander Bey, in strength a Jinn, whose sword two men can scarcely lift. He appeared before the army of the Sultan one day with a challenge. He whom thou seest yonder alone dared go forth to meet him. The fought from morning till noon; then they rested. 'Who art thou?' asked Iskander. 'I am a slave of Amurath, the Commander of the Faithful, who hath commissioned me to take thee to him dead or alive.' Iskander laughed, and said, 'I know by thy tongue now thou art not a Turk; and to see if the Commander of the Faithful, as thou callest him, hath it in soul to make much of thy merit as a warrior, I will leave thee the honors of the combat, and to go thy way.' Whereat they say he lifted his ponderous blade as not heavier than the leaf of a dead palm, and strode from the field."

The Prince listened, and at the end said, like a man in haste:

"Thou knowest Nilo, my black man. Bring him hither."

The Shaykh saluted gravely, and hurried away, leaving his patron with eyes fixed on the Emir, and muttering:

"So young!—and in such favor with the old Amurath! I will know him. If I fail, he may be useful to me. Who knows? Who knows?"

He looked upward as if speaking to some one there.

Meantime the Emir was questioning the ensign.

"This pilgrim," he said, "appears well provided."

And the ensign answered:

"He is the Indian Prince of whom I have been hearing since we left Medina."

"What hast thou heard?"

"That being rich, he is open-handed, making free with his aspers as sowers with their seed."

"What more?"

"He is devout and learned as an Imam. His people call him Malik. Of the prayers he knows everything. As the hours arrive, he lifts the curtains of his litter, and calls them with a voice like Belal's. The students in the mosque would expire of envy could they see him bend his back in the benedictions."

"*Bismillah!*"

"They say also that in the journey from El Katif to Medina he travelled behind the caravan when he might have been first."

"I see not the virtue in that. The hill-men love best to attack the van."

"Tell me, O Emir, which wouldst thou rather face, a hill-man or the Yellow Air?"

"The hill-man," said the other decidedly.

"And thou knowest when those in front abandon a man struck with the disease?"

"Yes."

"And then?"

"The vultures and the jackals have their rights."

"True, O Emir, but listen. The caravan left El Katif three thousand strong. Three hundred and more were struck with the plague, and left to die; of those, over one hundred were brought in by the Indian. They say it was for this he preferred to march in the rear. He himself teaches a saying of the *Hadis*, that Allah leaves his choicest blessings to be gathered from amidst the poor and the dying."

"If he thou describest be not a Prince of India as he claims, he is a"—

"A *Mashaikh*." [Footnote: Holier than a Dervish.]

"Ay, by the Most Merciful! But how did he save the castaways?"

"By a specific known only to kings and lords in his country. Can he but reach the plague-struck before death, a drop on the tongue will work a cure. Thou heardst what he did at Medina?"

"No."

"The Masjid El Nabawi [Footnote: Tomb of the Prophet.] as thou knowest, O Emir, hath many poor who somehow live in its holy shade."

"I know it," said the Emir, with a laugh. "I went in the house rich, and come out of it poorer than the poorest of the many who fell upon me at the doors."

"Well," the ensign continued, not heeding the interruption, "he called them in, and fed them; not with rice, and leeks, and bread ten days sour, but with dishes to rejoice a Kaliph; and they went away swearing the soul of the Prophet was returned to the world."

At this juncture a troop of horsemen ascending the hill brought the conversation to a stop. The uniformity of arms and armor, the furniture of the steeds, the order and regularity of the general movement, identified the body as some favorite corps of the Turkish army; while the music, the bristling lances, the many-folded turbans, and the half-petticoated trousers threw about it a glamor of purest orientalism.

In the midst of the troop, a vanguard in front, a rearguard behind them, central objects of care and reverence, moved the sacred camels, tall, powerful brutes, more gigantic in appearance because of their caparisoning and the extraordinary burdens they bore. They too were in full regalia, their faces visored in silk and gold, their heads resplendent with coronets of drooping feathers, their ample neck cloths heavy with tasselled metallic fringing falling to the knees. Each one was covered with a mantle of brocaded silk arranged upon a crinoline form to give the effect somewhat of the curved expansion on the rim of a bell. On the humps rose pavilions of silk in flowing draperies, on some of which the entire *Fatihah* was superbly embroidered. Over the pavilions arose enormous aigrettes of green and black feathers. Such were the *mahmals*, containing, among other things of splendor and fabulous value, the *Kiswah* which the Sultan was forwarding to the Scherif of Mecca to take the place of the worn curtains then draping the Tabernacle or House of God.

The plumed heads of the camels, and the yet more richly plumed pavilions, exalted high above the horsemen, moved like things afloat. One may not tell what calamities to body and soul would overtake the Emir El Hajj did he fail to deliver the *mahmals* according to consignment.

While the cavalry came up the hill the musicians exerted themselves; at the top, the column turned and formed line left of the Emir, followed by strings of camels loaded with military properties, and a horde of camp-followers known as *farrash*. Presently another camp was reared upon the eminence, its white roofs shining afar over the plain, and in their midst one of unusual dimensions for the Sultan's gifts.

The caravans in the meantime began to emerge from the dun cloud of their own raising, and spread at large over the land; and when the young Emir was most absorbed in the spectacle the Prince's Shaykh approached him.

"O Emir!" the Arab said, after a salaam.

A wild fanfare of clarions, cymbals, and drums drowning his voice, he drew nearer, almost to the stirrup.

"O Emir!" he said again.

This time he was heard.

"What wouldst thou?"

There was the slightest irritation in the tone, and on the countenance of the speaker as he looked down; but the feeling behind it vanished at sight of a negro whose native blackness was intensified by the spotless white of the Ihram in which he was clad. Perhaps the bright platter of beaten copper the black man bore, and the earthen bottle upon it, flanked by two cups, one of silver, the other of crystal, had something to do with the Emir's change of manner and mind.

"What wouldst thou?" he asked, slightly bending towards them.

The Shaykh answered:

"The most excellent Hadji, my patron, whom thou mayst see reclining at the door of his tent, sends thee greeting such as is lawful from one true believer to another travelling for the good of their souls to the most Holy of Cities; and he prays thou wilt accept from him a draught of this water of pomegranates, which he vouches cooling to the tongue and healthful to the spirit, since he bought it at the door of the House of the Prophet—to whom be prayer and praise forever."

During the speech, the negro, with a not unpractised hand, and conscious doubtless of the persuasion there was in the sound and sparkle of the beverage, especially to one not yet dismounted from a long ride on the desert, filled the cups, and held them up for acceptance.

Stripping the left hand of its steel-backed gauntlet, the Emir lifted the glass, and, with a bow to the pilgrim then arisen and standing by the tent-door, drank it at a draught; whereupon, leaving the ensign to pay like honor to the offered hospitality, he wheeled his horse, and rode to make acknowledgment in person.

"The favor thou hast done me, O Hadji," he said, dismounted, "is in keeping with the acts of mercy to thy fellow-men with which I hear thou hast paved the road from El Katif as with mother-of-pearl."

"Speak not of them, I pray," the Wanderer answered, returning the bow he received. "Who shall refuse obedience to the law?"

"I see plainly thou art a good man," the Emir said, bowing again.

"It would not become me to say so. Turning to something better, this tent in the wilderness is mine, and as the sun is not declined to its evening quarter, perhaps, O gallant Emir, it would be more to thy comfort were we to go within. I, and all I have, are at thy command."

"I am grateful for the offer, most excellent Hadji—if the address be lower than thy true entitlement, thou shouldst bring the Shaykh yonder to account for misleading a stranger—but the sun and I have become unmindful of each other, and duty is always the same in its demands at least. Here, because the valley is the *micath*, [Footnote: Meeting place.] the caravans are apt to run wild, and need a restraining hand. I plead the circumstance in excuse for presuming to request that thou wilt allow me to amend thy offer of courtesy."

The Emir paused, waiting for the permission.

"So thou dost accept the offer, amend it as thou wilt," and the Prince smiled.

Then the other returned, with evident satisfaction: "When our brethren of the caravans are settled, and the plain is quiet, and I too have taken the required vows, I will return to thee. My quarters are so close to thine it would please me to be allowed to come alone."

"Granted, O Emir, granted—if, on thy side, thou wilt consent to permit me to give thee of the fare I may yet have at disposal. I can promise thou shalt not go away hungry."

"Be it so."

Thereupon the Emir remounted, and went back to his stand overlooking the plain, and the coming of the multitude.

CHAPTER V
THE PASSING OF THE CARAVANS

From his position the Wanderer could see the advancing caravans; but as the spectacle would consume the afternoon, he called his three attendants, and issued directions for the entertainment of the Emir in the evening; this done, he cast himself upon the rug, and gave rein to his curiosity, thinking, not unreasonably, to find in what would pass before him something bearing on the subject ever present in his mind.

The sky could not be called blue of any tint; it seemed rather to be filled with common dust mixed with powder of crushed brick. The effect was of a semi-transparent ceiling flushed with heat from the direct down-beating action of the sun, itself a disk of flame. Low mountains, purplish black in hue, made a horizon on which the ceiling appeared set, like the crystal in the upper valve of a watch. Thus shut in, but still fair to view east and south of the position the spectator occupied, lay El Zaribah, whither, as the appointed meeting place, so many pilgrims had for days and weeks ever wearier growing been "walking with their eyes." In their thought the Valley was not so much a garden or landscape of beauty as an ante-chamber of the House of Allah. As they neared it now, journeying since the break of day, impatience seized them; so when the cry sped down the irregular column— "It is here! It is here!" they answered with a universal *labbayaki*, signifying, "Thou hast called us—here we are, here we are!" Then breaking into a rabble, they rushed multitudinously forward. To give the reader an idea of the pageant advancing to possess itself of the Valley, it will be well to refresh his memory with a few details. He should remember, in the first place, that it was not merely the caravan which left El Katif over on the western shore of the Green Sea, but two great caravans merged into one— *El Shemi*, from Damascus, and *Misri*, from Cairo. To comprehend these, the region they drained of pilgrims should be next considered. For example, at Cairo there was a concentration from the two Egypts, Upper and Lower, from the mysterious deserts of Africa, and from the cities and countries along the southern shore of the Mediterranean far as Gibraltar; while the whole East, using the term in its most comprehensive sense, emptied contingents of the devout into Damascus. In forwarding the myriads thus poured down upon them the Arabs were common carriers, like the Venetians to the hordes of western Europe in some of the later crusades; so to their thousands of votaries proper, the other thousands of them engaged in the business are also to be computed. El Medina was the great secondary rendezvous. Hardly could he be accounted of the Faithful who in making the pilgrimage would turn his back upon the bones of the Prophet; of such merit was the saying, "One prayer in this thy mosque is of more virtue than a thousand in other places, save only the Masjid El Haram." Once at Medina, how could the pilgrim refuse his presence, if not his tears, at El Kuba, forever sacred to the Mohammedan heart as the first place of public prayer in Islam? Finally, it should not be forgotten that the year we write of belonged to a cycle when readers of the Koran and worshippers at Mecca were more numerous than now, if not more zealous and believing. And it was to witness the passing of this procession, so numerous, so motley, so strangely furnished, so uncontrolled except as it pleased, the Prince of India was seated at the door of his tent upon the hill. Long before the spectacle was sighted in the distance, its approach was announced by an overhanging pillar of cloud, not unlike that which went before the Israelites in their exodus through similar wastes. Shortly after the interview with the Emir, the Prince, looking under the pillar, saw a darkening line appear, not more at first than a thread stretched across a section of the east.

The apparition was without a break; nor might he have said it was in motion or of any depth. A sound came from the direction not unlike that of a sibilant wind. Presently out of the perspective, which reduced the many to one and all sizes to a level, the line developed into unequal divisions, with intervals between them; about the same time the noise became recognizable as the voices fiercely strained and inarticulate of an innumerable host of men. Then the divisions broke into groups, some larger than others; a little later individuals became discernible; finally what had appeared a line resolved itself into a convulsing mass, without front, without wings, but of a depth immeasurable.

The pilgrims did not attempt to keep the road; having converted their march into a race, they spread right and left over the country, each seeking a near way; sometimes the object was attained, sometimes not; the end was a confusion beyond description. The very inequalities of the ground helped the confusion. A group was one moment visible on a height; then it vanished in a hollow. Now there were thousands on a level; then, as if sinking, they went down, down, and presently where they were there was only dust or a single individual.

Afterwhile, so wide was the inrolling tide, the field of vision overflowed, and the eye was driven to ranging from point to point, object to object. Then it was discernible that the mass was mixed of animals and men—here horses, there camels—some with riders, some without—all, the burdened as well as unburdened, straining forward under urgency of shriek and stick—forward for life—forward as if of the two "comforts," Success beckoned them in front, and Despair behind plied them with spears.

[Footnote: In the philosophy of the Arabs Success and Despair are treated as comforts.]

At length the eastern boundary of the Valley was reached. There one would suppose the foremost of the racers, the happy victors, would rest or, at their leisure, take of the many sites those they preferred; but no—the penalty attaching to the triumph was the danger of being run down by the thousands behind. In going on there was safety—and on they went.

To this time the spectacle had been a kind of panoramic generality; now the details came to view, and accustomed as he was to marvels of pageantry, the Prince exclaimed: "These are not men, but devils fleeing from the wrath of God!" and involuntarily he went nearer, down to the brink of the height. It seemed the land was being inundated with camels; not the patient brutes we are used to thinking of by that name, with which domestication means ill-treatment and suffering—the slow-going burden-bearers, always appealing to our sympathy because always apparently tired, hungry, sleepy, worn-out—always reeling on as if looking for quiet places in which to slip their loads of whatever kind, and lie down and die; but the camel aroused, enraged, frightened, panic-struck, rebellious, sending forth strange cries, and running with all its might—an army of camels hurling their gigantic hulks along at a rate little less than blind impetus. And they went, singly, and in strings, and yonder a mass. The slower, and those turned to the right or left of the direct course, and all such as had hesitated upon coming to a descent, were speedily distanced or lost to sight; so the ensemble was constantly shifting. And then the rolling and tossing of the cargoes and packages on the backs of the animals, and the streaming out of curtains, scarfs, shawls, and loose draperies of every shape and color, lent touches of drollery and bright contrasts to the scene. One instant the spectator on the hill was disposed to laugh, then to admire, then to shiver at the immensity of a danger; over and over again amidst his quick variation of feeling, he repeated the exclamation: "These are not men, but devils fleeing from the wrath of God!"

Such was the spectacle in what may be called the second act; presently it reached a third; and then the fury of the movement, so inconsistent with the habits and patient nature of the camel, was explained. In the midst of the hurly-burly, governing and directing it, were horsemen, an army of themselves. Some rode in front, and the leading straps on which they pulled with the combined strength of man and horse identified them as drivers; others rode as assistants of the drivers, and they were armed with goads which they used skilfully and without mercy. There were many collisions, upsets, and entanglements; yet the danger did not deter the riders from sharing the excitement, and helping it forward to their utmost. They too used knotted ropes, and stabbed with sharpened sticks; they also contributed to the unearthly tumult of sounds which travelled with the mob, a compound of prayers, imprecations, and senseless screams—the medley that may be occasionally heard from a modern mad-house.

In the height of the rush the Shaykh came up.

"How long," said the Prince—"in the Prophet's name, how long will this endure?"

"Till night, O most excellent Hadji—if the caravans be so long in coming."

"Is it usual?"

"It has been so from the beginning."

Thereupon the curiosity of the Prince took another turn. A band of horsemen galloped into view—free riders, with long lances carried upright, their caftans flying, and altogether noble looking.

"These are Arabs. I know by their horses and their bearing," said he, with admiration; "but possibly thou canst give me the name of their tribe."

The Shaykh answered with pride: "Their horses are gray, and by the sign, O lover of the Prophet, they are the Beni-Yarb. Every other one of them is a poet; in the face of an enemy, they are all warriors."

The camps on the hill, with the yellow flag giving notice of the Emir's station, had effect upon others besides the Yarbis; all who wished to draw out of the *melange* turned towards them, bringing the spectacle in part to the very feet of the Wanderer; whereas he thought with a quicker beating of the heart, "The followers of the Prophet are coming to show me of what they are this day composed." Then he said to the Shaykh, "Stand thou here, and tell me as I shall ask."

The conversation between them may be thus summarized:

The current which poured past then, its details in perfect view, carried along with it all the conditions and nationalities of the pilgrimage. Natives of the desert on bare-backed camels, clinging to the humps with one hand, while they pounded with the other—natives on beautiful horses, not needing whip or spur—natives on dromedaries so swift, sure-footed, and strong there was no occasion for fear. Men, and often women and children, on ragged saddle-cloths, others in pretentious boxes, and now and then a person whose wealth and rank were published by the magnificence of the litter in which he was borne, swinging luxuriously between long-stepping dromedaries from El Sbark.

"By Allah!" the Prince exclaimed. "Here hath barbarism its limit! Behold!"

They of whom he spoke came up in irregular array mounted on dromedaries without housing. At their head rode one with a white lettered green flag, and beating an immense drum. They were armed with long spears of Indian bamboo, garnished below the slender points with swinging tufts of ostrich feathers. Each carried a woman behind him disdainful of a veil. The feminine screams of exultation rose high above the yells of the men, helping not a little to the recklessness with which the latter bore onward.

Woe to such in their way as were poorly mounted. In a twinkling they were ridden down. Nor did those fare better who were overtaken struggling with a string of camels. The crash of bursting boxes, the sharp report of rending ropes, the warning cry, the maddening cheer; a battle of men, another of beasts—and when the collision had passed, the earth was strewn with its wreck.

"They are Wahabbas, O Hadji," said the Shaykh. "Thou seest the tufts on their spears. Under them they carry *Jehannum.*"

"And these now coming?" asked the Prince. "Their long white hats remind me of Persia."

"Persians they are," replied the Shaykh, his lip curling, his eyes gleaming. "They will tear their clothes, and cut their shaven crowns, and wail, 'Woe's me, O Ali!' then kiss the Kaaba with defilement on their beards. The curse of the *Shaykaim* is on them—may it stay there!"

Then the Prince knew it was a Sunite speaking of Schiahs.

Yet others of the Cafila of Bagdad passed with the despised sons of Iran; notably Deccanese, Hindoos, Afghans, and people from the Himalayas, and beyond them far as Kathay, and China, and Siam, all better known to the Prince than to his Shaykh, who spoke of them, saying, "Thou shouldst know thine own, O Hadji! Thou art their father!"

Next, in a blending that permitted no choice of associates, along swept the chief constituents of the caravans—Moors and Blackamoors, Egyptians, Syrians, Turks, Kurds, Caucasians, and Arabs of every tribe, each a multitude of themselves, and their passing filled up the afternoon.

Towards sundown the hurry and rush of the movement perceptibly slackened. Over in the west there were signs of a halt; tents were rising, and the smoke of multiplying fires began to deepen the blue of the distance. It actually appeared as if settlement for the night would creep back upon the east, whence the irruption had burst.

At a moment when the Prince's interest in the scene was commencing to flag, and he was thinking of returning to his tent, the rearmost divisions of the pilgrims entered the Valley. They were composed of footmen and donkey-riders, for whom the speed of the advance bodies had been too great. High-capped Persians, and Turks whose turbans were reduced to faded fezes, marched in the van, followed closely by a rabble of Takruris, ragged, moneyless, living upon meat of abandoned animals. Last of all were the sick and dying, who yet persisted in dragging their fainting limbs along as best they could. Might they but reach the Holy City! Then if they died it would be as martyrs for whom the doors of Paradise are always open. With them, expectants of easy prey, like the *rakham* [Footnote: Vultures.] sailing in slow circles overhead, flocked the beggars, thieves, outcasts and assassins; but night came quickly, and covered them, and all the things they did, for evil and night have been partners from the beginning.

At last the Prince returned to his tent. He had seen the sun set over El Zaribah; he had seen the passing of the caravans. Out there in the Valley they lay. They—to him, and for his purposes, the Mohammedan world unchanged—the same in composition, in practice, in creed—only he felt now a consciousness of understanding them as never before. Mahomet, in his re-introduction of God to man, had imposed himself upon their faith, its master idea, its central figure, the superior in sanctity, the essential condition—the ONE! Knowingly or unknowingly, he left a standard of religious excellence behind him—Himself. And by that standard the thief in the wake of the mighty caravans robbing the dead, the Thug strangling a victim because he was too slow in dying, were worthy Paradise, and would attain it, for they believed in him. Faith in the Prophet of God was more essential than faith in God. Such was the inspiration of Islam. A sinking of spirit fell upon the unhappy man. He felt a twinge of the bitterness always waiting on failure, where the undertaking, whatever it be, has enlisted the whole heart. At such times instinctively we turn here and there for help, and in its absence, for comfort and consolation; what should he do now but advert to Christianity? What would Christians say of his idea? Was God lost in Christ as he was here in Mahomet?

CHAPTER VI
THE PRINCE AND THE EMIR

In the reception room of the Prince's tent the lamps are lighted; one fastened to the stout centre pole, and five others on as many palings planted in the ground, all burning brightly. The illumination is enriched by the admirable blending of colors in the canopy of shawls. Within the space defined by the five lamps, on a tufted rug, the Mystic and the Emir are seated, both in *Ihram*, and looking cool and comfortable, though the night outside still testifies to the heat of the day.

A wooden trencher, scoured white as ivory, separates the friends, leaving them face to face. In supping they have reached what we call the dessert.

On the trencher are slender baskets containing grapes, figs, and dates, the choicest of the gardens of Medina. A jar of honey, an assortment of dry biscuits, and two jugs, one of water, the other of juice of pomegranates, with drinking cups, complete the board.

At this age, Orientals lingering at table have the cheer of coffee and tobacco; unhappily for the two of whom we are writing, neither of the great narcotics was discovered. Nevertheless it should not be supposed the fruits, the honey, and the waters failed to content them. Behind the host is the negro we already know as Nilo. He is very watchful of his master's every motion.

As guest and host appear now the formalism of acquaintanceship just made has somewhat disappeared, and they are talking easily and with freedom. Occasionally a movement of one or the other brings his head to a favorable angle, whereat the light, dropping on the freshly shaven crown, is sharply glinted back.

The Emir has been speaking of the plague.

"At Medina I was told it had run its course," the host remarked.

"True, O Hadji, but it has returned, and with greater violence. The stragglers were its victims; now it attacks indiscriminately. Yesterday the guard I keep in the rear came to a pilgrim of rank. His litter was deserted, and he was lying in it dead."

"The man may have been murdered."

"Nay," said the Emir, "gold in large amount was found on his person."

"But he had other property doubtless?"

"Of great value."

"What disposition was made of it?"

"It was brought to me, and is now with other stores in my tent; a law of ancient institution vesting it in the Emir El Hajj."

The countenance of the Jew became serious.

"The ownership was not in my thought," he said, waving his hand. "I knew the law; but this scourge of Allah has its laws also, and by one of them we are enjoined to burn or bury whatever is found with the body."

The Emir, seeing the kindly concern of his host, smiled as he answered:

"But there is a higher law, O Hadji."

"I spoke without thinking danger of any kind could disturb thee."

The host drew forward the date basket, and the Emir, fancying he discerned something on his mind besides the fruit, waited his further speech.

"I am reminded of another matter, O brave Emir; but as it also is personal I hesitate. Indeed I will not speak of it except with permission."

"As you will," the other replied, "I will answer—May the Prophet help me!"

"Blessed be the Prophet!" said the Prince, reverently. "Thy confidence doeth me honor, and I thank thee; at the same time I would not presume upon it if thy tongue were less suggestive of a land whose name is music—Italy. It is in my knowledge, O Emir, that the Sultan, thy master—may Allah keep him in countenance!—hath in his service many excellent soldiers by birth of other countries than his own, broad as it is—Christians, who are none the less of the true faith. Wherefore, wilt thou tell me of thyself?"

The question did not embarrass the Emir.

"The answer must be brief," he answered, without hesitation, "because there is little to tell. I do not know my native country. The peculiarity of accent you have mentioned has been observed by others; and as they agreed with you in assigning it to Italy, I am nothing loath to account myself an Italian. The few shreds of circumstance which came to me in course of time confirmed the opinion, and I availed myself of a favorable opportunity to acquire the tongue. In our further speech, O Hadji, you may prefer its use."

"At thy pleasure," the host replied; "though there is no danger of our being overheard. Nilo, the slave behind me, has been a mute from birth."

Then, without the slightest interruption, the Emir changed his speech from Greek to Italian.

"My earliest remembrance is of being borne in a woman's arms out of doors, under a blue sky, along a margin of white sand, an orchard on one hand, the sea on the other. The report of the waves breaking upon the shore lives distinctly in my memory; so does the color of the trees in the orchard which has since become familiar to me as the green of olives. Equally clear is the recollection that, returning in-doors, I was carried into a house of stone so large it must have been a castle. I speak of it, as of the orchard, and the sea, and the roar of the breakers, quite as much by reference to what I have subsequently seen as from trust in my memory."

Here the host interrupted him to remark:

"Though an Eastern, I have been a traveller in the west, and the description reminds me of the eastern shore of Italy in the region of Brindisi."

"My next recollection," the Emir resumed, "is a child's fright, occasioned by furious flames, and thick smoke, and noises familiar now as of battle. There was then a voyage on the sea during which I saw none but bearded men. The period of perfect knowledge so far as my history is concerned began when I found myself an object of the love and care of the wife of a renowned Pacha, governor of the city of Brousa. She called me *Mirza*. My childhood was spent in a harem, and I passed from it into a school to enter upon my training as a soldier. In good time I became a Janissary. An opportunity presented itself one day, and I distinguished myself. My master, the Sultan, rewarded me by promotion and transfer to the *Silihdars*, [Footnote: D'Oheson.] the most ancient and favored corps of the Imperial army, it being the body-guard of the Padisha, and garrison of his palace. The yellow flag my ensign carries belongs to that corps. As a further token of his confidence, the Sultan appointed me Emir El Hajj. In these few words, O Hadji, you have my history."

The listener was impressed with the simplicity of the narrative, and the speaker's freedom from regret, sorrow, or passion of any kind.

"It is a sad story, O Emir," he said, sympathetically, "and I cannot think it ended. Knowest thou not more?"

"Nothing of incident," was the reply. "All that remains is inferential. The castle was attacked at night by Turks landed from their galleys."

"And thy father and mother?"

"I never knew them."

"There is another inference," said the Prince, suggestively—"they were Christians."

"Yes, but unbelievers."

The suppression of natural affection betrayed by the remark still more astonished the host.

"But they believed in God," he said.

"They should have believed Mahomet was his Prophet."

"I fear I am giving you pain, O Emir."

"Dismiss the fear, O Hadji."

Again the Jew sought the choicest date in the basket. The indifference of his guest was quick fuel to the misgivings which we have already noticed as taking form about his purpose, and sapping and weakening it. To be arbiter in the religious disputes of men, the unique consummation called for by his scheme, the disputants must concede him room and hearing. Were all Mohammedans, from whom he hoped most, like this one born of Christians, then the two conditions would be sternly refused him. By the testimony of this witness, there was nothing in the heredity of faith; and it went to his soul incisively that, in stimulating the passions which made the crusades a recurrence of the centuries, he himself had contributed to the defeat now threatening his latest ambition. The sting went to his soul; yet, by force of will, always at command in the presence of strangers, he repressed his feeling, and said:

"Everything is as Allah wills. Let us rejoice that he is our keeper. The determination of our fate, in the sense of what shall happen to us, and what we shall be, and when and where the end shall overtake us, is no more to him than deciding the tint of the rose before the bud is formed. O Emir, I congratulate you on the resignation with which you accept his judgment. I congratulate you upon the age in which he has cast your life. He who in a moment of uncertainty would inform himself of his future should not heed his intentions and hopes; by studying his present conditions, he will find himself an oracle unto himself. He should address his best mind to the question, 'I am now in a road; if I keep it, where will I arrive?' And wisdom will answer, 'What are thy desires? For what art thou fitted? What are the opportunities of the time?' Most fortunate, O Emir, if there be correspondence between the desire, the fitness, and the opportunity!"

The Emir did not comprehend, and seeing it, the host added with a directness approaching the abrupt:

"And now to make the reason of my congratulations clear, it is necessary that thou consent to my putting a seal upon your lips. What sayest thou?"

"If I engage my silence, O Hadji, it is because I believe you are a good man."

The dignity of the Emir's answer did not entirely hide the effect of the Prince's manner.

"Know thou then," the latter continued, with a steady, penetrating gaze— "know thou then, there is a Brahman of my acquaintance who is a Magus. I use the word to distinguish him from the necromancers whom the Koran has set in everlasting prohibition. He keeps school in a chapel hid away in the heart of jungles overgrowing a bank of the Bermapootra, not far from the mountain gates of the river. He has many scholars, and his intelligence has compassed all knowledge. He is familiar with the supernatural as with the natural. On my way, I visited him.... Know thou next, O Emir, I too have had occasion to make inquiries of the future. The vulgar would call me an astrologer—not a professional practising for profit, but an adept seeking information because it lifts me so much nearer Allah and his sublimest mysteries. Very lately I found a celestial horoscope announcing a change in the status of the world. The masterful waves, as you may know, have for many ages flowed from the West; but now, the old Roman impetus having at last spent itself, a refluence is to set in, and the East in its turn pour a dominating flood upon the West. The determining stars have slipped their influences. They are in motion. *Constantinople is doomed!*"

The guest drew a quick breath. Understanding was flooding him with light.

"And now, O Emir, say, if the revelation had stopped there—stopped, I mean, with the overthrow of the Christian capital—wouldst thou have been satisfied with it?"

"No, by Allah, no!"

"Further, Emir. The stars being communicable yet, what wouldst thou have asked them next?"

"I would not have rested until I had from them the name of him who is to be leader in the movement."

The Mystic smiled at the young man's fervor.

"Thou hast saved me telling what I did, and affirmed the logic of our human nature," he said. "Thy imperial master is old, and much worn by wars and cares of government, is he not?"

"Old in greatness," answered the Emir, diplomatically.

"Hath he not a son?"

"A son with all the royal qualities of the father."

"But young—not more than eighteen."

"Not more."

"And the Prophet hath lent him his name?"

"Even so."

The host released the eager face of the Emir from his gaze, while he sought a date in the basket.

"Another horoscope—the second"—he then said, quietly, "revealed everything but the hero's name. He is to be of kingly birth, and a Turk. Though a lad, he is already used to arms and armor."

"Oh! by Allah, Hadji," cried the guest, his face flushed, his words quick, his voice mandatory. "Release me from my pledge of silence. Tell me who thou art, that I may report thee, and the things thou sayest. There was never such news to warm a heroic heart."

The Prince pursued his explanation without apparently noticing the interruption noticing the interruption.

"To verify the confidences of the stars, I sought the Magus in his chapel by the sacred river. Together we consulted them, and made the calculations. He embraced me; but it was agreed between us that absolute verity of the finding could only be had by re-casting the horoscopes at Constantinople. Thou must know, O Emir, there is an astral alphabet which has its origin in the inter-relations of the heavenly bodies, represented by lines impalpable to the common eye; know also that the most favored adept cannot read the mystic letters with the assurance best comporting with verity, except he be at the place of the destined event or revolution. To possess myself of the advantage, I shall ere long visit the ancient capital. More plainly, I am on the way thither now."

Instead of allaying the eagerness of the Emir, the words excited it the more.

"Release me from my pledge," he repeated, entreatingly, "and tell me who thou art. Mahommed is my pupil; he rides, carries shield, lays lance, draws arrow, and strikes with sword and axe as I have taught him. Thou canst not name a quality characteristic of heroes he does not possess. Doth Allah permit me safe return from the Hajj, he will be first to meet me at his father's gate. Think what happiness I should have in saluting him there with the title—Hail Mahommed, Conqueror of Constantinople!"

The Jew answered:

"I would gladly help thee, O Emir, to happiness and promotion; for I see what afterwhile, if not presently, they would follow such a salutation of thy pupil, if coupled with a sufficient explanation; but his interests are paramount; at the same time it becomes me to be allegiant to the divinatory stars. What rivalries the story might awaken! It is not uncommon in history, as thou mayst know, that sons of promise have been cut off by jealous fathers. I am not accusing the great Amurath; nevertheless precautions are always proper."

The speaker then became dramatic.

"Nay, brave Emir, the will to help thee has been already seconded by the deed. I spoke but now of lines of correspondence between the shining lights that are the life of the sky at night. Let me illustrate my meaning. Observe the lamps about us. The five on the uprights. Between them, in the air, two stars of interwoven form are drawn. Take the lamps as determining points, and use thy fancy a moment."

The Emir turned to the lamps; and the host, swift to understand the impulse, gave him time to gratify it; then he resumed:

"So the fields of Heaven between the stars, where the vulgar see only darkness, are filled with traceries infinite in form yet separable as the letters of the alphabet. They are the ciphers in which Allah writes his reasons for every creation, and his will concerning it. There the sands are numbered, and the plants and trees, and their leaves, and the birds, and everything animate; there is thy history, and mine, and all of little and great and good and bad that shall befall us in this life. Death does not blot out the records. Everlastingly writ, they shall be everlastingly read—for the shame of some, for the delight of others."

"Allah is good," said the Emir, bending his head.

"And now," the Mystic continued, "thou hast eaten and drunk with me in the Pentagram of the Magii. Such is the astral drawing between the five lamps. Henceforth in conflicts of interest, fortune against fortune, influences undreamt of will come to thy assistance. So much have I already done for thee."

The Emir bowed lower than before.

"Nor that alone," the Jew continued. "Henceforth our lives will run together on lines never divergent, never crossing. Be not astonished, if, within a week, I furnish, to thy full satisfaction, proof of what I am saying."

The expression could not be viewed except as of more than friendly interest.

"Should it so happen," the Emir said, with warmth, "consider how unfortunate my situation would be, not knowing the name or country of my benefactor."

The host answered simply, though evasively:

"There are reasons of state, O Emir, requiring me to make this pilgrimage unknown to any one."

The Emir apologized.

"It is enough," the host added, "that thou remember me as the Prince of India, whose greatest happiness is to believe in Allah and Mahomet his Prophet; at the same time I concede we should have the means of certainly knowing each other should communication become desirable hereafter."

He made a sign with his right hand which the negro in waiting responded to by passing around in front of him.

"Nilo," the master said in Greek, "bring me the two malachite rings—those with the turquoise eyes."

The slave disappeared.

"Touching the request to be released from the promise of secrecy, pardon me, O Emir, if I decline to grant it. The verification to be made in Constantinople should advise thee that the revolution to which I referred is not ripe for publication to the world. A son might be excused for dishonoring his parents; but the Magus who would subject the divine science to danger of ridicule or contempt by premature disclosure is fallen past hope—he would betray Allah himself."

The Emir bowed, but with evident discontent. At length the slave returned with the rings.

"Observe, O Emir," the Jew said, passing them both to his guest, "they are rare, curious, and exactly alike."

The circlets were of gold, with raised settings of deep green stone, cut so as to leave a drop of pure turquoise on the top of each, suggestive of birds' eyes.

"They are exactly the same, O Prince," said the Emir, tendering them back.

The Jew waved his hand.

"Select one of them," he said, "and I will retain the other. Borne by messengers, they will always identify us each to the other."

The two grew more cordial, and there was much further conversation across the board, interspersed with attentions to the fruit basket and pomegranate water. About midnight the Emir took his departure. When he was gone, the host walked to and fro a long time; once he halted, and said aloud—"I hear his salute, 'Hail Mahommed, Conqueror of Constantinople!' It is always well to have a store of strings for one's bow."

And to himself he laughed heartily.

Next day at dawn the great caravan was afoot, every man, woman, and child clad in *Ihram*, and whitening the pale green Valley.

CHAPTER VII
AT THE KAABA

The day before the pilgrimage.

A cloud had hung over the valley where Mecca lies like drift in the bed of a winding gorge. About ten o'clock in the morning the cloud disappeared over the summit of Abu Kubays in the east. The promise of rain was followed by a simoom so stifling that it plunged every breathing thing into a struggle for air. The dogs burrowed in the shade of old walls; birds flew about with open beaks; the herbage wilted, and the leaves on the stunted shrubs ruffled, then rolled up, like drying cinnamon. If the denizens of the city found no comfort in their houses of stone and mud, what suffering was there for the multitude not yet fully settled in the blistering plain beyond the bluffs of Arafat?

The zealous pilgrim, obedient to the law, always makes haste to celebrate his arrival at the Holy City by an immediate visit to the Haram. If perchance he is to see the enclosure for the first time, his curiosity, in itself pardonable, derives a tinge of piety from duty. The Prince of India but illustrated the rule. He left his tents pitched close to those of the Emir El Hajj and the Scherif of Mecca, under the Mountain of Mercy, as Arafat was practically translated by the very faithful. Having thus assured the safety of his property, for conveniency and greater personal comfort he took a house with windows looking into the Mosque. By so doing, he maintained the dignity of his character as a Prince of India. The beggars thronging his door furnished lively evidence of the expectations his title and greatness had already excited.

With a guide, his suite, and Nilo shading his head with an umbrella of light green paper, the Prince appeared in front of the chief entrance to the sacred square from the north. [Footnote: The Bab el Vzyadeh.]

The heads of the party were bare; their countenances becomingly solemn; their *Ihram* fresh and spotlessly white. Passing slowly on, they were conducted under several outside arches, and down a stairway into a hall, where they left the umbrella and their shoes.

The visitor found himself then in a cloister of the Mosque with which the area around the Kaaba is completely enclosed. There was a pavement of undressed flags, and to the right and left a wilderness of tall pillars tied together by arches, which in turn supported domes. Numbers of people, bareheaded and barefooted, to whom the heat outside was insupportable, were in refuge there; some, seated upon the stones, revolved their rosaries; others walked slowly about. None spoke. The silence was a tribute to the ineffable sanctity of the place. The refreshing shade, the solemn hush, the whiteness of the garments were suggestive of sepulchres and their spectral tenantry.

In the square whither the Prince next passed, the first object to challenge his attention was the Kaaba itself. At sight of it he involuntarily stopped.

The cloisters, seen from the square, were open colonnades. Seven minarets, belted in red, blue and yellow, arose in columnar relief against the sky and the mountains in the south. A gravelled plot received from the cloisters; next that, toward the centre, was a narrow pavement of rough stone in transverse extension down a shallow step to another gravelled plot; then another pavement wider than the first, and ending, like it, in a downward step; after which there was a third sanded plot, and then a third pavement defined by gilded posts upholding a continuous row of lamps, ready for lighting at the going down of the sun. The last pavement was of gray granite polished mirror-like by the friction of millions of bare feet; and upon it, like the pedestal of a monument upon a plinth, rested the base of the Holy House, a structure of glassy white marble about two feet in height, with a bench of sharp inclination from the top. At intervals it was studded with massive brass rings. Upon the base the Kaaba rose, an oblong cube forty feet tall, eighteen paces lengthwise, and fourteen in breadth, shrouded all in black silk wholly unrelieved, except by one broad band of the appearance of gold, and inscriptions from the Koran, of a like appearance, wrought in boldest lettering. The freshness of the great gloomy curtain told how quickly the gift of the Sultan had been made available, and that whatever else might betide him, the young Emir was already happily discharged of his trust.

Of the details, the only one the Jew actually coupled with a thought was the Kaaba. A hundred millions of human beings pray five times every day, their faces turned to this funereal object! The idea, though commonplace, called up that other always in waiting with him. In a space too brief for the formulation of words, he felt the Arbitership of his dreams blow away. The work of the founder of Islam was too well done and now too far gone to be disturbed, except with the sanction of God. Had he the sanction? A writhing of the soul, accompanied with a glare, like lightning, and followed, like lightning, by an engulfing darkness, wrung his features, and instinctively he covered them with his hands. The guide saw the action, and misjudged it.

"Let us not be in haste," he said. "Others before you have found the House at first sight blinding. Blessed be Allah!"

The commiseration affected the Prince strangely. The darkness, under pressure of his hands upon the eyeballs, gave place to an atmosphere of roseate light, in the fulness of which he saw the House of God projected by Solomon and rebuilt by Herod. The realism of the apparition was absolute, and comparison unavoidable. That he, familiar with the glory of the conception of the Israelite, should be thought blinded by this *Beit Allah* of the Arab, so without grace of form or lines, so primitive and expressionless, so palpably uninspired by taste, or genius, or the Deity it was designed to honor, restored him at once: indeed, in the succeeding reaction, he found it difficult to keep down resentment. Dropping his hands, he took another survey of the shrouded pile, and swept all the square under eye.

He beheld a crowd of devotees at the northeast corner of the House, and over their heads two small open structures which, from descriptions often heard, he recognized as praying places. A stream of worshippers was circling around the marble base of the Most Holy, some walking, others trotting; these, arriving at the northeast corner, halted—the Black Stone was there! A babel of voices kept the echoes of the enclosure in unremitting exercise. The view taken, the Jew said, calmly:

"Blessed be Allah! I will go forward."

In his heart he longed to be in Constantinople—Islam, it was clear, would lend him no ear; Christendom might be more amenable.

He was carried next through the Gate of the Sons of the Old Woman; thence to the space in front of the well Zem-Zem; mindful of the prayers and prostrations required at each place, and of the dumb servants who went with him.

The famous well was surrounded by a throng apparently impassable.

"Room for the Royal Hadji—for the Prince of India!" the guide yelled. "There are no poor where he is—make way!"

A thousand eyes sought the noble pilgrim; and as a path opened for him, a score of *Zem-Zemis* refilled their earthen cups with the bitter water afresh. A Prince of Hind did not come to them every day.

He tasted from a cup—his followers drank—and when the party turned away there were jars paid for to help all the blind in the caravan back to healthful vision.

"There is no God but Allah! Be merciful to him, O Allah," the crowd shouted, in approval of the charity.

The press of pilgrims around the northeastern corner of the Kaaba, to which the guide would have conducted the Prince next, was greater than at the well. Each was waiting his turn to kiss the Black Stone before beginning the seven circuits of the House.

Never had the new-comer seen a concourse so wrought upon by fanaticism; never had he seen a concourse so peculiarly constituted. All complexions, even that of the interior African, were a reddish desert tan. Eyes fiercely bright appeared unnaturally swollen from the colirium with which they were generally stained. The diversities the penitential costume would have masked were effectually exposed whenever mouths opened for utterance. Many sang, regardless of time or melody, the *tilbiye* they had hideously vocalized in their advance toward the city. For the most part, however, the effort at expression spent itself in a long cry, literally rendered—"Thou hast called me—I am here! I am here!" The deliverance was in the vernacular of the devotee, and low or loud, shrill or hoarse, according to the intensity of the passion possessing him.

To realize the discordancy, the reader must recall the multiplicity of the tribes and nations represented; then will he fancy the agitation of the mass, the swaying of the white-clad bodies, the tossing of bare arms and distended hands, the working of tearful faces turned up to the black-curtained pile regardless of the smiting of the sun—here men on their knees, there men grovelling on the pavement—yonder one beating his breast till it resounds like an empty cask—some comprehension of the living obstruction in front of the Jew can be had.

Then the guide, calling him, tried the throng.

"The Prince of India!" he shouted, at the top of his voice. "Room for the beloved of the Prophet! Stand not in his way—Room, room!"

After much persistence the object was achieved. A pilgrim, the last one in front of the Prince, with arms extended along the two sides of the angle of the wall where the curtain was looped up, seemed struggling to embrace the House; suddenly, as in despair he beat his head frantically against the sharp corner—a second thrust more desperate than the first—then a groan, and he dropped blindly to the pavement. The guide rejoicing made haste to push the Prince into the vacant place.

Without the enthusiasm of a traveller, calmly as a philosopher, the Jew, himself again, looked at the Stone which more nearly than any other material thing commanded idolatrous regard from the Mohammedan world. He had known personally most of the great men of that world—its poets, lawmakers, warriors, ascetics, kings—even the Prophet. And now they came one by one, as one by one they had come in their several days, and kissed the insensate thing; and between the coming and going time was scarcely perceptible. The mind has the faculty of compressing, by one mighty effort, the incidents of a life, even of centuries, into a flash-like reenactment.

As all the way from the first view of the sanctuary to arrival at the gate, and thence to this point, the Jew had promptly followed his guide, especially in recitation of the prescribed prayers, he was about to do so now; already his hands were raised.

"Great God! O my God! I believe in Thee—I Believe in thy Book—I believe in thy Word—I believe in thy Promise," the zealous prompter said, and waited.

For the first time the votary was slow to respond. How could he, at such a juncture, refuse a thought to the Innumerables whose ghosts had been rendered up in vain struggles to obey the law which required them to come and make proof of faith before this Stone! The Innumerables, lost at sea, lost in the desert—lost body and soul, as in their dying they themselves had imagined! Symbolism! An invention of men—a necessity of necromancers! God had his ministers and priests, the living media of his will, but of symbols—nothing!

"Great God! O my God!" the guide began again. A paroxysm of disgust seized the votary. The Phariseeism in which he was born and bred, and which he could no more outlive than he could outlive his body asserted itself.

In the crisis of the effort at self-control, he heard a groan, and, looking down, saw the mad devotee at his feet. In sliding from the shelf of the base, the man had been turned upon his back, so that he was lying face upward. On the forehead there were two cruel wounds; and the blood, yet flowing, had partially filled the hollows of the eyes, making the countenance unrecognizable.

"The wretch is dying," the Prince exclaimed.

"Allah is merciful—let us attend to the prayers," the guide returned, intent on business.

"But he will die, if not helped."

"When we have finished, the porters will come for him."

The sufferer stirred, then raised a hand.

"O Hadji—O Prince of India!" he said faintly, in Italian.

The Wanderer bent down to get a nearer view.

"It is the Yellow Air—save me!"

Though hardly articulate, the words were full of light to the listener.

"The virtues of the Pentagram endure," he said, with absolute self-possession. "The week is not ended, and, lo!—I save him."

Rising to his full stature, he glanced here and there over the throng, as if commanding attention, and proclaimed:

"A mercy of the Most Merciful! It is the Emir El Hajj."

There was a general silence. Every man had seen the martial figure of the young chief in his arms and armor, and on horseback; many of them had spoken to him.

"The Emir El Hajj—dying," passed rapidly from mouth to mouth.

"O Allah!" burst forth in general refrain; after which the ejaculations were all excerpted from prayers.

"'O Allah! This is the place of him who flies to thee from fire!—Shadow him, O Allah, in thy shadow!—Give him drink from the cup of thy Prophet!'"

A Bedouin, tall, almost black, and with a tremendous mouth open until the red lining was exposed between the white teeth down to the larynx, shouted shrilly the inscription on the marble over the breast of the Prophet—"In the name of Allah! Allah have mercy upon him!"—and every man repeated the words, but not one so much as reached a hand in help.

The Prince waited—still the *Amins*, and prayerful ejaculations. Then his wonder ceased. Not a pilgrim but envied the Emir—that he should die so young was a pity—that he should die at the base of the sanctuary, in the crowning act of the Hajj, was a grace of God. Each felt Paradise stooping low to receive a martyr, and that its beatitude was near. They trembled with ecstasy at hearing the gates opening on their crystal hinges, and seeing light as from the robe of the Prophet glimmering through them. O happy Emir!

The Jew drew within himself. Compromise with such fanaticism was impossible. Then, with crushing distinctness, he saw what had not before occurred to him. In the estimation of the Mohammedan world, the role of Arbiter was already filled; that which he thought of being, Mahomet was. Too late, too late! In bitterness of soul he flung his arms up and shouted:

"The Emir is dying of the plague!"

He would have found satisfaction in seeing the blatant crowd take to its heels, and hie away into the cloisters and the world outside; not one moved!

"By Allah!" he shouted, more vehemently than before. "The Yellow Air hath blown upon the Emir—is blowing upon you—Fly!"

"*Amin! Amin!*—Peace be with thee, O Prince of Martyrs! O Prince of the Happy! Peace be with thee, O Lion of Allah! O Lion of the Prophet!" Such the answers returned him.

The general voice became a howl. Surely here was something more than fanaticism. Then it entered his understanding. What he beheld was Faith exulting above the horrors of disease, above the fear of death—Faith bidding Death welcome! His arms fell down. The crowd, the sanctuary, the hopes he had built on Islam, were no more to him. He signed to his three attendants, and they advanced and raised the Emir from the pavement.

"To-morrow I will return with thee, and complete my vows;" he said to his guide. "For the present, lead out of the square to my house."

The exit was effected without opposition.

Next day the Emir, under treatment of the Prince, was strong enough to tell his story. The plague had struck him about noon of the day following the interview in the tent at El Zaribah. Determined to deliver the gifts he had in keeping, and discharge his trust to the satisfaction of his sovereign, he struggled resolutely with the disease. After securing the Scherif's receipt he bore up long enough to superintend the pitching his camp. Believing death inevitable, he was carried into his tent, where he issued his final orders and bade his attendants farewell. In the morning, though weak, half-delirious, his faith the strongest surviving impulse, he called for his horse, and being lifted into the saddle, rode to the city, resolved to assure himself of the blessings of Allah by dying in the shadow of the sanctuary.

The Prince, listening to the explanation, was more than ever impressed with the futility of attempting a compromise with people so devoted to their religion. There was nothing for him but to make haste to Constantinople, the centre of Christian sentiment and movement. There he might meet encouragement and ultimate success.

In the ensuing week, having performed the two pilgrimages, and seen the Emir convalescent, he took the road again, and in good time reached Jedda, where he found his ship waiting to convey him across the Red Sea to the African coast. The embarkation was without incident, and he departed, leaving a reputation odorous for sanctity, with numberless witnesses to carry it into every quarter of Islam.

CHAPTER VIII
THE ARRIVAL IN CONSTANTINOPLE

Uel, the son of Jahdai, was in the habit of carrying the letter received from the mysterious stranger about with him in a breast pocket. How many times a day he took it out for reexamination would be difficult to say. Observing the appearance of signs of usage, he at length wrapped it in an envelope of yellow silk. If he had thought less of it, he would have resorted to plain linen.

There were certain points in the missive which seemed of greater interest to him than others. For example, the place whence it had been addressed was an ever recurring puzzle; he also dwelt long upon the sentence which referred so delicately to a paternal relationship. The most exigent passages, however, were those relative to the time he might look for the man's coming. As specially directed, he had taken note of the day of the delivery of the letter, and was greatly surprised to find the messenger had arrived the last day of the year permitted him. The punctuality of the servant might be in imitation of a like virtue of the master. If so, at the uttermost, the latter might be expected six months after receipt of the letter. Or he might appear within the six months. The journeys laid out were of vast distances, and through wild and dangerous countries, and by sea as well. Only a good traveller could survive them at all; to execute them in such brief space seemed something superhuman.

So it befell that the son of Jahdai was at first but little concerned. The months—three, four, five—rolled away, and the sixth was close at hand; then every day brought him an increase of interest. In fact, he found himself looking for the arrival each morning, and at noon promising it an event of the evening.

November was the sixth and last month of the time fixed. The first of that month passed without the stranger. Uel became anxious. The fifteenth he turned the keeping of his shop over to a friend; and knowing the passage from Alexandria must be by sea, he betook himself, with Syama, to the port on the Golden Horn known as the Gate of St. Peter, at the time most frequented by Egyptian sailing masters. In waiting there, he saw the sun rise over the heights of Scutari, and it was the morning of the very last day. Syama, meantime, occupied himself in final preparation of the house for the reception. He was not excited, like Uel, because he had no doubt of the arrival within the period set. He was also positively certain of finding his master, when at length he did appear, exactly as when he separated from him in Cipango. He was used to seeing Time waste itself upon the changeless man; he had even caught from him a kind of contempt for what other men shrank from as dangers and difficulties.

The site of the house has been described; it remains to give the reader an idea of its interior. There were four rooms on the ground floor furnished comfortably for servants, of whom the arrangement indicated three besides Syama. The first floor was of three apartments communicable by doorways with portieres of camel's hair. The furniture was Roman, Greek, and Egyptian mixed. Of the three the middle chamber was largest, and as its fittings were in a style of luxury supposed to be peculiar to princes, the conclusion was fair that it was designed for the proprietor's occupancy during his waking hours. A dark blue rug clothed the floor. In the centre, upon a shield of clear copper, arose a silver brazier. The arms and legs of the stools here and there on the rug were carven in grotesque imitation of reptiles and animals of the ultra dragonish mode. The divans against the walls were of striped silk. In each corner stood a tall post of silvered bronze, holding at the end of a graceful crook several lamps of Pompeiian model. A wide window in the east end, filled with plants in bloom, admitted ample light, which, glancing through the flowers, fell on a table dressed in elegant cloth, and bearing a lacquered waiter garnished with cups of metal and glass, and one hand-painted porcelain decanter for drinking water. An enormous tiger-skin, the head intact and finished with extraordinary realism, was spread on the floor in front of the table. The walls were brilliant with fresh Byzantine frescoing. The air of the room was faintly pervaded with a sweet incense of intoxicating effect upon one just admitted to it. Indeed the whole interior partook of this sweetness.

The care of the faithful servant had not been confined to the rooms; he had constructed a summer house upon the roof, knowing that when the weather permitted his master would pass the nights there in preference to the chambers below. This structure looked not unlike a modern belfry, except that the pillars and shallow dome of the top were of Moorish lightness. Thence, to a familiar, the heavens in the absence of the sun would be an unrolled map.

When the last touch of the preparation had been given, and Syama said to himself, "He may come now," one point was especially noticeable— nowhere in the house was there provision for a woman.

The morning of the last day Syama accompanied Uel to the port reluctantly. Feeling sure his master had not arrived in the night, he left his friend on the watch, and returned home early.

The noise and stir of business at the ancient landing were engaging. With a great outcry, a vessel would be drawn up, and made fast, and the unloading begun. A drove of donkeys, or a string of camels, or a mob of porters would issue from the gate, receive the cargo and disappear with it. Now and then a ship rounded the classic Point, its square sail bent and all the oars at work: sweeping past Galata on the north side of the Horn, then past the Fish Market Gate on the south, up it would come gracefully as a flying bird; if there was place for it at the quay, well; if not, after hovering around awhile, it would push out to a berth in the open water. Such incidents were crises to Uel. To this one and to that he would run with the question:

"Where is she from?"

If from the upper sea, he subsided; but if from the Marmora, he kept eager lookout upon her, hoping to recognize in every disembarkee the man he was expecting.

That he had never seen the person was of little consequence. He had thought of him so much awake, and seen him so repeatedly in dreams, he was confident of knowing him at sight. Imagining a stranger's appearance is for the most part a gentle tribute of respect; the mistakes we make are for the most part ludicrous.

No one answering the preconception came. Noon, and still no one; then, cast down and disappointed, Uel went home, ate something, held the usual childish dialogue with his little girl, and about mid afternoon crossed the street to the new residence. Great was his astonishment at finding a pyramid of coals glowing in the silver brazier, and the chill already driven from the sitting-room. Here—there—upstairs, downstairs—the signs were of present occupancy. For a moment he thought the master had slipped by him or landed at some other port of the city.

"Is he here? Has he come?" he asked, excitedly, and Syama answered with a shake of the head.

"Then why the fire?"

Syama, briefly waving his hand as if following the great Marmorean lake, turned the finger ends into the other palm, saying plainly and emphatically:

"He is coming—he will be here directly."

Uel smiled—faith could not be better illustrated—and it was so in contrast with his own incredulity!

He lingered awhile. Restlessness getting the mastery, he returned home, reflecting on the folly of counting so implicitly upon the conclusion to a day of a tour so vast. More likely, he thought, the traveller's bones were somewhere whitening the desert, or the savages of Kash-Cush had eaten him. He had heard of their cannibalism.

Want of faith, however, did not prevent the shopkeeper from going to his friend's house after supper. It was night, and dark, and the chilling moisture of a winter wind blowing steadily from the Black Sea charged the world outside with discomfort. The brazier with its heap of living coals had astonished him before; now the house was all alight! He hastened upstairs. In the sitting-room the lamps were burning, and the illumination was brilliant. Syama was there, calm and smiling as usual.

"What—he is here?" Uel said, looking from door to door.

The servant shook his head, and waved his hand negatively, as to say:

"Not yet—be patient—observe me."

To indulge his wonder, Uel took seat. Later on he tried to get from Syama an explanation of his amazing confidence, but the latter's substitute for speech was too limited and uncertain to be satisfactory.

About ten o'clock Syama went below, and presently returned with food and drink on a large waiter.

"Ah, good Lord!" Uel thought. "He is making a meal ready. What a man! What a master!"

Then he gave attention to the fare, which was of wheaten wafers, cold fowl, preserved fruits, and wine in a stoneware bottle. These Syama set on a circular table not higher than the divan in front of which it was drawn. A white napkin and a bowl for laving the fingers completed the preparation, as Uel supposed. But no. Syama went below again, and reappeared with a metal pot and a small wooden box. The pot he placed on the coals in the brazier, and soon a delicate volume of steam was pouring from the spout; after handling the box daintily as if the contents were vastly precious, he deposited it unopened by the napkin and bowl. Then, with an expression of content upon his face, he too took seat, and surrendered himself to expectancy. The lisping of the steam escaping from the pot on the fire was the only sound in the room.

The assurance of the servant was contagious. Uel began to believe the master would come. He was congratulating himself upon the precaution he had taken in leaving a man at the port to conduct him rightly when he heard a shuffling of feet below stairs. He listened startled. There were several men in the company. Steps shook the floor. Uel and Syama arose.

The latter's countenance flushed with pleasure; giving one triumphal glance at his friend, much as to say, There—did I not tell you so? he walked forward quickly, and reached the head of the steps just as a stranger finished their ascent. In a moment Syama was on his knees, kissing the hand held out to him. Uel needed no prompter—it was the master!

If only on account of the mutuality of affection shown between the two, the meeting was a pleasant sight. That feature, however, was lost to the shopkeeper, who had no thought except of the master's appearance. He had imagined him modelled after the popular conceptions of kings and warriors—tall, majestic, awe-inspiring. He saw instead a figure rather undersized, slightly stoop-shouldered, thin; at least it seemed so then, hid as it was under a dark brown burnoose of the amplitude affected by Arab sheiks. The head was covered by a woollen handkerchief of reddish tint, held by a scarlet cord. The edge of the handkerchief projected over the forehead enough to cast the entire face in shade, leaving to view only a mass of white beard overflowing the breast.

The master ended the reception at the head of the stairs by gently raising Syama to his feet. Then he subjected the room to a swift inspection, and, in proof of satisfaction, he patted the happy retainer on the shoulder. Invited by the fire, and the assurance of comfort in its glow, he advanced to the brazier, and while extending his hands over it, observed Uel. Without surprise or hesitation he walked to him.

"Son of Jahdai!" he said, offering his hand.

The voice was of exceeding kindness. As an overture to peace and goodwill, it was reenforced by very large eyes, the intense blackness of which was softened by a perceptible glow of pleasure. Uel was won on the instant. A recollection of the one supreme singularity of the new acquaintance—his immunity from death—recurred to him, and he could not have escaped its effect had he wished. He was conscious also that the eyes were impressing him. Without distinct thought, certainly without the slightest courtierly design, he obeyed the impulse of the moment, and stooped and touched the extended hand with his lips. And before rising he heard the beginning of further speech:

"I see the truth of my judgment. The family of my ancient friends has trodden the ways of righteousness under the commandments of the Lord until it has become a kind unto itself. I see too my trust has been verified. O Son of Jahdai, you did assist my servant, as I requested, and to your kindness, doubtless, I am indebted for this home full of comforts after a long absence among strangers. I hold you my creditor."

The tendency of the speech was to relieve Uel of embarrassment.

"Do not thank me," he answered. "The business was ordinary, and strictly within Syama's capacity. Indeed, the good man could have finished it without my help."

The master, rich in experience, noticed the deferential manner of the reply, and was agreeably assured on his side.

"Very well. There will be no harm in reserving an opinion," he said. "The good man, as you call him, is making ready a drink with which he has preceded me from his country, and which you must stay and share, as it is something unknown in the West."

"Let me first welcome you here," Uel returned.

"Oh, I saw the welcome in your face. But let us get nearer the fire. The night is chilling. If I were owner of a garden under whatever hill along the Bosphorus, verily I should tremble for my roses."

Thus briefly, and in such simple manner, the wise Mystic put the shopkeeper perfectly at ease.

At the brazier they watched Syama in the operation since become of universal knowledge under title of "drawing tea." The fragrance of the decoction presently filled the room to the suppression of the incense, and they drank, ate, and were sociable. The host outlined his travels. Uel, in return, gave him information of the city. When the latter departed, it was with a light heart, and an elastic step; the white beard and patriarchal manner of the man had laid his fears, and the future was to him like a cloudless sky.

Afterwhile the master signified a wish to retire; whereupon his household came, as was their wont, to bid him good-night. Of these there were two white men. At sight of Syama, they rushed to embrace him as became brethren of old acquaintance long in the same service. A third one remained at the door. Syama looked at him, and then at the master; for the man was a stranger. Then the Jew, with quick intuition of the requirement of the time, went, and took him by the hand, and led him to the others. Addressing Syama, he said gravely:

"This is Nilo, son of the Nilo whom you knew. As you held the father in love, so you shall hold the son."

The man was young, very black, and gigantic in stature. Syama embraced him as he had the others.

In the great city there was not a more united household under roof than that of the shopkeeper's friend.

CHAPTER IX
THE PRINCE AT HOME

A wise man wishing to know another always attends him when he is in narrative. The reader may be familiar with the principle, and a believer in it; for his better satisfaction, therefore, a portion of the Prince's conversation with Uel over the tea-table the night of his arrival in Constantinople shall be reported nearly as possible in his own words. It will be found helpful to the story as well as an expose of character.

"I said in my letter, as thou mayst remember, O son of Jahdai"—the voice of the speaker was low, but earnest, and admirably in harmony with the sentiment, "that I hoped thou wouldst allow me to relate myself to thee as father to son. Thou hast not forgotten it, I am sure."

"I recall it distinctly," Uel answered, respectfully.

"Thou wilt remember not less clearly then that I added the words, 'in all things a help, in nothing a burden.'"

Uel assented.

"The addition I thought of great importance," the Prince continued; "for it was very desirable that thou shouldst not imagine me coming to sit down upon thee, and in idleness fatten upon the fruits of thy industry. As something of even greater importance, thou shouldst know now, at this earliest moment of our intercourse, that I am abundantly able from what I have of goods and treasure to keep any condition I may choose to assume. Indeed thou shouldst not be too much astonished did I practise the style and manner of the nobles who are privileged in the palaces of thy Caesar. At home I shall be as thou seest me now, thy friend of simplest habits, because my tastes really incline to them; when I go abroad, the officials of the Church and State whom I chance to encounter shall be challenged to comparison of appearance, and be piqued to inquire about me. Then when the city observes thou art intimate with me, the demand for thy wares will increase; thou mayst even be put to stress to keep apace with it. In speaking thus, I trust thy natural shrewdness, sharpened as it must have become by much dealing as a merchant."

He paused here to give his cup to Syama for replenishment; whereupon Uel said: "I have followed thy discourse with interest, and I hope with understanding; yet I am conscious of a disadvantage. I do not know thy name, nor if thou hast a title."

"Yes, and thou mightest have set down in the table of defaults," the Wanderer began pleasantly in reply, but broke off to receive the cup smoking hot from the servant, and say—"Thanks, Syama. I see thy hand hath not lost its deftness; neither has the green leaf suffered from its long journey over the sea."

Uel noticed with what intentness Syama watched the master's lips while he was speaking, and the gratification that beamed from his face in answer to the compliment; and he thought, "Verily this must be a good man to be so beloved by his dependents."

"I was saying, O son of Jahdai, that thou mightest have set down the other points of information equally necessary to our intercourse—Whence I come? And why? And I will not leave thee in the dark respecting them. Only let me caution thee—It is not required that the public should be taken into our confidence. I have seen a flower good to look upon, but viscous, and with a scent irresistible to insects. That flower represents the world; and what is the folly of its victims but the madness of men who yield themselves with too easy faith to the seductions of the world? Nay, my son—observe thou the term—I use it to begin the relationship I seek— observe also I begin the relationship by confidences which were unwisely given without the injunction that they are intended to be put away in thy inner-conscience. Tell me if I am understood."

The question was emphasized by a look whose magnetism thrilled Uel's every nerve.

"I believe I understand you," he replied.

Then, as if the Prince knew the effect he had wrought, and that it relieved him from danger of betrayal, he returned to his former easy manner.

"And yet, as thou shalt see, my son, the confidences are not crimes—But thy cup is empty, and Syama waiting for it."

"The drink is new to me," Uel replied, yielding to the invitation.

"New? And wilt thou not also say it is better than wine? The world of which we are talking, will one day take up the admission, and be happier of it."

Turning then to serious matter:

"Afterwhile," he said, "thou wilt be importuned by the curious to know who I am, and thou shouldst be able to answer according to the fact—He is a Prince of India. The vulgar will be satisfied with the reply. Others will come demanding more. Refer them to me. As to thyself, O son of Jahdai, call me as I have instructed thee to speak of me—call me Prince. At the same time I would have thee know that on my eighth day I was carried into a temple and registered a son of a son of Jerusalem. The title I give thee for my designation did not ennoble me. The birthright of a circumcised heritor under the covenant with Israel is superior to every purely human dignity whatever its derivation."

"In other words, O Prince, thou art"—Uel hesitated.

"A Jew!" the other answered promptly—"A Jew, as thy father was—as thou art."

The look of pleasure that appeared on the shopkeeper's face was swiftly interpreted by the Prince, who felt he had indeed evoked a tie of blood, and bound the man with it.

"So much is despatched," he said, with evident satisfaction; then, after a draught from the tea-cup, and a re-delivery to Syania for more, he continued: "Possibly thou wilt also remember my letter mentions a necessity for my crossing from India to Mecca on the way to Kash-Cush, and that, despite the stoppage, I hoped to greet thee in person within six months after Syama reported himself. How stands the time?"

"This is the last day of the six months," Uel answered.

"Yes, there was never man"—the Prince paused, as if the thought were attended with a painful recollection—"never a man," he presently resumed, "who kept account of time more exactly than myself."

A copious draught of tea assuaged the passing regret.

"I wrote the letter while in Cipango, an island of the great eastern sea. Thirty years after I set foot upon its shore, theretofore unvisited by a white man, a countryman of ours from this city, the sole survivor of a shipwreck, joined me. From him I heard of thy father's death. He also gave me thy name.... My life on the island was comparatively untroubled. Indeed, for thy perfect comprehension, my son, it is best to make an explanation now; then thou wilt have a key to many things in my conduct to come as well as conduct gone which would otherwise keep thee in doubtful reflection. The study of greatest interest is religion. I have travelled the world over—I mean the inhabited parts—and in its broad extent there is not a people without worship of some kind. Wherefore my assertion, that beyond the arts, above the sciences, above commerce, above any or all other human concernments, religion is the superlative interest. It alone is divine. The study of it is worship. Knowledge of it is knowledge of God. Can as much be said of any other subject?"

Uel did not answer; he was following the speech too intently, and the Prince, seeing it, drank again, and proceeded:

"The divine study took me to Cipango. Fifty years thou mayst say to thyself was a long term in such a country. Not so, my son. I found there two faiths; the one Sin-Siu, which I turned my back upon as mythologic, without the poetry of the Greek and Roman; the other—well, a life given to the laws of Buddha were well spent. To say truth, there is such similitude between them and the teachings of him we are in the habit of calling the carpenter's son that, if I did not know better, it were easy to believe the latter spent the years of his disappearance in some Buddhistic temple.... Leaving explanation to another time, the same study carried me to Mecca. The binding of men, the putting yokes about their necks, trampling them in the dust, are the events supposed most important and therefore most noticeable in history; but they are as nothing in comparison with winning belief in matters indeterminable by familiar tests. The process there is so mysterious, the achievement so miraculous that where the operator is vastly successful one may well look under them for the permission of God. The day was when Islamism did but stir contemptuous laughter; now it is the faith acceptable to more men than any other. Is it not worthy the vigils of a student? And then it happens, my son, that in the depths of their delusion, people sometimes presume to make their own gods, and reform them or cast them out. Deities have been set up or thrown down by their makers in the changes of a moon. I wanted to see if such calamity had befallen the Allah of Mahomet.... My going to Kash-Cush was on what thou wouldst call business, and of it I will also tell thee. At Jedda, whither I betook myself after making the pilgrimages at Mecca, I regained my ship, and descended the Red Sea, landing at a village on the extreme inland shore of the bay of Tajurrah, below the Straits of Bab-el-Mandel. I was then in Kash-Cush. From the village on the coast, I passed into the interior, travelling in a litter on the shoulders of native porters, and, after many days, reached my destination—a collection of bungalows pitched on the bank of a tributary of the Blue Nile called the Dedhesa. The journey would have been difficult and tedious but that one of my attendants—a black man— had been king of the tribe I sought. His name was Nilo, and his tribe paramount throughout the uncivilized parts of Kash-Cush. More than fifty years before,—prior, in fact, to my setting out for Cipango,—I made the same tour, and found the king. He gave me welcome; and so well did he please me that I invited him to share my wanderings. He accepted the proposal upon condition that in his old age he should be returned home, and exchanged for a younger man of his blood. I agreed, provided one younger could be found who, besides the requisite physique and the virtues of intellect and courage, was also deaf and dumb, like himself. A treaty was thus perfected. I call it a treaty as distinct from a purchase, for Nilo was my friend and attendant—my ally, if you please—never my slave. There was a reception for us the like of which for feasting and merriment was without mention in the traditions of the tribe. A grandson filled my friend's throne; but he gave it back to him, and voluntarily took his place with me. Thou shalt see him to-morrow. I call him Nilo, and spend the morning hours teaching him to talk; for while he keeps me reminded of a Greek demi-god—so tall, strong and brave is he—he is yet deaf and dumb, and has to be taught as Syama was. When thou hast to do with him be gentle and courteous. I wish it kept in mind he is my friend and ally, bound to me by treaty as his grandfather was.... The only part of the tour given thee in my letter which I omitted was the descent of the Nile. Having performed it before, my curiosity was sated, and I allowed my impatience to be in thy city here to determine my course. I made way back to the village on the bay of Tajurrah where, in anticipation of such a change, my vessel was held in detention. Thence, up the sea and across the Isthmus, I proceeded to Alexandria, and to-night happily find myself at home, in hope of rest for my body and renewal of my spirit."

With this, the explanation appeared concluded; for the Prince notified Syama that he did not desire more tea, and lapsed into a thoughtful silence. Presently Uel arose, saying: "You must be weary. With permission I will take my leave now. I confess you have given me much to think over, and made me happy by taking me into your confidence. If it be agreeable, I will call at noon to-morrow."

The Prince went with him to the head of the stairs, and there bade him peace and good-night.

CHAPTER X
THE ROSE OF SPRING

The Prince, as the Jew preferred to be called, kept his house closely quite a month, resting, not hibernating. He took exercise daily on the flat roof; and walking to and fro there, found three objects of attraction: the hill to the southwest with the church upon it, the Palace of Blacherne off further in the west, and the Tower of Galata. The latter, across the Golden Horn in the north, arose boldly, like a light-house on a cliff; yet, for a reason— probably because it had connection with the subject of his incessant meditations—he paused oftenest to gaze at the Palace.

He was in his study one day deeply absorbed. The sun, nearing meridian, poured a stream of white light through the south window, flooding the table at which he sat. That the reader may know something of the paths the Mystic most frequented when in meditation, we will make free with one of the privileges belonging to us as a chronicler.

The volume directly in front of him on the table, done in olive wood strengthened at the corners with silver, was near two feet in length, and one and a half in width; when closed, it would be about one foot thick. Now he had many wonderful rare and rich *antiques*, but none so the apple of his eye as this; for it was one of the fifty Holy Bibles of Greek transcription ordered by Constantine the Great.

At his right, held flat by weights, were the *Sacred Books* of China, in form a roll of broad-leafed vellum.

At his left, a roll somewhat similar in form and at the moment open, lay the *Rig-Veda* of the Aryans in Sanscrit.

The fourth book was the *Avesta* of Zoroaster—a collection of MSS. stitched together, and exquisitely rendered by Parse devas into the Zend language.

A fifth book was the *Koran*.

The arrangement of the volumes around the Judean Bible was silently expressive of the student's superior respect; and as from time to time, after reading a paragraph from one of the others, he returned to the great central treasure, it was apparent he was making a close comparison of texts with reference to a particular theme, using the Scriptures as a standard. Most of the time he kept the forefinger of his left hand on what is now known as the fourteenth verse of the third chapter of Exodus—"And God said unto

Moses, I AM THAT I AM: and he said, Thus shalt thou say unto the children of Israel, I AM hath sent me unto you." If, as the Prince himself had declared, religion were indeed the study of most interest to the greatest number of men, he was logically consistent in comparing the definitions of *God* in the Bibles of theistic nations. So had he occupied himself since morning. The shrewd reader will at once discern the theme of his comparative study.

At length he grew weary of bending over the books, and of the persistent fixedness of attention required for the pursuit of fine shades of meaning in many different languages. He threw his arms up in aid of a yawn, and turned partly around, his eyes outrunning the movement of his body. The half-introverted glance brightened with a gleam, and remained fixed, while the arms dropped down. He could only look in wonder at what he saw— eyes black and almost large as his own gazing at him in timid surprise. Beholding nothing but the eyes, he had the awesome feeling which attends imagining a spirit suddenly risen; then he saw a forehead low, round, and white, half shaded by fluffs of dark hair; then a face of cherubic color and regularity, to which the eyes gave an indefinable innocency of expression.

Every one knows the effect of trifles on the memory. A verse or a word, the smell of a flower, a lock of hair, a turn in music, will not merely bring the past back, but invest it with a miraculous recurrency of events. The Prince's gaze endured. He stretched his hand out as if fearful lest what he saw might vanish. The gesture was at once an impulse and an expression. There was a time—tradition says it was the year in which he provoked the curse—when he had wife and child. To one of them, possibly both, the eyes then looking into his might have belonged. The likeness unmanned him. The hand he stretched forth fell lightly upon the head of the intruder.

"What are you?" he said.

The vagueness of the expression will serve excellently as a definition of his condition; at the same time it plunged the child addressed into doubt. Presently she answered:

"I am a little girl."

Accepting the simplicity of the reply as evidence of innocency too extreme for fear, he took the visitor in his arms, and sat her on his knee.

"I did not mean to ask what you are, but who?" he said.

"Uel is my father."

"Uel? Well, he is my friend, and I am his; therefore you and I should be friends. What is your name?"

"He calls me Gul Bahar."

"Oh! That is Turkish, and means Rose of Spring. How came you by it?"

"My mother was from Iconium."

"Yes—where the Sultans used to live."

"And she could speak Turkish."

"I see! Gul Bahar is an endearment, not a real name."

"My real name is Lael."

The Prince paled from cheek to brow; his lips trembled; the arm encircling her shook; and looking into his eyes, she saw tears dim them. After a long breath, he said, with inexpressible tenderness, and as if speaking to one standing just behind her—"Lael!" Then, the tears full formed, he laid his forehead on her shoulder so his white hair blent freely with her chestnut locks; and sitting passively, but wondering, she heard him sob and sob again and again, like another child. Soon, from pure sympathy, unknowing why, she too began sobbing. Several minutes passed thus; then, raising his face, and observing her responsive sorrow, he felt the need of explanation.

"Forgive me," he said, kissing her, "and do not wonder at me. I am old— very old—older than thy father, and there have been so many things to distress me which other men know nothing of, and never can. I had once"—

He stopped, repeated the long breath, and gazed as at a far object.

"I too had once a little girl."

Pausing, he dropped his eyes to hers.

"How old are you?"

"Next spring I shall be fourteen," she answered.

"And she was just your age, and so like you—so small, and with such hair and eyes and face; and she was named Lael. I wanted to call her *Rimah*, for she seemed a song to me; but her mother said, as she was a gift from the Lord, she wanted in the fulness of days to give her back to him, and that the wish might become a covenant, she insisted on calling her Lael, which, in Hebrew—thy father's tongue and mine—means To God."

The child, listening with all her soul, was now not in the least afraid of him; without waiting, she made the application.

"You loved her, I know," she said

"How much—Oh, how much!"

"Where is she now?"

"At Jerusalem there was a gate called the Golden Gate. It looked to the east. The sun, rising over the top of Mount Olivet, struck the plates of gold and Corinthian brass more precious than gold, so it seemed one rosy flame. The dust at its rocky sill, and the ground about it are holy. There, deep down, my Lael lies. A stone that tasked many oxen to move it covers her; yet, in the last day, she will be among the first to rise—Of such excellence is it to be buried before that Golden Gate."

"Oh! she is dead!" the child exclaimed.

"She is dead;" and seeing her much affected, he hastened to say, "I shed many tears thinking of her. Ah, how gentle and truthful she was! And how beautiful! I cannot forget her. I would not if I could; but you who look so like her will take her place in my heart now, and love me as she did; and I will love you even as I loved her. I will take you into my life, believing she has come again. In the morning I will ask first, Where is my Lael? At noon, I will demand if the day has been kind to her; and the night shall not be half set in except I know it has brought her the sweetness of sleep. Will you be my Lael?"

The question perplexed the child, and she was silent.

Again he asked, "Will you be my Lael?"

The earnestness with which he put the question was that of a hunger less for love than an object to love. The latter is not often accounted a passion, yet it creates necessities which are peremptory as those of any passion. One of the incidents of the curse he was suffering was that he knew the certainty of the coming of a day when he must be a mourner for whomsoever he should take into his heart, and in this way expiate whatever happiness the indulgence might bring him. Nevertheless the craving endured, at times a positive hunger. In other words, his was still a human nature. The simplicity and beauty of the girl were enough to win him of themselves; but when she reminded him of the other asleep under a great rock before the gate of the Holy City, when the name of the lost one was brought to him so unexpectedly, it seemed there had been a resurrection, making it possible for him to go about once more as he was accustomed to in his first household. A third time he asked, "You will be my Lael?"

"Can I have two fathers?" she returned.

"Oh, yes!" he answered quickly. "One in fact, the other by adoption; and they can both love you the same."

Immediately her face became a picture of childish trust.

"Then I will be your Lael too."

He clasped her close to his breast, and kissed her, crying:

"My Lael has come back to me! God of my fathers, I thank thee!"

She respected his emotion, but at length, with her hand upon his shoulder, said:

"You and my father are friends, and thinking he came here, I came too."

"Is he at home?"

"I think so."

"Then we will go to him. You cannot be my Lael without his consent."

Presently, hand in hand, they descended the stairs, crossed the street, and were in the shopkeeper's presence.

The room was plainly but comfortably furnished as became the proprietor's fortune and occupation. Closer acquaintance, it is to be said, had dissipated the latent dread, which, as has been seen, marked Uel's first thought of intimacy between the stranger and the child. Seeing him old, and rich, and given to study, not to say careless of ordinary things, the father was beginning to entertain the idea that it might in some way be of advantage to the child could she become an object of interest to him. Wherefore, as they entered now, he received them with a smile.

Traces of the emotion he had undergone were in the Prince's face, and when he spoke his voice was tremulous.

"Son of Jahdai," he said, standing, "I had once a wife and child. They perished-how and when, I cannot trust myself to tell. I have been faithful to their memory. From the day I lost them, I have gone up and down the world hunting for many things which I imagined might renew the happiness I had from them. I have been prodigal of gratitude, admiration, friendship, and goodwill, and bestowed them singly and together, and often; but never have I been without consciousness of something else demanding to be given. Happiness is not all in receiving. I passed on a long time before it came to me that we are rich in affections not intended for hoarding, and that no one can be truly content without at least one object on which to lavish them. Here"—and he laid his hand on the child's head—"here is mine, found at last."

"Lael is a good girl," Uel said with pride.

"Yes, and as thou lovest her let me love her," the Prince responded. Then, seeing Uel become serious, he added, "To help thee to my meaning, Lael was my child's name, and she was the image of this one; and as she died

- 84 -

when fourteen, thy Lael's age, it is to me as if the tomb had miraculously rendered its victim back to me."

"Prince," said Uel, "had I thought she would not be agreeable to you, I should have been sorry."

"Understand, son of Jahdai," the other interposed, "I seek more of thee than thy permission to love her. I want to do by her as though she were mine naturally."

"You would not take her from me?"

"No. That would leave thee bereft as I have been. Like me, thou wouldst then go up and down looking for some one to take her place in thy heart. Be thou her father still; only let me help thee fashion her future."

"Her birthrights are humble," the shopkeeper answered, doubtfully; for while in his secret heart he was flattered, his paternal feeling started a scruple hard to distinguish from fear.

A light shone brightly in the eyes of the elder Jew, and his head arose.

"Humble!" he said. "She is a daughter of Israel, an inheritor of the favor of the Lord God, to whom all things are possible. He keeps the destinies of his people. He—not thou or I—knows to what this little one may come. As we love her, let us hope the happiest and the highest, and prepare her for it. To this end it were best you allow her to come to me as to another father. I who teach the deaf and dumb to speak—Syama and Nilo the elder—will make her a scholar such as does not often grace a palace. She shall speak the Mediterranean tongues. There shall be no mysteries of India unknown to her. Mathematics shall bring the heavens to her feet. Especially shall she become wise in the Chronicles of God. At the same time, lest she be educated into unfitness for the present conditions of life, and be unsexed, thou shalt find a woman familiar with society, and instal her in thy house as governess and example. If the woman be also of Israel, so much the better; for then we may expect faithfulness without jealousy. And further, son of Jahdai, be niggardly in nothing concerning our Lael. Clothe her as she were the King's daughter. At going abroad, which she shall do with me in the street and on the water, I would have her sparkle with jewels, the observed of everybody, even the Emperor. And ask not doubtingly, 'Whence the money for all this?' I will find it. What sayest thou now?"

Uel did not hesitate.

"O Prince, as thou dost these things for her—so far beyond the best I can dream of—take her for thine, not less than mine."

With a beaming countenance, the elder raised the child, and kissed her on the forehead.

"Dost hear?" he said to her. "Now art thou my daughter."

She put her arms about his neck, then held them out to Uel, who took her, and kissed her, saying:

"Oh my Gul Bahar!"

"Good!" cried the Prince. "I accept the name. To distinguish the living from the dead, I too will call her my Gul Bahar."

Thereupon the men sat, and arranged the new relation, omitting nothing possible of anticipation.

Next day the Prince's house was opened with every privilege to the child. A little later on a woman of courtly accomplishment was found and established under Uel's roof as governess. Thereupon the Mystic entered upon a season during which he forgot the judgment upon him, and all else save Gul Bahar, and the scheme he brought from Cipango. He was for the time as other men. In the lavishment of his love, richer of its long accumulation, he was faithful to his duty of teacher, and was amply rewarded by her progress in study.

BOOK III
THE PRINCESS IRENE

CHAPTER I
MORNING ON THE BOSPHORUS

Our narrative proceeds now from a day in the third year after Lael, the daughter of the son of Jahdai, dropped into the life of the Prince of India—a day in the vernal freshness of June.

From a low perch above the mountain behind Becos, the sun is delivering the opposite European shore of the Bosphorus from the lingering shades of night. Out on the bosom of the classic channel vessels are swinging lazily at their anchorages. The masthead of each displays a flag bespeaking the nationality of the owner; here a Venetian, there a Genoese, yonder a Byzantine. Tremulous flares of mist, rising around the dark hulls, become entangled in the cordage, and as if there were no other escape, resolve themselves into air. Fisher boats are bringing their owners home from night-work over in the shallows of Indjerkeui. Gulls and cormorants in contentious flocks, drive hither and thither, turning and tacking as the schools of small fish they are following turn and tack down in the warm blue-green depths to which they are native. The many wings, in quick eccentric motion, give sparkling life to the empurpled distance.

The bay of Therapia, on the same European shore over against Becos, was not omitted from rescue by the sun. Within its lines this morning the ships were in greater number than out in the channel—ships of all grades, from the sea going commercial galley to the pleasure shallop which, if not the modern *caique*, was at least its ante-type in lightness and grace.

And as to the town, one had but to look at it to be sure it had undergone no recent change—that in the day of Constantine Dragases it was the same summer resort it had been in the day of Medea the sorceress—the same it yet is under sway of the benignant Abdul-Hamid.

From the lower point northwardly jutting finger-like into the current of the channel, the beach swept in a graceful curve around to the base of the promontory on the south. Then as now children amused themselves gathering the white and black pebbles with which it was strewn, and danced in and out with the friendly foam-capped waves. Then as now the houses seemed tied to the face of the hill one above another in streetless disarrangement; insomuch that the stranger viewing them from his boat below shuddered thinking of the wild play which would ensue did an earthquake shake the hill ever so lightly.

And then as now the promontory south served the bay as a partial land-lock. Then as now it arose boldly a half mountain densely verdurous, leaving barely space enough for a roadway around its base. Then as now a descending terrace of easy grade and lined with rock pine trees of broadest umbrella tops, slashed its whole townward front. Sometime in the post-Medean period a sharp-eyed Greek discerned the advantages it offered for aesthetic purposes, and availed himself of them; so that in the age of our story its summit was tastefully embellished with water basins, white-roofed pavilions, and tessellated pavements Roman style. Alas, for the perishability of things human! And twice alas, that the beautiful should ever be the most perishable!

But it is now to be said we have spoken thus of the Bosphorus, and the bay and town of Therapia, and the high promontory, as accessories merely to a plot of ground under the promontory and linked to it by the descending terrace. There is no word fitly descriptive of the place. Ravine implies narrowness; gorge signifies depth; valley means width; dell is too toylike. A summer retreat more delicious could not be imagined. Except at noon the sun did but barely glance into it. Extending hundreds of yards back from the bay toward the highlands west of the town, it was a perfected garden of roses and flowering vines and shrubs, with avenues of boxwood and acacias leading up to ample reservoirs hidden away in a grove of beeches. The water flowing thence became brooks or was diverted to enliven fountains. One pipe carried it in generous flow to the summit of the promontory. In this leafy Eden the birds of the climate made their home the year round. There the migratory nightingale came earliest and lingered longest, singing in the day as well as in the night. There one went regaled with the breath of roses commingled with that of the jasmine. There the bloom of the pomegranate flashed through the ordered thicket like red stars; there the luscious fig, ripening in its "beggar's jacket," offered itself for the plucking; there the murmur of the brooks was always in the listening ear.

Along the whole front of the garden, so perfectly a poet's ideal, stretched a landing defended from the incessant swash of the bay by a stone revetment. There was then a pavement of smoothly laid flags, and then a higher wall of dark rubble-work, coped with bevelled slabs. An open pavilion, with a bell-fashioned dome on slender pillars, all of wood red painted, gave admission to the garden. Then a roadway of gray pebbles and flesh-tinted shells invited a visitor, whether afoot or on horseback, through clumps of acacias undergrown with carefully tended rosebushes, to a palace, which was to the garden what the central jewel is to the cluster of stones on "my lady's" ring.

Standing on a tumulus, a little removed from the foot of the promontory, the palace could be seen from cornice to base by voyagers on the bay, a quadrangular pile of dressed marble one story in height, its front relieved by a portico of many pillars finished in the purest Corinthian style. A stranger needed only to look at it once, glittering in the sun, creamy white in the shade, to decide that its owner was of high rank—possibly a noble—possibly the Emperor himself.

It was the country palace of the Princess Irene, of whom we will now speak.[Footnote: During the Crimean war a military hospital was built over the basement vaults and cisterns of the palace here described. The hospital was destroyed by fire. For years it was then known as the "Khedive's Garden," being a favorite resort for festive parties from the capital. At present the promontory and the retreat it shelters pertain to the German Embassy, a munificent gift from His Majesty, Sultan Abdul-Hamid.]

CHAPTER II
THE PRINCESS IRENE

[Footnote: This name is of three syllables, and is pronounced as if spelled E-ren-ay; the last syllable to rhyme with day, say, may.]

During the reign of the last Manuel, in 1412, as a writer has placed the incident—that is to say, about thirty-nine years prior to the epoch occupying us—a naval battle occurred between the Turks and Christians off Plati, one of the Isles of the Princes. The issue was of interest to all the peoples who were in the habit of commercial resort in the region, to the Venetians and Genoese as well as the Byzantines. To the latter it was of most vital moment, since defeat would have brought them a serious interruption of communication with the islands which still remained to the Emperor and the powers in the West upon which their dependency grew as year after year their capacity for self-defence diminished.

The Turkish ships had been visible in the offing several days. At last the Emperor concluded to allow his mariners to go out and engage them. His indecision had been from a difficulty in naming a commander. The admiral proper was old and inexperienced, and his fighting impulses, admitting they had ever really existed, had been lost in the habitudes of courtierly life. He had become little more than a ceremonial marker. The need of the hour was a genuine sailor who could manoeuvre a squadron. On that score there was but one voice among the seamen and with the public—

"Manuel—give us Manuel!"

The cry, passing from the ships to the multitude in the city, assailed the palace.

The reader should understand the Manuel wanted was not the Emperor, but one of his brothers who could lay no claim to birth in the purple. His mother had not been a lawful spouse; yet the Manuel thus on the tongues of the many had made a hero of himself. He proved his temper and abilities in many successful affairs on the sea, and at length became a popular idol; insomuch that the imperial jealousy descended upon him like a cloud, and hid him away. Nor could his admirers say he lived; he had a palace and a family, and it was not known that any of the monasteries in the city or on the Isles of the Princes had opened to receive him.

On these shreds of evidence, affirmative and negative, slender as they may appear, it was believed he was yet alive. Hence the clamor; and sooth to say it suffced to produce the favorite; so at least the commonalty were pleased to think, though a sharper speculation would have scored the advent quite as much to the emergency then holding the Empire in its tightening grip.

Restored to active life, Manuel the sailor was given a reception in the Hippodrome; then after a moment of gladness with his family, and another in which he was informed of the situation and trial before him, he hurried to assume the command.

Next morning, with the rising of the sun, the squadron under oar and sail issued gallantly from its retreat in the Golden Horn, and in order of battle sought the boastful enemy of Plati. The struggle was long and desperate. Its circumstances were dimly under view from the seaward wall in the vicinity of the Seven Towers. A cry of rejoicing from the anxious people at last rose strong enough to shake the turrets massive as they were—"Kyrie Eleison! Kyrie Eleison!" Christ had made his cause victorious. His Cross was in the ascendant. The Turks drew out of the defeat as best they could, and made haste to beach the galleys remaining to them on the Asiatic shore behind the low-lying islands.

Manuel the sailor became more than a hero; to the vulgar he was a savior. All Byzantium and all Galata assembled on the walls and water along the famous harbor to welcome him when, with many prizes and a horde of prisoners, he sailed back under the sun newly risen over the redeemed Propontis. Trumpets answered trumpets in brazen cheer as he landed. A procession which was a reminder of the triumphs of the ancient and better times of the Empire escorted him to the Hippodrome. The overhanging gallery reserved for the Emperor there was crowded with the dignitaries of the court; the factions were out with their symbols of blue and green; the scene was gorgeous; yet the public looked in vain for Manuel the Emperor; he alone was absent; and when the dispersion took place, the Byzantine spectators sought their homes shaking their heads and muttering of things in store for their idol worse than had yet befallen him. Wherefore there was little or no surprise when the unfortunate again disappeared, this time with his whole family. The victory, the ensuing triumph, and the too evident popularity were more than the jealous Emperor could overlook.

There was then a long lapse of years. John Palaeologus succeeded Manuel on the throne, and was in turn succeeded by Constantine, the last of the Byzantine monarchs.

Constantine signalized his advent, the great Greek event of 1448, by numerous acts of clemency, for he was a just man. He opened many prison doors long hopelessly shut. He conferred honors and rewards that had been remorselessly erased from account. He condoned offences against his predecessors, mercifully holding them wanting in evil against himself. So it came to pass that Manuel, the hero of the sea fight off Plati, attained a second release, or, in better speech, a second resurrection. He had been all the years practically buried in certain cells of the convent of St. Irene on the island of Prinkipo, and now he came forth an old man, blind and too enfeebled to walk. Borne into private audience, he was regarded by Constantine with tender sympathy.

"And thou art that Manuel who made the good fight at Plati?"

"Say rather I am he who was that Manuel," the ancient replied. "Death despises me now because he could not call my decease a victory."

The inquisitor, visibly affected, next spoke in an uncertain voice.

"Is what I have heard true, that at thy going into the Monastery thou hadst a family?"

The eyes of the unfortunate were not too far gone for tears; some rolled down his cheeks; others apparently dropped into his throat.

"I had a wife and three children. It is creditable to the feeling called love that they chose to share my fate. One only survives, and"—he paused as if feebly aware of the incoherency—"and she was born a prisoner."

"Born a prisoner!" exclaimed Constantine. "Where is she now?"

"She ought to be here."

The old man turned as he spoke, and called out anxiously:

"Irene—Irene, where art thou, child?"

An attendant, moved like his master, explained.

"Your Majesty, his daughter is in the ante-room."

"Bring her here."

There was a painful hush in the chamber during the waiting. When the daughter appeared, all eyes were directed to her—all but the father's, and even he was instantly aware of her presence; for which, doubtless, the sensibility known only to the long-time blind was sufficiently alive.

"Where hast thou been?" he asked, with a show of petulance.

"Calm thee, father, I am here."

She took his hand to assure him, and then returned the look of the Emperor; only his was of open astonishment, while hers was self-possessed.

Two points were afterwards remembered against her by the courtiers present; first, contrary to the custom of Byzantine women, she wore no veil or other covering for the face; in the next place, she tendered no salutation to the Emperor. Far from prostrating herself, as immemorial etiquette required, she did not so much as kneel or bow her head. They, however, excused her, saying truly her days had been passed in the Monastery without opportunity to acquire courtly manners. In fact they did not at the time notice the omissions. She was so beautiful, and her beauty reposed so naturally in an air of grace, modesty, intelligence, and purity that they saw nothing else. Constantine recovered himself, and rising from his seat, advanced to the edge of the dais, which in such audiences, almost wholly without state, raised him slightly above his guests and attendants, and spoke to the father:

"I know thy history, most noble Greek—noble in blood, noble in loyalty, noble by virtue of what thou hast done for the Empire—and I honor thee. I grieve for the suffering thou hast endured, and wish myself surrounded with many more spirits like thine, for then, from my exalted place, I could view the future and its portents with greater calmness of expectation, if not with more of hope. Perhaps thou hast heard how sadly my inheritance has been weakened by enemies without and within; how, like limbs lopped from a stately tree, the themes [Footnote: Provinces.] richest in their yield of revenue have been wrested from the body of our State, until scarce more than the capital remains. I make the allusion in apology and excuse for the meagreness of what I have to bestow for thy many heroic services. Wert thou in the prime of manhood, I would bring thee into the palace. That being impossible, I must confine myself to amends within my power. First, take thou liberty."

The sailor sunk to his knees; then he fell upon his hands, and touched the floor with his forehead. In that posture, he waited the further speech. Such was the prostration practised by the Greeks in formally saluting their Basileus.

Constantine proceeded.

"Take next the house here in the city which was thine when the judgment fell upon thee. It has been tenantless since, and may be in need of repairs; if so, report the cost they put thee to, and I will charge the amount to my civil list." Looking then at the daughter, he added: "On our Roumelian shore, up by Therapia, there is a summer house which once belonged to a learned Greek who was the happy possessor of a Homer written masterfully on stainless parchment. He had a saying that the book should be opened only in a palace specially built for it; and, being rich, he indulged the fancy. He brought the marble from the Pentelic quarries; nothing grosser was permitted in the construction. In the shade of a portico of many columns of Corinthian model he passed his days reading to chosen friends, and living as the Athenians were wont to live in the days of Pericles. In my youth I dwelt much with him, and he so loved me that at dying he gave me the house, and the gardens and groves around it. They will help me now to make partial amends for injustice done; and when will a claimant appear with better right than the daughter of this brave man? In speaking but now, did he not call thee Irene?"

A flush overspread her neck and face, but she answered without other sign of feeling:

"Irene."

"The house—it may be called a palace—and all that pertains to it, are thine," he continued. "Go thither at will, and begin thy life anew."

She took one step forward, but stopped as suddenly, her color coming and going. Never had Constantine seen wife or maid more beautiful. He almost dreaded lest the spell she cast over him would be broken by the speech trembling upon her lips. She moved quickly to the dais then, and taking his hand, kissed it fervently, saying:

"Almost I believe we have a Christian Emperor."

She paused, retaining the hand, and looking up into his face.

The spectators, mostly dignitaries of high degree, with their attendants, were surprised. Some of them were shocked; for it should be remembered the court was the most rigidly ceremonial in the world. The rules governing it were the excerpt of an idea that the Basileus or Emperor was the incarnation of power and majesty. When spoken to by him, the proudest of his officials dropped their eyes to his embroidered slippers; when required to speak to him, they fell to their knees, and kept the posture till he was pleased to bid them rise. Not one of them had ever touched his fingers, except when he deigned to hold them out to be most humbly saluted. Their manner at such times was more than servility; in appearance, at least, it was worship. This explanation will enable the reader to understand the feeling with which they beheld the young woman keep the royal hand a prisoner in hers. Some of them shuddered and turned their faces not to witness a familiarity so closely resembling profanation.

Constantine, on his part, looked down into the eyes of his fair kinswoman, knowing her speech was not finished. The slight inclination of his person toward her was intended for encouragement. Indeed, he made no attempt to conceal the interest possessing him.

"The Empire may be shorn, even as thou hast said," she resumed presently, in a voice slightly raised. "But is not this city of our fathers by site and many advantages as much the capital of the world as ever? A Christian

Emperor founded it, and his name was Constantine; may it not be its perfect restoration is reserved for another Constantine, also a Christian Emperor? Search thy heart, O my Lord! I have heard how noble impulses are often prophets without voices."

Constantine was impressed. From a young person, bred in what were really prison walls, the speech was amazing. He was pleased with the opinion she was evidently forming of himself; he was pleased with the hope she admitted touching the Empire; he was pleased with the Christian faith, the strength of mind, the character manifested. Her loyalty to the old Greek regime was unquestionable. The courtiers thought she might at least have made some acknowledgment of his princely kindness; but if he thought of the want of form, he passed it; enough for him that she was a lovely enthusiast. In the uncertainty of the moment, he hesitated; then, descending from the dais, he kissed her hand gracefully, courteously, reverently, and said simply:

"May thy hope be God's will."

Turning from her, he helped the blind man to his feet, and declared the audience dismissed.

Alone with his secretary, the Grand *Logothete*, he sat awhile musing.

"Give ear," he at length said. "Write it, a decree. Fifty thousand gold pieces annually for the maintenance of Manuel and Irene, his daughter."

The secretary at the first word became absorbed in studying his master's purple slippers; then, having a reply, he knelt.

"Speak," said Constantine.

"Your Majesty," the secretary responded, "there are not one thousand pieces in the treasury unappropriated."

"Are we indeed so poor?"

The Emperor sighed, but plucking spirit, went on bravely:

"It may be God has reserved for me the restoration, not only of this city, but of the Empire. I shall try to deserve the glory. And it may be that noble impulses *are* speechless prophets. Let the decree stand. Heaven willing, we will find a way to make it good."

CHAPTER III
THE HOMERIC PALACE

The reader is now informed of the history of Irene, which is to he remembered as of an important personage in the succeeding pages. Knowing also how she became possessed of the palace we have been at some pains to describe, he is prepared to see her at home.

The night has retreated from the European shore of the Bosphorus, although the morning is yet very young. The sun in the cloudless sky beyond Becos, where it appears standing as if to rest from the fatigue of climbing the hills, is lifting Therapia bodily out of its sparkling waters. In the bay moreover there are many calls of mariner to mariner, and much creaking of windlasses, and clashing of oars cast loose in their leather slings. To make the scene perfectly realistic there is a smell of breakfast cooking, not unpleasant to those within its waftage who are yet to have their appetites appeased. These sights, these sounds, these smells, none of them reach the palace in the garden under the promontory opposite the town. There the birds are singing their matin songs, the flowers loading the air with perfume, and vine and tree drinking the moisture borne down to them from the unresting sea so near in the north. [Footnote: The Black Sea.]

Under the marble portico the mistress is sitting exactly in the place we can imagine the old Greek loved most what time he read from his masterful copy of Homer. Between columns she saw the Bosphorean expanse clear to the wooded Asiatic shore. Below was a portion of the garden through which the walk ran, with a graceful curve, to the red kiosk by the front gate. Just beyond it the landing lay. Around her were palm and rose trees in painted tubs, and in their midst, springing from a tall vase carven over with mythologic figures, a jasmine vine affected all the graces of its most delicate nature. Within reach of her right hand there were platters of burnished brass on a table of ebony, its thin, spider legs inlaid with silver in lines. One of the platters bore a heap of white biscuits such as at this day are called crackers; the others supported pitchers, and some drinking cups, all of silver.

The mistress sat in an arm-chair very smooth in finish despite the lineations sunk into its surfaces, and so roomy as to permit her to drop easily into a half-reclining posture. A footstool dressed in dark stamped leather was ready to lend its aid to gracefulness and comfort.

We will presume now to introduce the reader to the Princess Irene, though, as the introduction must be in the way of description, our inability to render the subject adequately is admitted in advance.

At the moment of first sight, she is sitting erect, her head turned slightly to the left shoulder, and both hands resting on the dog's head garnishing the right arm of the chair. She is gazing abstractedly out at the landing, as if waiting for some one overdue. The face is uncovered; and it is to be said here that, abhorring the custom which bound her Byzantine sisterhood to veils, except when in the retiracy of their chambers, she was at all times brave enough to emphasize the abhorrence by discarding the encumbrance. She was never afraid of the effects of the sun on her complexion, and had the art of moving modestly and with composure among men, who, on their side, were used in meeting her to conceal their admiration and wonder under cover of grave respect.

Her figure, tall, slender, perfectly rounded, is clad in drapery of the purest classic mode. Outwardly it consists of but two garments—a robe of fine white woollen stuff, and over it a mantle of the same texture and hue, hanging from a yoke of close-fitting flesh-colored silk richly embroidered with Tyrian floss. A red rope loosely twisted girdles her body close under the breasts, from which, when she is standing, the gown in front falls to the feet, leaving a decided train. The mantle begins at a point just in front of the arm, under which, and along the sides, it hangs, like a long open sleeve, being cut away behind about half down the figure. The contrivance of the yoke enabled the artist, by gathering the drapery, to determine the lines in which it should drop, and they were few but positive. In movement, the train was to draw the gown to the form so its outlines could be easily followed from the girdle.

The hair, of the tint of old gold, is dressed in the Grecian style; and its abundance making the knot unusually ample, there was necessity for the two fillets of pink silk to keep it securely in place.

The real difficulty in the description is now reached. To a reader of sharp imagination it might be sufficient to say the face of the Princess Irene, seen the morning in question, was perfectly regular, the brows like pencilling, the nose delicate, the eyes of violet shading into blackness, the mouth small with deep corners and lips threads of scarlet, the cheeks and brow precisely as the received law of beauty would have them. This would authorize a conception of surpassing loveliness; and perhaps it were better did we stop with the suggestions given, since the fancy would then be left to do its own painting. But patience is besought, for vastly more than a face of unrivalled perfection, the conjuration is a woman who yet lives in history as such a combination of intellect, spirit, character, and personal charm that men, themselves rulers and conquerors, fell before her at sight. Under necessity therefore of going on with the description, what words are at command to convey an idea of the complexion—a property so wholly unartificial with her that the veins at the temples were as transparent shadows on snow, and the coloring of the cheeks like a wash of roses? What more is there than to point to the eyes of the healthful freshness peculiar to children of tender nurture; the teeth exquisitely regular and of the whiteness of milk and the lustre of pearls; the ears small, critically set, and tinted pink and white, like certain shells washed ashore last night? What more? Ah, yes! There are the arms bare from the shoulder, long and round as a woman's should be, and terminating in flexile wrists, and hands so gracefully modelled we shrink from thought of their doing more than making wreaths of flowers and playing with harp strings. There too is the pose of the head expressive of breeding and delicacy of thought and feeling, of pride and courage—the pose unattainable by effort or affectation, and impossible except where the head, itself faultless, is complemented by a neck long, slender, yet round, pliant, always graceful, and set upon shoulders the despair of every one but the master who found perfection of form and finish in the lilies of the Madonna. Finally there is the correspondence, in action as well as repose, of body, limbs, head, and face, to which, under inspiration of the soul, the air and manner of lovely women are always referable.

The Princess was yet intensely observing the stretch of water before her, and the rapid changes of the light upon its face, when a boat, driven by a single oarsman, drew up to the landing, and disembarked a passenger. That he was not the person she was expecting became instantly apparent. She glanced at him once, and then, satisfied he was a stranger in whom she had no interest, resumed study of the bay. He, however, after dropping something in the boatman's hand, turned, and walked to the gateway, and through it towards the palace.

Ere long a servant, whose very venerable appearance belied the steel-pointed javelin he carried, hobbled slowly along the floor of the portico marshalling a visitor. She touched the golden knot at the back of her head to be assured of its arrangement, arose, shook out the folds of her gown and mantle, and was prepared for the interruption.

The costume of the stranger was new to the Princess. A cassock of mixed white and brown wool that had gone through a primitive loom with little of any curative process except washing, hung from his neck to his heels. Aside from the coarseness of warp and woof, it fitted so closely that but for a slit on each side of the skirt walking would have been seriously impeded. The sleeves were long and loose, and covered the hands. From the girdle of untanned skin a double string of black horn beads, each large as a walnut, dropped to his knees. The buckle of the girdle, which might have been silver deeply oxidized, was conspicuously large, and of the rudest workmanship. But withal much the most curious part of the garb was the cowl, if such it may be called. Projecting over the face so far as to cast the features in shadow, it carried on the sides of the head broad flaps, not unlike the ears of an elephant. This envelope was hideous, yet it served to exalt the man within to giantesque proportions.

The Princess surveyed the visitor with astonishment hardly concealed. What part of the world could produce a creature so utterly barbarous? What business could he have with her? Was he young or old? Twice she scanned him from head to foot. He was a monk; so much the costume certified; and while he stopped before her with one foot advanced from the edge of the skirt, and resting lightly in the clasp of the thongs of a very old-fashioned sandal, she saw it was white, and blue veined, and at the edges pink, like a child's, and she said to herself, "He is young—a young monastic."

The stranger drew from his girdle a linen package carefully folded, kissed it reverently, and said:

"Would the Princess Irene be pleased if I open the favor for her?"

The voice was manly, the manner deferential.

"Is it a letter?" she asked.

"A letter from the Holy Father, the Archimandrite of the greatest of the northern Lavras." [Footnote: Monasteries.]

"Its name?"

"Bielo-Osero."

"The Bielo-Osero? Where is it?"

"In the country of the Great Prince." [Footnote: Russia.]

"I knew not that I had an acquaintance in so distant a region as the north of Russia. You may open the letter."

Unmindful of the indifferent air of the Princess, the monk removed the cloth, leaving its folds hanging loosely from his hand. A sheet of vellum was exposed lying on the covered palm.

"The Holy Father bade me when I delivered the writing, O Princess, to deliver his blessing also; which—the saying is mine, not his—is of more worth to the soul than a coffer of gold for the wants of the body."

The pious comment was not lost; but without a word, she took the vellum, and resuming her seat, addressed herself to the reading. First, her eyes dropped to the signature. There was a look of surprise—another of uncertainty—then an exclamation:

"Hilarion! Not my Father Hilarion! He is but a sacred memory! He went away and died—and yet this is his hand. I know it as I know my own."

The monk essayed to remove the doubt.

"Permit me," he said, then asked, "Is there not an island hereabouts called Prinkipo?"

She gave him instant attention.

"And on the side of the island over against the Asiatic coast, under a hill named Kamares, is there not a convent built centuries ago by an Empress?"

"Irene," she interposed.

"Yes, Irene—and was not Father Hilarion for many years Abbot of the convent? Then, on account of his fame for learning and piety, did not the Patriarch exalt him to attendance on his own person as Doctor of the Gospels? Still later, was he not summoned to serve the Emperor in the capacity of Warden of the Purple Ink?"

"From whom have you all these things?" she asked.

"Excellent Princess, from whom could I have them save the good Father himself?"

"Thou art then his messenger?"

"It becomes me better to refer you to what he has there written."

So saying, the monk stepped backward, and stood a little way off in a respectful attitude. She raised the missive, and kissed the signature several times, exclaiming:

"Now hath God taken care of his own!"

Then she said to the monk, "Thou art indeed a messenger with good tidings."

And he, accepting the welcome, uncovered his head, by raising the hideous *klobouk*, [Footnote: Cowl.] and letting it fall back pendant from his shoulders. The violet eyes of the Princess opened wider, brightening as with a sudden influx of light. She could not remember a finer head or a face more perfect in manly beauty, and at the same time so refined and gentle.

And he was so young—young even as herself—certainly not more than twenty. Such was her first general impression of him. For the pleasure there was in the surprise, she would not allow it to be observed, but said:

"The Father in his letter, no doubt, tells me thy name, but since I wish to reserve the reading, I hope thou wilt not be offended if I ask it directly."

"The name my mother gave me is Andre; but when I came to be a deacon in our Bielo-Osero, Father Hilarion, who presided at the raising, asked me how I wished to be known in the priesthood, and I answered him, Sergius. Andre was a good christening, and serves well to remind me of my dear mother; but Sergius is better, because at hearing it I am always reminded that by vows and solemn rites of ordination I am a servant of God."

"I will endeavor to remember thy preference," the Princess said; "but just now, good Sergius, it is of next importance to know if thou hast yet had breakfast?"

A smile helped his face to even more of pleasantness.

"No," he answered, "but I am used to fasting, and the great city is not more than two hours away."

She looked concerned.

"Thy patron Saint hath not deserted thee. Here is a table already set. He for whom I held it is long on the road; thou shalt take his place, and be not less welcome." To the old servant she added: "We have a guest, not an enemy, Lysander. Put up thy javelin, and bring a seat for him; then stand behind him, lest it happen one service of the cups be not enough."

Directly the two were at the table opposite each other.

CHAPTER IV
THE RUSSIAN MONK

Sergius took a glass of red wine from the old attendant, and said:

"I should like your permission, O Princess, to make a confession."

His manner was that of one unused to the society of women. He was conscious she was studying him, and spoke to divert her. As she was slow answering, he added: "That you may not think me disposed to abuse the acquaintance you honor me with, especially as you have not yet read the letter of the good Father Hilarion upon which I rely for your better regard, I ask the permission rather to show the degree of your kindness to me. It may interest you also to learn of the confirmation of a certain faith you are perhaps unwittingly lending a novice in the ways of the world."

She had been studying him, and her first impression was now confirmed. His head in shape and pose was a poet's; the long, wavy, flaxen hair, parted in the middle, left small space for the forehead, which was nevertheless broad and white, with high-arched, well-defined brows for base. The eyes were gray. In repose they had a dreamy introspectional expression. The mustache and beard, the first growth of youth spent entirely indoors, were as yet too light to shade any part of the face. The nose was not enough *retrousse* to be irregular. In brief, the monk was of the type now well known as Russian. Aside from height and apparent muscularity, he very nearly realized the Byzantine ideal of Christ as seen in the cartoons excellently preserved in a mosque of Stamboul not far from the gate anciently San Romain now *Top Kapoussi*.

The appearance of the young monk, so strikingly suggestive of the being most sacred in the estimation of the Princess, was at the moment less curious to her than a certain habit observable in him. The look of brightness attendant upon the thought he was putting into form would, when the utterance was through, suffer a lapse which, for want of strictly definite words, may be described as a sombering of the eyes when they were widest open, a gazing beyond at something else than the opposite speaker; implying that the soul was become mysteriously occupied apart from the mind. The effect was as if she had before her two widely different characters making themselves present at the same time in one person. Unquestionably, though rarely, there is a duality of nature in men, by which, to put it extremely, a seeming incapable may be vastly capable, outward gentleness a mask for a spirit of Neronian violence, dulness a low-lying cloud surcharged with genius. What shall be done with such a nature? When may it be relied upon? Who shall ever come to really know it?

Occupied with the idea, the Princess heard but the conclusion of the monk's somewhat awkward apology, and she answered:

"The confession must be of something lighter than a sin. I will listen."

"A sin!" he exclaimed, with a blush. "Pardon me, O Princess. It was a trifle of which I spoke too seriously. I promise thou shalt take from it nothing worse than a laugh at my simplicity. See thou these things?"

He gave her a glance full of boyish humor, and from a breast pocket of his cassock drew a bag of coarse yellow silk; thrusting a hand into its mouth, he then brought out a number of square leathern chips stamped with sunken letters, and laid them on the table before her.

"This you must know is our money." The Princess examined the pieces, and said:

"I doubt if our tradesmen would accept them."

"They will not. I am a witness to the fact. Nevertheless they will carry a traveller, go he either way, from one end of our Great Prince's realm to the other. When I left the Lavra, setting out on my journey, Father Hilarion gave me the bag, saying, as he put it into my hand, 'Now upon coming to the port where the ship awaits thee, be sure to exchange the money with the merchants there for Byzantine gold; else, unless God come to thy aid, thou wilt be turned into a mendicant.' And so I fully meant to do; but when I reached the port, I found it a city large, and full of people and sights wonderful to me, demanding to be seen. I forgot the injunction. Indeed I never thought of it until this morning."

Here he laughed at himself, proving he was not yet seriously alive to the consequences of his negligence. Presently he resumed:

"I landed only last night, and sick from the tossing of the sea, put up at an inn in the town yonder. I ordered breakfast, and, according to a custom of my people, offered to pay before tasting. The master of the house looked at my money, and told me to show him coin of gold; if not that, then copper or brass, or even iron, in pieces bearing the name of the Emperor. Being told I had only this, he bade me look elsewhere for breakfast. Now I had designed going to the great city to kiss the hand of the Patriarch, of whom I have always heard as the wisest of men, before coming to thee; but the strait I was in was hard. Could I expect better of the innkeepers there? I had a button of gold—a memorial of my entry into the Lavra. That day Father Hilarion blessed it three times; and it bore a cross upon its face which I thought might make it acceptable as if it were lettered with the name of Constantine. A boatman consented to take it for rowing me to thy landing. Behold! Thou hast my confession!"

His speech to this time had been in Greek singularly pure and fluent; now he hesitated, while his eyes, open to the full, sombered, as if from a field in the brain back of them a shadow was being cast through his face. When next he spoke it was in his native tongue.

The Princess observed her guest with increasing interest; for she was wholly unused to such artlessness in men. How could Father Hilarion have intrusted business of importance to an envoy so negligent? His confession, as he termed it, was an admission, neither more nor less, that he had no money of the country into which he was come. And further, how could the habit of lapsing in thought, or more simply, of passing abruptly from the present subject, be explained except on the theory of something to which he had so given himself it had become overmastering and all absorbent? This, she saw intuitively, would prove the key to the man; and she set about finding it out.

"Your Greek, good Sergius, is excellent; yet I did not understand the words with which you concluded."

"I beg pardon," he replied, with a change of countenance. "In my mother's tongue I repeated a saying of the Psalmist, which you shall have voice and look as Father Hilarion has given it to me oftener than I am days old." Then his voice lowered into a sweet intensity fitting the text: "'The Lord is my shepherd; I shall not want.' Those were the words, Princess; and who shall say they do not comprehend all there is of religion?"

The answer was unexpected, the manner affecting; never had she heard conviction and faith more perfectly affirmed. More than a monk, the young man might be a preacher! And Father Hilarion might have grown wiser of his years! Perhaps he knew, though at a vast distance, that the need of the hour in Constantinople was not a new notable—a bishop or a legate—so much as a voice with power of persuasion to still the contentions with which her seven hills were then resounding. The idea, though a surmise, was strong enough to excite a desire to read the holy man's letter. She even reproached herself for not having done so.

"The worthy priest gave me the same saying in the same words," she said, rising, "and they lose nothing of their meaning by thy repetition. We may speak of them hereafter. For the present, to keep thee from breakfast were cruel. I will go and make terms with my conscience by reading what thou hast brought me from the Father. Help thyself freely as if thou wert the most favored of guests; or rather "—she paused to emphasize the meaning—"as though I had been bidden to prepare for thy coming. Should there be failure in anything before thee, scruple not to ask for more. Lysander will be at thy service. I may return presently."

The monk arose respectfully, and stood until she disappeared behind the vases and flowers, leaving in his memory a fadeless recollection of graciousness and beauty, which did not prevent him from immediately addressing himself as became a hungry traveller.

CHAPTER V
A VOICE FROM THE CLOISTER

While the Princess Irene traversed the portico, she repeated the words, The Lord is my shepherd; I shall not want; and she could see how the negligent, moneyless monk, turned away at the inn, was provided for in his moment of need, and also that she was the chosen purveyor; if so, by whom chosen? The young man had intended calling on the Patriarch first; who brought him to her? The breakfast was set for an invited guest; what held him back, if not the power that led the stranger to her gate?

In saying now that one of the consequences of the religious passion characteristic of the day in the East—particularly in Constantinople—a passion so extreme as to induce the strongest minds to believe God, and the Son, and even the Holy Mother discernible in the most commonplace affairs—our hope is to save the Princess from misjudgment. Really the most independent and fearless of spirits, if now and then she fell into the habit of translating the natural into the supernatural, she is entitled to mercy, since few things are harder to escape than those of universal practice.

Through a doorway, chiselled top and jambs, she entered a spacious hall nude of furniture, though richly frescoed, and thence passed into a plain open, court coolly shaded, having in the centre a jet of water which arose and fell into a bowl of alabaster. The water overflowing the bowl was caught again in a circular basin which, besides the ornamental carving on the edge and outside, furnished an ample pool for the gold fish disporting in it.

In the court there were also a number of women, mostly young Greeks, sewing, knitting, and embroidering vestments. Upon her entrance they arose, let their work drop on the spotless white marble at their feet, and received her in respectful silence. Signing them to resume their labor, she took a reserved chair by the fountain. The letter was in her hand, but a thought had the precedence.

Admitting she had been chosen to fulfil the saying quoted, was the call for the once only? When the monk went up to the city, was her ministry to end? Would not that be a half-performance? How much farther should she go? She felt a little pang of trouble, due to the uncertainty that beset her, but quieted it by an appeal to the letter. Crossing herself, and again kissing the signature, she began the reading, which, as the hand was familiar to her, and the composition in the most faultless Greek of the period, was in nowise a perplexity.

"BIELO-OSERO, 3d *June*, 1452.

"From Hilarion, the Hegumen, to Irene, his well-beloved daughter.

"Thou hast thought of me this longtime as at rest forever—at rest with the Redeemer. While there is nothing so the equivalent of death as silence, there is no happiness so sweet as that which springs upon us unexpectedly. In the same sense the resurrection was the perfect complement of the crucifixion. More than all else, more than the sermon on the mount, more than His miracles, more than His unexampled life, it lifted our Lord above the repute of a mere philosopher like Socrates. We have tears for His much suffering; but we sing as Miriam sang when we think of His victory over the grave. I would not compare myself to Him; yet it pleases me believing these lines, so unexpected, will give thee a taste of the feeling the Marys had, when, with their spices in hand, they sought the sepulchre and found only the Angels there.

"Let me tell thee first of my disappearance from Constantinople. I repented greatly my taking from the old convent by the Patriarch; partly because it separated me from thee at a time when thy mind was opening to receive the truth and understand it. Yet the call had a sound as if from God. I feared to disobey it.

"Then came the summons of the Emperor. He had heard of my life, and, as a counteraction of vice, he wanted its example in the palace. I held back. But the Patriarch prevailed on me, and I went up and suffered myself to be installed Keeper of the Purple Ink. Then indeed I became miserable. To such as I, what is sitting near the throne? What is power when not an instrument of mercy, justice and charity? What is easy life, except walking in danger of habits enervating to the hope of salvation? Oh, the miseries I witnessed! And how wretched the sight of them, knowing they were beyond my help! I saw moreover the wickedness of the court. Did I speak, who listened except to revile me? Went I to celebrations in this or that church, I beheld only hypocrisy in scarlet. How often, knowing the sin-stains upon the hands of the celebrants at the altar in Sta. Sophia, the house in holiness next to the temple of Solomon—how often, seeing those hands raise the blood of Christ in the cup before the altar, have I trembled, and looked for the dome above to let consuming vengeance in upon us, the innocent with the guilty!

"At last fear filled all my thoughts, and forbade sleep or any comfort. I felt I must go, and quickly, or be lost for denial of covenants made with Him, the ultimate Judge, in whose approval there is the peace that passeth understanding. I was like one pursued by a spirit making its presence known to me in sobs and plaints, stinging as conscience stings.

"Consent to my departure was not to be expected; for great men dislike to have their favors slighted. It was not less clear that formal resignation of the official honor I was supposed to be enjoying would be serviceable to the courtiers who were not so much my enemies personally as they were enemies of religion and contemners of all holy observances. And there were so many of them! Alas, for the admission! What then was left but flight?

"Whither? I thought first of Jerusalem; but who without abasement can inhabit with infidels? Then Hagion Oras, the Holy Hill, occurred to me; the same argument applied against it as against return to the convent of Irene-I would be in reach of the Emperor's displeasure. One can study his own heart. Holding mine off, and looking at it alive with desires holy and unholy, I detected in it a yearning for hermitage. How beautiful solitude appears! In what condition can one wishing to change his nature for the better more certainly attain the end than without companionship except of God always present? The spirit of prayer is a delicate minister; where can we find purer nourishment for it than in the silence which at noon is deep as at midnight?

"In this mood the story of the Russian St. Sergius reverted to me. He was born at Rostoff. Filled with pious impulses more than dissatisfied with the world, of which he knew nothing, with a brother, he left his father's house when yet a youth and betook himself to a great woods in the region Radenego; there he dwelt among savage beasts and wild men, fasting and praying and dependent like Elijah of old. His life became a notoriety. Others drew to him. With his own hands he built a wooden church for his disciples, giving it the name of Troitza or Thrice Holy Trinity. Thither I wandered in thought. A call might be there for me, so weary of the egotism, envy, detraction, greed, grind and battle of the soulless artificiality called society.

"I left Blacherne in the night, and crossing the sea in the north—no wonder it is so terrible to the poor mariner who has to hunt his daily bread upon its treacherous waves—I indulged no wait until, in the stone church of the Holy Trinity, I knelt before the remains of the revered Russian hermit, and thanked God for deliverance and freedom.

"The Troitza was no longer the simple wooden church of its founder. I found it a collection of monasteries. The solitude of my dreams was to be sought northward further. Some years before, a disciple of Sergius—Cyrill by name, since canonized—unterrified by winters which dragged through three quarters of the year, wandered off to a secluded place on the shore of the White Lake, where he dwelt until, in old age, a holy house was required to accommodate his following. He called it Bielo-Osero. There I installed myself, won by the warmth of my welcome.

"Now when I departed from Blacherne, I took with me, besides the raiment I wore, two pieces of property; a copy of the Rule of the Studium Monastery, and a *panagia* given me by the Patriarch—a medallion portrait of the Blessed Mother of our Lord the Saviour, framed in gold, and set in brilliants. I carry it hanging from my neck. Even in sleep it is always lying just above my heart. The day is not far now when my need of it will be over; then I will send it to thee in notice that I am indeed at rest, and that in dying I wished to lend thee a preservative against ills of the soul and fear of death.

"The Rule was acceptable to the Brotherhood. They adopted it, and its letter and spirit prevailing, the house came in time to be odorous for sanctity. Eventually, though against my will, they raised me their Hegumen. And so my story reaches its end. May it find thee enjoying the delight of the soul's rest I have been enjoying without interruption since I began life anew in this retreat, where the days are days of prayer, and the nights illuminated by visions of Paradise and Heaven.

"In the next place, I pray thou wilt take the young brother by whom this will be delivered into friendly care. I myself raised him to a deaconship of our Monastery. His priestly name is Sergius. He was scarcely out of boyhood when I came here; it was not long, however, before I discovered in him the qualities which drew me to thee during thy prison life at the old convent of Irene—a receptive mind, and a native proneness to love God. I made his way easy. I became his teacher, as I had been thine; and as the years flew by he reminded me more and more of thee, not merely with respect to mental capacity, but purity of soul and aspiration as well. Need I say how natural it was for me to love him? Had I not just come from loving thee?

"The brethren are good men, though unmannerly, and for the most part the Word reaches them from some other's tongue. Filling the lad's mind was like filling a lamp with oil. How precious the light it would one day shed abroad! And how much darkness there was for it to dispel! And in the darkness—Mercy, Mercy! How many are in danger of perishing!

"Never did I think myself so clearly a servant of God as in the time Sergius was under my instruction. Thou, alas! being a woman, wert like a strong-winged bird doomed at best to a narrow cage. The whole world was before him.

"Of the many notes I have been compelled to take of the wants of religion in this our age, none so amazes me as the lack of preachers. We have priests and monks. Their name is Legion. Who of them can be said to have been touched with the fire that fell upon the faithful of the original twelve? Where among them is an Athanasius? Or a Chrysostom? Or an Augustine? Slowly, yet apace with his growth, I became ambitious for the young man. He showed quickness and astonishing courage. No task appalled him. He mastered the tongues of the nationalities represented around him as if he were born to them. He took in memory the Gospels, the Psalms, and the prophetic books of the Bible. He replies to me in Greek undistinguishable from mine. I began to dream of him a preacher like St. Paul. I have heard him talking in the stone chapel, when the sleet-ridden winds without had filled it with numbing frost, and seen the Brotherhood rise from their knees, and shout, and sing, and wrestle like madmen. It is not merely words, and ideas, and oratorical manner, but all of them, and more—when aroused, he has the faculty of pouring out his spirit, so that what he says takes hold of a hearer, making him calm if in a passion, and excited if in a calm. The willing listen to him from delight, the unwilling and opposite minded because he enchains them.

"The pearl seemed to me of great price. I tried to keep it free of the dust of the world. With such skill as I possess, I have worn its stains and roughnesses away, and added to its lustre. Now it goes from me.

"You must not think because I fled to this corner of the earth, there is any abatement of my affection for Constantinople; on the contrary, absence has redoubled the love for it with which I was born. Is it not still the capital of our holy religion? Occasionally a traveller comes this way with news of the changes it has endured. Thus one came and reported the death of the Emperor John, and the succession of Constantine; another told of justice finally done thy heroic father, and of thy prosperity; more lately a wandering monk, seeking solitude for his soul's sake, joined our community, and from him I hear that the old controversy with the Latins has broken out anew, and more hotly than ever; that the new Emperor is an *azymite*, and disposed to adhere to the compact of union of the churches east and west made with the Pope of Rome by his predecessor, leaving heart-blisters burning as those which divided the Jews. Indeed, I much fear the likeness may prove absolute. It certainly will when the Turk appears before our holy city as Titus before Jerusalem.

"This latest intelligence induced me at last to yield to Sergius' entreaties to go down to Constantinople, and finish there the courses begun here. It is true he who would move the world must go into the world; at the same time I confess my own great desire to be kept informed of the progress of the discussion between the churches had much to do with my consent to his departure. He has instructions to that effect, and will obey them.

Therefore I pray thee receive him kindly for his own sake, for mine, and the promise of good in him to the cause of Jesus, our beloved Master.

"In conclusion, allow me, daughter—for such thou wert to thy father, to thy mother, and to me—allow me to recur to circumstances which, after calm review, I pronounce the most interesting, the most delightful, the most cherished of my life.

"The house under the Kameses hill at Prinkipo was a convent or refuge for women rather than men; yet I was ordered thither when thy father was consigned to it after his victory over the Turks. I was then comparatively young, but still recollect the day he passed the gate going in with his family. Thenceforward, until the Patriarch took me away, I was his confessor.

"Death is always shocking. I remember its visits to the convent while I was of its people; but when it came and took thy sisters we were doubly grieved. As if the ungrateful Emperor could not be sufficiently cruel, it seemed Heaven must needs help him. The cloud of those sad events overhung the community a long time; at length there was a burst of sunshine. One came to my cell and said, 'Come, rejoice with us—a baby is born in the house.' Thou wert the baby; and thy appearance was the first of the great gladnesses to which I have referred.

"And not less distinctly I live over the hour we met in the chapel to christen thee. The Bishop was the chief celebrant; but not even the splendor of his canonicals—the cope with the little bells sewn down the sides and along the sleeves, the ompharium, the *panagia*, the cross, the crozier—were enough to draw my eyes from the dimpled pink face half-hidden in the pillow of down on which they held thee up before the font. And now the Bishop dipped his fingers in the holy water—'By what name is this daughter to be known?' And I answered, 'Irene.' Thy parents had been casting about for a name. 'Why not call her after the convent?' I asked. They accepted the suggestion; and when I gave it out that great day—to the convent it was holiday—it seemed a door in my heart of which I was unknowing opened of itself, and took thee into a love-lined chamber to be sweet lady at home forever. Such was the second of my greatest happinesses.

"And then afterwhile thy father gave thee over to me to be educated. I made thy first alphabet, illuminating each letter with my own hand. Dost thou remember the earliest sentence I heard thee read? Or, if ever thou dost think of it now, be reminded it was thy first lesson in writing and thy first in religion—'The Lord is my shepherd; I shall not want.' And thence what delight I found in helping thee each day a little further on in knowledge until at length we came to where thou couldst do independent thinking.

"It was in Sta. Sophia—in my memory not more than an occurrence of yesterday. Thou and I had gone from the island up to the holy house, where we were spectators of a service at which the Emperor, as Basileus, and the Patriarch were celebrants. The gold on cope and ompharium cast the space about the altar into a splendor rich as sunshine. Then thou asked me, 'Did Christ and His Disciples worship in a house like this? And were they dressed as these are?' I was afraid of those around us, and told thee to use eye and ear, but the time for questions and answers would be when we were back safely in the old convent.

"When we were there, thou didst renew the questions, and I did not withhold the truth. I told thee of the lowliness and simple ways of Jesus— how He was clothed—how the out-doors was temple sufficient for Him. I told thee of His preaching to the multitude on the shore of the Galilean sea—I told of His praying in the garden of Gethsemane—I told of the attempt to make a King of Him whether He would or not, and how He escaped from the people—of how He set no store by money or property, titles, or worldly honors.

"Then thou didst ask, 'Who made worship so formal?' And again I answered truthfully, there was no Church until after the death of our Lord; that in course of two hundred years kings, governors, nobles and the great of the earth were converted to the faith, and took it under their protection; that then, to conform it to their tastes and dignity, they borrowed altars from pagans, and recast the worship so sumptuously in purple and gold the Apostles would not have recognized it. Then, in brief, I began telling thee of the Primitive Church of Christ, now disowned, forgotten or lost in the humanism of religious pride.

"Oh, the satisfaction and happiness in that teaching! At each lesson it seemed I was taking thee closer to the dear Christ from whom the world is every year making new roads to get further away—the dear Christ in search of whom I plunged into this solitude.

"How is it with thee now, my daughter? Dost thou still adhere to the Primitive Church? Do not fear to speak thy mind to Sergius. He too is in the secret of our faith, believing it best to love our Lord from what our Lord hath Himself said.

"Now I bring this letter to a close. Let me have reply by Sergius, who, when he has seen Constantinople, will come back to me, unless He who holds every man's future in keeping discovers for him a special use.

"Do not forget me in thy prayers.

"Blessings on thee! HILARION."

The Princess read the letter a second time. When she came to the passage referring to the Primitive Church, her hands dropped into her lap, and she thought:

"The Father planted right well—better than he was aware, as he himself would say did he know my standing now."

A glow which might have been variously taken for half-serious, half-mocking defiance shone in her eyes as the thought ran on:

"Ay, dear man! Did he know that for asserting the Primitive Church as he taught it to me in the old convent, the Greeks and the Latins have alike adjudged me a heretic; that nothing saves me from the lions of the Cynegion, except my being a woman—a woman forever offending by going when and where I wist with my face bare, and therefore harmless except to myself. If he knew this, would he send me his blessing? He little imagined—he who kept his opinion to himself because he could see no good possible from its proclamation—that I, the prison-bred girl he so loved, and whom he helped make extreme in courage as in conviction, would one day forget my sex and condition, and protest with the vehemence of a man against the religious madness into which the Christian world is being swept. Oh, that I were a man!"

Folding the letter hastily, she arose to return to her guest. There was fixedness of purpose in her face.

"Oh, that I were a man!" she repeated, while passing the frescoed hall on the way out.

In the portico, with the white light of the marble whitening her whole person, and just as the monk, tall, strong, noble looking, despite the grotesqueness of his attire, was rising from the table, she stopped, and clasped her hands.

"I have been heard!" she thought, trembling. "That which it refused to make me, Heaven has sent me. Here is a man! And he is certified as of my faith, and has the voice, the learning, the zeal and courage, the passion of truth to challenge a hearing anywhere. Welcome Sergius! In want thou camest; in want thou didst find me. The Lord *is* shepherd unto us both."

She went to him confidently, and offered her hand. Her manner was irresistible; he had no choice but to yield to it.

"Thou art not a stranger, but Sergius, my brother. Father Hilarion has explained everything."

He kissed her hand, and replied:

"I was overbold, Princess; but I knew the Father would report me kindly; and I was hungry."

"It is my part now to see the affliction comes not back again. So much has the Shepherd already determined. But, speaking as thy sister, Sergius, thy garments appear strange. Doubtless they were well enough in the Bielo-Osero, where the Rule of the Studium is law instead of fashion; but here we must consult customs or be laughed at, which would be fatal to the role I have in mind for thee." Then with a smile, she added, "Observe the dominion I have already assumed."

He answered with a contented laugh: whereupon she went on, but more gravely:

"We have the world to talk over; but Lysander will now take you to your room, and you will rest until about mid-afternoon, when my boat will come to the landing to carry us to the city. The cowl you must exchange for a hat and veil, the sandals for shoes, the coarse cassock for a black gown; and, if we have time, I will go with you to the Patriarch."

Sergius followed Lysander submissively as a child.

CHAPTER VI
WHAT DO THE STARS SAY?

The sun which relieved the bay of Therapia from the thraldom of night did the same service for the Golden Horn; only, with a more potential voice, it seemed to say to the cities which were the pride of the latter, Awake! Arise! And presently they were astir indoor and out.

Of all the souls who, obedient to the early summons, poured into the street, and by the south window of the study of the Prince of India, some going this direction, some that, yet each intent upon a particular purpose, not one gave a thought to the Prince, or so much as wondered if he were awake. And the indifference of the many was well for him; it gave him immunity to pursue his specialty. But as we, the writer and the reader, are not of the many, and have an interest in the man from knowing more about him than they, what would have been intrusion in them may be excused in us.

Exactly at midnight the Prince, aroused by Syama, had gone to the roof, where there was a table, with a lamp upon it which he could shade at pleasure, an hour-glass, and writing materials. An easy chair was also set for him.

The view of the city offered for his inspection was circumscribed by the night. The famous places conspicuous in daytime might as well have been folded up and put away in a closet; he could not see so much as a glimmer of light from any of them. Pleased thereby, and arguing that even the wicked are good when asleep, he swept the heavens with a glance so long and searching there could be no doubt of the purpose which had brought him forth.

Next, according to the habit of astrologers, he proceeded to divide the firmament into Angles and Houses, and taking seat by the table, arranged the lamp to suit him, started the hour-glass running, and drew a diagram familiar to every adept in divinatory science—a diagram of the heavens with the Houses numbered from one to twelve inclusive.

In the Houses he then set the mystic symbols of the visible planets as they were at the moment in position, mindful not merely of the parallels, but of the degrees as well. Verifying the correctness of the diagram by a second survey of the mighty overarch more careful even than the first, he settled himself in the chair, saying complacently:

"Now, O Saturn, thou, the coldest and highest! Thy Houses are ready—come, and at least behold them. I wait the configurations."

Thereupon, perfectly at ease, he watched the stellar hosts while, to their own music, they marched past the Thrones of the Most High Planets unchallenged except by him.

Occasionally he sat up to reverse the hour-glass, though more frequently he made new diagrams, showing the changes in position of the several influential bodies relatively to each other and to the benefic or malific signs upon which so much of result depended; nor did his eyes once weary or his zeal flag.

Finally when the sun, yet under the horizon behind the heights of Scutari, began to flood the sky with a brilliance exceeding that of the bravest of the stars, he collected the drawings, extinguished the lamp, and descended to his study, but not to rest.

Immediately that the daylight was sufficient, he addressed himself to mathematical calculations which appeared exhaustive of every rule and branch of the disciplinary science. Hours flew by, and still he worked. He received Syama's call to breakfast; returning from the meal, always the simplest of the day with him, he resumed the problem. Either he was prodigiously intent on a scheme in mind, or he was occupying himself diligently in order to forget himself.

About noon he was interrupted.

"My father."

Recognizing the voice, he pushed the proofs of labor from him almost to the other side of the table, turned in his seat, and replied, his face suffused with pleasure:

"Thou enemy to labor! Did not some one tell thee of what I have on hand, and how I am working to finish it in time to take the water with thee this afternoon? Answer, O my Gul-Bahar, more beautiful growing as the days multiply!"

The Lael of the son of Jahdai, the Gul-Bahar of the mysterious Prince, was much grown, and otherwise greatly changed since we saw her last. Each intervening year had in passing left her a benediction. She was now about sixteen, slight, and Jewish in eyes, hair, and complexion. The blood enriched her olive cheeks; the lips took a double freshness from health; the smile resting habitually on the oval face had a tale it was always telling of a nature confiding, happy, satisfied with its conditions, hopeful of the future, and unaware from any sad experience that life ever admitted of changes. Her beauty bore the marks of intelligence; her manner was not enough self-contained to be called courtly; yet it was easy, and carried its own certificate of culture; it yielded too much to natural affection to deserve the term dignified. One listening to her, and noticing the variableness of her mood, which in almost the same instant could pass from gay to serious without ever reaching an extreme, would pronounce her too timid for achievement outside the purely domestic; at the same time he would think she appeared lovable to the last degree, and might be capable of loving in equal measure.

She was dressed in Byzantine fashion. In crossing the street from her father's house, she had thrown a veil over her head, but it was now lying carelessly about her neck. The wooden sandals with blocks under them, like those yet worn by women in Levantine countries to raise them out of the dust and mud when abroad, had been shaken lightly from her feet at the top of the stairs. Perfectly at home, she advanced to the table, and put one of her bare arms around the old man's neck, regardless of the white locks it crushed close down, and replied:

"Thou flatterer! Do I not know beauty is altogether in the eye of the beholder, and that all persons do not see alike? Tell me why, knowing the work was to be done, you did not send for me to help you? Was it for nothing you made me acquainted with figures until—I have your authority for the saying—I might have stood for professor of mathematics in the best of the Alexandrian schools? Do not shake your head at me—or"—

With the new idea all alight in her face, she ran around the table, and caught up one of the diagrams.

"Ah, it is as I thought, father! The work I love best, and can do best! Whose is the nativity? Not mine, I know; for I was born in the glad time when Venus ruled the year. Anael, her angel, held his wings over me against this very wry-faced, snow-chilled Saturn, whom I am so glad to see in the Seventh House, which is the House of Woe. Whose the nativity, I say?"

"Nay, child—pretty child, and wilful—you have a trick of getting my secrets from me. I sometimes think I am in thy hands no more than tawdry lace just washed and being wrung preparatory to hanging in the air from thy lattice. It is well for you to know there are some things out of your reach—for the time at least."

"That is saying you will tell me."

"Yes—some day."

"Then I will be patient."

Seeing him become thoughtful, and look abstractedly out of the window, she laid the diagram down, went back, and again put her arm around his neck.

"I did not come to interrupt you, father, but to learn two things, and run away."

"You begin like a rhetorician. What subdivisions lie under those two things? Speak!"

"Thank you," she replied, quickly. "First, Syama told me you were at some particular task, and I wanted to know if I could help you."

"Dear heart!" he said, tenderly.

"Next—and this is all—I did not want you to forget we are to go up the Bosphorus this afternoon—up to Therapia, and possibly to the sea."

"You wish to go?" he asked.

"I dreamt of it all night."

"Then we will; and to prove I did not forget, the boatmen have their orders already. We go to the landing directly after noon."

"Not too soon," she answered, laughing. "I have to dress, and make myself gorgeous as an empress. The day is soft and kind, and there will be many people on the water, where I am already known quite as well as here in the city as the daughter of the Prince of India."

He replied with an air of pride:

"Thou art good enough for an emperor."

"Then I may go and get ready."

She withdrew her arm, kissed him, and started to the door, but returned, with a troubled look.

"One thing more, father."

He was recovering his work, but stopped, and gave her ear.

"What is it?"

"You have said, good father, that as my studies were too confining, it would be well if I took the air every day in my sedan. So, sometimes with Syama, sometimes with Nilo, I had the men carry me along the wall in front of the Bucoleon. The view over the sea toward Mt. Ida is there very beautiful; and if I look to the landward side, right at my feet are the terraced gardens of the palace. Nowhere do the winds seem sweeter to me. For their more perfect enjoyment I have at moments alighted from the chair, and walked; always avoiding acquaintances new and old. The people appear to understand my preference, and respect it. Of late, however, one person— hardly a man—has followed me, and stopped near by when I stopped; he has even persisted in attempts to speak to me. To avoid him, I went to the Hippodrome yesterday, and taking seat in front of the small obelisks in that quarter, was delighted with the exhibition of the horsemen. Just when the entertainment was at its height, and most interesting, the person of whom I am speaking came and sat on the same bench with me. I arose at once. It is very annoying, father. What shall I do?"

The Prince did not answer immediately, and when he did, it was to ask, suggestively:

"You say he is young?"

"Yes."

"His dress?"

"He seems to be fond of high colors."

"You asked no question concerning him?"

"No. Whom could I ask?"

Again the Prince reflected. Outwardly he was unconcerned; yet his blood was more than warm—the blood of pride which, as every one knows, is easily started, and can go hissing hot. He did not wish her to think of the affair too much; therefore his air of indifference; nevertheless it awoke a new train of thought in him.

If one were to insult this second Lael of his love, what could he do? The idea of appeal to a magistrate was irritating. Were he to assume punishment of the insolence, from whom could he hope justice or sympathy—he, a stranger living a mysterious life?

He ran hastily over the resorts at first sight open to him. Nilo was an instrument always ready. A word would arouse the forces in that loyal but savage nature, and they were forces subject to cunning which never slept, never wearied, and was never in a hurry—a passionless cunning, like that of the Fedavies of the Old Man of the Mountain.

It may be thought the Prince was magnifying a fancied trouble; but the certainty that sorrow *must* overtake him for every indulgence of affection was a haunting shadow always attending the most trifling circumstance to set his imagination conjuring calamities. That at such times his first impulse was toward revenge is explicable; the old law, an eye for an eye, was part of his religion; and coupling it with personal pride which a thought could turn into consuming heat, how natural if, while the anticipation was doing its work, his study should be to make the revenge memorable!

Feeling he was not entirely helpless in the affair, he thought best to be patient awhile, and learn who was the offender; a conclusion followed by a resolution to send Uel with the girl next time she went to take the air.

"The young men of the city are uncontrolled by respect or veneration," he said, quietly. "The follies they commit are sometimes ludicrous. Better things are not to be looked for in a generation given to dress as a chief ambition. And then it may be, O my Gul-Bahar"—he kissed her as he uttered the endearment—"it may be he of whom you complain does not know who you are. A word may cure him of his bad manners. Do not appear to notice him. Have eyes for everything in the world but him; that is the virtuous woman's defence against vulgarity and insult under every circumstance. Go now, and make ready for the boat. Put on your gayest; forget not the last necklace I gave you—and the bracelets—and the girdle with the rubies. The water from the flying oars shall not outflash my little girl. There now—Of course we will go to the landing in our chairs."

When she disappeared down the stairs, he went back to his work.

CHAPTER VII
THE PRINCE OF INDIA MEETS CONSTANTINE

It is to be remembered now, as very material to our story, that the day the Prince of India resolved on the excursion up the Bosphorus with Lael the exquisite stretch of water separated the territorial possessions of the Greek Emperor and the Sultan of the Turks.

In 1355 the utmost of the once vast Roman dominions was "a corner of Thrace between the Propontis (Marmora) and the Black Sea, about fifty miles in length and thirty in breadth." [Footnote: Gibbon.]

When Constantine Dragases—he of whom we are writing—ascended the throne, the realm was even more diminished.

Galata, just across the Golden Horn, had become a Genoese stronghold.

Scutari, on the Asiatic shore almost *vis-a-vis* with Constantinople, was held by a Turkish garrison.

With small trouble the Sultan could have converted the pitiful margin between Galata and the Cyanean rocks on the Black Sea.

Once indeed he set siege to Constantinople, but was beaten off, it was said, by the Mother of God, who appeared upon the walls of the city, and in person took part in the combat. Thereafter he contented himself with a tribute from the Emperors Manuel and John Palaeologus.

The relations of the Christian and Moslem potentates being thus friendly, it can be seen how the Princess Irene could keep to her palace by Therapia and the Prince of India plan jaunts along the Bosphorus.

Still there is a point to be borne in mind. Ships under Christian flags seldom touched at a landing upon the Asiatic shore. Their captains preferred anchoring in the bays and close under the ivy-covered heights of Europe. This was not from detestation or religious intolerance; at bottom there was a doubt of the common honesty of the strong-handed Turk amounting to fear. The air was rife with stories of his treachery. The fishermen in the markets harrowed the feelings of their timid customers with tales of surprises, captures, and abductions. Occasionally couriers rushed through the gates of Constantinople to report red banners in motion, and the sound of clarions and drums, signifying armies of Moslems gathering for mysterious purposes.

The Moslems, on their part, it is but fair to say, were possessed of the same doubts of the Christians, and had answers to accusations always ready. The surprises, captures, and abductions were the unlicensed savageries of brigands, of whom they never knew one not a Greek; while the music and flags belonged to the militia.

Six or seven miles above Scutari a small river, born in the adjacent highlands, runs merrily down to meet and mingle with the tideless Bosphorus. The water it yields is clear and fresh; whence the name of the stream, The Sweet Waters of Asia. On its south side there is a prairie-like stretch, narrow, but green and besprent with an orchard of sycamores old and gnarled, and now much frequented on Mohammedan Sundays by ladies of the harems, who contrive to make it very gay. No doubt the modest river, and the grass and great trees were just as attractive ages before the first Amurath, with an army at his heels, halted there for a night. From that time, however, it was banned by the Greeks; and for a reason.

On the north bank of the little river there was a fortress known as the White Castle. An irregular, many-angled pile of undressed stone heavily merloned on top, its remarkable feature was a tall donjon which a dingy white complexion made visible a great distance, despite its freckling of loopholes and apertures for machine artillery. Seeing its military importance, the Sultan left a garrison to hold it. He was also pleased to change its name to Acce-Chisar.

The blood-red flag on this donjon was, at the era engaging us, the disenchanter of the Greeks; insomuch that in passing the Sweet Waters of Asia they hugged the opposite shore of the Bosphorus, crossing themselves and muttering prayers often of irreligious compound. A stork has a nest on the donjon now. As an apparition it is not nearly so suggestive as the turbaned sentinel who used to occupy its outlook.

The popular imagination located dungeons under the grim old Castle, whence, of the many Christian men and women immured there, it was said none ever came forth alive.

But for these things, whether true or false, the Prince of India cared little. He was not afraid of the Turks. If the Asiatic shore had been festooned with red flags from the City of the Blind down by the Isles of the Princes to the last of the gray fortresses overlooking the Symplegades, it would not have altered a plan of his jot or tittle. Enough that Lael wanted and needed an outing on the glorious Bosphorus.

Accordingly, shortly after noon two chairs were brought and set down in his house. That is to say, two upright boxes fixed centrally on poles, and differing in nowise from the sedans still the mode of carriage affected by ladies of Constantinople unless it might be in their richer appointments. Inside, all was silk, lace and cushions; outside, the inlaying of mother of pearl and vari-colored woods was suggestive of modern papier-mache. The entrance was by a door in the front. A window in the door, and lesser ones on the sides, afforded the inmate air and opportunity for speech. Not wanting to be seen, she had only to draw the curtains together. In this instance it must be said the decoration of the carriages had been carried to an extreme.

Soon as the chairs were set down in the house, the Prince and Lael descended the stairs. The latter was attired in a semi-Greek costume, very rich and becoming; to embroidery of gold, she added bracelets, and a necklace of large pearls strung between spheres of gold equally large. A coronet graced her head, and it was so bejewelled that in bright light it seemed some one was sprinkling her with an incessant shower of sparkles.

The two took their seats. The carriers, two to each litter, stalwart men, uniformly clad in loose white garments, raised the poles on their shoulders. Syama threw the door of the house open, and at a signal from the Prince the procession sallied into the street. The crowd, in expectant waiting there, received it in silent wonder.

It is due the truth to say now that the common eye was attracted by the appearance of Nilo as much as by the rarities wrought in the panelling of the carriages. He strode ten or twelve feet in advance of Lael who, in the place of honor, was completely under the Prince's observation. The negro's costume was of a King of Kash-Cush. The hair stood on end in stiff cues, sharply pointed, and held by a chain of silver medals; an immense ring of silver hung from the cartilage of his nose. The neck was defended by a gorget of leather bristling with the fangs and claws of tigers in alternating rows. A robe of scarlet cloth large enough to envelop the man was thrown behind the massive shoulders. The body, black as polished ebony, was naked to the waist, whence a white skirt fell to the knees. The arms and legs were adorned with bracelets and anklets of ivory, while the straps of the heavy sandals were bordered with snail-shells. On the left arm he bore a round shield of rhinoceros hide embossed in brass; in the right hand, a pointless lance. Towering high above the heads of the crowd which opened before him with alacrity, the admiration received by the Prince's ally and friend was but a well-deserved tribute.

"A tiger-hunter!" said one, to a friend at his elbow.

"I should call him king of the tiger-hunters," the friend replied.

"Only a Prince of India would carry such a pensioner with him," another remarked.

"What a man!" said a woman, half afraid.

"An infidel, no doubt," was the answer.

"It is not a Christian wish, I know," the first added; "still I should like to see him face a lion in the Cynegion."

"Ay, him they call Tamerlane, because he is shorn of two toes."

The Prince, casting a glance of scarce concealed contempt over the throng, sighed, as he muttered, "If now I could meet the Emperor!"

The exclamation was from his heart.

We have seen the idea which lured him to Mecca, and brought him to Constantinople. In the years since flown, it was held subordinate to his love of Lael—subordinate merely. Latterly it had revived with much of its original force, and he was now for the first time seriously scheming for an interview with the Emperor. No doubt a formal request would have secured the honor; but it was in his view better policy to be sought than seek, and with all his wealth, there was nothing he could so well afford to pay for success as time. In his study, he was continually saying to himself:

"It cannot be that the extravagances to which I am going will fail. He will hear of me, or we may meet—then the invitation!—And then I will propose the Brotherhood—God help me! But it is for him to invite me. Patience, O my soul!"

Extravagances!

The exclamation helps us to an understanding of the style he was carrying before the public—the silvering on his own black velvet robe, the jewels in Lael's coronet bursting with light, the gorgeous finish of the sedans, the barbaric costuming of Nilo. They were not significant of his taste. Except for what they might bring him, he did not care for jewels. And as for Lael, he would have loved her for her name's sake, and her honest, untarnished Jewish blood. Let us believe so at least until we find otherwise.

Nilo, by this time familiar with every quarter of the city, was told the boat was in readiness for the party at a landing near the Grand Gate of Blacherne; to make which, it being on the Golden Horn well up in the northwest, he must turn the hill back of the Prince's residence, and pursue one of the streets running parallel with the wall. Thither he accordingly bent his steps, followed by the porters of the sedans, and an increasing but respectful assemblage of curious citizens.

Scarcely had the progress begun before the Prince, watching through his front window, saw a man approach the side of Lael's chair, and peer into it. His wit served him well and instantly.

"'Tis he—the insolent!—Close up!" he cried, to his porters.

The intruder at the sound of his voice looked at him once, then disappeared in the throng. He was young, handsome, showily dressed, and beyond question the person of whom Lael had complained. Though smarting under the insult, and a suspicion, suddenly engendered, of a watch kept over his house, the Prince concluded the stranger was of noble connection, and that the warrant for his boldness was referable to family influence. While his subtle mind was pothering with schemes of detection, the affair presented itself in another light, and he laughed at his own dulness.

"'Tis nothing," he reflected—"nothing! The boy is in love, and allowing his passion to make a fool of him. I have only to see my pretty Gul-Bahar does not return the madness."

Deciding then to make inquiry and satisfy himself who the young admirer was, he dismissed the subject.

Presently Nilo turned into a street of some width compared with the generality of thoroughfares in the city. On the left hand were shops and pretentious houses; on the right, towered the harbor wall. The people attending the procession increased instead of dispersing; but as they continued in good nature, they gave him no concern. Their comments amongst themselves were about equally divided between Nilo and Lael.

"Beautiful, beautiful!" one said, catching sight of the latter through the windows of the chair.

"Who is she?"

"A daughter of a Prince of India."

"And the Prince—Who is he?"

"Ask some one who knows. There he is in the second chair."

Once a woman went close to Lael, snatched a look, and stepped back, with clasped hands, crying:

"'Tis the Sweet Mother herself!"

Without other incident, the procession passed the gate of St. Peter, and was nearing that of Blacherne, when a flourish of trumpets announced a counter pageant coming down the street from the opposite direction. A man near by shouted:

"The Emperor! The Emperor!"

Another seconded him.

"Long live the good Constantine!"

The words were hardly uttered before they were answered:

"The *azymite*! The *azymite*! Down with the betrayer of Christ!"

In less than a minute the Prince was being borne along in the midst of two howling factions. Scarcely knowing whether to take Lael into a house or go on, he tried to communicate with Nilo; but in unconsciousness of the tempest so suddenly risen, that grandson of a king marched on in unremitted stateliness, until directly a band of trumpeters in magnificent livery confronted him.

The astonishment was mutual. Nilo halted, dropping his headless lance in defence; the trumpeters quit blowing, and, opening order, filed hastily by him, their faces saying with a distinctness words could not have helped:

"A son of Satan! Beware!"

The chairs were also brought to a halt.

Thereupon the people, now a mob apparently ready to tear each other into bloody ribbons, refused to give way to the trumpeters. Nilo finally comprehending the situation returned to Lael just as the Prince on foot came up to her. She was pale and trembling with fear.

The deadlock between the musicians and the mob was brought to an end by the appearance of a detachment of the Imperial guard. A mounted officer, javelin in hand, rode up and shouted:

"The Emperor! Make way for the Emperor!"

While he was speaking, the horsemen behind him came on steadily. There was irresistible persuasion in the glitter of their spears; besides it was matter of universal knowledge that the steel panoply of each rider concealed a mercenary foreigner who was never so happy as when riding over a Greek. One yell louder and more defiant than any yet uttered—"The azymite, the azymite!"—and the mob broke and fled. At a signal from the officer, the guards, as they came on, opened right and left of the chairs, and passed them with scarce notice.

A few words from the Prince to Lael dispelled her fears.

"It is an every-day affair," he said, lightly; "an amusement of the people, the Roman factionists against the Greek. Nobody is ever hurt, except in howling he opens his jaws too wide."

The levity was affected, but mastering the irritation he really felt, the Prince was about to make acknowledgment to the officer for his timely intervention, when another personage appeared, claiming his attention.

Indeed his heart began beating unusually fast, and in spite of himself his face flushed—he knew he had his wish—the meeting with Constantine was come!

The last Emperor of the Byzantines sat in an open chair borne upon the shoulders of eight carriers in striking livery—a handsome man in his forty-sixth year, though apparently not more than thirty-eight or forty. His costume was that of Basileus, which was a religious dignity.

A close-fitting cap of red velvet covered his head, with a knot of purple silk triply divided on the top; while a pliable circlet of golden scales, clearing the brows, held the cap securely in place. On each scale a ruby of great size sparkled in solitaire setting. The circlet was further provided with four strings of pearls, two by each ear, dangling well down below in front of the shoulders. A loose drab robe or gown, drawn close at the waist, clothed him, neck, arms, body and nether limbs, answering excellently as ground for a cope the color of the cap, divided before and behind into embroidered squares defined by rows of pearls. Boots of purple leather, also embroidered, gave finish to the costume. Instead of sword or truncheon, he carried a plain ivory crucifix. The people staring at him from the doors and windows knew he was going to Sancta Sophia intent on some religious service.

While the Emperor was thus borne down upon the Prince, his dark eyes, kindly looking, glanced from Nilo to Lael, and finally came to rest full upon the face of the master. The officer returned to him. A few paces off, the imperial chair stopped, and a conversation ensued, during which a number of high officials who were of the sovereign's suite on foot closed up in position to separate their Lord from a mounted rear guard.

The Prince of India kept his mind perfectly. Having exchanged glances with the Emperor, he was satisfied an impression was made strong enough to pique curiosity, and at the same time fix him in the royal memory. With a quick sense of the proprieties, he thereupon addressed himself to moving his carriages to the left, that when the conference with the officers was concluded the Emperor might have the right of way with the least possible obstruction.

Presently the Acolyte—such the officer proved to be—approached the Prince.

"His Imperial Majesty," he said, courteously, "would be pleased could I inform him the name and title of the stranger whose progress he has been so unfortunate as to interrupt."

The Prince answered with dignity:

"I thank you, noble sir, for the fair terms in which you couch the inquiry, not less than the rescue I and my daughter owe you from the mob."

The Acolyte bowed.

"And not to keep his Imperial Majesty waiting," the Prince continued, "return him the compliments of a Prince of India, at present a resident of this royal and ancient capital. Say also it will give me happiness far beyond the power of words when I am permitted to salute him, and render the veneration and court to which his character and place amongst the rulers of the earth entitle him."

At the conclusion of the complex, though courtierly reply, the speaker walked two steps forward, faced the Emperor, and touched the ground with his palms, and rising, carried them to his forehead.

The answer duly delivered, the Emperor responded to the salaam with a bow and another message.

"His Imperial Majesty," the Acolyte said, "is pleased at meeting the Prince of India. He was not aware he had a guest of such distinction in his capital. He desires to know the place of residence of his noble friend, that he may communicate with him, and make amends for the hindrance which has overtaken him to-day."

The Prince gave his address, and the interview ended.

It is of course the reader's privilege to pass judgment upon the incidents of this rencounter; at least one of the parties to it was greatly pleased, for he knew the coveted invitation would speedily follow.

While the Emperor was borne past, Lael received his notice more especially than her guardian; when they were out of hearing, he called the Acolyte to his side.

"Didst thou observe the young person yonder?" he asked.

"The coronet she wears certifies the Prince of India to be vastly rich," the other answered.

"Yes, the Princes of India, if we may judge by common report, are all rich; wherefore I thought not of that, but rather of the beauty of his daughter. She reminded me of the Madonna on the Panagia in the transept of our church at Blacherne."

CHAPTER VIII
RACING WITH A STORM

One who has seen the boats in which fishermen now work the eddies and still waters of the Bosphorus will not require a description of the vessel the Prince and Lael stepped into when they arrived at the Grand Gate of Blacherne. He need only be told that instead of being pitch-black outside and in, it was white, except the gunwale which was freshly gilt. The untravelled reader, however, must imagine a long narrow craft, upturned at both ends, graceful in every line, and constructed for speed and beauty. Well aft there was a box without cover, luxuriously cushioned, lined with chocolate velvet, and wide enough to seat two persons comfortably; behind it, a decked space for a servant, pilot or guard. This arrangement left all forward for the rowers, each handling two oars.

Ten rowers, trained, stout, and clad in white headkerchiefs, shirts and trousers of the same hue, and Greek jackets of brilliant scarlet, profusely figured over with yellow braid, sat stolidly, blades in hand and ready dipped, when the passengers took their places, the Prince and Lael in the box, and Nilo behind them as guard. The vessel was too light to permit a ceremonious reception.

In front of the party, on the northern shore of the famous harbor, were the heights of Pera. The ravines and grass-green benches into which they were broken, with here and there a garden hut enclosed in a patch of filbert bushes—for Pera was not then the city it now is—were of no interest to the Prince; dropping his eyes to the water, they took in a medley of shipping, then involuntarily turned to the cold gray face of the wall he was leaving. And while seeing in vivid recollection the benignant countenance of Constantine bent upon him from the chair in the street, he thought of the horoscope he had spent the night in taking and the forenoon in calculating. With a darkened brow, he gave the word, and the boat was pushed off and presently seeking the broader channel of the Bosphorus.

The day was delightful. A breeze danced merrily over the surface of the water. Soft white summer clouds hung so sleepily in the southwest they scarce suggested motion. Seeing the color deepen in Lael's cheeks, and listening to her questions, he surrendered himself to the pleasures of the situation, not the least being the admiration she attracted.

By ships at anchor, and through lesser craft of every variety they sped, followed by exclamations frequently outspoken:

"Who is she? Who can she be?"

Thus pursued, they flew past the gate of St. Peter, turned the point of Galata, and left the Fish Market port behind; proceeding then in parallelism with the north shore, they glided under the great round tower so tall and up so far overhead it seemed a part of the sky. Off Tophane, they were in the Bosphorus, with Scutari at their right, and Point Serail at their backs.

Viewed from the harbor on the sea, the old historic Point leaves upon the well informed an impression that in a day long gone, yielding to a spasm of justice, Asia cast it off into the waves. Its beauty is Circean. Almost from the beginning it has been the chosen place in which men ran rounds gay and grave, virtuous and wanton, foolish and philosophic, brave and cowardly—where love, hate, jealousy, avarice, ambition and envy have delighted to burn their lights before Heaven—where, possibly with one exception, Providence has more frequently come nearer lifting its veil than in any other spot of earth.

Again and again, the Prince, loth to quit the view, turned and refilled his eyes with Sancta Sophia, of which, from his position, the wall at the water's edge, the lesser churches of the Virgin Hodegetria and St. Irene, and the topmost sections far extending of the palaces of Bucoleon seemed but foundations. The edifice, as he saw it then, depended on itself for effect, the Turk having not yet, in sign of Mohammedan conversion, broken the line of its marvellous dome with minarets. At length he set about telling stories of the Point.

Off the site of the present palace of Dolma-Batchi he told of Euphrosyne, the daughter of the Empress Irene; and seeing how the sorrowful fortune of the beautiful child engaged Lael's sympathies, he became interested as a narrator, and failed to notice the unusual warmth tempering the air about Tchiragan. Neither did he observe that the northern sky, before so clear and blue, was whitening with haze.

To avoid the current running past Arnoot-Kouy, the rowers crossed to the Asiatic side under the promontory of Candilli.

Other boats thronged the charming expanse; but as most of them were of a humbler class sporting one rower, the Prince's, with its liveried ten, was a surpassing attraction. Sometimes the strangers, to gratify their curiosity, drew quite near, but always without affronting him; knowing the homage was to Lael, he was happy when it was effusively rendered.

His progress was most satisfactory until he rounded Candilli. Then a flock of small boats came down upon him pell-mell, the rowers pulling their uttermost, the passengers in panic.

The urgency impelling them was equally recognized by the ships and larger vessels out in the channel. Anchors were going down, sails furling, and oars drawing in. Above them, moreover, much beyond their usual levels of flight troops of gulls were circling on rapid wings screaming excitedly.

The Prince had reached the part of greatest interest in the story he was telling—how the cruel and remorseless Emperor Michel, determined to wed the innocent and helpless Euphrosyne, shamelessly cheated the Church and cajoled the Senate—when Nilo touched his shoulder, and awoke him to the situation. A glance over the water—another at the sky—and he comprehended danger of some kind was impending. At the same moment Lael commenced shivering and complaining of cold. The air had undergone a sudden change. Presently Nilo's red cloak was sheltering her.

The boat was in position to bring everything into view, and he spoke to the rowers:

"A storm is rising."

They ceased work, and looked over their shoulders, each for himself.

"A blow from the sea, and it comes fast. What we shall do is for my Lord to say," one of them returned.

The Prince grew anxious for Lael. What was done must be for her—he had no thought else.

A cloud was forming over the whole northeastern quarter of the sky, along the horizon black, overhead a vast gray wave, in its heart copper-hued, seething, interworking, now a distended sail, now a sail bursted; and the wind could be heard whipping the shreds into fleece, and whirling them a confusion of vaporous banners. Yet glassy, the water reflected the tint of the cloud. The hush holding it was like the drawn breath of a victim waiting the first turn of the torturous wheel.

The Asiatic shore offered the Prince a long stretch, and he persisted in coasting it until the donjon of the White Castle—that terror to Christians— arrested his eye. There were houses much nearer, some of them actually overhanging the water; but the donjon seemed specially inviting; at all events, he coolly reflected, if the Governor of the Castle denied him refuge, the little river near by known as the Sweet Waters of Asia would receive him, and getting under its bank, he might hope to escape the fury of the wind and waves. He shouted resolutely:

"To the White Castle! Make it before the wind strikes, my men, and I will double your hire."

"We may make it," the rower answered, somewhat sullenly, "but"—

"What?" asked the Prince.

"The devil has his lodgings there. Many men have gone into its accursed gates on errands of peace, and never been heard of again."

The Prince laughed.

"We lose time—forward! If there be a fiend in the Castle, I promise you he is not waiting for us."

The twenty oars fell as one, and the boat jumped like a steed under a stab of the spur.

Thus boldly the race with the storm was begun. The judgment of the challenger, assuming the Prince to be such, may be questioned. The river was the goal.

Could he reach it before the wind descended in dangerous force?—That was the very point of contest.

The chances, it is to be remembered next, were not of a kind to admit weighing with any approach to certainty; it was difficult even to marshal them for consideration. The distance was somewhat less than three-quarters of a mile; on the other part, the competing cloud was wrestling with the mountain height of Alem Daghy, about four miles away. The dead calm was an advantage; unfortunately it was more than offset by the velocity of the current which, though not so strong by the littoral of Candilli as under the opposite bluffs of Roumeli-Hissar, was still a serious opposing force. The boatmen were skilful, and could be relied upon to pull loyally; for, passing the reward offered in the event of their winning, the dangers of failure were to them alike. Treating the contest as a race, with the storm and the boat as competitors, the Prince was not without chances of success.

But whatever the outcome of the venture, Lael would be put to discomfort. His care of her was so habitually marked by tender solicitude one cannot avoid wondering at him now.

After all he may have judged the affair more closely than at first appears. The sides of the boat were low, but danger from that cause might be obviated by the skill of the rowers; and then Alem Daghy was not a trifling obstacle in the path of the gale. It might be trusted to hold the cloud awhile; after which a time would be required by the wind to travel the miles intervening.

Certainly it had been more prudent to make the shore, and seek refuge in one of the houses there. But the retort of the spirited Jew of that day, as in this, was a contemptuous refusal of assistance, and the degree to which this son of Israel was governed by the eternal resentment can be best appreciated by recalling the number of his days on earth.

At the first response to the vigorous pull of the oarsmen, Lael drew the red cloak over her face, and laid her head against the Prince. He put his arm around her, and seeing nothing and saying nothing, she trusted in him.

The rowers, pulling with strength from the start, gradually quickened the stroke, and were presently in perfect harmony of action. A short sough accompanied each dip of the blades; an expiration, like that of the woodman striking a blow with his axe, announced the movement completed. The cords of their brawny necks played fast and free; the perspiration ran down their faces like rain upon glass. Their teeth clinched. They turned neither right nor left; but with their straining eyes fixed upon him, by his looks they judged both their own well-doing and the progress of their competitor.

Seeing the boat pointed directly toward the Castle, the Prince watched the cloud. Occasionally he commended the rowers.

"Well done, my men!—Hold to that, and we will win!"

The unusual brightness of his eyes alone betrayed excitement. Once he looked over the yet quiet upper field of water. His was the only vessel in motion. Even the great ships were lying to. No—there was another small boat like his own coming down along the Asiatic shore as if to meet him. Its position appeared about as far above the mouth of the river as his was below it; and its three or five rowers were plainly doing their best. With grim pleasure, he accepted the stranger as another competitor in the race.

The friendly heights of Alem, seen from the Bosphorus, are one great forest always beautifully green. Even as the Prince looked at them, they lost color, as if a hand out of the cloud had suddenly dropped a curtain of white gauze over them. He glanced back over the course, then forward. The donjon was showing the loopholes that pitted its southern face. Excellent as the speed had been, more was required. Half the distance remained to be overcome—and the enemy not four miles away.

"Faster, men!" he called out. "The gust has broken from the mountain. I hear its roaring."

They turned involuntarily, and with a look measured the space yet to be covered, the distance of the foe, and the rate at which he was coming. Nor less did they measure the danger. They too heard its warning, the muffled roar as of rocks and trees snatched up and grinding to atoms in the inner coils of the cloud.

"It is not a blow," one said, speaking quick, "but a"—

"Storm."

The word was the Prince's.

"Yes, my Lord."

Just then the water by the boat was rippled by a breath, purring, timorous, but icy.

The effect on the oarsmen was stronger than any word from the master could have been. They finished a pull long and united; then while the oars swung forward taking reach for another, they all arose to their feet, paused a moment, dipped the blades deeper, gave vent to a cry so continuous it sounded like a wail, and at the same time sunk back into their seats, pulling as they fell. This was their ultimate exertion. A jet of water spurted from the foot of the sharp bow, and the bubbles and oar eddies flew behind indistinguishably.

"Well done!" said the Prince, his eyes glowing.

Thenceforward the men continued to rise at the end of a stroke, and fall as they commenced delivery of another. Their action was quick, steady, machine-like; they gripped the water deep, and made no slips; with a thought of the exhilaration an eagle must feel when swooping from his eyrie, the Prince looked at the cloud defiantly as a challenger might. Each moment the donjon loomed up more plainly. He saw now, not merely the windows and loopholes, but the joinery of the stones in their courses. Suddenly he beheld another wonder—an army of men mounted and galloping along the river bank toward the Castle.

The array stretched back into the woods. In its van were two flags borne side by side, one green, the other red. Both were surrounded by a troop in bright armor. No need for him to ask to whom they belonged. They told him of Mecca and Mahomet—on the red, he doubted not seeing the old Ottomanic symbols, in their meaning poetic, in their simplicity beautiful as any ever appropriated for martial purposes. The riders were Turks. But why the green flag? Where it went somebody more than the chief of a sanjak, more than the governor of a castle, or even a province, led the way.

The number trailing after the flags was scarcely less mysterious. They were too many to be of the garrison; and then the battlements of the Castle were lined with men also under arms. Not daring to speak of this new apparition lest his oarsmen might take alarm, the Prince smiled, thinking of another party to the race—a fourth competitor.

He sought the opposing boat next. It had made good time. There were five oarsmen in it; and, like his own, they were rising and falling with each stroke. In the passengers' place, he could make out two persons whom he took to be women.

A roll of thunder from the cloud startled the crew. Clear, angry, majestic, it filled the mighty gorge of the Bosphorus. Under the sound the water seemed to shrink away. Lael looked out from her hiding, but as quickly drew back, crowding closer to the Prince. To calm her he said, lightly,

"Fear nothing, O my Gul Bahar! A pretty race we are having with the cloud yonder; we are winning, and it is not pleased. There is no danger."

She answered by doubling the folds of the gown about her head.

Steadily, lithely, and with never an error the rowers drove through the waves—steadily, and in exact time, their cry arose cadencing each stroke. They did their part truly. Well might the master cry them, "Good, good." But all the while the wind was tugging mightily at its cloudy car; every instant the rattle of its wheels sounded nearer. The trees on the hills behind the Castle were bending and bowing; and not merely around the boat, but far as could be seen the surface of the ancient channel was a-shirr and a-shatter under beating of advance gusts.

And now the mouth of the Sweet Waters, shallowed by a wide extended osier bank, came into view; and the Castle was visible from base to upper merlon, the donjon, in relief against the blackened sky, rising more ghostly than ever. And right at hand were the flags, and the riders galloping with them. And there, coming bravely in, was the competing boat.

Over toward Roumeli-Hissar the sea birds congregated in noisy flocks, alarmed at the long line of foam the wind was whisking down the current. Behind the foam, the world seemed dissolving into spray.

Then the boats were seen from the Castle, and a company of soldiers ran out and down the bank. A noise like the rushing of a river sounded directly overhead. The wind struck the Castle, and in the thick of the mists and flying leaves hurled at it, the donjon disappeared.

"We win, we win, my men!" the Prince shouted. "Courage—good spirit—brave work—treble wages! Wine and wassail to-morrow!"

The boat, with the last word, shot into the little river, and up to the landing of the Castle just as the baffled wind burst over the refuge. And simultaneously the van of the army galloped under the walls and the competing boat arrived.

CHAPTER IX
IN THE WHITE CASTLE

The landing was in possession of dark-faced, heavily bearded men, with white turbans, baggy trousers, gray and gathered at the ankles, and arms of every kind, bows, javelins, and cimeters.

The Prince, stepping from his boat, recognized them as Turkish soldiers. He had hardly time to make the inspection, brief as it was, before an officer, distinguished by a turban, kettle-shaped and elaborately infolded, approached him.

"You will go with me to the Castle," he said.

The official's tone and manner were imperative. Suppressing his displeasure, the Prince replied, with dignity:

"The Governor is courteous. Return to him with my thanks, and say that when I decided to come on in the face of the storm, I made no doubt of his giving me shelter until it would be safe to resume my journey. I fear, however, his accommodations will be overtaxed; and since the river is protected from the wind, it would be more agreeable if he would permit me to remain here."

The response betrayed no improvement in manner:

"My order is to bring you to the Castle."

Some of the boatmen at this raised their eyes and hands toward heaven; others crossed themselves, and, like men taking leave of hope, cried out, "O Holy Mother of God!"

Yet the Prince restrained himself. He saw contention would be useless, and said, to quiet the rowers: "I will go with you. The Governor will be reasonable. We are unfortunates blown to his hands by a tempest, and to make us prisoners under such circumstances would be an abuse of one of the first and most sacred laws of the Prophet. The order did not comprehend my men; they may remain here."

Lael heard all this, her face white with fear.

The conversation was in the Greek tongue. At mention of the law, the Turk cast a contemptuous look at the Prince, much as to say, Dog of an unbeliever, what dost thou with a saying of the Prophet? Then dropping his eyes to Lael and the boatmen, he answered in disdain of argument or explanation:

"You—they—all must go."

With that, he turned to the occupants of the other boat, and raising his voice the better to be heard, for the howling of the wind was very great, he called to them:

"Come out."

They were a woman in rich attire, but closely veiled, and a companion at whom he gazed with astonishment. The costume of the latter perplexed him; indeed, not until that person, in obedience to the order, erected himself to his full stature upon the landing, was he assured of his sex.

They were the Princess Irene and Sergius the monk.

The conversation between them in the Homeric palace has only to be recalled to account for their presence. Departing from Therapia at noon, according to the custom of boatmen wishing to pass from the upper Bosphorus, they had been carried obliquely across toward the Asiatic shore where the current, because of its greater regularity, is supposed to facilitate descent. When the storm began to fill the space above Alem Daghy, they were in the usual course; and then the question that had been put to the Prince of India was presented to the Princess Irene. Would she land in Asia or recross to Europe?

The general Greek distrust of the Turks belonged to her. From infancy she had been horrified with stories of women prisoners in their hands. She preferred making Roumeli-Hissar; but the boatmen protested it was too late; they said the little river by the White Castle was open, and they could reach it before the storm; and trusting in their better judgment, she submitted to them.

Sergius, on the landing, pushed the cowl back, and was about to speak, but the wind caught his hair, tossing the long locks into tangle. Seeing him thus in a manner blinded, the Princess took up the speech. Drawing the veil aside, she addressed the officer:

"Art thou the Governor of the Castle?"

"No."

"Are we to be held guests or prisoners?"

"That is not for me to say."

"Carry thou then a message to him who may be the Governor. Tell him I am the Princess Irene, by birth near akin to Constantine, Emperor of the Greeks and Romans; that, admitting this soil is lawfully the property of his master the Sultan, I have not invaded it, but am here in search of temporary refuge. Tell him if I go to his Castle a prisoner, he must answer for the trespass to my royal kinsman, who will not fail to demand reparation; on the other hand, if I become his guest, it must be upon condition that I shall be free to depart as I came, with my friend and my people, the instant the wind and waves subside. Yes, and the further condition, that he wait upon me as becomes my station, and personally offer such hospitality as his Castle affords. I shall receive his reply here."

The officer, uncouth though he was, listened with astonishment not in the least disguised; and it was not merely the speech which impressed him, nor yet the spirit with which it was given; the spell was in the unveiled face. Never in his best dream of the perfected Moslem Paradise had he seen loveliness to compare with it. He stood staring at her.

"Go," she repeated. "There will be rain presently."

"Who am I to say thou art?" he asked.

"The Princess Irene, kinswoman of the Emperor Constantine."

The officer made a low salaam to her, and walked hurriedly off to the Castle.

His soldiers stood in respectful remove from the prisoners—such the refugees must for the present be considered—leaving them grouped in close vicinity, the Prince and the monk ashore, the Princess and Lael seated in their boats.

Calamity is a rough master of ceremonies; it does not take its victims by the hand, and name them in words, but bids them look to each other for help. And that was precisely what the two parties now did.

Unsophisticated, and backward through inexperience, Sergius was nevertheless conscious of the embarrassing plight of the Princess. He had also a man's quick sense of the uselessness of resistance, except in the way of protest. To measure the stranger's probable influence with the Turks, he looked first at the Prince, and was not, it must be said, rewarded with a return on which to found hope or encouragement. The small, stoop-shouldered old man, with a great white beard, appeared respectable and well-to-do in his black velvet cap and pelisse; his eyes were very bright, and his cheeks hectic with resentment at the annoyance he was undergoing; but that he could help out of the difficulty appeared absurd.

Having by this time rescued his hair from the wind, and secured it under his cowl, he looked next at Lael. His first thought was of the unfitness of her costume for an outing in a boat under the quietest of skies. A glance at the Princess, however, allayed the criticism; while the display of jewelry was less conspicuous, her habit was quite as rich and unsubstantial. It dawned upon him then that custom had something to do with the attire of Greek women thus upon the water. That moment Lael glanced up at him, and he saw how childlike her face was, and lovely despite the anxiety and fear with which it was overcast. He became interested in her at once.

The monk's judgment of the little old man was unjust. That master of subtlety had in mind run forward of the situation, and was already providing for its consequences.

He shared the surprise of the Turk when the Princess raised her veil. Overhearing then her message to the Governor, delivered in a manner calm, self-possessed, courageous, dignified, and withal adroit, he resolved to place Lael under her protection.

"Princess," he said, doffing his cap unmindful of the wind, and advancing to the side of her boat, "I crave audience of you, and in excuse for my unceremoniousness, plead community in misfortune, and a desire to make my daughter here safe as can be."

She surveyed him from head to foot; then turned her eyes toward Lael, sight of whom speedily exorcised the suspicion which for the instant held her hesitant.

"I acknowledge the obligation imposed by the situation." she replied; "and being a Christian as well as a woman, I cannot without reason justifiable in sight of Heaven deny the help you ask. But, good sir, first tell me your name and country."

"I am a Prince of India exercising a traveller's privilege of sojourning in the imperial city."

"The answer is well given; and if hereafter you return to this interview, O Prince, I beg you will not lay my inquiry to common curiosity."

"Fear not," the Prince answered; "for I learned long ago that in the laws prescribed for right doing prudence is a primary virtue; and making present application of the principle, I suggest, if it please you to continue a discourse which must be necessarily brief, that we do so in some other tongue than Greek."

"Be it in Latin then," she said, with a quick glance at the soldiers, and observing his bow of acquiescence, continued, "Thy reverend beard, O Prince, and respectable appearance, are warranties of a wisdom greater than I can ever attain; wherefore pray tell me how I, a feeble woman, who may not be able to release herself from these robbers, remorseless from religious prejudice, can be of assistance to thy daughter, now my younger sister in affliction."

She accompanied the speech with a look at Lael so kind and tender it could not be misinterpreted.

"Most fair and gentle Princess, I will straight to the matter. Out on the water, midway this and the point yonder, when too late for me to change direction or stay my rowers, I saw a body of horsemen, whom I judged to be soldiers, moving hurriedly down the river bank toward the Castle. A band richly caparisoned, carrying two flags, one green, the other red, moved at their head. The former, you may know, has a religious signification, and is seldom seen in the field except a person of high rank be present. It is my opinion, therefore, that our arrest has some reference to the arrival of such a personage. In confirmation you may yet hear the musical flourish in his honor."

"I hear drums and trumpets," she replied, "and admit the surmise an ingenious accounting for an act otherwise unaccountable."

"Nay, Princess, with respect to thyself at least, call it a deed intolerable, and loud with provocation."

"From your speech, O Prince, I infer familiarity with these faithless barbarians. Perhaps you can make your knowledge of them so far serviceable as to tell me the great man's name."

"Yes, I have had somewhat to do with Turks; yet I cannot venture the name, rank or purpose of the newcomer. Pursuing the argument, however, if my conjecture be true, then the message borne the Governor, though spirited, and most happily accordant with your high degree, will not accomplish your release, simply because the reason of the capture in the first place must remain a reason for detaining you in the next. In brief, you may anticipate rejection of the protest."

"What, think you they will hold me prisoner?"

"They are crafty."

"They dare not!" and the Princess' cheek reddened with indignation. "My kinsman is not powerless—and even the great Amurath"—

"Forgive me, I pray; but there was never mantle to cover so many crimes as the conveniences kings call 'reasons of state.'"

She looked vaguely up the river which the tempest was covering with promiscuous air-blown drifting; but recovering, she said: "It is for me to pray pardon, Prince. I detain you."

"Not at all," he answered. "I have to remark next, if my conjecture prove correct, a lady of imperial rank might find herself ill at ease and solitary in a hold like this Castle, which, speaking by report, is now kept to serve some design of war to come more particularly than domestic or social life."

The imagination of the Princess caught the idea eagerly, and, becoming active, presented a picture of a Moslem lair without women or apartments for women. Her mind filled with alarm.

"Oh, that I could recall the message!" she exclaimed. "I should not have tempted the Governor by offering to become his guest upon any condition."

"Nay, do not accuse yourself. The decision was brave and excellent in every view," he said, perceiving his purpose in such fair way. "For see—the storm increases in strength; yonder"—he pointed toward Alem Daghy—"the rain comes. Not by thy choice, O Princess, but the will of God, thou art here!"

He spoke impressively, and she bent her head, and crossed herself twice.

"A sad plight truly," he continued. "Fortunately it may be in a measure relieved. Here is my daughter, Lael by name. The years have scarcely outrun her childhood. More at mercy than thyself, because without rank to make the oppressor careful, or an imperial kinsman to revenge a wrong done her, she is subject to whatever threatens you—a cell in this infidel stronghold, ruffians for attendants, discomforts to cast her into fever, separation from me to keep her afraid. Why not suffer her to go with you? She can serve as tirewoman or companion. In villany the boldest often hesitate when two are to be overcome."

The speech was effective.

"O Prince, I have not words to express my gratitude. I am thy debtor. Heaven may have brought this crisis, but it has not altogether deserted me—And in good time! See—my messenger, with a following! Let thy daughter come, and sit with me now—and do thou stand by to lend me of thy wisdom in case appeal to it become necessary. Quick! Nay, Prince, Sergius is young and strong. Permit him to bring the child to me."

The monk made haste. Drawing the boat close to the shore, he gave Lael his strong hand. Directly she was delivered to the Princess, and seated beside her.

"Now they may come!"

Thus the Princess acknowledged the strength derivable from companionship. The result was perceptible in her voice once more clear, and her face actually sparkling with confidence and courage.

Then, drawn together in one group, the refugees awaited the officer.

"The Governor is coming," that worthy said, saluting the Princess.

Looking toward the Castle, the expectants beheld a score or more men issuing from the gate on foot. They were all in armor, and each complemented the buckler on his arm with a lance from which a colored pennon blew out straight and stiff as a panel. One walked in front singly, and immediately the Prince and Princess fixed upon him as the Governor, and kept him in eye curiously and anxiously.

That instant rain in large drops began to fall. The Governor appeared to notice the premonition, for looking at the angry sky he halted, and beckoned to his followers, several of whom ran to him, received an order, and then hastily returned to the Castle. He came on in quickened gait.

Here the Prince, with his greater experience, noticed a point which escaped his associates; and that was the extraordinary homage paid the stranger.

At the landing the officer and soldiers would have prostrated themselves, but with an imperious gesture, he declined the salutation.

The observers, it may be well believed, viewed the man afar with interest; when near, they scanned him as persons under arraignment study the judge, that from his appearance they may glean something of his disposition. He was above the average height of men, slender, and in armor—the armor of the East, adapted in every point to climate and light service. A cope or hood, intricately woven of delicate steel wire, and close enough to refuse an arrow or the point of a dagger, defended head, throat, neck, and shoulders, while open at the face; a coat, of the same artistic mail, beginning under the hood, followed closely the contour of the body, terminating just above the knees as a skirt. Amongst Teutonic and English knights, on account of its comparative lightness, it would have been distinguished from an old-fashioned hauberk, and called *haubergeon*. A sleeveless *surcoat* of velvet, plain green in color, overlaid the mail without a crease or wrinkle, except at the edge of the skirt. *Chausses*, or leggins, also of steel, clothed the nether limbs, ending in shoes of thin lateral scales sharply pointed at the toes. A slight convexity on top, and the bright gold-gilt band by which, with regular interlacement, the cope was attached, gave the cap surmounting the head a likeness to a crown.

In style this armor was common. The preference Eastern cavaliers showed it may have been due in part at least to the fact that when turned out by a master armorer, after years of painstaking, it left the wearer his natural graces of person. Such certainly was the case here.

The further equipment of the man admits easy imagining. There were the gauntlets of steel, articulated for the fingers and thumbs; a broad flexible belt of burnished gold scales, intended for the cimeter, fell from the waist diagonally to the left hip; light spurs graced the heels; a dagger, sparkling with jewels, was his sole weapon, and it served principally to denote the peacefulness of his errand. As there was nothing about him to rattle or clank his steps were noiseless, and his movements agile and easy.

These martial points were naturally of chief attraction to the Prince of India, whose vast acquaintanceship with heroes and famous warriors made comparison a habit. On her side, the Princess, to whom accoutrement and manner were mere accessories, pleasing or otherwise, and subordinate, sought the stranger's face. She saw brown eyes, not very large, but exceedingly bright, quick, sharp, flying from object to object with flashes of bold inquiry, and quitting them as instantly; a round forehead on brows high-arched; a nose with the curvature of a Roman's; mouth deep-cornered, full-lipped, and somewhat imperfectly mustached and bearded; clear, though sunburned complexion—in brief, a countenance haughty, handsome, refined, imperious, telling in every line of exceptional birth, royal usages, ambition, courage, passion, and confidence. Most amazing, however, the stranger appeared yet a youth. Surprised, hardly knowing whether to be pleased or alarmed, yet attracted, she kept the face in steady gaze.

Halting when a few steps from the group, the stranger looked at them as if seeking one in especial.

"Have a care, O Princess! This is not the Governor, but he of whom I spoke—the great man."

The warning was from the Prince of India and in Latin. As if to thank him for a service done—possibly for identifying the person he sought—the subject of the warning slightly bowed to him, then dropped his eyes to the Princess. A light blown out does not vanish more instantly than his expression changed. Wonder—incredulity—astonishment—admiration chased each other over his face in succession. Calling them emotions, each declared itself with absolute distinctness, and the one last to come was most decided and enduring. Thus he met her gaze, and so ardent, intense and continuous was his, that she reddened cheek and forehead, and drew down the veil; but not, it should be understood, resentfully.

The disappearance of the countenance, in effect like the sudden extinguishment of a splendor, aroused him. Advancing a step, he said to her, with lowered head and perceptible embarrassment:

"I come to offer hospitality to the kinswoman of the Emperor Constantine. The storm shows no sign of abatement, and until it does, my Castle yonder is at her order. While not sumptuous in appointment as her own palace, fortunately there are comfortable apartments in it where she can rest securely and with reserve. The invitation I presume to make in the name of my most exalted master Sultan Amurath, who takes delight in the amity existing between him and the Lord of Byzantium. To lay all fear, to dispel hesitation, in his name again, together with such earnest of good faith as lies in an appeal to the most holy Prophet of God, I swear the Princess Irene shall be safe from interruption while in the Castle, and free to depart from it at her pleasure. If she chooses, this tender of courtesy may, by agreement, here in the presence of these witnesses, be taken as an affair of state. I await her answer."

The Prince of India heard the speech more astonished by the unexceptional Latin in which it was couched than the propriety of the matter or the grace of its delivery, though, he was constrained to admit, both were very great. He also understood the meaning of the look the stranger had given him at the conclusion of his warning to the Princess, and to conceal his vexation, he turned to her.

That moment two covered chairs, brought from the Castle, were set down near by, and the rain began to fall in earnest.

"See," said the Governor, "the evidence of my care for the comfort of the kinswoman of the most noble Emperor Constantine. I feared it would rain before I could present myself to her; nor that alone, fair Princess—the chair must convict me of a wholesome dread of accusation in Constantinople; for what worse could be said than that I, a faithful Moslem, to whom hospitality is an ordination of religion, refused to open my gates to women in distress because they were Christians. Most noble and fair lady, behold how much I should esteem acceptance of my invitation!"

Irene looked at the Prince of India, and seeing assent in his face, answered:

"I will ask leave to report this courtesy as an affair of state that my royal kinsman may acknowledge it becomingly."

The Governor bowed very low while saying:

"I myself should have suggested the course."

"Also that my friends"—she pointed to the Prince of India, and the monk—"and all the boatmen, be included in the safeguard."

This was also agreed to; whereupon she arose, and for assistance offered her hand to Sergius. Lael was next helped from the boat. Then, taking to the chairs, the two were carried into the Castle, followed by the Prince and the monk afoot.

CHAPTER X
THE ARABIAN STORY-TELLER

The reader will doubtless refer the circumstance to the jealousy which is supposed to prompt the Faithful where women are required to pass before men; yet the best evidence of the Governor's thoughtfulness for his female guests met them at their approach to the Castle. There was not a man visible except a sentinel on the battlement above the gate, and he stood faced inwardly, making it impossible for him to see them when they drew near.

"Where are the horsemen of whom you spoke? And the garrison, where are they?" Sergius asked the Prince.

The latter shrugged his shoulders, as he answered:

"They will return presently."

Further proof of the same thoughtfulness was presented when the two chairs were set down in the broad stone-paved passage receiving from the front door. The sole occupant there was a man, tall as the monk, but unnaturally slender; indeed, his legs resembled those of a lay figure, so thin were they, while the residue of his person, although clad in a burnoose gorgeously embroidered, would have reminded a modern of the skeletons surgeons keep for office furniture. Besides blackness deep as the unlighted corner of a cellar, he had no beard. The Prince of India recognized him as one of the indispensables of an Eastern harem, and made ready to obey him without dissent—only the extravagance of the broidery on the burnoose confirmed him in the opinion that the chief just arrived outranked the Governor. "This is the Kislar Aga of a Prince," he said to himself.

The eunuch, like one accustomed to the duty, superintended the placement of the chairs; then, resting the point of a very bright crescent-shaped sword on the floor, he said, in a voice more incisive than the ordinary feminine tenor:

"I will now conduct the ladies, and guard them. No one will presume to follow."

The Prince replied: "It is well; but they will be comforted if permitted to abide together."

He spoke with deference, and the black responded:

"This is a fort, not a palace. There is but one chamber for the two."

"And if I wish to communicate with them or they with me?"

"*Bismillah!*" the eunuch replied. "They are not prisoners. I will deliver what thou hast for them or they for thee."

Thereupon the Princess and Lael stepped from the chairs, and went with their guide. When they were gone, word sped through the Castle, and with clamor and clangor, doors opened, and men poured forth in companies. And again the Prince reflected: "Such discipline pertains to princes only."

Now the office of eunuch was by no means an exclusive pagan institution; time out of mind it had been a feature of Byzantine courts; and Constantine Dragases, the last, and probably the most Christian of Greek emperors, not only tolerated, but recognized it as honorable. With this explanation the reader ought not to be surprised if the Princess Irene accepted the guidance offered her without fear or even hesitation. Doubtless she had been in similar keeping many times.

Climbing a number of stairways, the eunuch brought his fair charges into a part of the Castle where there were signs of refinement. The floors were swept; the doors garnished with rugs; a delicate incense lingered in the air; and to rescue the tenants, whoever they might be, from darkness, lighted lamps swung from the ceiling, and were affixed to the walls. Stopping finally before a portiere, he held it aside while saying:

"Enter here, and be at home. Upon the table yonder there is a little bell; ring, and I will answer."

And seeing Lael clinging closely to the Princess, he added: "Be not afraid. Know ye rather that my master, when a child, heard the story of Hatim, a warrior and poet of the Arabs, and ever since he has lived believing hospitality a virtue without which there can be no godliness. Do not forget the bell."

They entered and were alone.

To their amazement the room was more than comfortably furnished. What may be termed a chandelier swung from the ceiling with many lamps ready for lighting; under it there was a circular divan; then along the four sides a divan extended continuously, with pillows at the corners in heaps. Matting covered the floor, and here and there rugs of gay dyes offered noticeable degrees of warmth and coloring. Large trays filled the deep recesses of the windows, and though the smell of musk overpowered the sweet outgivings of the roses blooming in them, they sufficed to rouge the daylight somewhat scantily admitted. The roughness and chill of the walls were provided against by woollen drapery answering for arras.

They went first to one of the windows, and peered out. Below them the world was being deluged with fiercely driven rain. There was the Bosphorus lashed into waves already whitened with foam. The European shore was utterly curtained from sight. Gust after gust raved around the Castle, whistling and moaning; and as she beheld the danger escaped, the Princess thought of the saying of the Prince of India and repeated it in a spirit of thanksgiving: "By the will of God thou art here."

The reflection reconciled her to the situation, and led on till presently the face and martial figure of the Governor reproduced themselves to her fancy. How handsome he appeared—how courteous—how young!—scarcely older than herself! How readily she had yielded to his invitation! She blushed at the thought.

Lael interrupted the revery, which was not without charm, and for that reason would likely return, by bringing her a child's slipper found near the central divan; and while examining the embroidery of many-colored beads adorning it, she divined the truth.

Isolated as the Castle was on a frontier of the Islamic world, and crowded with men and material of war, yet the Governor was permitted his harem, and this was its room in common. Here his wives, many or few, for the time banished to some other quarters, were in the habit of meeting for the enjoyment of the scant pleasantries afforded by life like theirs.

Again she was interrupted. The arras over one of the walls was pushed aside, and two women came in with refreshments. A third followed with a small table of Turkish pattern which she placed on the floor. The viands, very light and simple, were set upon the table; then a fourth one came bringing an armful of shawls and wraps. The last was a Greek, and she explained that the Lord of the Castle, her master, was pleased to make his guests comfortable. In the evening later a more substantial repast would be served. Meantime she was appointed to wait on them.

The guests, assured by the presence of other women in the Castle, partook of the refection; after which the table was removed, and the attendants for the present dismissed. Wrapping themselves then in shawls, for they had not altogether escaped the rain, and were beginning to feel the mists stealing into the chamber through the unglazed windows, they took to the divan, piling the cushions about them defensively.

In this condition, comfortable, cosey, perfectly at rest, and with the full enjoyment of the sensations common to every one in the midst of a novel adventure, the Princess proceeded to draw from Lael an account of herself; and the ingenuousness of the girl proved very charming, coupled as it was with a most unexpected intelligence. The case was the not unusual one of education wholly unsupported by experience. The real marvel to the inquisitor was that she should have made discovery of two such instances the same day, and been thrown into curious relation with them. And as women always run parallels between persons who interest them, the Princess was struck with the similarities between Sergius and Lael. They were both young, both handsome, both unusually well informed and at the same time singularly unsophisticated. In the old pagan style, what did Fate mean by thus bringing them together? She determined to keep watch of the event.

And when, in course of her account, Lael spoke of the Prince of India, Irene awoke at once to a mystery connected with him. Lacking the full story, the narrator could give just enough of it to stimulate wonder. Who was he? Where was Cipango? He was rich—learned—knew all the sciences, all the languages—he had visited countries everywhere, even the inhabited islands. To be sure, he had not appeared remarkable; indeed, she gave him small attention when he was before her; she recalled him chiefly by his eyes and velvet pelisse. While she was mentally resolving to make better study of him, the eunuch appeared under the portiere, and, coming forward, said, with a half salaam to the Princess:

"My master does not wish his guests to think themselves forgotten. The kinswoman of the most august Emperor Constantine, he remembers, is without employment to lighten the passage of a time which must be irksome to her. He humbly prays her to accept his sympathy, and sends me to say that a famous story-teller, going to the court of the Sultan at Adrianople, arrived at the Castle to-day. Would the Princess be pleased to hear him?"

"In what tongue does he recite?" she asked.

"Arabic, Turkish, Greek, Latin, Hebrew," was the reply.

"Oh, a most wise man!"

Irene consulted Lael, and thinking to offer her amusement, assented to the suggestion, with thanks to the Governor.

"Have the veils ready," the eunuch said, as he retreated backward to the door. "The story-teller is a man, and he will come directly."

The story-teller was ushered in. He walked to the divan where his auditors sat, slowly, as if he knew himself under close observation, and courted it.

Now caravans were daily shows in Constantinople. The little bell of the donkey leading its string of laden camels through the narrow streets might be heard any hour, and the Shaykh in charge was almost invariably an Arab. So the Princess had seen many of the desert-born, and was familiar with their peculiarities; never, however, had chance brought a nobler specimen of the race before her. As he approached, stepping as modern stage heroes are wont, she saw the red slippers, the white shirt falling to the ankles and girdled at the waist, its bosom a capacious pocket, the white and red striped cloak over the shoulders. She marked the material of which they were made, the shirt of selected Angora wool, the cloak of camel's hair, in its fineness iridescent and soft as velvet. She saw in the girdle an empty scabbard for a yatagan elaborately covered with brilliants. She saw on the head a kerchief of mixed silk and cotton, tasselled, heavily striated red and yellow, and secured by the usual cord; but she scarcely more than noticed them—the air of the man, high, stately, king-like, was a superior attraction, and she gazed at his face unconscious that her own was uncovered.

The features were regular, the complexion sunburned to the hue of reddish copper, the beard thin, the nose sharp, the cheeks hollow, the eyes, through the double shade of brows and kerchief, glittered like balls of polished black amber. His hands were crossed above the girdle after the manner of Eastern servants before acknowledged superiors; his salutation was expressive of most abject homage; yet when he raised himself, and met the glance of the Princess, his eyes lingered, and brightened, and directly he cast off or forgot his humility, and looked lordlier than an Emir boasting of his thousand tents, with ten spears to each, and a score of camels to the spear. She endured the gaze awhile; for it seemed she had seen the face before—where, she could not tell; and when, as presently happened, she began to feel the brightness of the eyes intenser growing, the sensation reminded her of the Governor at the landing. Could this be he? No, the countenance here was of a man already advanced in life. And why should the Governor resort to disguise? The end, nevertheless, was the same as on the landing—she drew down the veil. Then he became humble again, and spoke, his eyes downcast, his hands crossed:

"This faithful servant"—he pointed to the eunuch "my friend"—the eunuch crossed his hands, and assumed an attitude of pleased attention—"brought me from his master—may the most Merciful and Compassionate continue a pillow to the good man here and to his soul hereafter!—how a kinswoman of the Emperor whose capital is to the earth a star, and he as the brightness thereof, had taken refuge with him from the storm, and was now his guest, and languishing for want of amusement. Would I tell her a story? I have a horde of parables, tales, and traditions, and many nations have contributed to it; but, alas, O Princess! they are simple, and such as beguile tentmen and tentwomen shut in by the desert, their fancies tender as children's. I fear your laughter. But here I am; and as the night bird sings when the moon is risen, because the moon is beautiful and must be saluted, even so I am obedient. Command me."

The speech was in Greek, with the slightest imperfection of accent; at the conclusion the Princess was silent.

"Knowest thou"—she at length said—"knowest thou of one Hatim, renowned as a warrior and poet of the Arabs?"

The eunuch saw the reference, and smiled. Asking of Hatim now was only another form of inquiry after his master; not merely had the latter been in her mind; she wished to know more about him. On his part, the story-teller arose from his servile posture, and asked with the animation of one to whom a favorite theme is presented:

"Noble lady, know you aught of the desert?"

"I have never been there," the Princess answered.

"Though not beautiful, it is the home of mysteries," he said, with growing enthusiasm. "When he whom in the same breath you worship as God and the Son of God—an opposition beyond the depth of our simple faith—made ready to proclaim himself, he went for a time into the Wilderness, and dwelt there. So likewise our Prophet, seeing the dawn of his day, betook himself to Hiva, a rock, bleak, barren, waterless. Why, O Princess, if not for purification, and because God of preference has founded his dwelling there, wasting it indeed the better to nurse his goodness in a perfected solitude? Granting this, why may I not assert without shocking you that the sons of the desert are the noblest of men?—

"Such was Hatim!

"In the Hijaz and the Nejd, they tell of him thus:

"In the day the Compassionate set about world-making, which is but a pastime with him, nor nearly so much as nest-building to a mother-dove, he rested. The mountains and rivers and seas were in their beds, and the land was variegated to please him, here a forest, there a grassy plain; nothing remained unfinished except the sand oceans, and they only wanted water. He rested.

"Now, if, with their sky, a sun-field in the day, a gallery of stars at night, and their winds, flying from sea to sea, but gathering no taint, the deserts are treeless, and unknowing the sweetness of gardens and the glory of grass, it was not by accident or forgetfulness; for with him, the Compassionate, the Merciful, there are no accidents or lapses of any kind. He is all attention and ever present. Thus the Throne verse—'Drowsiness overcomes him not nor sleep.... His firmament spans the Heaven and the Earth, and the care of them does not distress him.'

"Why then the yellowness and the burning, the sameness and solitude, and the earth intolerant of rain and running stream, and of roads and paths—why, if there was neither accident nor forgetfulness?

"He is the High and the Great! Accuse him not!

"In that moment of rest, not from weariness or overburden, but to approve the work done, and record the approval as a judgment, he said, speaking to his Almightiness as to a familiar: 'As it is it shall stay. A time will come when with men I, and the very name of me, shall go out utterly like the green of last year's leaf. He who walks in a garden thinks of it only; but he who abides in a desert, wanting to see the beautiful, must look into the sky, and looking there he shall be reminded of me, and say aloud and as a lover, 'There is no God but him, the Compassionate, the Merciful.... The eyes see him not, but he seeth the eyes; and He is the Gracious, the Knowing'.... So also comes a time when religion shall be without heart, dead, and the quickening of worship lost in idolatry; when men shall cry, God, my God, to stones and graven images, and sing to hear their singing, and the loud music it goes with. And that time shall be first in lands of growth and freshness, in cities where comforts and luxuries are as honey in hives after the flowering of palms. Wherefore—Lo, the need of deserts. There I shall never be forgotten. And out of them, out of their hardness and heat, out of their yellow distances and drouth, religion shall arise again, and go forth purified unto universality; for I shall be always present there, a life-giver. And against those days of evil, I shall keep men there, the best of their kind, and their good qualities shall not rust; they shall be brave, for I may want swords; they shall keep the given word, for as I am the Truth, so shall my chosen be; there shall be no end to charity among them, for in such lands charity is life, and must take every form, friendship, love of one another, love of giving, and hospitality, unto which are riches and plenty. And in their worship, I shall be first, and honor next. And as Truth is the Soul of the World, it being but another of my names, for its salvation they shall speak with tongues of fire, this one an orator, that one a poet; and living in the midst of death, they shall fear me not at all, but dishonor more. Mine are the Sons of the Desert—the Word-Keepers!—the Unconquered and Conquerless! For my name's sake, I nominate them Mine, and I alone am the High and the Great.... And there shall be amongst them exemplars of this virtue and that one singly; and at intervals through the centuries standards for emulation among the many, a few, in whom all the excellences shall be blent in indivisible comeliness.'

"So came Hatim, of the Bene-Tayyi, lustrous as the moon of Ramazan to eager watchers on high hilltops, and better than other men, even as all the virtues together are better than any one of them, excepting charity and love of God.

"Now Hatim's mother was a widow, poor, and without relations, but beloved by the Compassionate, and always in his care, because she was wise beyond the men of her time, and kept his laws, as they were known, and taught them to her son. One day a great cry arose in the village. Everybody rushed to see the cause, and then joined in the clamor.

"Up in the north there was an appearance the like of which had never been beheld, nor were there any to tell what it was from hearsay. Some pooh-poohed, saying, contemptuously:

"''Tis only a cloud.'

"Others, observing how rapidly it came, in movement like a bird sailing on outspread motionless wings, said:

"'A roc! A roc!'

"When the object was nearer, a few of the villagers, in alarm, ran to their houses, shrieking:

"'Israfil, Israfil! He is bringing the end of time!'

"Soon the sight was nearly overhead; then it was going by, its edge overhead, the rest of it extending eastwardly; and it was long and broad as a pasture for ten thousand camels, and horses ten thousand. It had no likeness earthly except a carpet of green silk; nor could those standing under describe what bore it along. They thought they heard the sound of a strong wind, but as the air above far and near was full of birds great and small, birds of the water as well as the land, all flying evenly with the carpet, and making a canopy of their wings, and shade deeper than a cloud's, the beholders were uncertain whether the birds or the wind served it. In passing, it dipped gently, giving them a view of what it carried—a throne of pearl and rainbow, and a crowned King sitting in majesty; at his left hand, an army of spirits, at his right, an army of men in martial sheen.

"While the prodigy was before them, the spectators stirred not; nor was there one brave enough to speak; most of them with their eyes devoured it all, King and throne, birds, men and spirits; though afterwards there was asking:

"'Did you see the birds?'

"'No.'

"'The spirits?'

"'No.'

"'The men?'

"'I saw only the King upon His throne.'

"In the passing, also, a man, in splendor of apparel, stood on the carpet's edge and shouted:

"'God is great! I bear witness there is no God but God.'

"The same instant something fell from his hand. When the marvel was out of sight in the south, some bethought them, and went to see what it was which fell. They came back laughing, 'It was only a gourd, and as we have much better on our camel-saddles, we threw it away.'

"But the mother of Hatim, listening to the report, was not content. In her childhood she heard what was tradition then; how Solomon, at the completion of his temple in Jerusalem, journeyed to Mecca upon a carpet of silk wafted by the wind, with men, spirits, and birds. Wherefore, saying to herself, 'It was Solomon going to Mecca. Not for nothing threw he the gourd,' she went alone, and brought it in, and opened it, finding three seeds—one red, like a ruby; a second blue, like a sapphire; the third green, like an emerald.

"Now she might have sold the seeds, for they were beautiful as gems cut for a crown, and enriched herself; but Hatim was all the world to her. They were for him, she said, and getting a brown nut such as washes up from vines in the sea, she cut it, put the treasures into it, sealed them there, and tied them around the boy's neck.

"'Thanks, O Solomon,' she said. 'There is no God but God; and I shall teach the lesson to my Hatim in the morning, when *al hudhud* flies for water; at noon, when it whistles to itself in the shade; and at night, when it draws a wing over its head to darken the darkness, and sleep.'

"And from that day through all his days Hatim wore the brown nut with the three seeds in it; nor was there ever such an amulet before or since; for, besides being defended by the genii who are Solomon's servants, he grew one of the exemplars promised by God, having in himself every virtue. No one braver than he; none so charitable; none so generous and merciful; none so eloquent; none on whose lips poetry was such sweet speech for the exalting of souls; above all, never had there been such a keeper of his word of promise.

"And of this judge you by some of the many things they tell of him.

"A famine fell upon the land. It was when Hatim had become Sheik of his tribe. The women and children were perishing. The men could no more than witness their suffering. They knew not whom to accuse; they knew no one to receive a prayer. The time predicted was come—the name of God had gone out utterly, like the green of last year's leaf. In the Sheik's tent even, as with the poorest, hunger could not be allayed—there was nothing to eat. The last camel had been devoured—one horse remained. More than once the good man went out to kill him, but the animal was so beautiful—so affectionate—so fleet! And the desert was not wide enough to hold his fame! How much easier to say, 'Another day—to-morrow it may rain.'

"He sat in his tent telling his wife and children stories, for he was not merely the best warrior of his day; he was the most renowned poet and storyteller. Riding into battle, his men would say, 'Sing to us, O Hatim—sing, and we will fight.' And they he loved best, listening to him, had nigh forgot their misery, when the curtain of the tent was raised.

"'Who is there?' he asked.

"'Thy neighbor,' and the voice was a woman's. 'My children are anhungred and crying, and I have nothing for them. Help, O Sheik, help or they die.'

"'Bring them here,' he said, rising.

"'She is not worse off than we,' said his wife, 'nor are her children more hungry than ours. What will you do?'

"'The appeal was to me,' he answered.

"And passing out, he slew the horse, and kindled a fire; then, while the stranger and her children were sharing piece by piece with his own, 'Shame, shame!' he said, 'that ye alone should eat;' and going through the dowar, he brought the neighbors together, and he only went hungry. There was no more of the meat left. Was ever one merciful like Hatim? In combat, he gave lives, but took none. Once an antagonist under his foot, called to him: 'Give me thy spear, Hatim,' and he gave it.

"'Foolish man!' his brethren exclaimed.

"'What else was there?' he answered. 'Did not the poor man ask a gift of me?'

"Never a captive besought his help vainly. On a journey once, a prisoner begged him to buy his liberty; but he was without the money required, and on that account he was sorely distressed. To his entreaties, the strangers listened hard-heartedly; at last he said to them:

"Am not I—Hatim—good as he? Let him go, and take me.'

"And knocking the chains from the unfortunate, he had them put on himself, and wore them until the ransom came.

"In his eyes a poet was greater than a king, and than singing a song well the only thing better was being the subject of a song. Perpetuation by tombs he thought vulgar; so the glory unremembered in verse deserved oblivion. Was it wonderful he gave and kept giving to story-tellers, careless often if what he thus disposed of was another's?

"Once in his youth—and at hearing this, O Princess, the brown-faced sons of the desert, old and young, laugh, and clap their hands—he gave of his grandfather's store until the prudent old man, intending to cure him of his extravagance, sent him to tend his herds in the country. Alas!

"Across the plain Hatim one day beheld a caravan, and finding it escorting three poets to the court of the King of El-Herah, he invited them to stop with him, and while he killed a camel for each of them, they recited songs in his praise, and that of his kin. When they wished to resume the journey, he detained them.

"'There is no gift like the gift of song,' he said. 'I will do better by you than will he, the King to whom you are going. Stay with me, and for every verse you write I will give you a camel. Behold the herd!'

"And at departing, they had each a hundred camels, and he three hundred verses.

"'Where is the herd?' the grandfather asked, when next he came to the pasture.

"'See thou. Here are songs in honor of our house,' Hatim answered, proudly—'songs by great poets; and they will be repeated until all Arabia is filled with our glory.'

"'Alas! Thou hast ruined me!' the elder cried, beating his breast.

"'What!' said Hatim, indignantly. 'Carest thou more for the dirty brutes than for the crown of honor I bought with them?'"

Here the Arab paused. The recitation, it is to be remarked, had been without action, or facial assistance—a wholly unornate delivery; and now he kept stately silence. His eyes, intensely bright in the shadow of the *kufiyeh,* may have produced the spell which held the Princess throughout; or it may have been the eyes and voice; or, quite as likely, the character of Hatim touched a responsive chord in her breast.

"I thank you," she said, adding presently: "In saying I regret the story ended so soon, I pray you receive my opinion of its telling. I doubt if Hatim himself could have rendered it better."

The Arab recognized the compliment with the faintest of bows, but made no reply in words. Irene then raised her veil, and spoke again.

"Thy Hatim, O eloquent Arab, was warrior and poet, and, as thou hast shown him to me, he was also a philosopher. In what age did he live?"

"He was a shining light in the darkness preceding the appearance of the Prophet. That period is dateless with us."

"It is of little consequence," she continued. "Had he lived in our day, he would have been more than poet, warrior and philosopher—he would be a Christian. His charity and love of others, his denial of self, sound like the Christ. Doubtless he could have died for his fellow-men. Hast thou not more of him? Surely he lived long and happily."

"Yes," said the Arab, with a flash of the eyes to denote his appreciation of the circumstance. "He is reported to have been the most wretched of men. His wife—I pray you will observe I am speaking by the tradition—his wife had the power, so dreadful to husbands, of raising Iblis at pleasure. It delighted her to beat him and chase him from his tent; at last she abandoned him."

"Ah!" the Princess exclaimed. "His charities were not admirable in her eyes."

"The better explanation, Princess, may be found in a saying we have in the desert—'A tall man may wed a small woman, but a great soul shall not enter into bonds with a common one.'"

There was silence then, and as the gaze of the story-teller was again finding a fascination in her face, Irene took refuge behind her veil, but said, presently:

"With permission, I will take the story of Hatim for mine; but here is my friend—what hast thou for her?"

The story-teller turned to Lael.

"Her pleasure shall be mine," he said.

"I should like something Indian," the girl answered, timidly, for the eyes oppressed her also.

"Alas! India has no tales of love. Her poetry is about gods and abstract religions. Wherefore, if I may choose, I will a tale from Persia next. In that country there was a verse-maker called Firdousi, and he wrote a great poem, *The Shah Nameh*, with a warrior for hero. This is how Rustem, in single combat, killed Sohrab, not knowing the youth was his son until after the awful deed was done."

The tale was full of melancholy interest, and told with singular grace; but it continued until after nightfall; of which the party was admonished by the attendants coming to light the lamps. At the conclusion, the Arab courteously apologized for the time he had wrested from them.

"In dealing with us, O Princess," he said, "patience is full as lovely as charity."

Lifting the veil again, she extended her hand to him, saying, "The obligation is with us. I thank you for making light and pleasant an afternoon which else had been tedious."

He kissed her hand, and followed the eunuch to the door. Then the supper was announced.

CHAPTER XI
THE TURQUOISE RING

The Prince of India, left in the passage of the Castle with Sergius, was not displeased with the course the adventure appeared to be taking. In the first place, he felt no alarm for Lael; she might be uncomfortable in the quarter to which she had been conducted, but that was all, and it would not last long. The guardianship of the eunuch was in his view a guaranty of her personal safety. In the next place, acquaintance with the Princess might prove serviceable in the future. He believed Lael fitted for the highest rank; she was already educated beyond the requirements of the age for women; her beauty was indisputable; as a consequence, he had thought of her a light in the court; and not unpleasantly it occurred to him now that the fair Princess might carry keys for both the inner and outer doors of the royal residence.

Generally the affair which was of concern to Lael was an affair of absorbing interest to the Prince; in this instance, however, another theme offered itself for the moment a superior attraction.

The impression left by the young master of ceremonies in the reception at the landing was of a kind to arouse curiosity. His appearance, manner, speech and the homage paid him denoted exalted rank; while the confidence with which he spoke for Sultan Amurath was most remarkable. His acceptance of the terms presented by the Princess Irene was little short of downright treaty-making; and what common official dared carry assumption to such a height? Finally the Prince fell to thinking if there was any person the actual governor of the Castle would quietly permit to go masquerading in his authority and title.

Then everything pointed him to Prince Mahommed. The correspondence in age was perfect; the martial array seen galloping down the bank was a fitting escort for the heir-apparent of the gray Sultan; and he alone might with propriety speak for his father in a matter of state.

"A mistake cannot be serious," said the Prince to himself, at the end of the review. "I will proceed upon the theory that the young man is Prince Mahommed."

This was no sooner determined than the restless mind flew forward to an audience. The time and place—midnight in the lonesome old Castle—were propitious, and he was prepared for it.

Indeed it was the very purpose he had in view the night of the repast in his tent at El Zaribah where he so mysteriously intrusted the Emir Mirza with revelations concerning the doom of Constantinople.

Once more he ran over the scheme which had brought him from Cipango. If Islam could not be brought to lead in the project, Christendom might be more amenable to reason. The Moslem world was to be reached through the Kaliph whom he expected to find in Egypt; wherefore his contemplated trip down the Nile from Kash-Cush. If driven to the Christian, Constantine was to be his operator. Such in broadest generality was the plan of execution he had resolved upon.

But to these possibilities he had appended another of which it is now necessary to speak.

Enough has been given to apprise the reader of the things to which the Prince preferably devoted himself. These were international affairs, and transcendently war. If indeed the latter were not the object he had always specially in mind, it was the end to which his management usually conducted. For mere enjoyment in the sight of men facing the death which strangely passed him by, he delighted in hovering on the edge of battle until there was a crisis, and then plunging into its heated heart.

He had also a peculiar method of bringing war about. This consisted in providing for punishments in case his enterprises miscarried. Invariably somebody suffered for such failures. In that way he soothed the pangs of wounded vanity.

When he was inventing the means for executing his plots, and forming the relations essential to them, it was his habit to select instruments of punishment in advance.

Probably no better illustration of this feature of his dealings can be given than is furnished by the affair now engaging him. If he failed to move the Kaliph to lead the reform, he would resort to Constantine; if the Emperor also declined, he would make him pay the penalty; then came the reservation. So soon after his arrival from Cipango as he could inform himself of the political conditions of the world to which he was returning, he fixed upon Mahommed to avenge him upon the offending Greek.

The meeting with Mirza at El Zaribah was a favorable opportunity to begin operating upon the young Turk. The tale the Emir received that night under solemn injunctions of secrecy was really intended for his master. How well it was devised for the end in view the reader will be able to judge from what is now to follow.

The audience with Mahommed determined upon by the Prince of India, our first point of interest is in observing how he set about accomplishing it. His promptness was characteristic.

Directly the ladies had disappeared with the eunuch, the soldiers poured from their hiding places in the Castle, and seeing one whom he judged an officer, the Prince called to him in Turkish:

"Ho, my friend!"

The man was obliging.

"Present my salutations to the Governor of the Castle, and say the Prince of India desires speech with him."

The soldier hesitated.

"Understand," said the Prince, quickly, "my message is not to the great Lord who received me at the landing. But the Governor in fact. Bring him here."

The confident manner prevailed.

Presently the messenger returned with a burly, middle-aged person in guidance. A green turban above a round face, large black eyes in muffling of fleshy lids, pallid cheeks lost in dense beard, a drab gown lined with yellow fur, a naked cimeter in a silk-embroidered sash, bespoke the Turk; but how unlike the handsome, fateful-looking masquerader at the river side!

"The Prince of India has the honor of speech with the Governor of the Castle?"

"God be praised," the Governor replied. "I was seeking your Highness. Besides wishing to join in your thanks for happy deliverance from the storm, I thought to discharge my duty as a Moslem host by conducting you to refreshments and repose. Follow me, I pray."

A few steps on the way, the Governor stopped:

"Was there not a companion—a younger man—a Dervish?"

"A monk," said the Prince; "and the question reminds me of my attendant, a negro. Send for him—or better, bring them both to me. I wish them to share my apartment."

In a short time the three were in quarters, if one small room may be so dignified. The walls were cold gray stone; one oblong narrow port-hole admitted scanty light; a rough bench, an immense kettle-drum shaped like the half of an egg-shell, and propped broadside up, some piles of loose straw, each with folded sheepskins on it, constituted the furnishment.

Sergius made no sign of surprise or disappointment. Possibly the chamber and its contents were reproductions of his cell up in Bielo-Osero. Nilo gave himself to study of the drum, reminded, doubtless, of similar warlike devices in Kash-Cush. The Prince alone expostulated. Taking a stand between the Governor and the door, he said:

"A question before thou goest hence."

The Turk gazed at him silently.

"To what accommodations have the Princess Irene and her attendant been taken? Are they vile as these?"

"The reception room of my harem is the most comfortable the Castle affords," the Governor answered.

"And they?"

"They are occupying it."

"Not by courtesy of thine. He who could put the hospitality of the Prince Mahommed to shame by maltreating one of his guests."

He paused, and grimly surveyed the room.

"Such a servant would be as evil-minded to another guest; and that the other is a woman, would not affect his imbruited soul."

"The Prince Mahommed!" the Governor exclaimed.

"Yes. What brings him here, matters not; his wish to keep the Romans in ignorance of his near presence, I know as well as thou; none the less, it was his royal word we accepted. As for thee—thou mightest have promised faith and hospitality with thy hand on the Prophet's beard, yet would I have bidden the Princess trust herself to the tempest sooner."

Sergius was now standing by, but the conversation being in Turkish, he listened without understanding.

"Thou ass!" the Prince continued. "Not to know that the kinswoman of the Roman Emperor, under this roof by treaty with the mighty Amurath, his son the negotiator, is our guardian! When the storm shall have spent itself, and the waters quieted down, she will resume her journey. Then—it may be in the morning—she will first ask for us, and then thy master will require to know how we have passed the night. Ah, thou beginnest to see!"

The Governor's head was drooping; his hands crossed themselves upon his stomach; and when he raised his eyes, they were full of deprecation and entreaty.

"Your Highness—most noble Lord—condescend to hear me."

"Speak. I am awake to hear the falsehood thou hast invented in excuse of thy perfidy to us, and thy treason to him, the most generous of masters, the most chivalrous of knights."

"Your Highness has greatly misconceived me. In the first place you have forgotten the crowded state of the Castle. Every room and passage is filled with the suite and escort of"—

He hesitated, and turned pale, like a man dropped suddenly into a great danger. The shrewd guest caught at the broken sentence and finished it:

"Of Prince Mahommed!"

"With the suite and escort," the Governor repeated.... "In the next place, it was not my intention to leave you unprovided. From my own apartments, light, beds and seats were ordered to be brought here, with meats for refreshment, and water for cleansing and draught. The order is in course of execution now. Indeed, your Highness, I swear by the first chapter of the Koran"—

"Take something less holy to swear by," cried the Prince.

"Then, by the bones of the Faithful, I swear I meant to make you comfortable, even to my own deprivation."

"By thy young master's bidding?"

The Governor bent forward very low.

"Well," said the Prince, softening his manner—"the misconception was natural."

"Yes—yes."

"And now thou hast only to prove thy intention by making it good."

"Trust me, your Highness."

"Trust thee? Ay, on proof. I have a commission"—

The Prince then drew a ring from his finger.

"Take this," he said, "and deliver it to the Emir Mirza."

The assurance of the speech was irresistible; so the Turk held out his hand to receive the token.

"And say to the Emir, that I desire him to thank the Most Compassionate and Merciful for the salvation of which we were witnesses at the southwest corner of the Kaaba."

"What!" exclaimed the Governor. "Art thou a Moslem?"

"I am not a Christian."

The Governor, accepting the ring, kissed the hand offering it, and took his departure, moving backward, and with downcast eyes, his manner declarative of the most abject humility.

Hardly was the door closed behind the outgoing official, when the Prince began to laugh quietly and rub his hands together—quietly, we say, for the feeling was not merriment so much as self-gratulation.

There was cleverness in having doubted the personality of the individual who received the refugees at the landing; there was greater cleverness in the belief which converted the Governor into the Prince Mahommed; but the play by which the fact was uncovered—if not a stroke of genius, how may it be better described? The Prince of India thought as he laughed:

"Not long now until Amurath joins his fathers, and then—Mahommed."

Presently he stopped, a step half taken, his gaze upon the floor, his hands clasped behind him. He stood so still it would not have been amiss to believe a thought was all the life there was in him. He certainly did believe in astrology. Had not men been always ruled by what they imagined heavenly signs? How distinctly he remembered the age of the oracle and the augur! Upon their going out he became a believer in the stars as prophets, and then an adept; afterwhile he reached a stage when he habitually mistook the commonest natural results, even coincidences, for confirmations of planetary forecasts. And now this halting and breathlessness was from sudden recollection that the horoscope lying on his table in Constantinople had relation to Mahommed in his capacity of Conqueror. How marvellous also that from the meeting with Constantine in the street of the city, he should have been blown by a tempest to a meeting with Mahommed in the White Castle!

These circumstances, trifling to the reader, were of deep influence to the Prince of India. While he stands there rigid as a figure marbleized in mid action, he is saying to himself:

"The audience will take place—Heaven has ordered it. Would I knew what manner of man this Mahommed is!"

He had seen a handsome youth, graceful in bearing, quick and subtle in speech, cultivated and evidently used to governing. Very good, but what an advantage there would be in knowing the bents and inclinations of the royal lad beforehand.

Presently the schemer's head arose. The boyish Prince was going about in armor when soft raiment would be excusable—and that meant ambition, dreams of conquest, dedication to martial glory. Very good indeed! And then his manner under the eyes of the girlish Princess—how quickly her high-born grace had captivated him! Something impossible were he not of a romantic turn, a poet, sentimentalist, knight errant.

The Prince clapped his hands. He knew the appeals effective with such natures. Let the audience come.... Ah, but—

Again he sunk into thought. Youths like Mahommed were apt to be wilful. How was he to be controlled? One expedient after another was swiftly considered and as swiftly rejected. At last the right one! Like his ancestors from Ertoghrul down, the young Turk was a believer in the stars. Not unlikely he was then in the Castle by permission of his astrologer. Indeed, if Mirza had repeated the conversation and predictions at El Zaribah, the Prince of India was being waited for with an impatience due a master of the astral craft. Again the Wanderer cried, "Let the audience come!" and peace and confidence were possessing him when a loud report and continuous rumble in the room set the solid floor to quaking. He looked around in time to see the big drum quivering under a blow from Nilo.

From the negro his gaze wandered to Sergius standing before the one loophole by which light and air were let into the dismal chamber; and recalling the monk as the sole attendant of the Princess Irene, he thought it best to speak to him.

Drawing near, he observed the cowl thrown back, and that the face was raised, the eyes closed, the hands palm to palm upon the breast. Involuntarily he stopped, not because he was one of those who always presume the most Holy Presence when prayer is being offered—he stopped, wondering where he had seen that countenance. The delicate features, the pallid complexion, the immature beard, the fair hair parted in the middle, and falling in wavy locks over the shoulders, the aspect manly yet womanly in its refinement, were strangely familiar to him. It was his first view of the monk's face. Where had he seen it? His memory went back, far back of the recent. A chill struck his heart. The features, look, air, portrait, the expression indefinable except as a light of outcoming spirit, were those of the man he had helped crucify before the Damascus gate in the Holy City, and whom he could no more cast out of mind than he could the bones from his body. His feet seemed rooting into the flinty flags beneath them. He heard the centurion call to him: "Ho, there! If thou knowest the Golgotha, come show it." He felt the sorrowful eyes of the condemned upon him. He struck the bloody cheek, and cried as to a beast: "Go faster, Jesus!" And then the words, wrung from infinite patience at last broken:

"I am going, but do thou TARRY TILL I COME."

For relief, he spoke:

"What dost thou, my friend?"

Sergius opened his eyes and answered simply, "I am praying."

"To whom?"

"To God."

"Art thou a Christian?"

"Yes."

"God is for the Jew and the Moslem."

"Nay," said Sergius, looking at the Prince without taking down his hands, "all who believe in God find happiness and salvation in Him—the Christian as well as the Jew and the Moslem."

The questions had been put with abrupt intensity; now the inquisitor drew back astonished. He heard the very postulate of the scheme to which he was devoting himself—and from a boy so like the dead Christ he was working to blot out of worship he seemed the Christ arisen!

The amazement passed slowly, and with its going the habitual shrewdness and capacity to make servants of circumstances apparently the most untoward returned. The youth had intellect, impressiveness, aptitude in words, and a sublime idea. But what of his spirit—his courage—his endurance in the Faith?

"How came this doctrine to thee?"

The Prince spoke deferentially.

"From the good father Hilarion."

"Who is he?"

"The Archimandrite of Bielo-Osero."

"A monastery?"

"Yes."

"How did he receive it?"

"From the Spirit of God, whence Christ had his wisdom—whence all good men have their goodness—by virtue of which they, like Him, become sons of God."

"What is thy name?"

"Sergius."

"Sergius"—the Prince, now fully recovered, exerted his power of will—"Sergius, thou art a heretic."

At this accusation, so terrible in those days, the monk raised the rosary of large beads dangling from his girdle, kissed the cross, and stood surveying the accuser with pity.

"That is," the Prince continued with greater severity, "speak thou thus to the Patriarch yonder"—he waved a hand toward Constantinople—"dare repeat the saying to a commission appointed to try thee for heresy, and thou wilt thyself taste the pangs of crucifixion or be cast to the beasts."

The monk arose to his great height, and replied, fervently:

"Knowest thou when death hath the sweetness of sleep? I will tell thee"—A light certainly not from the narrow aperture in the wall collected upon his countenance, and shone visibly—"It is when a martyr dies knowing both of God's hands are a pillow under his head."

The Prince dropped his eyes, for he was asking himself, was such sweetness of sleep appointed for him? Resuming his natural manner, he said: "I understand thee, Sergius. Probably no man in the world, go thou East or West, will ever understand thee better. God's hands under my head, welcome death!—Let us be friends."

Sergius took his offered hand.

Just then there was a noise at the door, and a troop of servants entered with lighted lamps, rugs, a table, stools, and beds and bedding, and it was not long until the apartment was made habitable. The Prince, otherwise well satisfied, wanted nothing then but a reply from Mirza; and in the midst of his wonder at the latter's delay, a page in brilliant costume appeared, and called out:

"The Emir Mirza!"

CHAPTER XII
THE RING RETURNS

The Prince, at the announcement of Mirza, took position near the centre of the room where the light was ample. His black velvet pelisse contrasting strongly with his white hair and beard, he looked a mysterious Indian potentate to whom occult Nature was a familiar, and the stars oracular friends.

Mirza's cheeks were scarcely so sun and sand stained as when we first beheld him in conduct of the caravan to Mecca; in other respects he was unchanged. His attire, like the lord Mahommed's at the reception on the landing, was of chain mail very light and flexible. He carried a dagger in his belt, and to further signify confidence in the Prince, the flat steel cap forming his headgear was swinging loosely from his left arm; or he might have intended to help his friend to a more ready recognition by presenting himself bareheaded. He met his survey with unaffected pleasure, took the hand extended in greeting, and kissed it reverentially.

"Forgive me, O Prince, if my first greeting have the appearance of a reproach," Mirza said, as he gave up the hand. "Why have you kept us waiting so long?"

The Prince's countenance assumed a severe expression.

"Emir, I gave you confidence under seal."

The Emir flushed deeply.

"Was it knightly to betray me? To whom have you told the secret? How many have been waiting for my coming?"

"Be merciful, I pray."

"But the stars. You have made me culprit with them. I may pardon you; can you assure me of their pardon?"

The Emir raised his head, and with an expostulatory gesture, was about to reply, when the Prince continued, "Put thy words in the tongue coinage of Italy, for to be overheard now were to make me an offender like unto thyself."

Mirza glanced hastily at Sergius, still praying before the loophole, and at Nilo; then he surveyed the cell critically, and said, in Italian, "This is the prison of the Castle—and thou—can it be I see thee a prisoner?"

The Prince smiled. "The Governor led me here with my friends; and what you behold of accommodations he sent in afterwards, saying the better rooms were filled with soldiery."

"He will rue the deed. My Lord is swift at righting a wrong, and trust me, O Prince, to make report. But to return"—Mirza paused, and looked into the Prince's eyes earnestly—"Is your accusation just? Hear me; then by the motive judge. When I stood before my master, Prince Mahommed, a returned pilgrim, if not taller in fact, his bearing was more majestic. I kissed his hand wondering if some servant of the Compassionate, some angel or travelling Jinn, had not arrived before me, and whispered him of what you told me, speaking for the stars. And when we were alone, he would have account of the countries journeyed through, of the people met, of Medina and Mecca, and the other holy places; nor would he rest until he had from me the sayings I had heard on the way, everything from calls to prayer to the Khatib's sermon. When I told him I had not heard the sermon, nor seen the preacher or his camel, he demanded why, and—what else was there to do, O Prince?—I related how we had been pursued by the terrible Yellow Air; how it had overtaken me; how I fell down dying at the corner of the Kaaba, and by whom I was saved even as the life was departing. This last directed him to you. My efforts to put him off but whetted his desire. He would not be diverted or denied. He insisted—urged—threatened. At last I told him all—of your joining us with the Hajj from El Khatif—your rank and train—your marches in the rear—the hundreds of miserables you saved from the plague—of our meeting at Zaribah, your hospitality, your learning in all that pertains to the greatest of the prophets, your wisdom above the wisdom of other men. And you grew upon him as I proceeded. 'Oh, a good man truly!' 'What courage!' 'What charity!' 'The Prophet himself!' 'Oh, that I had been you!' 'O foolish Mirza, to suffer such a man to escape!' With such exclamations he kept breaking up my story. It was not long until he fastened upon our meeting in the tent. He plied me to know of what we talked—what you said, and all you said. O Prince, if you did but know him; if you knew the soul possessing him, the intellectual things he has mastered, his sagacity, his art, his will, his day-dreams pursuing him in sleep, the deeds he is prepared to do, the depth and strength of his passions, his admiration for heroes, his resolve to ring the world with the greatness of his name—Oh, knew you the man as I do, were you his lover as I am, his confidant—had you, for teaching him to ride and strike with sword and spear, his promise of a share in the glory beckoning him on, making his mighty expectations a part of you even as they are of him, would you—ah, Prince, could you have withheld the secret? Think of the revelation! The old East to awake, and march against the West! Constantinople doomed! And he the leader for whom the opportunity is waiting! And to call my weakness betrayal! Unsay it, unsay it, Prince!"

The face of the auditor as Mirza proceeded with his defence would have been a profitable study. He saw himself succeeding in the purpose of his affected severity; he was drawing from Mahommed's intimate the information he most desired; and thus advised in advance, his role in the interview coming would be of easy foresight and performance. Not to appear too lightly satisfied, however, he said gravely, "I see the strain you underwent, my gallant friend. I see also the earnestness of your affection for your most noble pupil. He is to be congratulated upon the possession of a servant capable of such discernment and devotion. But I recall my question—How many are there waiting for me?"

"Your revelations, O Prince, were imparted to my master alone; and with such certainty as you know yourself, you may believe them at rest in his bosom. No one better than he appreciates the importance of keeping them there under triple lock. More than one defeat—I think he would permit the confession—has taught him that secrecy is the life of every enterprise."

"Say you so, Emir? I feel warmth returning to my hope. Nay, listening to you, and not believing in improvised heroes, I see how your course may have been for the best. The years gone since you yielded to his importunities, wisely used, have doubtless served him providentially."

The Prince extended his hand again, and it was ardently taken; then, on his part, more than pleased, Mirza said, "I bring you a message from my Lord Mahommed. I was with him when the Governor came and delivered your ring to me—and, lest I forget a duty, Prince, here it is—take it at some future time it may be serviceable as today."

"Yes, well thought!" the Jew exclaimed, replacing the signet on his finger, and immediately, while looking at the turquoise eye, he dropped his tone into the solemn, "Ay, the obligations of the Pentagram endure—they are like a decree of God."

The words and manner greatly impressed Mirza.

"My Lord Mahommed," he said, "observed the delivery of the ring to me by the Governor; and when we were alone, and I had recounted the story of the jewels, 'What!' my Lord cried, quite as transported as myself. 'That wonderful man—he here—here in this Castle! He shall not escape me. Send for him at once. I brook no delay.' He stamped his foot. 'Lest he vanish in the storm—go!' When I was at the door, he bade me come back. 'The elder man with the white beard and black eyes, said you? It were well for me to begin by consulting his comfort. He may be tired, and in want of repose; his accommodations may be insufficient; wherefore go see him first, and ascertain his state and wishes.' And as I was going, he summoned me to return again. 'A moment—stay!' he said.'The circumstance enlarges with thought. Thou knowest, Mirza, I did not come here with a special object; I was drawn involuntarily; now I see it was to meet him. It is a doing of the stars. I shall hear from them!' O Prince"—Mirza's eyes sparkled, arid he threw up both his hands—"if ever man believed what he said, my master did."

"A wise master truly," said the Jew, struggling with his exultation. "What said he next?"

"'While I am honoring their messenger'—thus my Lord continued—'why not honor the stars? Their hour is midnight, for then they are all out, from this horizon and that calling unto each other, and merging their influences into the harmony the preachers call the Will of the Most Merciful. A good hour for the meeting. Hear, Mirza—at midnight—in this room. Go now.' And so it is appointed."

"And well appointed, Emir."

"Shall I so report?"

"With my most dutiful protestations."

"Look for me then at midnight."

"I shall be awake, and ready."

"Meantime, Prince, I will seek an apartment more in correspondence with the degree of my Lord's most honored guest."

"Nay, good Mirza, suffer me to advise in that matter. The bringing me into this place was a mistake of the Governor's. He could not divine the merit I have in your master's eyes. He took me for a Christian. I forgive him, and pray he may not be disturbed. He may be useful to me. Upon the springing of a mischance—there is one such this instant in my mind's eye—I may be driven to come back to this Castle. In such an event, I prefer him my servant rather than my enemy."

"O Prince!"

"Nay, Emir, the idea is only a suggestion of one of the Prophets whom Allah stations at the turns in every man's career."

"But every man cannot see the Prophets."

The Jew finished gravely: "Rather than disturb the Governor further, soothe him for me; and when the Lord Mahommed goes hence, do thou see an instruction is left putting the Castle and its chief at my order. Also, as thou art a grateful friend, Mirza, serve me by looking into the kettles out of which we are to have our refreshment, and order concerning them as for thyself. I feel a stir of appetite."

The Emir backed from the apartment, leaving a low salaam just outside the door.

If the reader thinks the Prince content now, he is not mistaken. True he paced the floor long and rapidly; but, feeling himself close upon a turn in his course, he was making ready for it perfectly as possible by consulting the Prophet whom he saw waiting there.

And as the Lord Mahommed failed not to remember them what time he betook himself to supper, the three guests up in the prison fared well, nor cared for the howling of the wind, and the bursting and beating of the rain still rioting without the walls.

CHAPTER XIII
MAHOMMED HEARS FROM THE STARS

The second recall of the Emir Mirza departing with the appointment for the Prince of India was remarkable, considering Mahommed's usual quickness of conclusion and steadiness of purpose; and the accounting for it is noteworthy.

So completely had the young Turk been taken up by study and military service that leisure for love had been denied him; else he either despised the passion or had never met a woman to catch his fancy and hold it seriously.

We have seen him make the White Castle by hard galloping before the bursting of the storm. While at the gate, and in the midst of his reception there, the boats were reported making all speed to the river landing; and not wishing his presence at the Castle to be known in Constantinople, he despatched an under officer to seize the voyagers, and detain them until he had crossed the Bosphorus *en route* to Adrianople. However, directly the officer brought back the spirited message of the Princess Irene to the Governor of the Castle, his mind underwent a change.

"What," he asked, "sayst thou the woman is akin to the Emperor Constantine?"

"Such is her claim, my Lord, and she looks it."

"Is she old?"

"Young, my Lord—not more than twenty."

Mahommed addressed the Governor:

"Stay thou here. I will take thy office, and wait upon this Princess."

Dismounting, then, in the capacity of Governor of the Castle, he hastened to the landing, curious as well as desirous of offering refuge to the noble lady.

He saw her first a short way off, and was struck with her composed demeanor. During the discussion of his tender of hospitality, her face was in fair view, and it astonished him. When finally she stepped from the boat, her form, delicately observable under the rich and graceful drapery, and so exquisitely in correspondence with her face, still further charmed him.

Before the chairs were raised, he sent a messenger to the Castle with orders to place everybody in hiding, and for his Kislar-Aga, or chief eunuch, to be in the passage of entrance to receive and take charge of the kinswoman of the Emperor and her attendant. By a further order the Governor proper was directed to vacate his harem apartments for her accommodation.

In the Castle, after the Princess had been thus disposed of, the impression she made upon him increased.

"She is so high-born!—so beautiful!—She has such spirit and mind!—She is so calm under trial—so courageous—so decorous—so used to courtly life!"

Such exclamations attested the unwonted ferment going on in his mind. Gradually, as tints under the brush of a skilful painter lose themselves in one effect, his undefined ideas took form.

"O Allah! What a Sultana for a hero!"

And by repetition this ran on into what may be termed the chorus of a love song—the very first of the kind his soul had ever sung.

Such was Mahommed's state when Mirza received the turquoise ring, and, announcing the Prince of India, asked for orders. Was it strange he changed his mind? Indeed he was at the moment determining to see again the woman who had risen upon him like a moon above a lake; so, directly he had despatched the Emir to the Prince of India with the appointment for midnight, he sent for an Arab Sheik of his suite, arrayed himself in the latter's best habit, and stained his hands, neck, and face-turned himself, in brief, into the story-teller whom we have seen admitted to amuse the Princess Irene.

At midnight, sharply as the hour could be determined by the uncertain appliances resorted to by the inmates of the Castle, Mirza appeared at his master's door with the mystical Indian, and, passing the sentinel there, knocked like one knowing himself impatiently awaited. A voice bade them enter.

The young Turk, upon their entrance, arose from a couch of many cushions prepared for him under a canopy in the centre of the room.

"This, my Lord, is the Prince of India" said Mirza; then, almost without pause, he turned to the supposed Indian, and added more ceremoniously: "Be thou happy, O Prince! The East hath not borne a son so worthy to take the flower from the tomb of Saladin, and wear it, as my master here— the Lord Mahommed."

Then, his duty done, the Emir retired.

Mahommed was in the garb used indoors immemorially by his race— sharply pointed slippers, immense trousers gathered at the ankles, a yellow quilted gown dropping below the knees, and a turban of balloon shape, its interfolding stayed by an aigrette of gold and diamonds. His head was shaven up to the edge of the turban, so that, the light falling from a cluster of lamps in suspension from the ceiling, every feature was in plain exposure. Looking into the black eyes scarcely shaded by the upraised arching brows, the Prince of India saw them sparkle with invitation and pleasure, and was himself satisfied.

He advanced, and saluted by falling upon his knees, and kissing the back of his hands laid palm downward on the floor. Mahommed raised him to his feet.

"Rise, O Prince!" he said—"rise, and come sit with me."

From behind the couch, the Turk dragged a chair of ample seat, railed around except at the front, and provided with a cushion of camel's hair—a chair such as teachers in the Mosques use when expounding to their classes. This he placed so while he sat on the couch the visitor would be directly before him, and but little removed. Soon the two were sitting cross-legged face to face.

"A man devout as the Prince of India is reported to me," Mahommed began, in a voice admirably seconding the respectful look he fixed upon the other, "must be of the rightly guided, who believe in God and the Last Day, and observe prayer, and pay the alms, and dread none but God—who therefore of right frequent the temples."

"Your words, my Lord, are those of the veritable messenger of the most high Heaven," the Wanderer responded, bending forward as if about to perform a prostration. "I recognize them, and they give me the sensation of being in a garden of perpetual abode, with a river running beneath it." Mahommed, perceiving the quotation from the Koran, bent low in turn, saying: "It is good to hear you, for as I listen I say to myself, This one is of the servants of the Merciful who are to walk upon the earth softly. I accost you in advance, Welcome and Peace."

After a short silence, he continued: "A frequenter of mosques, you will see, O Prince, I have put you in the teacher's place. I am the student. Yours to open the book and read; mine to catch the pearls of your saying, lest they fall in the dust, and be lost."

"I fear my Lord does me honor overmuch; yet there is a beauty in willingness even where one cannot meet expectation. Of what am I to speak?"

Mahommed knit his brows, and asked imperiously, "Who art thou? Of that tell me first."

Happily for the Prince, he had anticipated this demand, and, being intensely watchful, was ready for it, and able to reply without blenching: "The Emir introduced me rightly. I am a Prince of India."

"Now of thy life something."

"My Lord's request is general—perhaps he framed it with design. Left thus to my own judgment, I will be brief, and choose from the mass of my life."

There was not the slightest sign of discomposure discernible in the look or tone of the speaker; his air was more than obliging—he seemed to be responding to a compliment.

"I began walk as a priest—a disciple of Siddhartha, whom my Lord, of his great intelligence, will remember as born in Central India. Very early, on account of my skill in translation, I was called to China, and there put to rendering the Thirty-five Discourses of the father of the Budhisattwa into Chinese and Thibettan. I also published a version of the Lotus of the Good Law, and another of the Nirvana. These brought me a great honor. To an ancestor of mine, Maha Kashiapa, Buddha happened to have intrusted his innermost mysteries—that is, he made him Keeper of the Pure Secret of the Eye of Right Doctrine. Behold the symbol of that doctrine."

The Prince drew a leaf of ivory, worn and yellow, from a pocket under his pelisse, and passed it to Mahommed, saying, "Will my lord look?"

Mahommed took the leaf, and in the silver sunk into it saw this sign:

[Illustration]

"I see," he said, gravely. "Give me its meaning."

"Nay, my Lord, did I that, the doctrine of which, as successor of Kashiapa, though far removed, they made me Keeper—the very highest of Buddhistic honors—would then be no longer a secret. The symbol is of vast sanctity. There is never a genuine image of Buddha without it over his heart. It is the monogram of Vishnu and Siva; but as to its meaning, I can only say every Brahman of learning views it worshipfully, knowing it the compression of the whole mind of Buddha."

Mahommed respected the narrator's compunction, and returned the symbol, saying simply, "I have heard of such things."

"To pursue," the Prince then said, confident of the impression he was producing: "At length I returned to my own country enriched beyond every hope. A disposition to travel seized me. One day, passing the desert to Baalbec, some Bedouin made me prisoner, and carrying me to Mecca, sold me to the Scherif there; a good man who respected my misfortune and learning—may the youths ever going in Paradise forget not his cup of flowing wine!—and wrought with me over the Book of the One God until I became a believer like himself. Then, as I had exchanged the hope of Nirvana for the better and surer hope of Islam, he set me free.... Again in my native land, I betook myself to astrologic studies, being the more inclined thereto by reason of the years I had spent in contemplating the abstrusities of Siddhartha. I became an adept—something, as my Lord may already know, impossible to such as go about unknowing the whole earth and heavens, and the powers superior, those of the sky, and those lesser, meaning Kings, Emperors, and Sultans."

"How!" exclaimed Mahommed. "Is not every astrologer an adept?"

The Prince answered softly, seeing the drift was toward the professor in the young Turk's service. "There is always a better until we reach the best. Even the stars differ from each other in degree."

"But how may a man know the superior powers?"

"The sum of the observations kept by the wise through the ages, and recorded by them, is a legacy for the benefit of the chosen few. Had my Lord the taste, and were he not already devoted by destiny, I could take him to a college where what is now so curious to him is simple reading."

The hard and doubting expression on Mahommed's face began to soften, yet he persisted: "Knowing the superior, why is it needful to know the inferior powers?"

"My Lord trenches now upon the forbidden, yet I will answer as his shrewdness deserves. Never man heard from the stars in direct speech— that were almost like words with God. But as they are servants, they also have servants. Moreover what we have from them is always in answer. They love to be sought after by the diligent. Some ages ago an adept seeking this and that of them conjecturally, had reply, 'Lo! A tribe of poor wanderers in the East. Heed them, for they shall house their dominion in palaces now the glory of the West, and they shall dig the pit to compass the fall of the proud.' Is it this tribe? Is it that? But the seeker never knew. The children of Ertoghrul were yet following their herds up and down the pastures they had from Ala-ed-din, the Iconian. Not knowing their name, he could not ask of them from the decree-makers?"

The Mystic beheld the blood redden Mahommed's open countenance, and the brightening of his eyes; and as he was speaking to his pride, he knew he was not amiss.

"The saying of the stars," he went on, "descended to succeeding adepts. Time came to their aid. When at length your fathers seated themselves in Broussa, the mystery was in part revealed. Anybody, even the low-browed herdsman shivering in the currents blowing from the Trojan heights, could then have named the fortunate tribe. Still the exposure was not complete; a part remained for finding out. We knew the diggers of the pit; but for whom was it? To this I devoted myself. Hear me closely now—my Lord, I have traversed the earth, not once, but many times—so often, you cannot name a people unknown to me, nor a land whither I have not been—no, nor an island. As the grandson of Abd-el-Muttalib was a Messenger of God, I am a Messenger of the Predicting Stars—not their prophet, only their Interpreter and Messenger. The business of the stars is my business." Mahommed's lips moved, and it was with an effort he kept silent.

The Prince proceeded, apparently unconscious of the interest he was exciting: "Here and there while I travelled, I kept communication with the planets; and though I had many of their predictions to solve, I asked them oftenest after the unnamed proud one for whom thy Ottomanites were charged to dig a pit. I presented names without number—names of persons, names of peoples, and lest one should be overlooked, I kept a record of royal and notable families. Was a man-child horn to any of them, I wrote down the minute of the hour of his birth, and how he was called. By visitations, I kept informed of the various countries, their conditions, and their relations with each other; for as the state of the earth points favorably or unfavorably to its vegetation, so do the conditions of nations indicate the approach of changes, and give encouragement to those predestined to bring the changes about. Again I say, my Lord, as the stars are the servants of God, they have their servants, whom you shall never know except as you are able to read the signs their times offer you for reading. Moreover the servants are sometimes priests, sometimes soldiers, sometimes kings; among them have been women, and men of common origin; for the seed of genius falls directly from God's hand, and He chooses the time and field for the sowing; but whether high or low, white or black, good or bad, how shall a Messenger interpret truly for the stars except by going before their elect, and introducing them, and making their paths smooth? Must he not know them first?"

A mighty impulse here struck Mahommed. Recurring rather to what he had heard from Mirza of the revelation dropped by the strange person met by him during the pilgrimage, he felt himself about to be declared of the elect, and unable to control his eagerness, he asked abruptly:

"Knowest thou me, O Prince?"

The manner of the Mystic underwent a change. He had been deferential, even submissive; seldom a teacher so amiable and unmasterful; now he concentrated his power of spirit, and shot it a continuing flash from his large eyes.

"Know thee, Lord Mahommed?" he answered, in a low voice, but clear and searching, and best suited to the conflict he was ushering in—the conflict of spirit and spirit. "Thou knowest not thyself as well."

Mahommed shrank perceptibly—he was astonished.

"I mean not reference to thy father—nor to the Christian Princess, thy mother,—nor to thy history, which is of an obedient son and brave soldier,—nor to thy education, unusual in those born inheritors of royal power—I mean none of these, for they are in mouths everywhere, even of the beggars nursing their sores by the waysides.... In thy father's palace there was a commotion one night—thou wert about to be born. A gold-faced clock stood in the birth chamber, the gift of a German King, and from the door of the chamber eunuchs were stationed. Exactly as the clock proclaimed midnight, mouth and mouth carried the cry to a man on the roof—'A Prince is born! A Prince is born! Praised be Allah!' He on the roof was seated at a table studying a paper with the signs of the Zodiac in the usual formulary of a nativity. At the coming of the cry, he arose, and observed the heavens intently; then he shouted, 'There is no God but God! Lo, Mars, Lord of the Ascendant—Mars, with his friends, Saturn, Venus, and Jupiter in happy configuration, and the moon nowhere visible. Hail the Prince!' And while his answer was passing below, the man on the roof marked the planets in their Houses exactly as they were that midnight between Monday and Tuesday in the year 1430. Have I in aught erred, my lord?"

"In nothing, O Prince."

"Then I proceed.... The nativity came to me, and I cast and recast it for the aspects, familiarities, parallels and triplicities of the hour, and always with the same result. I found the sun, the angles and the quality of the ambient signs favorable to a career which, when run, is to leave the East radiant with the glory of an unsetting sun."

Here the Jew paused, and bowed—"Now doth my Lord doubt if I know him best?"

CHAPTER XIV
DREAMS AND VISIONS

Mahommed sat awhile in deep abstraction, his face flushed, his hands working nervously in their own clasp. The subject possessing him was very pleasurable. How could it be else?

On his side the Prince waited deferentially, but very observant. He was confident of the impression made; he even thought he could follow the young Turk's reflections point by point; still it was wisest to let him alone, for the cooling time of the sober second thought would come, and then how much better if there were room for him to believe the decision his own.

"It is very well, Prince," Mahommed said, finally, struggling to keep down every sign of excitement. "I had accounts of you from Mirza the Emir, and it is the truth, which neither of us will be the worse of knowing, that I see nothing of disagreement in what he told me, and in what you now tell me of yourself. The conceptions I formed of you are justified: you are learned and of great experience; you are a good man given to charity as the Prophet has ordered, and a believer in God. At various times in the world's history, if we may trust the writers, great men have had their greatness foretold them; now if I think myself in the way of addition to the list of those so fortunate, it is because I put faith in you as in a friendly Prophet."

At this the Prince threw up both hands.

"Friendly am I, my lord, more than friendly, but not a Prophet. I am only a Messenger, an Interpreter of the Superior Powers."

Much he feared the demands upon him if he permitted the impression that he was a Prophet to go uncontradicted; as an astrologer, he could in need thrust the stars between him and the unreasonable. And his judgment was quickly affirmed.

"As you will, O Prince," said Mahommed. "Messenger, interpreter, prophet, whichever pleases you, the burden of what you bring me is nevertheless of chiefest account. Comes a herald, we survey him, and ask voucher for his pretensions; are we satisfied with them, why then he gives place in our interest, and becomes secondary to the matter he bears. Is it not so?"

"It is righteously said, my Lord."

"And when I take up this which you have brought me"—Mahommed laid a hand upon his throat as if in aid of the effort he was making to keep calm and talk with dignity—"I cannot deny its power; for when was there an imaginative young man who first permitted ambition and love of glory to build golden palaces for their abiding in his heart, with self-control to stop his ears to promises apparently from Heaven? O Prince, if you are indeed my friend, you will not laugh at me when you are alone!... Moreover I would not you should believe your tidings received carelessly or as a morsel sweet on my tongue; but as wine warms to the blood coursing to the brain, it has started inquiries and anxieties you alone can allay. And first, the great glory whose running is to fill the East, like an unsetting sun, tell me of it; for, as we all know, glory is of various kinds; there is one kind reserved for poets, orators, and professors cunning in the arts, and another for cheer of such as find delight in swords and bossy shields, and armor well bedight, and in horses, and who exult in battle, and in setting armies afield, in changing boundary lines, and in taking rest and giving respite in the citadels of towns happily assaulted. And as of these the regard is various, tell me the kind mine is to be."

"The stars speak not doubtfully, my Lord. When Mars rises ascendant in either of his Houses, they that moment born are devoted to war, and, have they their bent, they shall be soldiers; nor soldiers merely, but as the conjunctions are good, conquerors, and fortunate, and Samael, his angel, becomes their angel. Has my Lord ever seen his nativity?"

"Yes."

"Then he knows whereof I speak."

Mahommed nodded affirmatively, and said, "The fame is to my taste, doubt not; but, Prince, were thy words duly weighed, then my glory is to be surpassing. Now, I am of a line of heroes. Othman, the founder; Orchan, father of the Janissaries; Solyman, who accepted the crescent moon seen in a dream by the sea at Cyzicus as Allah's bidding to pass the Hellespont to Tzympe in Europe; Amurath, conqueror of Adrianople; Bajazet, who put an end to Christian crusading in the field of Nicopolis—these filled the East with their separate renowns; and my father Amurath, did he not subdue Hunyades? Yet, Prince, you tell me my glory is to transcend theirs. Now—because I am ready to believe you—say if it is to burst upon me suddenly or to signalize a long career. The enjoyment of immortality won in youth must be a pleasant thing."

"I cannot answer, my Lord"

"Cannot?"

And Mahommed's eagerness came near getting the better of his will.

"I have nothing from the stars by which to speak, and I dare not assume to reply for myself."

Then Mahommed's eyes became severely bright, and the bones of his hands shone white through the skin, so hard did he compress them.

"How long am I to wait before the glory you promise me ripens ready for gathering? If it requires long campaigns, shall I summon the armies now?"

A tone, a stress of voice in the question sent a shiver through the Prince despite his self-command. His gaze upon Mahommed's countenance, already settled, intensified, and almost before the last word passed he saw the idea he was expected to satisfy, and that it was the point to which his interrogator had been really tending from the commencement of the interview. To gain a moment, he affected not to clearly understand; after a repetition, he in turn asked, with a meaning look:

"Is not thy father, O Prince, now in his eighty-fifth year?"

Mahommed leaned further forward.

"And is it not eight and twenty years since he began reigning wisely and well?"

Mahommed nodded assent.

"Suffer me to answer now. Besides his age which pleads for him, your father has not allowed greatness and power to shade the love he gave you heartily the hour he first took you in his arms. Nature protests against his cutting off, and in this instance, O Prince, the voice of Nature is the voice of Allah. So say I speaking for myself."

Mahommed's face relaxed its hardness, and he moved and breathed freely while replying: "I do not know what the influences require of me."

"Speak you of the stars, my Lord," the other returned, "hear me, and with distinctness. As yet they have intrusted me with the one prediction, and that you have. In other words, they are committed to a horoscope based upon your nativity, and from it your glory has been rightly delivered. So much is permitted us by the astrologic law we practise. But this now asked me, a circumstance in especial, appertains to you as chief of forces not yet yours. Wherefore—heed well, my Lord—I advise you to make note of the minute of the hour of the day you gird yourself with the sword of sovereignty which, at this speaking, is your great father's by sanction of Heaven; then will I cast a horoscope for Mahommed the Sultan, not Mahommed, son of Amurath merely—then, by virtue of my office of Interpreter of the Stars, having the proper writing in my hand, I will tell you this you now seek, together with all else pertaining to your sovereignty intrusted me for communication. I will tell you when the glory is open to you, and the time for setting forward to make it yours—even the dawning of the term of preparation necessarily precedent to the movement itself. Now am I understood? Will my Lord tell me I am understood?"

An observation here may not be amiss. The reader will of course notice the clever obtrusion of the stars in the speech; yet its real craft was in the reservations covered. Presuming it possible for the Prince to have fixed a time to Mahommed's satisfaction, telling it would have been like giving away the meat of an apple, and retaining the rind. The wise man who sets out to make himself a need to another will carefully husband his capital. Moreover it is of importance to keep in mind through this period of our story that with the Prince of India everything was subsidiary to his scheme of unity in God. To which end it was not enough to be a need to Mahommed; he must also bring the young potentate to wait upon him for the signal to begin the movement against Constantinople; for such in simplicity was the design scarcely concealed under the glozing of "the East against the West." That is to say, until he knew Constantine's disposition with respect to the superlative project, his policy was delay. What, in illustration, if the Emperor proved a friend? In falconry the hawk is carried into the field hooded, and cast off only when the game is flushed. So the Prince of India thought as he concluded his speech, and looked at the handsome face of the Lord Mahommed.

The latter was disappointed, and showed it. He averted his eyes, knit his brows, and took a little time before answering; then a flash of passion seized him.

"With all thy wisdom, Prince, thou knowest not how hard waiting will be. There is nothing in Nature sweeter than glory, and on the other hand nothing so intolerably bitter as hungering for it when it is in open prospect. What irony in the providence which permits us to harvest greatness in the days of our decline! I dream of it for my youth, for then most can be made of it. There was a Greek—not of the Byzantine breed in the imperial kennel yonder"—he emphasized the negative with a contemptuous glance in the direction of Constantinople—"a Greek of the old time of real heroes, he who has the first place in history as a conqueror. Think you he was happy because he owned the world? Delight in property merely, a horse, a palace, a ship, a kingdom, is vulgar: any man can be owner of something; the beggar polishes his crutch for the same reason the king gilds his throne—it belongs to him. Possession means satiety. But achieve thou immortality in thy first manhood, and it shall remain to thee as the ring to a bride or as his bride to the bridegroom.—Let it be as you say. I bow to the stars. Between me and the sovereignty my father stands, a good man to whom I give love for love; and he shall not be disturbed by me or any of mine. In so far I will honor your advice; and in the other matter also, there shall be one ready to note the minute of the hour the succession falls to me. But what if then you are absent?"

"A word from my Lord will bring me to him; and His Majesty is liable to go after his fathers at any moment"—

"Ay, and alas!" Mahommed interposed, with unaffected sorrow, "a king may keep his boundaries clean, and even extend them thitherward from the centre, and be a fear unto men; yet shall death oblige him at last. All is from God."

The Prince was courtier enough to respect the feeling evinced.

"But I interrupted you," Mahommed presently added. "I pray pardon."

"I was about to say, my Lord, if I am not with you when His Majesty, your father, bows to the final call—for the entertainment of such was Paradise set upon its high hill!—let a messenger seek me in Constantinople; and it may even serve well if the Governor of this Castle be instructed to keep his gates always open to me, and himself obedient to my requests."

"A good suggestion! I will attend to it. But"—

Again he lapsed into abstraction, and the Prince held his peace watchfully.

"Prince," Mahommed said at length, "it is not often I put myself at another's bidding, for freedom to go where one pleases is not more to a common man than is freedom to do what pleases him to a sovereign; yet so will I with you in this matter; and as is the custom of Moslems setting out on a voyage I say of our venture, 'In the name of God be its courses and its moorings.' That settled, hearken further. What you have given me is not all comprehensible. As I understand you, I am to find the surpassing glory in a field of war. Tell me, lies the field far or near? Where is it? And who is he I am to challenge? There will be room and occasion for combat around me everywhere, or, if the occasion exist not, my Spahis in a day's ride can make one. There is nothing stranger than how small a cause suffices us to set man against man, life or death. But—and now I come to the very difficulty—looking here and there I cannot see a war new in any respect, either of parties, or objects, or pretence, out of which such a prodigious fame is to be plucked. You discern the darkness in which I am groping. Light, O Prince—give me light!"

For an instant the mind of the Jew, sown with subtlety as a mine with fine ore, was stirred with admiration of the quality so strikingly manifested in this demand; but collecting himself, he said, calmly, for the question had been foreseen:

"My Lord was pleased to say a short while ago that the Emir Mirza, on his return from the Hajj, told him of me. Did Mirza tell also of my forbidding him to say anything of the predictions I then intrusted him?"

"Yes," Mahommed answered, smiling, "and I have loved him for the disobedience. He satisfied me to whom he thought his duty was first owing."

"Well, if evil ensue from the disclosure, it may be justly charged to my indiscretion. Let it pass—only, in reporting me, did not Mirza say, Lord Mahommed, that the prohibition I laid upon him proceeded from a prudent regard for your interests?"

"Yes."

"And in speaking of the change in the status of the world I then announced, and of the refluent wave the East was to pour upon the West"—

"And of the doom of Constantinople!" Mahommed cried, in a sudden transport of excitement.

"Ay, and of the hero thou wert to be, my Lord! Said he nothing of the other caution I gave him, how absolute verity could only be had by a recast of the horoscope at the city itself? And how I was even then on my way thither?"

"Truly, O Prince. Mirza is a marvel!"

"Thanks, my Lord. The assurance prepares me to answer your last demand."

Then, lowering his voice, the Prince returned to his ordinary manner.

"The glory you are to look for will not depend upon conditions such as parties to the war, or its immediate cause, or the place of its wagement."

Mahommed listened with open mouth.

"My Lord knows of the dispute long in progress between the Pope of Rome and the Patriarch of Constantinople; one claiming to be the head of the Church of Christ, the other insisting on his equality. The dispute, my Lord also knows, has been carried from East to West, and back and back again, prelate replying to prelate, until the whole Church is falling to pieces, and on every Christian tongue the 'Church East' and the 'Church West' are common as morning salutations."

Mahommed nodded.

"Now, my Lord," the Prince continued, the magnetic eyes intensely bright, "you and I know the capital of Christianity is yonder "—he pointed toward Constantinople—"and that conquering it is taking from Christ and giving to Mahomet. What more of definition of thy glory wilt thou require? Thus early I salute thee a Sword of God."

Mahommed sprang from his couch, and strode the floor, frequently clapping his hands. Upon the passing of the ecstasy, he stopped in front of the Prince.

"I see it now—the feat of arms impossible to my father reserved for me."

Again he walked, clapping his hands.

"I pray your pardon," he said, when the fit was over. "In my great joy I interrupted you."

"I regret to try my Lord's patience further," the Prince answered, with admirable diplomacy. "It were better, however, to take another step in the explanation now. A few months after separating from Mirza in Mecca, I arrived in Constantinople, and every night since, the heavens being clear, I have questioned the stars early and late. I cannot repeat to my Lord all the inquiries I made of them, so many were they, and so varied in form, nor the bases I laid hold of for horoscopes, each having, as I hoped, to do with the date of the founding of the city. What calculations I have made—tables of figures to cover the sky with a tapestry of algebraic and geometrical symbols: The walks of astrology are well known—I mean those legitimate—nevertheless in my great anxiety, I have even ventured into the arcana of magic forbidden to the Faithful. The seven good angels, and the seven bad, beginning with Jubanladace, first of the good, a celestial messenger, helmeted, sworded with flame, and otherwise beautiful to behold, and ending with Barman, the lowest of the bad, the consort and ally of witches—I besought them all for what they could tell me. Is the time of the running of the city now, to-morrow, next week—when? Such the burden of my inquiry. As yet, my Lord, no answer has been given. I am merely bid keep watch on the schism of the Church. In some way the end we hope has connection with that rancor, if, indeed, it be not the grand result. With clear discernment of the tendencies, the Roman Pontiff is striving to lay the quarrel; but he speaks to a rising tide. We cannot hasten the event; neither can he delay it. Our role is patience—patience. At last Europe will fall away, and leave the Greek to care of himself; then, my Lord, you have but to be ready. The end is in the throes of its beginning now."

"Still you leave me in the dark," Mahommed cried, with a frown.

"Nay, my Lord, there is a chance for us to make the stars speak."

The beguiler appeared to hesitate.

"A chance?" Mahommed asked.

"It is dependent, my Lord."

"Upon what?"

"The life of the Sultan, thy father."

"Speak not in riddles, O Prince."

"Upon his death, thou wilt enter on the sovereignty."

"Still I see not clearly."

"With the horoscope of Mahommed the Sultan in my hand, then certainly as the stars perform their circuits, being set thereunto from the first morning, they must respond to me; and then, find I Mars in the Ascendant, well dignified essentially and accidentally, I can lead my Lord out of the darkness."

"Then, Prince?"

"He may see the Christian capital at his mercy."

"But if Mars be not in the Ascendant?"

"My Lord must wait."

Mahommed sprang to his feet, gnashing his teeth.

"My Lord," said the Prince, calmly, "a man's destiny is never unalterable; it is like a pitcher filled with wine which he is carrying to his lips—it may be broken on the way, and its contents spilled. Such has often happened through impatience and pride. What is waiting but the wise man's hour of preparation?"

The quiet manner helped the sound philosophy. Mahommed took seat, remarking, "You remind me, Prince, of the saying of the Koran, 'Whatsoever good betideth thee, O man, it is from God, and whatsoever evil betideth, from thyself is it.' I am satisfied. Only"—

The Prince summoned all his faculties again.

"Only I see two periods of waiting before me; one from this until I take up the sovereignty; the other thence till thou bringest me the mandate of the stars. I fear not the second period, for, as thou sayest, I can then lose myself in making ready; but the first, the meantime—ah, Prince, speak of it. Tell me how I can find surcease of the chafing of my spirit."

The comprehension of the wily Hebrew did not fail him. His heart beat violently. He was master! Once more he was in position to change the world. A word though not more than "now," and he could marshal the East, which he so loved, against the West, which he so hated. If Constantinople failed him, Christianity must yield its seat to Islam. He saw it all flash-like; yet at no time in the interview did his face betoken such placidity of feeling. The *meantime* was his, not Mahommed's—his to lengthen or shorten—his for preparation. He could afford to be placid.

"There is much for my Lord to do," he said.

"When, O Prince—now?"

"It is for him to think and act as if Constantinople were his capital temporarily in possession of another."

The words caught attention, and it is hard saying what Mahommed's countenance betokened. The reader must think of him as of a listener just awakened to a new idea of infinite personal concern.

"It is for him now to learn the city within and without," the Jew proceeded; "its streets and edifices; its halls and walls; its strong and weak places; its inhabitants, commerce, foreign relations; the character of its ruler, his resources and policies; its daily events; its cliques and clubs, and religious factions; especially is it for him to foment the differences Latin and Greek."

It is questionable if any of the things imparted had been so effective upon Mahommed as this one. Not only did his last doubt of the man talking disappear; it excited a boundless admiration for him, and the freshest novitiate in human nature knows how almost impossible it is to refuse trust when once we have been brought to admire. "Oh!" Mahommed cried. "A pastime, a pastime, if I could be there!"

"Nay, my Lord," said the insidious counsellor, with a smile, "how do kings manage to be everywhere at the same time?"

"They have their Ambassadors. But I am not a king."

"Not yet a king"—the speaker laid stress upon the adverb—"nevertheless public representation is one thing; secret agency another."

Mahommed's voice sank almost to a whisper.

"Wilt thou accept this agency?"

"It is for me to observe the heavens at night, while calculations will take my days. I trust my Lord in his wisdom will excuse me."

"Where is one for the service? Name him, Prince—one as good."

"There is one better. Bethink you, my Lord, the business is of a long time; it may run through years."

Mahommed's brow knit darkly at the reminder.

"And he who undertakes it should enter Constantinople and live there above suspicion. He must be crafty, intelligent, courtly in manner, accomplished in arms, of high rank, and with means to carry his state bravely, for not only ought he to be conspicuous in the Hippodrome; he should be welcome in the palace. Along with other facilities, he must be provided to buy service in the Emperor's bedroom and council chamber— nay, at his elbow. It is of prime importance that he possesses my Lord's confidence unalterably. Am I understood?"

"The man, Prince, the man!"

"My Lord has already named him."

"I?"

"Only to-night my Lord spoke of him as a marvel."

"Mirza!" exclaimed Mahommed, clapping his hands.

"Mirza," the Prince returned, and proceeded without pause: "Despatch him to Italy; then let him appear in Constantinople, embarked from a galley, habited like a Roman, and with a suitable Italian title. He speaks Italian already, is fixed in his religion, and in knightly honor. Not all the gifts at the despot's disposal, nor the blandishments of society can shake his allegiance—he worships my Lord."

"My servant has found much favor with you, O Prince?"

Accepting the remark as a question, the other answered:

"Did I not spend the night with him at El Zaribah? Was I not witness of his trial of faith at the Holy Kaaba? Have I not heard from my Lord himself how, when put to choice, he ignored my prohibition respecting the stars?"

Mahommed arose, and again walked to and fro.

"There is a trouble in this proposal, Prince," he said, halting abruptly. "So has Mirza become a part of me, I am scarcely myself without him."

Another turn across the floor, and he seemed to become reconciled. "Let us have done for to-night," he next said. "The game is imperative, but it will not be harmed by a full discussion. Stay with me to-morrow, Prince."

The Prince remembered the Emperor. Not unlikely a message from that high personage was at his house, received in course of the day.

"True, very true, and the invitation is a great honor to me," he replied, bowing; "but I am reminded that the gossips in Byzantium will feast each other when to-morrow it passes from court to bazaar how the Princess Irene and the Prince of India were driven by the storm to accept hospitality in the White Castle. And if it get abroad, that Mahommed, son of the great Amurath, came also to the Castle, who may foretell the suspicions to hatch in the city? No, my Lord, I submit it is better for me to depart with the Princess at the subsidence of the waters."

"Be it so," Mahommed returned, cordially. "We understand each other. I am to wait and you to communicate with me; and now, morning comes apace, good night."

He held his hand to the Jew; whereat the latter knelt and kissed the hand, but retained it to say:

"My Lord, if I know him rightly, will not sleep to-night; thought is an enemy to sleep; and besides the inspiration there is in the destiny promised, its achievement lies all before him. Yet I wish to leave behind me one further topic, promising it is as much greater than any other as the Heavens are higher than the earth."

"Rise, Prince," said Mahommed, helping him to his feet. "Such ceremonious salutation whether in reception or at departure may be dispensed with hereafter; thou art not a stranger, but more than a guest. I count thee my friend whom everything shall wait upon—even myself. Speak now of what thou callest the greater scheme. I am most curious."

There was a silence while one might count ten slowly. The Jew in that space concentrated the mysterious force of which he was master in great store, so it shone in his eyes, gave tone to his voice, and was an outgoing of WILL in overwhelming current. "Lord Mahommed," he said, "I know you are a believer in God."

The young Turk was conscious of a strange thrill passing through him from brain to body.

"In nature and every quality the God of the Jew, the Christian, and the Moslem is the same. Take we their own sayings. Christ and Mahomet were witnesses sent to testify of Him first, highest and alone—Him the universal Father. Yet behold the perversity of man. God has been deposed, and for ages believers in Him have been divided amongst themselves; wherefore hate, jealousies, wars, battle and the smoke of slaughter perpetually. But now is He at last minded to be restored. Hear, Lord Mahommed, hear with soul and mortal ear!"

The words and manner caught and exalted Mahommed's spirit. As Michael, with a sweep of his wings, is supposed to pass the nether depths, an impulsion bore the son of Amurath up to a higher and clearer plane. He could not but hear.

"Be it true now that God permits His presence to be known in human affairs only when He has a purpose to justify His interposition; then, as we dare not presume the capital of Christendom goes to its fall without His permission, why your designation for the mighty work? That you may be personally glorified, my Lord? Look higher. See yourself His chosen instrument—and this the deed! From the seat of the Caesars, its conquest an argument, He means you to bring men together in His name. Titles may remain—Jew, Moslem, Christian, Buddhist—but there shall be an end of wars for religion—all mankind are to be brethren in Him. This the deed, my Lord—Unity in God, and from it, a miracle of the ages slow to come but certain, the evolution of peace and goodwill amongst men. I leave the idea with you. Good night!"

Mahommed remained so impressed and confounded that the seer was permitted to walk out as from an empty room. Mirza received him outside the door.

CHAPTER XV
DEPARTURE FROM THE WHITE CASTLE

The storm continued till near daybreak. At sunrise the wind abated, and was rapidly succeeded by a dead calm; about the same time the last cloud disappeared, leaving the sky an azure wonder, and the shores of the Bosphorus far and near refreshed and purified.

After breakfast, Mirza conducted the Prince of India to another private audience with Mahommed. As the conference had relation to the subjects gone over in the night, the colloquy may be dispensed with, and only the conclusions given.

Mahommed admitted he had not been able to sleep; in good spirits, however, he agreed, if the Prince were accountable for the wakefulness, he was to be forgiven, since he had fairly foretold it, and, like other prophets, was entitled to immunity. The invitation to remain at the Castle was renewed, and again declined.

Mahommed next conceded the expediency of his waiting to hear what further the stars might say with respect to the great business before him, and voluntarily bound himself to passive conduct and silence; in assuagement of the impatience he knew would torment him, he insisted, however, upon establishing a line of couriers between his place of residence, wherever it might be, and the White Castle. Intelligence could thus be safely transmitted him from Constantinople. In furtherance of this object the Governor of the Castle would be instructed to honor the requests of the Prince of India.

Mahommed condescended next to approve the suggestion of a secret agency in Constantinople. Respecting a person for the service, the delicacy of which was conceded, he had reached the conclusion that there was no one subject to his control so fitted in every respect as Mirza. The selection of the Emir might prove troublesome since he was a favorite with the Sultan; if investigations consequent on his continued absence were instituted, there was danger of their resulting in disagreeable exposure; nevertheless the venture was worth the while, and as time was important, the Emir should be sent off forthwith under instructions in harmony with the Prince's advice. Or more clearly, he was to betake himself to Italy immediately, and thence to the Greek capital, a nobleman amply provided with funds for his maintenance there in essential state and condition. His first duty when in the city should be to devise communication with the White Castle, where connection with the proposed line of couriers should be made for safe transmission of his own reports, and such intelligence as the Prince should from time to time consider it advisable to forward.

This of course contemplated recognition and concert between the Emir and the Prince. In token of his confidence in the latter, Mahommed would constitute him the superior in cases of difference of opinion; though from his knowledge of Mirza's romantic affection acquired in Mecca and on the road thither, he had little apprehension of such a difference.

Mahommed and the Prince were alike well satisfied with the conclusions between them, and their leave-taking at the end of the audience was marked with a degree of affection approaching that of father and son.

About mid-afternoon the Prince and Sergius sallied from the Castle to observe the water, and finding it quiet, they determined to embark.

The formalities of reception in the Castle were not less rigidly observed at the departure. In care of the eunuch the Princess and Lael descended to the hall of entrance where they were received by the supposed Governor, who was in armor thoroughly cleansed of dust and skilfully furbished. His manner was even more gallant and dignified. He offered his hand to assist the Princess to seat in the chair, and upon taking it she glanced furtively at his face, but the light was too scant for a distinct view.

In the Castle and out there were no spectators.

Passing the gate, the Princess bethought her of the story-teller, and looked for him well as she could through the narrow windows. At the landing, when the Governor had in silence, though with ease and grace, helped her from the carriage, the porters being withdrawn, she proceeded to acknowledgments.

"I am sorry," she said, through her veil, "that I must depart without knowing the name or rank of my host."

"Had I greater rank. O Princess," he returned, gravely. "I should have pleasure in introducing myself; for then there would be a hope that my name supported by a title of dignity, would not be erased from your memory by the gayeties of the city to which you are going. The White Castle is a command suitable to one of humble grade, and to be saluted Governor, because I am charged with its keeping, satisfies my pride for the present. It is a convenient title, moreover, should you ever again honor me with a thought or a word."

"I submit perforce," she said. "Yet, Sir Governor, your name would have saved me from the wonder of my kinsman, if not his open question, when, as I am bound to, I tell him of the fair treatment and high courtesy you have shown me and my friends here while in refuge in your Castle walls. He knows it natural for the recipient of bounty to learn who the giver is, with name and history; but how amazed and displeased he will be when I barely describe your entertainment. Indeed, I fear he will think me guilty of over description or condemn me for ingratitude."

She saw the blood color his face, and noticed the air of sincerity with which he replied. "Princess, if payment for what you have received at my hands were worthy a thought, I should say now, and all my days through, down to the very latest, that to have heard you speak so graciously is an overprice out of computation."

The veil hid her responsive blush; for there was something in his voice and manner, possibly the earnestness marking them, which lifted the words out of the commonplace and formal. She could not but see how much more he left implied than actually expressed. For relief, she turned to another subject.

"If I may allude to a part of your generous attention, Sir Governor, distinguishing it from the whole, I should like to admit the pleasure had from the recitation of the Arabian story-teller. I will not ask his name; still it must be a great happiness to traverse the world with welcome everywhere, and everywhere and all the time accompanied and inspired by a mind stored with themes and examples beautiful as the history of El Hatim."

A light singularly bright shone in the Governor's eyes, significant of a happy idea, and with more haste than he had yet evinced, he replied:

"O Princess, the name of the Arab is Aboo-Obeidah; in the desert they call him the Singing Sheik, and among Moslems, city bred and tent born alike, he is great and beloved. Such is his sanctity that all doors he knocks at open to him, even those of harems zealously guarded. When he arrives at Adrianople, in his first day there he will be conducted to the Hanoum of the Sultan, and at her signal the ladies of the household will flock to hear him. Now, would it please you, I will prevail on him to delay his journey that he may visit you at your palace."

"The adventure might distress him," she replied.

"Say not so. In such a matter I dare represent and pledge him. Only give me where you would have him come, and the time, O Princess, and he will be there, not a star in the sky more constant."

"With my promise of good welcome to him then," she said, well pleased, "be my messenger, Sir Governor, and say in the morning day after to-morrow at my palace by Therapia. And now thanks again, and farewell."

So saying she held her hand to him, and he kissed it, and assisted her into the boat.

The adieux of the others, the Prince of India, Sergius and Lael, were briefer. The Governor was polite to each of them; at the same time, his eyes, refusing restraint, wandered to where the Princess sat looking at him with unveiled face.

In the mouth of the river the boats were brought together, and, while drifting, she expressed the pleasure she had from the fortunate meeting with the Prince; his presence, she doubted not, contributed greatly to the good conclusion of what in its beginning seemed so unpromising.

"Nor can I convey an idea of the confidence and comfortable feeling I derived from the society of thy daughter," she added, speaking to the Prince, but looking at Lael. "She was courageous and sensible, and I cannot content myself until she is my guest at Therapia."

"I would be greatly pleased," Lael said, modestly.

"Will the Princess appoint a time?" the Wanderer asked.

"To-morrow—or next week—at your convenience. These warm months are delightful in the country by the water side. At Therapia, Prince—thou and thine. The blessing of the Saints go with you—farewell."

Then though the boats kept on down toward Constantinople, they separated, and in good time the Prince of India and Lael were at home; while the Princess carried Sergius to her palace in the city. Next day, having provided him with the habit approved by metropolitan Greek priests, she accompanied him to the patriarchal residence, introduced him with expressions of interest, and left him in the holy keeping.

Sergius was accepted and rated a neophyte, the vanity of the Byzantine clergy scorning thought of excellence in a Russian provincial. He entered upon the life, however, with humility and zeal, governed by a friendly caution from the Princess.

"Remember," she said to him, as they paused on the patriarchal doorsteps for permission to enter, "remember Father Hilarion is regarded here as a heretic. The stake, imprisonment in darkness for life, the lions in the Cynegion, punishment in some form of approved cruelty awaits a follower of his by open avowal. Patience then; and when endurance is tried most, and you feel it must break, come to me at Therapia. Only hold yourself in readiness, by reading and thought, to speak for our Christian faith unsullied by human inventions, and bide my signal."

And so did he observe everything and venture nothing that presently he was on the road to high favor.

CHAPTER XVI
AN EMBASSY TO THE PRINCESS IRENE

When the Princess Irene returned to Therapia next day, she found awaiting her the Dean of the Court, an official of great importance to whom the settlement of questions pertinent to rank was confided. The state barge of fifteen oars in which he arrived was moored to the marbles of the quay in front of her palace, a handsomely ornamented vessel scarcely needing its richly liveried rowers to draw about it the curious and idle of the town in staring groups. At sight of it, the Princess knew there was a message for her from the Emperor. She lost no time in notifying the Dean of her readiness to receive him. The interview took place in the reception room.

The Dean was a venerable man who, having served acceptably through the preceding reign, was immensely discreet, and thoroughly indurate with formalism and ceremony; wherefore, passing his speech and manner, it is better worth the while to give, briefly as may be, the substance of the communication he brought to the Princess.

He was sure she remembered all the circumstances of the coronation of His Majesty, the Emperor, and of His Majesty's entry into Constantinople; he was not so certain, however, of her information touching some matters distinguishable as domestic rather than administrative. Or she might know of them, but not reliably. Thus she might not have heard authentically that, immediately upon his becoming settled in the imperial seat, His Majesty decided it of first importance to proceed to the selection of a spouse.

The Dean then expatiated on the difficulty of finding in all the world a woman suitable for the incomparable honor. So many points entered into the consideration—age, appearance, rank, education, religion, dowry, politics—upon each of which he dwelt with the gravity of a philosopher, the assurance of a favorite, and the garrulity of age. Having at length presented the problem, and, he thought, sufficiently impressed the Princess with its unexampled intricacies and perils, he next unfolded the several things resolved upon and attempted in the way of solution.

Every royal house in the West had been searched for its marriageable females. At one time a daughter of the Doge of Venice was nearly chosen. Unfortunately there were influential Greeks of greater pride than judgment to object to the Doge. He was merely an elective chief. He might die the very day after celebrating the espousals, and then—not even the ducal robes were inheritable. No, the flower to deck the Byzantine throne was not in the West.

Thereupon the East was explored. For a time the election trembled between a Princess of Trebizond and a Princess of Georgia. As usual the court divided on the question, when, to quiet the factions, His Majesty ordered Phranza, the Grand Chamberlain, a courtier of learning and diplomatic experience, who held the Emperor's confidence in greater degree than any other court official, unless it might be the Dean himself, to go see the rivals personally, and report with recommendation. The ambassador had been gone two years. From Georgia he had travelled to Trebizond; still nothing definite. The embassy, having been outfitted in a style to adequately impress the semi-barbarians, was proving vastly expensive. His Majesty, with characteristic wisdom, had determined to take the business in his own keeping. There were many noble families in Constantinople. Why not seek a consort among them?

The scheme had advantages; not least, if a Byzantine could be found, the Emperor would have the happiness of making the discovery and conducting the negotiations himself—in common parlance, of doing his own courting. There might be persons, the Dean facetiously remarked, who preferred trusting the great affair of wife-choosing to ambassadors, but he had never seen one of them.

The ground covered by the ancient in his statement is poorly represented by these paragraphs, ample as they may seem to the reader. Indeed, the sun was falling swiftly into the lap of night when he thought of concluding. Meantime the Princess listened silently, her patience sustained by wonder at what it all meant. The enlightenment at last came.

"Now, my dear Princess," he said, lowering his voice, "you must know "— he arose, and, as became one so endued with palace habits, peered cautiously around.

"Be seated, my Lord," she said; "there are no eyes in my doors nor ears in my walls."

"Oh, the matter is of importance—a state secret!" He drew the stool nearer her.

"You must know, dear Princess, that the Grand Chamberlain, Phranza, has been negligent and remiss in the time he has consumed, saying nothing of his lavishment of treasure so badly needed at home. Notaras, the Admiral, and the Grand Domestic, are both pursuing His Majesty vigorously for funds and supplies; worse still, the Patriarch lets slip no opportunity to bid him look at the furniture of the churches going to ruin. The imperial conscience being tender in whatever pertains to God and religion, he has little peace left for prayers. Wherefore, there are of us who think it would be loyalty to help secure a bride for His Majesty at home, and thus make an end to the wasteful and inconclusive touring of Phranza."

The Dean drew yet nearer the Princess, and reduced his voice to a tone slightly above a whisper.

"Now you must know further—I am the author and suggestor of the idea of His Majesty's choosing an Empress from the many noble and beautiful dames and maidens of this our ancient city of Byzantium, in every respect the equals, and in many points mentionable the superiors of the best foreigner possible of finding."

The Dean pursed his white-bearded mouth, and posed himself proudly; but his auditor still holding her peace, he leaned forward further, and whispered, "My dear Princess, I did more. I mentioned you to His Majesty"—

The Princess started to her feet, whiter than whitest marble in the Pentelic panelling of the room; yet in total misapprehension of her feeling, the venerable intriguant went on without pause: "Yes, I mentioned you to His Majesty, and to-morrow, Princess—to-morrow—he will come here in person to see you, and urge his suit."

He dropped on his knees, and catching her hand, kissed it.

"O Princess, fairest and most worthy, suffer me first of all the court to congratulate you on the superlative honor to which you will he invited. And when you are in the exalted position, may I hope to be remembered"—

He was not permitted to finish the petition. Withdrawing her hand with decisive action, she bade him be silent or speak to her questions. And he was silent through surprise.

In such manner she gained an interval for thought. The predicament, as she saw it, was troublesome and unfortunate. Honor was intended her, the highest in the imperial gift, and the offer was coming with never a doubt of its instantaneous and grateful acceptance. Remembering her obligations to the Emperor, her eyes filled with tears. She respected and venerated him, yet could not be his Empress. The great title was not a sufficient inducement. But how manage the rejection? She called on the Virgin for help. Directly there was a way exposed. First, she must save her benefactor from rejection; second, the Dean and the court must never know of the course of the affair or its conclusion.

"Rise, my Lord," she said, kindly though with firmness. "The receiver of great news, I thank you, and promise, if ever I attain the throne to hold you in recollection. But now, so am I overwhelmed by the prospect, I am not myself. Indeed, my Lord, would you increase my indebtedness to its utmost limit, take every acknowledgment as said, and leave me—leave me for preparation for the morrow's event. God, his Son and angels only know the awfulness of my need of right direction and good judgment."

He had the wit to see her agitation, and that it was wisest for him to depart.

"I will go, Princess," he said, "and may the Holy Mother give you of her wisdom also." She detained him at the door to ask: "Only tell me, my Lord, did His Majesty send you with this notice?"

"His Majesty honored me with the message."

"At what hour will he come?"

"In the forenoon."

"Report, I pray you then, that my house will be at his service."

CHAPTER XVII
THE EMPEROR'S WOOING

About ten o'clock the day following the extraordinary announcement given, a galley of three banks of oars, classed a *trireme*, rounded the seaward jut of the promontory overhanging the property of the Princess Irene at Therapia.

The hull of the vessel was highly ornate with gilding and carving. At the bow, for figure-head, there was an image of the Madonna of the *Panagia*, or Holy Banner of Constantinople. The broad square sail was of cherry-red color, and in excellent correspondence, the oars, sixty to a side, were painted a flaming scarlet. When filled, the sail displayed a Greek cross in golden filament. The deck aft was covered with a purple awning, in the shade of which, around a throne, sat a grave and decorous company in gorgeous garments; and among them moved a number of boys, white-shirted and bare of head, dispensing perfume from swinging censers. Forward, a body guard, chosen from the household troops and full armed, were standing at ease, and they, with a corps of trumpeters and heralds in such splendor of golden horns and tabards of gold as to pour enrichment over the whole ship, filled the space from bulwark to bulwark. The Emperor occupied the throne.

This galley, to which the harmonious movement of the oars gave a semblance of life, in the distance reminding one of a great bird fantastically feathered and in slow majestic motion, was no sooner hove in sight than the townspeople were thrown into ferment. A flotilla of small boats, hastily launched, put out in racing order to meet and escort it into the bay, and before anchorage was found, the whole shore was astir and in excited babblement.

A detachment of the guard was first landed on the quay in front of the Princess' gate. Accepting the indication, thither rushed the populace; for in truth, since the occupation of the Asiatic shore of the Bosphorus by the Turks, the Emperor seldom extended his voyages far as Therapia. Then, descending the sides by carpeted stairs, the suite disembarked, and after them, amidst a tremendous flourish from the trumpet corps, Constantine followed.

The Emperor, in his light boat, remained standing during the passage to the shore that he might be seen by the people; and as he then appeared, helmed and in close-fitting cuirass, his arms in puffed sleeves of red silk, his legs, below a heavily embroidered narrow skirt, clothed in pliant chain mail intricately linked, his feet steel-shod, a purple cloak hanging lightly at the back from neck to heel, and spurred and magnificently sworded, and all agleam with jewels and gold, it must be conceded he justified his entitlement.

At sight of his noble countenance, visible under the raised visor, the spectators lifted their voices in hearty acclamations—"God and Constantine! Live the Emperor!"

It really seemed as if the deadly factiousness of the capital had not reached Therapia. In the lifted head, the brightened eyes, the gracious though stately bows cast right and left, Constantine published the pleasure the reception was giving him.

A long flourish timed his march through the kiosk of the gate, and along the shell-strewn, winding road, to the broad steps leading to the portico of the palace; there, ascending first, he was received by the Princess.

Amid a group of maids in attendance, all young, fair, high-born, she stood, never more tastefully attired, never more graceful and self-possessed, never more lovely, not even in childhood before the flitting of its virginal bloom; and though the portico was garden-like in decoration, vines, roses and flowering shrubs everywhere, the sovereign had eyes for her alone.

Just within the line of fluted pillars he halted, and drew himself up, smiling as became a suitor, yet majestic as became a king. Then she stepped forward, and knelt, and kissed his hand, and when he helped her to her feet, and before the flush on her forehead was gone, she said:

"Thou art my sovereign and benefactor; nor less for the goodnesses thou hast done to thy people, and art constantly doing, welcome, O my Lord, to the house thou didst give me."

"Speak not so," he replied. "Or if it please thee to give me credit, be it for the things which in some way tried me, not those I did for reward."

"Reward!"

"Ay, for such are pleasure and peace of mind."

Then one by one, she naming them as they advanced, her attendants knelt, and kissed the floor in front of him, and had each a pleasant word, for he permitted none to excel him in decorous gallantry to good women.

In return, he called the officers of his company according to their rank; his brother, who had afterward the grace to die with him; the Grand Domestic, general of the army; the Grand Duke Notaras, admiral of the navy; the Grand Equerry (*Protostrator*); the Grand Chancellor of the Empire (*Logothete*); the Superintendent of Finance; the Governor of the Palace

(*Curopalate*); the Keeper of the Purple Ink; the Keeper of the Secret Seal; the First Valet; the Chief of the Night Guard (*Grand Drumgaire*); the Chief of the Huntsmen (*Protocynege*); the Commander of the Body Guard of Foreigners (*Acolyte*); the Professor of Philosophy; the Professor of Elocution and Rhetoric; the Attorney General (*Nornophylex*); the Chief Falconer (*Protojeracaire*) and others—these he called one by one, and formally presented to the Princess, not minding that with many of them she was already acquainted.

They were for the most part men advanced in years, and right well skilled in the arts of courtiership. The *empressement* of manner with which they saluted her was not lost upon her woman's instinct; infinitely quick and receptive, she knew without a word spoken, that each left his salute on her hand believing it the hand of his future Empress. Last of those presented was the Dean of the Court. He was noticeably formal and distant; besides being under the eye of his master, the wily diplomat was more doubtful of the outcome of the day's visit than most of his colleagues.

"Now," the Princess said, when the presentation was finished, "will my most noble sovereign suffer me to conduct him to the reception room?"

The Emperor stepped to her side, and offered his hand. "Pardon, Sire," she added, taking the hand. "It is necessary that I speak to the Dean."

And when the worthy came to her, she said to him: "Beyond this, under the portico, are refreshments for His Majesty's suite. Serve me, I pray, by leading thy colleagues thither, and representing me at the tables. Command the servants whom thou wilt find there."

Now the reader must not suppose he is having in the foregoing descriptions examples of the style of ceremonials most in fashion at the Greek court. Had formality been intended, the affair would have been the subject of painstaking consideration at a meeting of officials in the imperial residence, and every point within foresight arranged; after which the revolution of the earth might have quickened, and darkness been unnaturally precipitated, without inducing the slightest deviation from the programme.

When resolving upon the visit, Constantine considerately thought of the Princess' abhorrence of formality, and not to surprise her, despatched the Dean with notice of the honor intended. Whereupon she arranged the reception to suit herself; that is, so as to remain directress of the occasion. Hence the tables under the portico for the entertainment of the great lords, with the garden open to them afterward. This management, it will be perceived, left Constantine in her separate charge.

So, while the other guests went with the Dean, she conducted the Emperor to the reception room, where there were no flowers, and but one armless chair. When he was seated, the two alone, she knelt before him, and without giving him time to speak, said, her hands crossed upon her bosom: "I thank my Lord for sending me notice of his coming, and of his purpose to invite me to share his throne. All night I have kept the honor he intended me in mind, believing the Blessed Mother would listen to my prayers for wisdom and right direction; and the peace and confidence I feel, now that I am at my Lord's feet, must be from her.... Oh, my Lord, the trial has not been what I should do with the honor, but how to defend you from humiliation in the eyes of your court. I wish to be at the same time womanly and allegiant. How gentle and merciful you have been to me! How like a benignant God to my poor father! If I am in error, may Heaven forgive me; but I have led you here to say, without waiting for the formal proposal, that while you have my love as a kinswoman and subject, I cannot give you the love you should have from a wife."

Constantine was astonished.

"What!" he said.

Before he could get further, she continued, sinking lower at his feet:

"Ah me, my Lord, if now thou art thinking me bold and forward, and outcast from natural pride, what can I but plead the greater love I bear you as my benefactor and sovereign? ... It may be immodest to thus forestall my Lord's honorable intent, and decline being his wife before he has himself proposed it; yet I pray him to consider that with this avowal from me, he may go hence and affirm, God approving the truth, that he thought better of his design, and did not make me any overture of marriage, and there will be no one to suffer but me.... The evil-minded will talk, and judge me punished for my presumption. Against them I shall always have a pure conscience, and the knowledge of having rescued my Lord from an associate on his throne who does not love him with wifely devotion."

Pausing there, the Princess looked into his face, her own suffused. His head drooped; insomuch that the tall helmet with its glitter, and the cuirass, and fine mail reenforced by the golden spurs and jewelled sword and sword-harness, but deepened the impression of pain bewrayed on his countenance.

"Then it is as I have heard," he said, dejectedly. "The rustic hind may have the mate of his choice, and there is preference allowed the bird and wild wolf. The eye of faith beholds marriages of love in meeting waters and in clouds brought together from diverse parts. Only Kings are forbidden to select mates as their hearts declare. I, a master of life and death, cannot woo, like other men."

The Princess moved nearer him.

"My Lord," she said, earnestly, "is it not better to be denied choice than to be denied after choosing?"

"Speakest thou from experience?" he asked.

"No," she answered, "I have never known love except of all God's creatures alike."

"Whence thy wisdom then?"

"Perhaps it is only a whisper of pride."

"Perhaps, perhaps! I only know the pain it was intended to relieve goes on." Then, regarding her moodily, not angrily, nor even impatiently, he continued: "Did I not know thee true as thou art fair, O Princess, and good and sincere as thou art brave, I might suspect thee."

"Of what, my Lord?"

"Of an intent to compass my misery. Thou dost stop my mouth. I may not declare the purpose with which I came—I to whom it was of most interest—or if I do, I am forestopped saying, 'I thought better of it, and told her nothing.' Yet it was an honorable purpose nursed by sweet dreams, and by hopes such as souls feed upon, strengthening themselves for trials of life; I must carry it back with me, not for burial in my own breast, but for gossips to rend and tear, and make laughter of—the wonder and amusement of an unfeeling city. How many modes of punishment God keeps in store for the chastening of those who love Him!"

"It is beggarly saying I sympathize"—

"No, no—wait!" he cried, passionately. "Now it breaks upon me. I may not offer thee a seat on my throne, or give a hand to help thee up to it; for the present I will not declare I love thee; yet harm cannot come of telling thee what has been. Thou hadst my love at our first meeting. I loved thee then. As a man I loved thee, nor less as an Emperor because a man. Thou wast lovely with the loveliness of the angels. I saw thee in a light not of earth, and thou wert transparent as the light. I descended from the throne to thee thinking thou hadst collected all the radiance of the sun wasting in the void between stars, and clothed thyself in it."

"Oh, my Lord"—

"Not yet, not yet"—

"Blasphemy and madness!"

"Be it so!" he answered, with greater intensity. "This once I speak as a lover who was—a lover making last memories of the holy passion, to be henceforth accounted dead. Dead? Ah, yes!—to me—dead to me!"

She timidly took the hand he dropped upon his knee at the close of a long sigh.

"It may rest my Lord to hear me," she said, tearfully. "I never doubted his fitness to be Emperor, or if ever I had such a doubt, it is no more. He has conquered himself! Indeed, indeed, it is sweet to hear him tell his love, for I am woman; and if I cannot give it back measure for measure, this much may be accepted by him—I have never loved a man, and if the future holds such a condition in store for me, I will think of my Lord, and his strength and triumph, and in my humbler lot do as he has so nobly done. He has his Empire to engage him, and fill his hours with duties; I have God to serve and obey with singleness. Out of the prison where my mother died, and in which my father grew old counting his years as they slowly wore away, a shadow issued, and is always at hand to ask me, 'Who art thou? What right hast thou to happiness?' And if ever I fall into the thought so pleasant to woman, of loving and being loved, and of marriage, the shadow intervenes, and abides with me until I behold myself again bounden to religion, a servant vowed to my fellow creatures sick, suffering, or in sorrow."

Then the gentle Emperor fell to pitying her, and asked, forgetful of himself, and thinking of things to lighten her lot, "Wilt thou never marry?"

"I will not say no, my Lord," she answered. "Who can foresee the turns of life? Take thou this in reply—never will I surrender myself to wedlock under urgency of love alone. But comes there some great emergency, when, by such sacrifice, I may save my country, or my countrymen in multitude, or restore our holy religion overthrown or in danger, then, for the direct God-service there may be in it, I could give myself in contract, and would."

"Without love?" he asked.

"Yes, without loving or being loved. This body is not mine, but God's, and He may demand it of me for the good of my fellow-men; and, so there be no tarnishment of the spirit, my Lord, why haggle about the husk in which the spirit is hidden?"

She spoke with enthusiasm. Doubt of her sincerity would have been blasphemous. That such fate should be for her, so bright, pure and heroic! Not while he had authority! And in the instant he vowed himself to care of her by resolution strong as an oath. In thought of the uncertainties lowering over his own future, he saw it was better she should remain vowed to Heaven than to himself; thereupon he arose, and standing at her side, laid a hand lightly upon her head, and said solemnly:

"Thou hast chosen wisely. May the Blessed Mother, and all the ministering angels, in most holy company, keep guard lest thou be overtaken by calamity, sorrow and disappointment. And, for me, O Irene!"—his voice shook with emotion—"I shall be content if now thou wilt accept me for thy father."

She raised her eyes, as to Heaven, and said, smiling: "Dear God! How Thou dost multiply goodnesses, and shower them upon me!"

He stooped, and kissed her forehead.

"Amen, sweet daughter!"

Then he helped her to her feet.

"Now, while thou wert speaking, Irene, it was given me to see how the betrothal I was determined upon would have been a crime aside from wresting thee from the service of thy choice. Phranza is a true and faithful servant. How know I but, within his powers, and as he lawfully might, he has contracted me by treaty to acceptance of the Georgian? Thou hast saved me, and my ancient Chamberlain. Those under the portico are conspirators. But come, let us join them."

CHAPTER XVIII
THE SINGING SHEIK

IT was about ten o'clock when the Emperor and Princess Irene appeared on the portico, and, moving toward the northern side, wended slowly through the labyrinth of flowers, palms, and shrubs. The courtiers and dignitaries, upon their approach, received them in respectful silence, standing in groups about the tables.

A chair, with arms, high back, and a canopy, looking not unlike a sedilium, had been set in an open space. The reservation was further marked by a table in front of the chair, and two broad-branched palm trees, one on each side. Thither the Princess conducted the sovereign; and when he was seated, at a signal from her, some chosen attendants came bearing refreshments, cold meats, bread, fruits, and wines in crystal flagons, which they placed on the table, and retiring a little way, remained in waiting, while their mistress, on a stool at the left of the board, did the honors.

The introduction of a queen into a palace is usually the signal for a change of the existing domestic regime. Old placeholders go out; new favorites come in; and not seldom the revolution reaches the highest official circles of the government. The veterans of the suite, to some of whom this bit of knowledge had come severely home, were very watchful of the two superior personages. Had His Majesty really exposed his intent to the Princess? Had he declared himself to her? Had she accepted? The effect was to trebly sharpen the eyes past which the two were required to go on their way to the reserved table.

Mention has been made of Phranza, the Grand Chamberlain, at the moment absent on a diplomatic search for an imperial consort. Of all attaches of the court, he was first in his master's regard; and the distinction, it is but just to say, was due to his higher qualities and superior character. The term *favorite*, as a definition of relationship between a despot and a dependent, is historically cloudy; wherefore it is in this instance of unfair application. Intimate or confidante is much more exactly descriptive. But be that as it may, the good understanding between the Emperor and his Grand Chamberlain was amply sufficient to provoke the jealousy of many of the latter's colleagues, of whom Duke Notaras, Grand Admiral, and the most powerful noble of the Empire, was head and front. The scheme for the elevation of the Princess to the throne originated with him, and was aimed malevolently at Phranza, of whom he was envious, and Constantine, whom he hated on religious grounds. Interest in the plot brought him to Therapia;

yet he held himself aloof, preferring the attitude of a spectator coldly polite to that of an active partisan in the affair. He declined sitting at a table, but took position between two of the columns whence the view of the bay was best. There were numbers of the suite, however, who discredited the motive with which he chose the place.

"See Notaras," said one of a group, whispering to friends drinking wine a little way off. "The scene before him is charming, but is he charmed with it as he appears?"

"There was an old demi-god with an eye in his forehead. Notaras' best orb just now is in the back of his head. He may be looking at the bay; he is really watching the portico"—such was the reply.

"Out! He cares nothing for us."

"Very true—we are not the Emperor."

"My Lord Duke is not happy to-day," was remarked in another coterie.

"Wait, my dear friend. The day is young."

"If this match should not be made after all"—

"He will know it first."

"Yes, nothing from the lovers, neither smile nor sigh, can escape him."

The Professor of Philosophy and his brother the Professor of Rhetoric ate and drank together, illustrating the affinity of learning.

"Our Phranza is in danger," said the latter, nervously. "As thou art a subscriber to the doctrine of the *Phaedon*, I wish we could disembody our souls, if only for an hour."

"Oh, a singular wish! What wouldst thou?"

"Tell it not; but"—the voice dropped into a whisper—"I would despatch mine in search of the wise Chamberlain to warn him of what is here in practice."

"Ah, my brother, thou didst me the honor to read and approve my treatise on the Philosophy of Conspiracy. Dost thou remember the confounding elements given in the thesis?"

"Yes—Goodness is one."

"Under condition; that is, when the result is dependent upon a party of virtuous disposition."

"I remember now."

"Well, we have the condition here."

"The Princess!"

"And therefore the Duke, not our Phranza, is in danger. She will discomfit him."

"May Heaven dispose so!" And the Rhetorician almost immediately added, "Observe thou. Notaras has established himself within easy hearing of the two. He has actually invaded the space reserved for them."

"As if to confirm my forecast!"

Then the Philosopher raised a cup.

"To Phranza!"

"To Phranza!" the Rhetorician responded.

This episode hardly concluded when the Emperor's brother sauntered to the Duke's side; and on the appearance of the Emperor and the Princess, he exclaimed, enthusiastically:

"Come of it what may, my Lord, the damsel is comely, and I fear not to compare her with the best of Trebizond or Georgia."

The Duke did not answer. Indeed, the lords were all intent upon exactly the same subject. Whether there had been an overture and an acceptance, or an overture and a declination, they believed the principals could not conceal the result; a look, a gesture, or something in the manner of one or both of them, would tell the tale to eyes of such practical discernment. By the greater number the information would be treated as news for discussion merely; a few had hopes or fears at stake; none of them was so perilously involved as Notaras; in his view, failure meant the promotion of Phranza, of all consequences, not excepting his own loss of favor and prestige, the most intolerable.

On the other part, Constantine was not less concerned in misleading his court. At the proper time he would give out that he had changed his mind at the last moment; before engaging himself to the Princess, he had concluded it best to wait and hear from Phranza. Accordingly, in passing along the portico, he endeavored to look and behave like a guest; he conversed in an ordinary tone; he suffered his hostess to precede him; and, well seconded by her, he was installed in the state chair, without an argument yes or no for the sharp reviewers. At the table he appeared chiefly solicitous to appease an unusual hunger, which he charged to the early morning air on the Bosphorus.

Notaras, whom nothing of incident, demeanor or remark escaped, began very early to be apprehensive. Upon beholding his master's unlover-like concession to appetite, he remarked sullenly, "Verily, either his courage failed, and he did not submit a proposal, or she has rejected him."

"My Lord Duke," the Emperor's brother replied, somewhat stung, "dost thou believe it in woman to refuse such an honor?"

"Sir," the Duke retorted, "women who go about unveiled are above or below judgment."

The Princess, in her place at the table, began there to recount her adventure at the White Castle, but when far enough in the recital to indicate its course the Emperor interrupted her.

"Stay, daughter," he said, gently. "The incident may prove of international interest. If not objectionable to you, I should be pleased to have some of my friends hear it." Then raising his voice, he called out: "Notaras, and thou, my brother, come, stand here. Our fair hostess had yesterday an astonishing experience with the Turks on the other shore, and I have prevailed on her to narrate it." The two responded to the invitation by drawing nearer the Emperor at his right hand.

"Proceed now, daughter," the latter said.

"Daughter, daughter, indeed!" the Duke repeated to himself, and so bitterly it may be doubted if his master's diplomacy availed to put him at rest. The paternalism of the address was decisive—Phranza had won.

Then, presently overcoming her confusion, the Princess succeeded in giving a simple but clear account of how she was driven to the Castle, and of what befell her while there. When she finished, the entire suite were standing about the table listening.

Twice she had been interrupted by the Emperor.

"A moment!" he said to her, while she was speaking of the Turkish soldiery whose arrival at the ancient stronghold had been so nearly simultaneous with her own. Then he addressed himself to the Grand Domestic and the Admiral. "My Lords, in passing the Castle, on our way up, you remember I bade the pilot take our ship near the shore there. It seemed to me the garrison was showing unusually large, while the flags on the donjon were strange, and the tents and horses around the walls implied an army present. You remember?"

"And we have now, Sire, the justification of your superior wisdom," the Grand Domestic replied, rising from a low salutation.

"I recall the circumstance, my Lords, to enjoin you not to suffer the affair to slip attention when next we meet in council—I pray pardon, daughter, for breaking the thread of your most interesting and important narrative. I am prepared to listen further."

Then, after description of the Governor, and his reception of the fugitives on the landing, His Majesty, with apologies, asked permission to offer another inquiry.

"Of a truth, daughter, the picture thou hast given us under the title of Governor beareth no likeness to him who hath heretofore responded to that dignity. At various times I have had occasion to despatch messengers to the commandant, and returning, they have reported him a coarse, unrefined, brutish-looking person, of middle age and low rank; and much I marvel to hear the freedom with which this person doth pledge my august friend and ally, Sultan Amurath. My Lords, this will furnish us an additional point of investigation. Obviously the Castle is of military importance, requiring an old head full of experience to keep it regardful of peace and clear understanding between the powers plying the Bosphorus. We are always to be apprehensive of the fire there is in young blood."

"With humility, Your Majesty," said the Grand Domestic, "I should like to hear from the Princess, whose loveliness is now not more remarkable than her courage and discretion, the evidence she has for the opinion that the young man is really the Governor."

She was about to reply when Lysander, the old servant, elbowed himself through the brilliant circle, and dropped his javelin noisily by her chair.

"A stranger calling himself an Arab is at the gate," he said to her, with the semblance of a salutation.

The simplicity of the ancient, his zeal in the performance of his office, his obliviousness to the imperial presence, caused a ripple of amusement.

"An Arab!" the Princess exclaimed, in momentary forgetfulness. "How does the man appear?"

Lysander was in turn distraught; after a short delay, however, he managed to answer: "His face is dark, almost black; his head is covered with a great cloth of silk and gold; a gown hides him from neck to heels; in his girdle there is a dagger. He has a lordly air, and does not seem in the least afraid. In brief, my mistress, he looks as if he might be king of all the camel drivers in the world."

The description was unexpectedly graphic; even the Emperor smiled, while many of the train, presuming license from his amusement, laughed aloud.

In the midst of the merriment, the Princess, calmly, and with scarce a change from her ordinary tone, proceeded to an explanation.

"Your Majesty," she said, "I am reminded of an invitation left with the person whose identity was in discussion the instant of this announcement. In the afternoon, while I was sojourning in the White Castle, an Arab story-teller was presented to me under recommendation of my courteous host. He was said to be of great professional renown in the East, a Sheik travelling to Adrianople for the divertisement of the Hanoum of the Sultan. In the desert they call him endearingly the *Singing Sheik*. I was glad to have the hours assisted in their going, and he did not disappoint me. So charmed was I by his tales and manner of telling them, by his genius, that in taking my departure from what proved a most agreeable retreat, and in acknowledging the hospitable entertainment given me, I referred to the singer, and requested the Governor to prevail on him to extend his journey here, in order to favor me with another opportunity to hear him. Had I then known it was in my Lord's purposes to visit me with such a company of most noble gentlemen, or could I have even anticipated the honor, I should not have appointed to-day for the audience with him. But he is in attendance; and now, with full understanding of the circumstances, it is for Your Majesty to pronounce upon his admission. Perhaps"—she paused with a look of deprecation fairly divisible share and share alike between the Emperor and the Lords around her—"perhaps time may hang heavy with my guests this morning; if so, I shall hold myself obliged to the Singing Sheik if he can help me entertain them."

Now, was there one present to attach a criticism to the favor extended the Arab, he dismissed it summarily, wondering at her easy grace. The Emperor no doubt shared the admiration with his suite; but concealing it, he said, with an air of uncertainty, "Thy recommendation, daughter, is high; and if I remain, verily, it will be with expectation wrought up to a dangerous degree; yet having often heard of the power of the strolling poets of whom this one is in probability an excellent example, I confess I should be pleased to have thee admit him."

Of the Admiral, he then asked, "We were to set out in return about noon, were we not?"

"About noon, Your Majesty."

"Well, the hour is hardly upon us. Let the man appear, daughter; only, as thou lovest us, contrive that he keep to short recitals, which, without holding us unwillingly, will yet suffice to give an idea of his mind and methods. And keep thyself prepared for an announcement of our departure, and when received, mistake it not for discontent with thyself. Admit the Arab."

CHAPTER XIX
TWO TURKISH TALES

The situation now offered the reader is worth a pause, if only to fix it in mind.

Constantine and Mahommed, soon to be contestants in war, are coming face to face, lovers both of the same woman. The romance is obvious; yet it is heightened by another circumstance. One of them is in danger.

We of course know Aboo-Obeidah, the Singing Sheik, is Prince Mahommed in disguise; we know the Prince also as heir of Amurath the Sultan, a very old man liable to vacate place and life at any moment. Suppose now the rash adventurer—the term fits the youth truly as if he were without rank—should be discovered and denounced to the Emperor. The consequences can only be treated conjecturally.

In the first place, to what extremities the Prince would be put in explaining his presence there. He could plead the invitation of the Princess Irene. But his rival would be his judge, and the judge might find it convenient to laugh at the truth, and rest his decision on the prisoner's disguise, in connection with his own presence—two facts sufficiently important to serve the most extreme accusation.

Constantine, next, was a knightly monarch who knew to live nobly, and dared die as he lived; yet, thinking of what he might do with Mahommed fallen into his hands under circumstances so peculiar, there was never a Caesar not the slave of policy. In the audience to Manuel the sailor, we have seen how keenly sensitive he was to the contraction the empire had suffered. Since that day, to be sure, he had managed to keep the territory he came to; none the less, he felt the Turk to whom the stolen provinces invariably fell was his enemy, and that truce or treaty with him did not avail to loosen the compression steadily growing around his capital. Over and over, daytime and night, the unhappy Emperor pondered the story of the daughter of Tantalus; and often, starting from dreams in which the Ottoman power was a serpent slowly crawling to its victim, he would cry in real agony—"O Constantinople—Niobe! Who can save thee but God? And if He will not—alas, alas!" The feeling thus engendered was not of a kind to yield readily to generosity. Mahommed once securely his, everything might be let go—truth, honor, glory—everything but the terms of advantage purchasable with such an hostage.

The invitation to the imaginary Sheik had been a last act of grace by Irene, about to embark for the city. Mahommed, when he accepted, knew Therapia by report a village very ancient historically, but decaying, and now little more than a summer resort and depot of supplies for fishermen. That its proverbial quietude would be disturbed, and the sleepy blood of its inhabitants aroused, by a royal galley anchoring in the bay to discharge the personnel of the empire itself, could have had no place in his anticipations. So when he stepped into a boat, the Aboo-Obeidah of his eulogy, and suffered himself, without an attendant, to be ferried across to Roumeli-Hissar; when he there took an humble wherry of two oars, and bade the unliveried Greeks who served them pull for Therapia, it was to see again the woman who was taking his fancy into possession, not Constantine and his court bizarre in splendor and habitude. In other words, Mahommed on setting out had no idea of danger. Love, or something very like it, was his sole inspiration.

The trireme, with the white cross on its red sail, its deck a martial and courtly spectacle, had been reported to him as the hundred and twenty flashing scarlet blades, in their operation a miracle of unity, whisked it by the old Castle, and he had come forth to see it. Where are they going? he asked those around him; and they, familiar with the Bosphorus, its shipping and navigation, answered unanimously, To exercise her crew up in the Black Sea; and thinking of the breadth of the dark blue fields there, the reply commended itself, and he dismissed the subject.

The course chosen by his boatmen when they put off from Roumeli-Hissar kept him close to the European shore, which he had leisure to study. Then, as now, it was more favored than its Asiatic opposite. The winds from the sea, southward blowing, unloaded their mists to vivify its ivy and myrtle. The sunlight, tarrying longest over its pine-clad summits, coaxed habitations along the shore; here, a palace; there, under an overhanging cliff, a hamlet; yonder, a long extended village complaisantly adapting itself to the curvatures of the brief margin left it for occupancy. Wherever along the front of the heights and on the top there was room for a field the advantage had been seized. So the Prince had offered him the sight of all others most significant of peace among men—sight of farmers tilling the soil. With the lucid sky above him summer-laden, the water under and about him a liquid atmosphere, the broken mountain-face changing from lovely to lovelier, and occasionally awakening him with a superlative splendor, the abodes so near, and the orchards and strawberry and melon patches overhead, symbolizing goodwill and fraternity and happiness amongst the poor and humble—with these, and the rhythmic beating of the oars to soothe his spirit, fierce and mandatory even in youth, he went, the time divided between views fair enough for the most rapturous dreams, and the Greek, of whom, with all their brightness, they were but dim suggestions. Past the stream-riven gorge of Balta-Liman he went; past Emirghian; past the haven of Stenia, and the long shore-town of Yenikeui; then, half turning the Keuibachi bend, lo! Therapia, draggling down the stony steep, like a heap of bangles on a brown-red cheek. And there, in the soft embracement of the bay, a bird with folded wings asleep—the *trireme!*

The sight startled the Prince. He spoke to the rowers, and they ceased fighting the current, and with their chins over their shoulders, looked whither he pointed. From ship to shore he looked; then, pursuing the curve inland to the bridge at the upper end; thence down what may be called the western side, he beheld people crowding between a quay and a red kiosk over which pended a wooded promontory.

"There is a Princess living in this vicinity," said he to one of the rowers, slightly lifting the handkerchief from his face. "Where is her palace?"

"In the garden yonder. You see the gate over the heads of the men and women."

"What is her name?"

"Princess Irene. She is known on this shore as the Good Princess."

"Irene—a sound pleasant to the ear"—Mahommed muttered. "Why is she called good?"

"Because she is an angel of mercy to the poor."

"That is not usual with the great and rich," he said next, yielding to a charm in the encomiums.

"Yes," the boatman responded, "she is great, being akin to the Emperor, and rich, too, though"—

Here the man broke off to assist in bringing the boat back from its recession with the current, at this point boisterously swift.

"You were saying the Princess is rich," Mahommed said, when the oars were again at rest.

"Oh, yes! But I cannot tell you, my friend, how many are partners in her wealth. Every widow and orphan who can get to her comes away with a portion. Isn't it so?"

His companion grunted affirmatively, adding: "Down yonder a man with a crooked back lives in an arched cell opening on the water. Perhaps the stranger saw it as he came up."

"Yes," Mahommed answered.

"Well, in the back part of the cell he has an altar with a crucifix and a picture of the Blessed Mother on it, and he keeps a candle burning before them day and night—something he could not do if we did not help him, for candles of wax are costly. He has named the altar after the Princess, Sta. Irene. We often stop and go in there to pray; and I have heard the blessings in the light of that candle are rich and many as the Patriarch has for sale in Sta. Sophia."

These praises touched Mahommed; for, exalted as he was in station, he was aware of the proneness of the poor to berate the rich and grumble at the great, and that such had been a habit with them from the commencement of the world. Again the boat slipped down the current; when it was brought back, he asked: "When did the ship yonder come up?"

"This morning."

"Oh, yes! I saw it then, but thought the crew were being taken to the sea for practice."

"No," the boatman replied, "it is the state galley of His Majesty the Emperor. Did you not see him? He sat on the throne with all his ministers and court around him."

Mahommed was startled.

"Where is the Emperor now?" he inquired.

"I should say, seeing the crowd yonder, that His Majesty is in the palace with the Princess."

"Yes," said the second rower, "they are waiting to see him come out."

"Row out into the bay. I should like to have the view from that quarter."

While making the detour, Mahommed reflected. Naturally he remembered himself the son of Amurath; after which it was easy to marshal the consequences of exposure, if he persisted in his venture. He saw distinctly how his capture would be a basis of vast bargaining with his father, or, if the sturdy old warrior preferred revenge to payment of a ruinous ransom, how the succession and throne might slip to another, leaving him a prisoner for life.

Yet another matter presented itself to him which the reader may decide worthy a separate paragraph. Its mention has been waiting this opportunity. The Prince from Magnesia, his seat of government, was on the way to Adrianople, called thither by his father, who had chosen a bride for him, daughter of a renowned Emir. Regularly he would have crossed the Hellespont at Gallipoli; a whim, however, took him to the White Castle— whim or destiny, one being about as satisfactory as the other. Pondering silently whether it were not best to return, he thought, apropos the Princess Irene, of the nuptials to be celebrated, and of his bride expectant; and a Christian, pausing over the suggestion, may be disposed to condemn him for inconstancy.

In countries where many wives are allowed the same husband he is not required to love any of them. Indeed, his fourth spouse may be the first to command him; hers the eyes for his enslavement; hers the voice of the charmer charming both wisely and forever. Mahommed did now think of the Emir's daughter, but not with compunction, nor even in comparison. He had never seen her face, and would not until after the wedding days. He thought of her but to put her aside; she could not be as this Christian was, neither so accomplished nor courtly; besides which, it was dawning upon him that there were graces of mind and soul as well as of person, while perfection was a combination of all the graces in equal degree. Gleams of the latter had visited him while gazing into the radiant face of the Emperor's kinswoman; and how, at such favoring times, his fancy had gone out to her and come back warmed, enlivened, glorified! There is a passion of the mind and a passion of the blood; and though one and one make two, two is still a multiple of one.

Looking thus at the galley, Mahommed thought of the tales in the East not less common than in the West, and believed in them faithfully, for chivalry was merely on the wane—tales of beauteous damsels shut up in caves or adamantine castles, with guardian lions couchant at the gates, and of well-sworded heroes who marched boldly up to the brutes, and slew them, and delivered the captives always with reward. Of course, in making the application, the Princess was the prisoner, the ship the lion, and himself—well, in want of a sword, he laid hand upon his dagger, precisely as a liberating knight up to the ideal would do.

Nor was this all. The revelations of the Prince of India were still fresh to him. He wished to see his competitor. How did he look? Was there enough of him to make battle? He smiled thinking of the pleasure there would be in slyly studying the Princess and the Emperor at the same time. He drew the handkerchief down, looked at his brown-stained hands, and adjusted the folds of his burnoose. The disguise was perfect.

"Take me to the landing—there before the gate of the Good Princess," he said, with the air of a traveller above suspicion.

His resolution was taken. Challenging all chances, he would respond to the invitation of the Princess. And so completely were doubt and hesitation dismissed with our adventurer, that it was not Mahommed who stepped from the boat where the populace was in densest assemblage, but Aboo-Obeidah, the Singing Sheik, and as such we will speak of him.

The guard at the gate, viewing him askance, detained him until he could be reported.

A fair conception of the scene presented when the Sheik stood on the floor of the portico is probably in the reader's mind; yet a glance at it may be pardoned. It was at first like a sudden introduction to an oriental garden. There were the vines, flowering shrubs, fruiting trees, many-fronded palms, and the effect of outdoors derived from the shadows of the pillars, and the sunshine streaming brilliantly through the open intervals. The tables bore proofs of the collation served upon them. Overhead was the soft creaminess of pure marble in protected state mellowed by friendly touches of time. At the end of the vista, the company was indistinctly visible through the verdure of obtruding branches. Voices came to him from that part, and gleams of bright garments; and to get to them it seemed he must pass through a viridescent atmosphere flecked with blooms, and faintly sweet with odors. For in losing the masculinity of their race the Greeks devoted themselves more and more to refined effeminacies.

Moving slowly forward under the guidance of Lysander, whose javelin beating the floor accentuated the rasping shuffle of his sandals, the Sheik came presently to a full view of the concourse.

He stopped, partly in obedience to a fine instinct of propriety teaching him he was now subject to the pleasure of his hostess, and partly to single out the royal enemy against whom he believed he was about to be pitted by destiny.

Constantine was sitting at ease, his left elbow resting on an arm of the sedilium, his forefinger supporting his cheek, his cloak across his lap. The attitude was reflective; the countenance exposed under the lifted visor of the helmet, was calm and benignant; except there was no suggestion of an evil revery holding the current of his thought, or casting a shade of uncertainty over his soul, he looked not unlike the famous Il Penseroso familiar to art-seekers in the Medici Chapel of Florence. Then the eyes of the rivals met. The Greek was in no wise moved. How it would have been with him could he have seen through the disguise of the Sheik may never be said. On the other part, the Sheik lifted his head, and seemed taking on increase of stature. A projecting fold of the head-kerchief overhung his face, permitting nothing to be seen but red-hued cheeks, a thin beard, and eyes black and glittering. The review he felt himself undergoing did not daunt him; it only sent his pride mounting, like a leap of flame. "By the Virgin!" said one of the courtiers to another, in a louder tone than the occasion demanded. "We may indeed congratulate ourselves upon having seen the king of camel drivers." There was a disposition to laugh amongst the lighter-minded of the guests, but the Princess checked it by rising. "Bid the Sheik approach," she said, to the old domestic; and, at a sign from her, the waiting-women drew closer about her chair. The figure of the Princess clad all in white, a bracelet of plain gold upon her left arm, fillets in her hair, one red, the other blue, a double strand of pearls about her neck—this figure, with the small head, perfect in turn, set matchlessly upon the sloping shoulders, the humid eyes full of violet light, the cheeks flushed with feeling—this figure so bright in its surroundings, admitted no rivalry in attention, none in admiration; the courtiers, old and young, turned from the Sheik, and the Sheik from the Emperor. In a word, every eye centred upon the Princess, every tongue bade hush lest what she said might be lost. Etiquette required the Sheik's presentation to the Emperor first, but seeing her about to comply with the rule, he prostrated himself at her feet. As he arose, she said: "When I invited you to come and give me more of the cheer there is in your art, O Sheik, I did not know my gracious kinsman, to whom every Greek is proud and happy to be allegiant, designed visiting me to-day. I pray you will not suffer too much from his presence, but regard him a royal auditor who delights in a tale well told, and in verses when the theme and measure go lovingly together. His Majesty, the Emperor!"

"Hist! Didst hear?" whispered the Professor of Philosophy to the Professor of Rhetoric. "Thyself couldst not have spoken better."

"Ay, truly," the other answered. "Save a trifle of stiffness, the speech might have served Longinus."

With her last word, the Princess stepped aside, leaving Mahommed and Constantine front to front.

Had the Sheik been observant of the monarch's dues, he would have promptly prostrated himself; but the moment for the salutation passed, and he remained standing, answering the look he received calmly as it was given. The reader and the writer know the reason governing him; the suite, however, were not so well informed, and they began to murmur. The Princess herself appeared embarrassed.

"Lord of Constantinople," the Sheik said, seeing speech was his, "were I a Greek, or a Roman, or an Ottoman, I should make haste to kiss the floor before you, happy of the privilege; for—be the concession well noted"—he glanced deferentially around him as he spoke—"the report which the world has of you is of a kind to make it your lover. After a few days—Allah willing—I shall stand before Amurath the Sultan. Though in reverencing him I yield not to any one simply his friend, he will waive prostration from me, knowing what Your Majesty may not. In my country we cleanse the ground with our beards before no one but God. Not that we are unwilling to conform to the rules of the courts in which we find ourselves; with us it is a law—To kiss a man's hand maketh him the master; prostrate thyself to him, and without other act, thou becomest his subject. I am an Arab!"

The Sheik was not in the least defiant; on the contrary, his manner was straightforward, simple, sincere, as became one interposing conscience against an observance in itself rightful enough. Only in the last exclamation was there a perceptible emphasis, a little marked by a lift of the head and a kindling of the eyes.

"I see Your Majesty comprehends me," he said, continuing; "yet to further persuade your court, and especially the fair and high-born lady, whose guest, with all my unworthiness, I am, from believing me moved in this matter by disrespect for their sovereign, I say next, if by prostration I made myself a Roman, the act would be binding on the tribe whose Sheik I am by lawful election. And did I that, O thou whose bounties serve thy people in lieu of rain! though my hand were white, like the first Prophet's, when, to assure the Egyptian, he drew it from his bosom, it would char blacker than dust of burned willow—then, O thou, lovelier than the queen the lost lapwing reported to Solomon! though my breath were as the odor of musk, it would poison, like an exhalation from a leper's grave—then, O my lords! like Karoon in his wickedness, I should hear Allah say of me, O Earth, swallow him! For as there are crimes and crimes, verily the chief who betrays his brethren born to the practice of freedom, shall wander between tents all his days, crying, Oh, alas! oh, alas! Who now will defend me against God?"

When the Sheik paused, as if for judgment, he was not only acquitted of intentional disrespect; the last grumbler was anxious to hear him further.

"What astonishing figures!" the Philosopher whispered to the Rhetorician. "I begin to think it true that the East hath a style of its own."

"I commend thy sagacity, my brother," the other replied. "His peroration was redolent of the Koran—A wonderful fellow nevertheless!"

Presently the whole concourse was looking at the Emperor, with whom it rested whether the Sheik should be dismissed or called on for entertainment.

"Daughter," said Constantine to the Princess, "I know not enough of the tribal law of thy guest to have an opinion of the effect upon him and his of the observance of our ancient ceremony; wherefore we are bound to accept his statement. Moreover it does not become our dignity to acquire subjects and dominion, were they ever so desirable, in a method justly liable to impeachment for treachery and coercion. Besides which—and quite as important, situated as we are—thy hospitality is to be defended."

Here the Sheik, who had been listening to the Emperor, and closely observing him, thrice lightly clapped his hands.

"It remains for us, therefore, to waive the salutation in this instance."

A ripple of assent proceeded from the suite.

"And now, daughter," Constantine pursued, "thy guest being present to give thee of his lore, it may be he will be pleased to have us of his audience as well. Having heard much of such performances, and remembering their popularity when we were in our childhood, we will esteem ourselves fortunate if now favored by one highly commended as a master in his guild."

The Sheik's eyes sparkled brighter as he answered, "It is written for us in our Holiest, the very Word of the Compassionate,—'If ye are greeted with a greeting, then greet ye with a better greeting, or at least return it.' Verily my Lord dispenseth honor with so light a hand as not to appear aware of the doing. When my brethren under the black tents are told of my having won the willing ear of their Majesties of Byzantium and Adrianople, they will think of me as one who has been permitted to walk in the light of two suns simultaneous in shining."

So saying, he bowed very low.

"My only unhappiness now is in not knowing the direction in which my Lord's preferences run; for as a stream goes here and there, but all the time keeps one general course, seeking the sea, so with taste; though it yield a nod now, and then a smile, it hath always a deeper delight for the singer's finding. I have the gay and serious—history, traditions—the heroics of men and nations, their heart-throbs in verse and prose—all or any for the Lord of Constantinople and his kinswoman, my hostess,—may her life never end until the song of the dove ceases to be heard in the land!"

"What say you, my friends?" asked Constantine, glancing graciously at those around him.

Then they looked from him to the Princess, and in thought of the betrothal, replied, "Love—something of love!"

"No," he returned, unflinchingly. "We are youths no longer. There is enlightenment in the traditions of nations. Our neighbors, the Turks—what hast thou of them, Sheik?"

"Didst thou hear?" said Notaras to one at his elbow. "He hath recanted; the Empress will not be a Greek."

There was no answer; for the Sheik, baring his head, hung the kerchief and cord upon his arm, preliminaries which gave him perfectly to view. A swarthy face; hair black, profuse, closely cut along the temples; features delicate but manly—these the bystanders saw in a general way, being more attracted by the repressed fire in the man's eyes, and his air high and severely noble.

When the Princess caught sight of the countenance, she fell into a confusion. She had seen it, but where and when? The instant he was beginning he gazed at her, and in the exchange of glances she was reminded of the Governor bidding her adieu on the shore of the Sweet Waters. But he was youthful, while this one—could it be he was old? The feeling was a repetition of that she had in the Castle when the storyteller appeared the first time.

"I will tell how the Turks became a Nation."

Then, in Greek but a little broken, the Sheik began a recital.

ALAEDDIN AND ERTOGHRUL

I

A tale of Ertoghrul!—
      How when the Chief
Lay one day nooning with his stolen herds,
A sound of drumming smote him from the East,
And while he stood to see what came of it,
The West with like notes fainter, echo-like,
Made answer; then two armies rode in view,
Horses and men in steel, the sheen of war
About them and above, and wheeling quick
From column into line, drew all their blades,
Shook all their flags, and charged and lost themselves
In depths of dusty clouds, which yet they tore
With blinding gleams of light, and yells of rage,
And cheers so high and hoarse they well might seem
The rolling thunder of a mountain storm.
Long time the hosts contended; but at last
The lesser one began to yield the ground,
Oppressed in front, and on its flanks o'erwhelmed:
And hasted then the end, a piteous sight,
Most piteous to the very brave who know
From lessons of their lives, how seldom 'tis
Despair can save where valor fails to win.
Then Ertoghrul aroused him, touched to heart.

"My children, mount, and out with cimeter!
I know not who these are, nor whence they come;

Nor need we care. 'Twas Allah led them here,
And we will honor Him—and this our law;
What though the weak may not be always right,
We'll make it always right to help the weak.
Deep take the stirrups now, and ride with me,
Allah-il-Allah!"

       Thus spake Ertoghrul;
And at the words, with flying reins, and all
His eager tribe, four hundred sworded men,
Headlong he rode against the winning host.

II

Beneath the captured flags, the spoils in heaps
Around him laid, the rescued warrior stood,
A man of kingly mien, while to him strode
His unexpected friend.

       "Now who art thou?"
The first was first to ask.

       "Sheik Ertoghrul
Am I."

   "The herds I see—who calls them his?"

Laughed Ertoghrul, and showed his cimeter.
"The sword obeys my hand, the hand my will,
And given will and hand and sword, I pray
Thee tell me, why should any man be poor?"

"And whose the plain?"

       "Comes this way one a friend
Of mine, and leaves his slippers at my door,
Why then, 'tis his."
       "And whose the hills that look
Upon the plain?"

       "My flocks go there at morn,
And thence they come at night—I take my right
Of Allah."

       "No," the stranger mildly said,
"'Twas Allah made them mine."

       Frowned Ertoghrul,
While darkened all the air; but from his side

Full pleasantly the stranger took a sword,
Its carven hilt one royal emerald,
Its blade both sides with legends overwrought,
Some from the Koran, some from Solomon,
All by the cunning Eastern maker burned
Into the azure steel-his sword he took,
And held it, belt, and scabbard too, in sign
Of gift.

     "The herds, the plain, the hills were mine;
But take thou them, and with them this in proof
Of title."

     Lifted Ertoghrul his brows,
And opened wide his eyes.

     "Now who art thou?"
He asked in turn.

     "Oh, I am Alaeddin—
Sometimes they call me Alaeddin the Great."

"I take thy gifts—the herds, the plain, the hills,"
Said Ertoghrul; "and so I take the sword;
But none the less, if comes a need, 'tis thine.
Let others call thee Alaeddin the Great;
To me and mine thou'rt Alaeddin the Good
And Great."

     With that, he kissed the good King's hand;
And making merry, to the Sheik's dowar
They rode. And thus from nothing came the small;
And now the lonely vale which erst ye knew,
And scorned, because it nursed the mountain's feet,
Doth cradle mornings on the mountain's top.

     Mishallah!

The quiet which held the company through the recitation endured a space afterwards, and—if the expression be allowed—was in itself a commentary upon the performance.

"Where is our worthy Professor of Rhetoric?" asked Constantine.

"Here, Your Majesty," answered the man of learning, rising.

"Canst thou not give us a lecture upon the story with which thy Arabian brother hath favored us?"

"Nay, sire, criticism, to deal justly, waiteth until the blood is cool. If the Sheik will honor me with a copy of his lines, I will scan and measure them by the rules descended to us from Homer, and his Attic successors."

The eyes of the Emperor fell next upon the moody, discontented face of Duke Notaras.

"My lord Admiral, what sayest thou of the tale?"

"Of the tale, nothing; of the story-teller—I think him an insolent, and had I my way, Your Majesty, he should have a plunge in the Bosphorus."

Presuming the Sheik unfamiliar with Latin, the Duke couched his reply in that tongue; yet the former raised his head, and looked at the speaker, his eyes glittering with intelligence—and the day came, and soon, when the utterance was relentlessly punished.

"I do not agree with you, my Lord," Constantine said, in a melancholy tone. "Our fathers, whether we look for them on the Roman or the Greek side, might have played the part of Ertoghrul. His was the spirit of conquest. Would we had enough of it left to get back our own!—Sheik," he added, "what else hast thou in the same strain? I have yet a little time to spare— though it shall be as our hostess saith."

"Nay," she answered, with deference, "there is but one will here."

And taking assent from her, the Sheik began anew.

EL JANN AND HIS PARABLE

Bismillah!

> Ertoghrul pursued a wolf,
> And slew it on the range's tallest peak,
> Above the plain so high there was nor grass
> Nor even mosses more. And there he sat
> Him down awhile to rest; when from the sky,
> Or the blue ambiency cold and pure,
> Or maybe from the caverns of the earth
> Where Solomon the King is wont to keep
> The monster Genii hearkening his call,
> El Jann, vast as a cloud, and thrice as black,
> Appeared and spoke—

> "Art thou Sheik Ertoghrul?"

And he undaunted answered: "Even so."

"Well, I would like to come and sit with thee."

"Thou seest there is not room for both of us."

"Then rise, I say, and get thee part way down
The peak."

"'Twere easier," laughed Ertoghrul,
"Madest thou thyself like me as thin and small;
And I am tired."

A rushing sound ran round and up
And down the height, most like the whir of wings
Through tangled trees of forests old and dim.
A moment thus—the time a crisped leaf,
Held, armlength overhead, will take to fall—
And then a man was sitting face to face
With Ertoghrul.

"This is the realm of snow,"
He said, and smiled—"a place from men secure,
Where only eagles fearless come to nest,
And summer with their young."

The Sheik replied,
"It was a wolf—a gaunt gray wolf, which long
Had fattened on my flocks—that lured me here.
I killed it."

"On thy spear I see no blood;
And where, O Sheik, the carcass of the slain?
I see it not."

Around looked Ertoghrul—
There was no wolf; and at his spear—
Upon its blade no blood. Then rose his wrath,
A mighty pulse.

"The spear hath failed its trust—
I'll try the cimeter."

A gleam of light—
A flitting, wind-borne spark in murk of night—
Then fell the sword, the gift of Alaeddin;
Edge-first it smote the man upon his crown—
Between his eyes it shore, nor staying there,
It cut his smile in two—and not yet spent,
But rather gaining force, through chin and chine,
And to the very stone on which he sat

It clove, and finished with a bell-like clang
Of silvern steel 'gainst steel.

       "Aha! Aha!"—
But brief the shout; for lo! there was no stain
Upon the blade withdrawn, nor moved the man,
Nor changed he look or smile.

       "I was the wolf
That ran before thee up the mountain side;
'Twas I received thy spear as now thy sword;
And know thou further, Sheik, nor wolf nor man
Am I, nor mortal thing of any kind;
Only a thought of Allah's. Canst thou kill
A thought divine? Not Solomon himself
Could that, except with thought yet more divine.
Yield thee thy rage; and when thou think'st of me
Hereafter, be it as of one, a friend,
Who brought a parable, and made display
Before thee, saying—
       "Lo! what Allah wills."

Therewith he dropped a seed scarce visible
Into a little heap of sand and loam
Between them drawn.

       "Lo! Allah wills."

      And straight
The dust began to stir as holding life.
Again El Jann—

       "Behold what Allah wills!"

A tiny shoot appeared; a waxen point
Close shawled in many folds of wax as white,
It might have been a vine to humbly creep—
A lily soon to sunward flare its stars—
A shrub to briefly coquette with the winds.
Again the cabalism—

       "Lo! Allah's will."

The apparition budded, leafed, and branched,
And with a flame of living green lit all
The barrenness about. And still it grew—
Until it touched the pillars of the earth,
And lapped its boundaries, the far and near,

And under it, as brethren in a tent,
The nations made their home, and dwelt in peace
Forever.

"Lo!"—

And Ertoghrul awoke.

Mishallah!

This recitation commanded closer attention than the first one. Each listener had a feeling that the parable at the end, like all true parables, was of continuous application, while its moral was in some way aimed at him.

The looks the Sheik received were by no means loving. The spell was becoming unpleasant. Then the Emperor arose, as did the Princess, to whom, as hostess, the privilege of sitting had been alone conceded.

"Our playtime is up—indeed, I fear, it has been exceeded," he said, glancing at the Dean, who was acting master of ceremonies.

The Dean responded with a bow low as his surroundings admitted; whereupon the Emperor went to the Princess, and said, "We will take leave now, daughter, and for myself and my lords of the court, I acknowledge a most agreeable visit, and thank you for it."

She respectfully saluted the hand he extended to her.

"Our gate and doors at Blacherne are always open to you."

The adieu was specially observed by the courtiers, and they subsequently pronounced it decorous for a sovereign, cordial as became a relative, but most un-loverlike. Indeed, it was a strong point in the decision subsequently of general acceptance, by which His Majesty was relieved of the proposal of marriage to the Princess.

The latter took his offered arm, and accompanied him to the steps of the portico, where, when he had descended, the lords one by one left a kiss on her hand.

Nor should it be forgotten, that as Constantine was passing the Sheik, he paused to say to him in his habitually kind and princely manner: "The tree Sheik Ertoghrul saw in his dream has spread, and is yet spreading, but its shadow has not compassed all the nations; and while God keeps me, it will not. Had not I myself invited the parable, it might have been offensive. For the instruction and entertainment given me, accept thou this—and go in peace."

The Sheik took the ring offered him, and the gaze with which he followed the imperial giver was suggestive of respect and pity.

CHAPTER XX
MAHOMMED DREAMS

It was a trifle after noon. The trireme and the assemblage of admiring townspeople had disappeared, leaving the bay and its shores to their wonted quiet. The palace, however, nestling in the garden under the promontory, must be permitted to hold our interest longer.

Aboo-Obeidah had eaten and drunk, for being on a journey, he was within the license of the law as respects wine; and now he sat with the Princess alone at the end of the portico lately occupied by the Emperor and his suite. A number of her attendants amused themselves out of hearing of the two, though still within call. She occupied the sedilium; he a seat by the table near her. Save a fine white veil on an arm and a fan which she seldom used, her appearance was as in the morning.

It is to be admitted now that the Princess was finding a pleasure in the society of the Sheik. If aware of the fact, which was doubtful, it is still more doubtful if she could have explained it. We are inclined to think the mystery attaching to the man had as much to do with the circumstance as the man himself. He was polite, engaging, and handsome; the objection to his complexion, if such there were, was at least offset by a very positive faculty of entertaining; besides which, the unspeakable something in manner, always baffling disguises, always whispering of other conditions, always exciting suggestions and expectations, was present here.

If she thought him the Bedouin he assumed to be, directly a word changed the opinion; did she see the Governor of the old Castle in his face, an allusion or a bit of information dropped by him unaware spoke of association far beyond such a subordinate; most perplexing, however, where got the man his intelligence? Did learning like his, avoiding cloisters, academies, and teachers of classical taste, comport with camel-driving and tent-life in deserts harried by winds and sand?

The mystery, together with the effort to disentangle it, resolved the Princess into an attentive auditor. The advantages in the conversation were consequently with the Sheik; and he availed himself of them to lead as he chose.

"You have heard, O Princess, of the sacred fig-tree of the Hindus?"

"No."

"In one of their poems—the Bhagavad Gita, I think—it is described as having its roots above and its branches downward; thus drawing life from the sky and offering its fruit most conveniently, it is to me the symbol of a good and just king. It rose to my mind when thy kinsman—may Allah be thrice merciful to him!—passed me with his speech of forgiveness, and this gift "—he raised his hand, and looked at the ring on one of the fingers-"in place of which I was more deserving burial in the Bosphorus, as the black-browed Admiral said."

A frown dark as the Admiral's roughened his smooth brow.

"Why so?" she inquired.

"The tales I told were of a kind to be spared a Greek, even one who may not cover his instep with the embroidered buskin of an Emperor."

"Nay, Sheik, they did not ruffle him. On the tongue of a Turk, I admit, the traditions had been boastful, but you are not a Turk."

The remark might have been interrogative; wherefore with admirable address, he replied: "An Ottoman would see in me an Arab wholly unrelated to him, except as I am a Moslem. Let it pass, O Princess—he forgave me. The really great are always generous. When I took the ring, I thought, Now would the young Mahommed have so lightly pardoned the provocation?"

"Mahommed!" she said.

"Not the Prophet," he answered; "but the son of Amurath."

"Ah, you know him?"

"I have sat with him, O Princess, and at table often helped him to meat and bread. I have been his cupbearer and taster, and as frequently shared his outdoor sports; now hunting with hawk, and now with hound. Oh, it were worth a year of common days to gallop at his right hand, and exult with him when the falcon, from its poise right under the sun, drops itself like an arrow upon its enemy! I have discoursed with him also on themes holy and profane, and given and taken views, and telling him tales in prose and verse, have seen the day go out, then come again. In knightly practice I have tilted with him, and more than once, by his side in battle, loosened rein at the same cry and charged. His Sultana mother knows him well; but, by the lions and the eagles who served Solomon, I know him, beginning where her knowledge left off—that is, where the horizon of manhood stretched itself to make room for his enlarging soul."

The awakening curiosity of his listener was not lost upon the Sheik.

"You are surprised to hear a kindly speech of the son of Amurath," he said.

She flushed slightly.

"I am not a person, Sheik, whose opinions are dangerous to the peace of States, and of whom diplomacy is required; yet it would grieve me to give offence to you or your friend, the Prince Mahommed. If now I concede a wish to have some further knowledge of one who is shortly to inherit the most powerful of the Eastern Kingdoms, the circumstance ought not to subject me to harsh judgment."

"Princess," the Sheik said, "nothing so becomes a woman as care where words may be the occasion of mischief. As a flower in a garden, such a woman would rank as the sovereign rose; as a bird, she would be the bulbul, the sweetest of singers, and in beauty, a heron with throat of snow, and wings of pink and scarlet; as a star, she would be the first of the evening, and the last to pale in the morning—nay, she would be a perpetual morning. Of all fates what more nearly justifies reproach of Allah than to have one's name and glory at the mercy of a rival or an enemy? I am indeed Mahommed's friend—I know him—I will defend him, where sacred truth permits defence. And then"—his glance fell, and he hesitated.

"And what then?" she asked.

He gave her a grateful look, and answered: "I am going to Adrianople. The Prince will be there, and can I tell him of this audience, and that the Princess Irene regrets the evil reported of him in Constantinople, and is not his enemy, straightway he will number himself of those the most happy and divinely remembered, whose books are to be given them in their right hands."

The Princess looked at the singer, her countenance clear, serene, fair as a child's, and said:

"I am the enemy of no one living. Report me so to him. The Master I follow left a law by which all men and women are neighbors whom I am to love and pray for as I love and pray for myself. Deliver him the very words, O Sheik, and he will not misunderstand me."

A moment after she asked:

"But tell me more of him. He is making the world very anxious."

"Princess," the Sheik began, "Ebn Hanife was a father amongst Dervishes, and he had a saying, 'Ye shall know a plant by its flower, a vine by its fruit, and a man by his acts; what he does being to the man as the flower to the plant, and the fruit to the vine; if he have done nothing, prove him by his tastes and preferences, for what he likes best that he will do when left to himself.' By these tests let us presume to try the Prince Mahommed.... There is nothing which enthralls us like the exercise of power—nothing we so nearly carry with us into the tomb to be a motive there; for who shall say it has not a part in the promise of resurrection? If so, O Princess, what praise is too great for him who, a young man placed upon a throne by his father, comes down from it at his father's call?"

"Did Mahommed that?"

"Not once, O Princess, but twice."

"In so much at least his balance should be fair."

"To whom is the pleasant life in a lofty garden, its clusters always near at hand—to whom, if not to the just judges of their fellow-men?"

The Sheik saluted her twice by carrying his right hand to his beard, then to his forehead.

"Attend again, O Princess," he continued, more warmly than in the outset. "Mahommed is devoted to learning. At night in the field when the watches are set, the story-tellers, poets, philosophers, lawyers, preachers, experts in foreign tongues, and especially the inventors of devices, a class by themselves, supposed generally to live on dreams as others on bread—all these, finding welcome in his tent, congregate there. His palace in the city is a college, with recitations and lectures and instructive conversations. The objection his father recognized the times he requested him to vacate the throne was that he was a student. His ancestors having been verse makers, poetry is his delight; and if he does not rival them in the gentle art, he surpasses them in the number of his acquirements. The Arab, the Hebrew, the Greek, the Latin address him and have answers each in his mother's tongue. Knew you ever a scholar, O Princess, whose soul had utterly escaped the softening influence of thought and study? It is not learning which tames the barbarian so much as the diversion of mind from barbaric modes required of him while in the pursuit of learning."

She interrupted him, saying pleasantly: "I see, O Sheik, if to be at the mercy of an enemy is sad, how fortunate where one's picture is intended if the artist be a friend. Where had the Prince his instructors?"

There was a lurking smile in the Sheik's eyes, as he replied: "The sands in my country drink the clouds dry, and leave few fountains except of knowledge. The Arab professors in Cordova, whom the Moorish Kaliphs deemed themselves honored in honoring, were not despised by the Bishops of Rome. Amurath, wanting teachers for Mahommed, invited the best of them to his court. Ah—if I had the time!"

Observing his sigh had not failed its mark, he continued: "I would speak of some of the books I have seen on the Prince's table; for as a licensed friend, I have been in his study. Indeed, but for fear of too greatly recommending myself, I would have told you earlier, O Princess, how he favoured me as one of his teachers."

"Of poetry and story-telling, I suppose?"

"Why not?" he asked. "Our history is kept and taught in such forms. Have we a hero not himself a poet, he keeps one.... Upon the Prince's table, in the central place, objects of his reverence, the sources to which he most frequently addresses himself when in need of words and happy turns of expression, his standards of comparison for things beautiful in writing and speech, mirrors of the Most Merciful, whispering galleries wherein the voice of the Most Compassionate is never silent, are the Koran, with illustrations in gold, and the Bible in Hebrew, copied from *torahs* of daily use in the Synagogues."

"The Bible in Hebrew! Does he read it?"

"Like a Jewish elder."

"And the Gospels?"

The Sheik's face became reproachful.

"Art thou—even thou, O Princess—of those who believe a Moslem must reject Christ because the Prophet of Islam succeeded him with later teachings?"

Dropping then into the passionless manner, he continued:

"The Koran does not deny Christ or his Gospels. Hear what it says of itself: 'And this Koran is not a forgery of one who is no God, but it hath been sent down as a confirmation of those books which have been before it, and an explanation of the Scriptures from the Lord of the Worlds.' [Footnote: The Koran] ... That verse, O Princess, transcribed by the Prince Mahommed himself, lies between the Bible and the Koran; the two being, as I have said, always together upon his table."

"What then is his faith?" she asked, undisguisedly interested.

"Would he were here to declare it himself!"

This was said disconsolately; then the Sheik broke out:

"The truth now of the son of Amurath! Listen!—He believes in God. He believes in the Scriptures and the Koran, holding them separate wings of the divine Truth by which the world is to attain righteousness. He believes there have been three Prophets specially in the confidence of God: Moses, the first one; Jesus, who was greater than Moses; Mahomet, the very greatest—not for speaking better or sublimer things, but because he was last in their order of coming. Above all, O Princess, he believes worship due to the Most High alone; therefore he prays the prayer of Islam, God is God, and Mahomet is his Prophet—meaning that the Prophet is not to be mistaken for God."

The Sheik raised his dark eyes, and upon meeting them the Princess looked out over the bay. That she was not displeased was the most he could read in her face, the youthful light of which was a little shaded by thinking. He waited for her to speak.

"There were other books upon the Prince's table?" she presently asked.

"There were others, O Princess."

"Canst thou name some of them?"

The Sheik bowed profoundly.

"I see the pearls of Ebn Hanife's saying were not wasted. Mahommed is now to be tried by his tastes and preferences. Let it be so.... I saw there, besides dictionaries Greek, Latin, and Hebrew, the Encyclopaedia of Sciences, a rare and wonderful volume by a Granadian Moor, Ibn Abdallah. I saw there the Astronomy and Astronomical Tables of Ibn Junis, and with them a silver globe perfected from the calculations of Almamon the Kaliph, which helps us to the geographical principle not yet acknowledged in Rome, that the earth is round. I saw there the Book of the Balance of Wisdom by Alhazan, who delved into the laws of nature until there is nothing phenomenal left. I saw there the Philosophy of Azazzali the Arab, for which both Christian and Moslem should be grateful, since it has given Philosophy its true place by exalting it into a handmaiden of Religion. I saw there books treating of trade and commerce, of arms and armor, and machines for the assault and defence of cities, of military engineering, and the conduct of armies in grand campaigns, of engineering not military, dealing with surveying, and the construction of highways, aqueducts, and bridges, and the laying out of towns. There, also, because the soul of the student must have rest and diversion, I saw volumes of songs and music loved by lovers in every land, and drawings of mosques, churches and palaces, masterpieces of Indian and Saracenic genius; and of gardens there was the Zebra, created by Abderrahman for the best loved of his Sultanas. Of poetry, O Princess, I saw many books, the lord of them a copy of Homer in Arabic, executed on ivory from the translation ordered by Haroun Al-Raschid."

During this recital the Princess scarcely moved. She was hearing a new version of Mahommed; and the Sheik, like a master satisfied with his premises, proceeded to conclusions.

"My Lord has a habit of dreaming, and he does not deny it—he believes in it. In his student days, he called it his rest. He used to say, when his brain reeled in overtask dreaming was a pillow of down and lavender; that in moments of despair, dreaming took his spirit in its hands softer than air, and, nurse-like, whispered and sung to it, and presently it was strong again. Not many mornings ago he awoke to find that in a deep sleep some ministrant had come to him, and opened the doors of his heart, and let out its flock of boyish fantasies. He has since known but three visions. Would it please you, O Princess, to hear of them? They may be useful as threads on which to hang the Dervish father's pearls of saying."

She re-settled herself, resting her cheek on her hand, and her elbow on the arm of the chair, and replied:

"I will hear of them."

"The visions have all of them reference to the throne he is soon to ascend, without which they would be the mere jingling of a jester's rattle.

"First Vision.... He will be a hero. If his soul turned from war, he were not his father's son. But unlike his father, he holds war the servant of peace, and peace the condition essential to his other visions.

"Second Vision.... He believes his people have the genius of the Moors, and he will cultivate it in rivalry of that marvellous race."

"Of the Moors, O Sheik?" the Princess said, interrupting him. "Of the Moors? I have always heard of them as pillagers of sacred cities—infidels sunk in ignorance, who stole the name of God to excuse invasions and the spilling of rivers of blood."

The Sheik lifted his head haughtily.

"I am an Arab, and the Moors are Arabs translated from the East to the West."

"I crave thy pardon," she said, gently.

And calming himself, he rejoined: "If I weary you, O Princess, there are other subjects to which I can turn. My memory is like the box of sandal-wood a lady keeps for her jewelry. I can open it at will, and always find something to please—better probably because I have it from another."

"No," she returned, artlessly, "a hero in actual life transcends the best of fancies—and besides, Sheik, you spoke of a third vision of your friend, the Prince Mahommed."

He dropped his eyes lest she should see the brightness with which they filled.

"War, my Lord says, is a necessity which, as Sultan, he cannot avoid. Were he disposed to content himself with the empire descending from his great father, envious neighbors would challenge him to the field. He must prove his capacity in defence. That done, he vows to tread the path made white and smooth by Abderrahman, the noblest and best of the Western Kaliphs. He will set out by founding a capital somewhere on the Bosphorus. Such, O Princess, is my Lord Mahommed's Third Vision."

"Nay, Sheik—on the Marmora—at Broussa, perhaps."

"I am giving the Vision as he gave it to me, Princess. For where else, he asks, has the spreading earth diviner features than on the Bosphorus? Where bends a softer sky above a friendlier channel by Nature moulded for nobler uses? Where are there seas so bridled and reduced? Does not the rose bloom here all the year? Yonder the East, here the West—must they be strangers and enemies forever? His capital, he declares, shall be for their entertainment as elder and younger brother. Within its walls, which he will build strong as a mountain's base, with gates of brass invulnerable, and towers to descry the clouds below the horizon, he will collect unselfishly whatever is good and beautiful, remembering he serves Allah best who serves his fellow-men."

"All his fellow-men, Sheik?"

"All of them."

Then she glanced over the bay, and said very softly:

"It is well; for 'if ye salute your brethren only, what do ye more than others?'"

The Sheik smiled, saying:

"And thus the latest Prophet, O Princess. 'Turn away evil by that which is better; and lo, he between whom and thyself was enmity, shall become as though he were a warm friend.'" [Footnote: Koran]

She answered, "A goodly echo."

"Shall I proceed?" he then asked.

"Yes."

"I was speaking of the Third Vision.... To make his capital the centre of the earth, he will have a harbor where ships from every country, and all at once, can come and lie, oars slung and sails furled: and near by for trade, a bazaar with streets of marble, and roofed with glass, and broad and long enough for a city unto itself; and in the midst a khan for lodging the merchants and travellers who have not other houses. And as did Abderrahman, he will build a University of vast enclosure; here temples, there groves; nor may a study be named without its teacher, and he the most famous; so the votaries of Music and Poetry, Philosophy, Science, and the Arts, and the hundred-handed Mechanics shall dwell together like soldiers in a holy league. And comes that way one religious, of him but a question, Believest thou in God? and if he answer yes, then for him a ready welcome. For of what moment is it, my Lord asks, whether God bear this name or that? Or be worshipped with or without form? Or on foot or knee? Or whether the devout be called together by voice or bell? Is not Faith everything?"

The picture wrought upon the Princess. Her countenance was radiant, and she said half to herself, but so the Sheik heard her:

"It is a noble Vision."

Then the Sheik lowered his voice:

"If, with such schemes, excluding races and religions—hear me again, O Princess!—if with such schemes or visions, as thou wilt, the Lord Mahommed allows himself one selfish dream, wouldst thou condemn him?"

"What is the selfish dream?" she asked.

"He has an open saying, Princess, 'Light is the life of the world, while Love is the light of life.' Didst thou ever hear how Othman wooed and won his Malkatoon?"

"No."

"It is a Turkish tale of love. Mahommed had it from his mother when he was a lad, and he has been haunted ever since with a belief which, to his dreaming, is like the high window in the eastern front of a palace, outwardly the expression-giver, within the principal source of light. The idea is strongest what times the moon is in the full; and then he mounts a horse, and hies him, as did Othman, to some solitary place where, with imagination for cup-bearer, he drinks himself into happy drunkenness." The Sheik, bending forward, caught her eyes with his, and held them so not a glance escaped him.

"He thinks—and not all the Genii, the winged and the unwinged, of the wisest of Kings could win him from the thought—that he will sometime meet a woman who will have the mind, the soul of souls, and the beauty of the most beautiful. When she will cross his vision is one of the undelivered scriptories which Time is bringing him; yet he is looking for her, and the more constantly because the first sight of her will be his first lesson in the mystery called love. He will know her, for at seeing her a lamp will light itself in his heart, and by it, not the glare of the sun, his spirit will make sure of her spirit. Therefore in his absoluteness of faith, O Princess, there is a place already provided for her in his promised capital, and even now he calls it this House of Love. Ah, what hours he has spent planning that abode! He will seat it in the Garden of Perfection, for the glorifying which, trees, birds, flowers, summer-houses, water, hill-tops and shaded vales shall be conquered. Has he not studied the Zehra of Abderrahman? And divided it as it was into halls, courts and chambers, and formed and proportioned each, and set and reset its thousand and more columns, and restored the pearls and gold on its walls, and over the wide Alhambran arches hung silken doors sheened like Paradisean birds? And all that when he shall have found her, his Queen, his Malkatoon, his Spirit of Song, his Breath of Flowers, his Lily of Summer, his Pearl of Oman, his Moon of Radjeb, monotony shall never come where she dwells nor shall she sigh except for him absent. Such, O Princess Irene, is the one dream the Prince has builded with the world shut out. Does it seem to you a vanity of wickedness?"

"No," she returned, and covered her face, for the Sheik's look was eager and burning bright.

He knelt then, and kissed the marble at her feet.

"I am Prince Mahommed's ambassador, O Princess," he said, rising to his knees. "Forgive me, if I have dared delay the announcement."

"His ambassador! To what end?"

"I am afraid and trembling."

He kissed the floor again.

"Assure me of pardon—if only to win me back my courage. It is miserable to be shaken with fear."

"Thou hast done nothing, Sheik, unless drawing thy master's portrait too partially be an offence. Speak out."

"It is not three days, Princess, since you were Mahommed's guest."

"I his guest—Mahommed's!"

She arose from her chair.

"He received you at the White Castle."

"And the Governor?"

"He was the Governor."

She sunk back overcome with astonishment. The Sheik recalled her directly.

"Prince Mahommed," he said, "arrived at the Castle when the boats were discovered, and hastened to the landing to render assistance if the peril required it.... And now, O Princess, my tongue falters. How can I without offending tell of the excitement into which seeing you plunged him? Suffer me to be direct. His first impression was supported by the coincidences—your coming and his, so nearly at the same instant—the place of the meeting so out of the way and strange—the storm seemingly an urgency of Heaven. Beholding and hearing you, 'This is she! This is she! My Queen, my Malkatoon!' he cried in his heart. And yesterday"—

"Nay, Sheik, allow the explanation to wait. Bearest thou a message from him to me?"

"He bade me salute thee, Princess Irene, as if thou wert now the Lady of his House of Love in his Garden of Perfection, and to pray if he might come and in person kiss thy hand, and tell thee his hopes, and pour out at thy feet his love in heartfuls larger than ever woman had from man."

While speaking, the Sheik would have given his birthright to have seen her face.

Then, in a low voice, she asked:

"Does he doubt I am a Christian?"

The tone was not of anger; with beatings of heart trebly quickened, he hastened to reply:

"'That she is a Christian'—may God abandon my mouth, if I quote him unfaithfully!—'That she is a Christian, I love her the more. For see you, Sheik'—by the faith of an Arab, Princess, I quote him yet, word for word—'my mother was a Christian.'"

In the morning of this very day we have seen her put to like question by Constantine, and she did not hesitate; now the reply took a time.

"Say to Prince Mahommed," she at length returned, "that his message presents itself honorably, for which it is deserving a soft answer. His fancy has played him false. I cannot be the woman of his dream. She is young; I am old, though not with years. She is gay; I am serious. She is in love with life, hopeful, joyous; I was born to sorrow, and in sorrow brought up, and the religion which absorbed my youth is now life's hold on me. She will be delighted with the splendors he has in store for her; so might I, had not the wise man long since caught my ear and judgment by the awful text, Vanity of vanities, all is vanity. While her charms endure she will keep him charmed with the world; I could not so much, for the world to come has possession of me, and the days here are but so many of a journey thither. Tell him, O Sheik, while he has been dreaming of palaces and gardens in rivalry of Abderrahman the Kaliph, I have been dreaming of a house in splendor beyond the conception of architects; and asks he more about it, tell him I know it only as a house not made with hands. Tell him I speak not in denial of possibilities; for by the love I have never failed to accord the good and noble, I might bend my soul to his; to this hour, however, God and His Son the Christ, and the Holy Mother, and the Angels and deserving men and women have taken up my heart and imagination, and in serving them I have not aspired to other happiness. A wife I might become, not from temptation of gain or power, or in surrender to love—I speak not in derision of the passion, since, like the admitted virtues, it is from God—nay, Sheik, in illustration of what may otherwise be of uncertain meaning to him, tell Prince Mahommed I might become his wife could I by so doing save or help the religion I profess. Then, if I brought him love, the sacrifice would rescue it from every taint. Canst thou remember all this? And wilt thou deliver it truly?"

The Sheik's demeanor when she ended was greatly changed; his head was quite upon his breast; his attitude and whole appearance were disconsolate to the last degree.

"Alas, Princess! How can I carry such speech to him, whose soul is consuming with hunger and thirst for thy favor?"

"Sheik," she said in pity, "no master, I think, had ever a more faithful servant than thou hast proved thyself. Thy delivery of his message, could it be preserved, would be a model for heralds in the future."

Thereupon she arose, extended her hand to him, and he kissed it; and as she remained standing, he arose also.

"Be seated," she then said, and immediately that they were both in their chairs again, she took direction of the interview.

"You asked me, Sheik, if I had heard how Othman wooed and won his Malkatoon, and said it was a Turkish romance. The Othman, I take it, was founder of Prince Mahommed's house. Now, if thou art not too weary, tell me the story."

As the recital afforded him the opportunities to give poetic expression to his present feeling, he accepted the suggestion gladly, and, being in the right mood, was singularly effective. Half the time listening she was in tears. It was past three o'clock when he finished. The audience then terminated. In no part of it had her manner been more gracious than when she conducted him along the portico, or her loveliness so overwhelming as when she bade him adieu at the head of the steps.

Standing between columns near the sedilium, she saw him gain his boat, take something from the sitting-box, step ashore again, and return to her gate, where he remained awhile pounding with a stone. The action was curious, and when he was out of sight rounding the water front of the promontory, she sent Lysander to investigate.

"The infidel has fixed a brass plate to the right-hand post of the kiosk," the ancient reported, in bad humor. "It may be a curse." The Princess then called her attendants, and went with them to see the brass plate. There it was, an arm's reach overhead, and affixed firmly to the post, the corners turned down to serve the tacking. Graven on its polished surface was the following:

[Illustration]

Wholly unable to decipher it, she sent for a Dervish, long resident in the town, and returned to the portico.

"Princess," the old man said, having viewed the mysterious plate, "he who did the posting was a Turk; and if he were aged, I should say thou hast entertained unaware the great Amurath, Sultan of Sultans."

"But the man was young."

"Then was he the son of Amurath, Prince Mahommed."

The Princess turned pale.

"How canst thou speak so positively?" she asked.

"It is a *teukra*; in the whole world, O Princess, there are but two persons with authority to make use of it."

"And who are they?"

"The Sultan, and Mahommed, next him in the succession."

In the silence which ensued, Lysander officiously proposed to remove the sign. The Dervish interposed.

"Wilt thou hear me, O Princess," he said, with a low reverence, "whether the plate proceeded from Amurath or Mahommed, or by the order of either of them, the leaving it behind signifies more than friendship or favor—it is a safeguard—a proclamation that thou and thy people and property here are under protection of the master of all the Turks. Were war to break out to-morrow, thou mightest continue in thy palace and garden with none to make thee afraid save thine own countrymen. Wherefore consider well before acceding to the rancor of this ancient madman."

Thus the truth came to the Princess Irene. The Singing Sheik was Prince Mahommed!

Twice he had appeared before her; in the White Castle once, and now in her palace; and having announced himself her lover, and proposed marriage, he intended her to know him, and also that he was not departing in despair. Hence the plate on the gate! The circumstance was novel and surprising. Her present feelings were too vague and uncertain for definition: but she was not angry.

Meantime Mahommed, returning to the old Castle, debated with himself. He loved the Princess Irene with the passion of a soul unused to denial or disappointment, and before he reached the Roumelian Hissar he swore a Moslem oath to conquer Constantinople, less for Islam and glory, than for her. And from that hour the great accomplishment took hold of him to the exclusion of all else.

At Hissar he ascended the mountain, and, standing on the terreplein of the precipice in front of what is now Robert College, he marked the narrowness of the Bosphorus below, and thinking of the military necessity for a crossing defended on both shores, he selected a site for a castle on the European side opposite the White Castle in Asia. In due time we will have occasion to notice the creation of the walls and towers of the stupendous fortification yet standing between Bebek and Hissar, a monument to his energy and sagacity more imposing than anything left by him in Constantinople.

BOOK IV
THE PALACE OF BLACHERNE

CHAPTER I
THE PALACE OF BLACHERNE

The Prince of India was not given to idle expectations. He might deceive others, but he seldom deceived himself. His experience served him prophetically in matters largely dependent on motives ordinarily influential with men. He was confident the Emperor would communicate with him, and soon.

The third day after the adventure at the White Castle, a stranger, mounted, armed, and showily caparisoned, appeared at the Prince's door under guidance of Uel. In the study, to which he was hidden, he announced himself the bearer of a complimentary message from His Majesty, concluding with an invitation to the palace of Blacherne. If agreeable, His Majesty would be pleased to receive the Indian dignitary in the afternoon at three o'clock. An officer of the guard would be at the Grand Gate for his escort. The honor, needless to say, was accepted in becoming terms.

When the Prince descended to the hall of entry on the ground floor to take the sedan there, the unusual care given his attire was apparent. His beard was immaculately white. His turban of white silk, balloon in shape, and with a dazzle of precious stones in front, was a study. Over a shirt of finest linen, with ruffles of lace at the throat and breast, there was a plain gown of heavy black velvet, buttoned at the neck, but open down to a yellow sash around the waist. The sash was complemented by a belt which was a mass of pearls in relief on a ground of gold embroidery. The belt-plate and crescented sword scabbard were aflame with brilliants on blue enamelling. His trousers, ample as a skirt, were of white satin overflowing at the ankles. Pointed red slippers, sparkling with embroidery of small golden beads, completed the costume.

The procession in the street was most striking. First Nilo, as became a king of Kash-Cush, barbarously magnificent; the sedan next, on the shoulders of four carriers in white livery; at the rear, two domestics arrayed *a la Cipango*, their strange blue garments fitting them so close as to impede their walking; yet as one of them bore his master's paper sunshade and ample cloak, and the other a cushion bloated into the proportions of a huge pillow, they were by no means wanting in self-importance. Syama, similarly attired, though in richer material, walked at the side of the sedan, ready to open the door or answer such signal as he might receive from within.

The appearance of this retinue in the streets was a show to the idle and curious, who came together as if rendered out of the earth, and in such numbers that before fairly reaching the thoroughfare by which the Grand Gate of Blacherne was usually approached from the city side, the gilded box on the shoulders of its bearers looked, off a little way, not unlike a boat rocking in waves.

Fortunately the people started in good humor, and meeting nothing to break the mood, they permitted the Prince to accomplish his journey without interruption. The companionship of the crowd was really agreeable to him; he hardly knew whether it were pleasanter to be able to excite such respectful curiosity than to gratify it successfully. It might have been otherwise had Lael been with him.

The Very High Residence, as the Palace of Blacherne was generally spoken of by Greeks, was well known to the Prince of India. The exclamation with which he settled himself in the sedan at setting out from his house— "Again, again, O Blacherne!"—disclosed a previous personal acquaintance with the royal property. And over and over again on the way he kept repeating, "O Blacherne! Beautiful Blacherne! Bloom the roses as of old in thy gardens? Do the rivulets in thy alabaster courts still run singing to the mosaic angels on the walls?"

As to the date of these recollections, if, as the poets tell us, time is like a flowing river, and memory a bridge for the conveniency of the soul returning to its experiences, how far had this man to travel the structure before reaching the Blacherne he formerly knew? Over what tremendous spaces between piers did it carry him!

The street traversed by the Prince carried him first to the Grate of St. Peter on the Golden Horn, and thence, almost parallel with the city wall, to Balat, a private landing belonging to the Emperor, at present known as the gate of Blacherne.

At the edge of an area marble paved, the people stopped, it being the limit of their privilege. Crossing the pavement, the visitor was set down in front of the Grand Gate of the Very High Residence. History, always abominating lapses, is yet more tender of some places than others. There, between flanking towers, an iron-plated valve strong enough to defy attack by any of the ancient methods was swung wide open, ready nevertheless to be rolled to at set of sun. The guard halted the Prince, and an officer took his name, and apologizing for a brief delay, disappeared with it. Alighting from his sedan, the worthy proceeded to take observation and muse while waiting.

The paved area on which he stood was really the bottom of a well-defined valley which ran off and up irregularly toward the southeast, leaving an ascent on its right memorable as the seventh hill of Constantinople. A stone wall marked here and there by sentinel boxes, each with a red pennon on its top, straggled down along the foot of the ascent to the Grand Gate. There between octangular towers loopholed and finished battlement style was a covered passage suggestive of Egypt. Two Victories in high relief blew trumpets at each other across the entrance front. Ponderous benches of porphyry, polished smooth by ages of usage, sat one on each side for the guards; fellows in helmets of shining brass, cuirasses of the same material inlaid with silver, greaves, and shoes stoutly buckled. Those of them sitting sprawled their bulky limbs broadly over the benches. The few standing seemed like selected giants, with blond beards and blue eyes, and axes at least three spans in length along their whetted edges. The Prince recognized the imperial guards—Danes, Saxons, Germans, and Swiss—their nationalities merged into the corps entitled *Varangians*.

Conscious, but unmindful of their stare, he kept his stand, and swept the hill from bottom to top, giving free rein to memory.

In 449 A. D.—he remembered the year and the circumstance well—an earthquake threw down the wall then enclosing the city. Theodosius restored it, leaving the whole height outside of this northwestern part a preserve wooded, rocky, but with one possession which had become so infinitely sanctified in Byzantine estimation as to impart the quality to all its appurtenances, that was the primitive but Very Holy Church of Blacherne, dedicated to the Virgin.

Near the church there was a pleasure house to which the Emperors, vainly struggling to escape the ceremonies the clergy had fastened upon them to the imbitterment of life, occasionally resorted, and down on the shore of the Golden Horn a zoological garden termed the Cynegion had been established. The latter afterwhile came to have a gallery in which the public was sometimes treated to games and combats between lions, tigers, and elephants. There also criminals and heretics were frequently carried and flung to the beasts.

Nor did the Prince fail to recall that in those cycles the sovereigns resided preferably in the Bucoleon, eastwardly by the sea of Marmora. He remembered some of them as acquaintances with whom he had been on close terms—Justinian, Heraclius, Irene, and the Porphyrogentes.

The iconoclastic masters of that cluster of magnificent tenements, the Bucoleon, had especial claims upon his recollection. Had he not incited them to many of their savageries? They were incidents, it is true, sadly out of harmony with his present dream; still their return now was with a certain fluttering of the spirit akin to satisfaction, for the victims in nearly every case had been Christians, and his business of life then was vengeance for the indignities and sufferings inflicted on his countrymen.

With a more decided flutter, he remembered a scheme he put into effect just twenty years after the restoration of the wall by Theodosius. In the character of a pious Christianized Israelite resident in Jerusalem, he pretended to have found the vestments of the Holy Mother of Christ. The discovery was of course miraculous, and he reported it circumstantially to the Patriarchs Galvius and Candidus. For the glory of God and the exaltation of the Faith, they brought the relics to Constantinople. There, amidst most solemn pomp, the Emperor assisting, they were deposited in the Church of Saints Peter and Mark, to be transferred a little later to their final resting-place in the holier Church of the Virgin of Blacherne. There was a world of pious propriety in the idea that as the vestments belonged to the Mother of God they would better become her own house. The *Himation* or *Maphorion*, as the robe of the Virgin was called, brought the primitive edifice in the woods above the Cynegion a boundless increase of sanctity, while the discoverer received the freedom of the city, the reverence of the clergy, and the confidence of the Basileus.

Nor did the prodigious memory stay there. The hill facing the city was of three terraces. On the second one, half hidden among cypress and plane trees, he beheld a building, low, strong, and, from his direction, showing but one window. Some sixteen years previous, during his absence in Cipango, a fire had destroyed the Church of the Virgin, and owing to the poverty of the people and empire, the edifice had not been rebuilt. This lesser unpretentious structure was the Chapel of Blacherne which the flames had considerately spared. He recognized it instantly, and remembered it as full of inestimable relics—amongst them the *Himation*, considered indestructible; the Holy Cross which Heraclius, in the year 635, had brought from Jerusalem, and delivered to Sergius; and the *Panagia Blachernitissa*, or All Holy Banner of the Image of the Virgin. Then rose another reminiscence, and though to reach him it had to fly across a chasm of hundreds of years, it presented itself with the distinctness of an affair of yesterday. In 626, Heraclius being Emperor, a legion of Avars and Persians sacked Scutari, on the Asiatic side of the Bosphorus, and laid siege to Constantinople. The Byzantines were in awful panic; and they would have yielded themselves had not Sergius the Patriarch been in control. With a presence of mind equal to the occasion, he brought the *Panagia* forth, and supported by an army of clerics and monks, traversed the walls, waving the All Holy Banner. A volley of arrows from invisible archers fell upon the audacious infidels, and the havoc was dreadful; they fled, and their prince, the Khagan, fled with them, declaring he had seen a woman in shining garments but of awful presence on the walls. The woman was the Holy Mother; and with a conceit easily mistaken for gratitude, the Byzantines declared their capital thenceforward guarded by God. When they went out to the Church in the Woods and found it unharmed by the enemy, they were persuaded the Mother had adopted them; in return, what could they else than adopt her? Pisides, the poet, composed a hymn, to glorify her. The Church consecrated the day of the miraculous deliverance a fete day observable by Greeks forever. The Emperor removed the old building, and on its site raised another of a beauty more expressive of devotion. To secure it from ravage and profanation, he threw a strong wall around the whole venerated hill, and by demolishing the ancient work of Theodosius, made Blacherne a part of the city.

By and by the Church required enlargement, and it was then cruci-formed by the addition of transepts right and left. Still later, a Chapel was erected specially for the relics and the All Holy Banner. This was contiguous to the Church, and besides being fireproof, it covered a spring of pure water, afterwards essential in many splendid ceremonies civil as well as religious. The Chamber of Relics was prohibited to all but the Basileus. He alone could enter it. By great favor, the Prince of India was once permitted to look into the room, and he remembered it large and dimly lighted, its shadows alive, however, with the glitter of silver and gold in every conceivable form, offered there as the Wise Men laid their gifts before the Child in the Cave of the Nativity.

Again and again the Church was burned, yet the Chapel escaped. It seemed an object of divine protection. The sea might deliver tempests against the Seven Hills, earthquakes shake the walls down and crack the hanging dome of St. Sophia, cinders whiten paths from the porphyry column over by the Hippodrome to the upper terrace of Blacherne; yet the Chapel escaped— yet the holy fountain in its crypt flowed on purer growing as the centuries passed.

The Prince, whose memories we are but weaving into words, did not wonder at the increase of veneration attaching to the Chapel and its precious deposits—manuscripts, books, bones, flags, things personal to the Apostles, the Saints, the Son and His Mother, parings of their nails, locks of their hair, spikes and splinters of the Cross itself—he did not wonder at it, or smile, for he knew there is a devotional side to every man which wickedness may blur but cannot obliterate. He himself was going about the world convinced that the temple of Solomon was the House of God.

The guards sprawling on the benches kept staring at him; one of them let his axe fall without so much as attracting the Prince's attention. His memory, with a hold on him too firm to be disturbed by such trifles, insisted on its resurrectionary work, and returned him to the year 865. Constantinople was again besieged, this time by a horde from the Russian wilderness under the chiefs Dir and Askold. They had passed the upper sea in hundreds of boats, and disembarking on the European shore, marched down the Bosphorus, leaving all behind them desolate. Photius was then Patriarch. When the fleet was descried from the walls, he prevailed on the Emperor to ask the intervention of the Virgin. The *Maphorion* or Sacred Robe was brought out, and in presence of the people on their knees, the clergy singing the hymn of Pisides, the holy man plunged it into the waves.

A wind arose under which the water in its rocky trough was as water in a shaken bowl. The ships of the invaders sunk each other. Not one survived. Of the men, those who lived came up out of the vortexes praying to be taken to the Church of Blacherne for baptism. This was two hundred years and more after the first deliverance of the city, and yet the Mother was faithful to her chosen!—Constantinople was still the guarded of God!— The *Penagia* was still the All Holy! Having repulsed the Muscovite invasion, what excuse for his blasphemy would there be left the next to challenge its terrors?

The Prince of India saw the blackened walls of the burned Church, an appealing spectacle which the surrounding trees tried to cover with their foliage, but could not; then he lifted his eyes to the Palace upon the third terrace.

To the hour decay sets in the touches of Time are usually those of an artist who loves his subject, and wishes merely to soften or ennoble its expression. So had he dealt with the Very High Residence.

It began in the low ground down by the Cynegion, and arose with the city wall, which was in fact its southwestern front. Though always spoken of in the singular, like the Bucoleon, it was a collection of palaces, vast, irregular, and declarative of the taste of the different eras they severally memorialized. The spaces between them formed courts and *places* under cover; yet as the architects had adhered to the idea of a main front toward the northeast, there appeared a certain unity of design in the structures.

This main front, now under the Prince's view, was frequently broken, advancing here, retreating there; one section severely plain and sombre; another relieved by porticos with figured friezes resting on tall columns. The irregularities were pleasing; some of them were stately; and they were all helped not a little by domes and pavilions without which the roof lines would have been monotonous.

Lifting his gaze up the ascent from the low ground, it rested presently on a Tower built boldly upon the Heraclian wall. This was the highest pinnacle of the Palace, first to attract the observer, longest to hold his attention. No courier was required to tell its history to him through whose eyes we are now looking—it was the tower of Isaac Angelus. How clearly its outlines cut the cloudless sky! How strong it seemed up there, as if built by giants!

Yet with windows behind balconies, how airy and graceful withal! The other hills of the city, and the populated valleys between the hills, spread out below it, like an unrolled map. The warders of the Bucoleon, or what is now Point Serail, the home-returning mariner shipping oars off Scutari, the captain of the helmeted column entering the Golden Gate down by the Seven Towers, the insolent Genoese on the wharves of Galata, had only to look up, and lo! the perch of Isaac. And when, as often must have happened, the privileged lord himself sat midafternoons on the uppermost balcony of the Tower, how the prospect soothed the fever of his spirit! If he were weary of the city, there was the Marmora, always ready to reiterate the hues of the sky, and in it the Isles of the Princes, their verdurous shades permeated with dreamful welcome to the pleasure-seeker as well as the monk; or if he longed for a further flight, old Asia made haste with enticing invitation to some of the villas strewing its littoral behind the Isles; and yonder, to the eye fainting in the distance, scarce more than a pale blue boundary cloud, the mountain beloved by the gods, whither they were wont to assemble at such times as they wished to learn how it fared with Ilium and the sons of Priam, or to enliven their immortality with loud symposia. A prospect so composed would seem sufficient, if once seen, to make a blind man's darkness perpetually luminous.

Sometimes, however, the superlative magnate preferred the balcony on the western side of the Tower. There he could sit in the shade, cooled by waftures from a wide campania southward, or, peering over the balustrade, watch the peasantry flitting through the breaks of the Kosmidion, now the purlieus of Eyoub.

Again the Prince was carried back through centuries. It had been determined to build at Blacherne; but the hill was steep. How could spaces be gained for foundations, for courts and gardens? The architects pondered the problem. At last one of bolder genius came forward. We will accept the city wall for a western front, he said, and build from it; and for levels, allow us to commence at the foot of the height, and rear arches upon arches. The proposal was accepted; and thereafter for years the quarter was cumbered with brick and skeleton frames, and workingmen were numerous and incessantly busy as colonized ants. Thus the ancient pleasure house disappeared, and the first formal High Residence took its place; at the same time the Bucoleon, for so many ages the glory of Constantinople, was abandoned by its masters.

Who was the first permanent occupant of the Palace of Blacherne? The memory, theretofore so prompt, had now no reply. No matter—the Prince recalled sessions had with Angelus on the upper balcony yonder. He remembered them on account of his host one day saying: "Here I am safe." The next heard of him he was a captive and blind.

Passing on rapidly, he remembered the appearance of Peter the Hermit in the gorgeous reception room of the Palace in 1096. Quite as distinctly, he also remembered the audience Alexis I. tendered Godfrey of Bouillon and his Barons in the same High Residence.

What a contrast the host and his guests presented that day! The latter were steel clad from head to foot and armed for battle, while Alexis was a spectacle of splendor unheard of in the barbarous West. How the preachers and eunuchs in the silk-gowned train of the one trembled as the redoubtables of the West mangled the velvet carpets with their cruel spurs! How peculiarly the same redoubtables studied the pearls on the yellow stole of the wily Comnene and the big jewels in his Basilean mitre—as if they were counting and weighing them mentally, preliminary to casting up at leisure a total of value! And the table ware—this plate and yon bowl—were they really gold or some cunning deception? The Greeks were so treacherous! And when the guests were gone, the Greeks, on their part, were not in the least surprised at the list of spoons and cups subtly disappeared—gifts, they supposed, intended by the noble "Crosses" for the most Holy Altar in Jerusalem!

Still other remembrances of the Prince revived at sight of the Palace— many others—amongst them, how the Varangians beat the boastful Montferrat and the burly Count of Flanders in the assault of 1203, specially famous for the gallantry of old Dandolo, operating with his galleys on the side of the Golden Horn. Brave fellows, those Varangians! Was the corps well composed now as then? He glanced at the lusty examples before him on the stone benches, thinking they might shortly have to answer the question.

These reminiscences, it must not be forgotten, were of brief passage with the Prince, much briefer than the time taken in writing them. They were interrupted by the appearance of a military official whose uniform and easy manner bespoke palace life. He begged to be informed if he had the honor of addressing the Prince of India; and being affirmatively assured, he announced himself sent to conduct him to His Majesty. The hill was steep, and the way somewhat circuitous; did the Prince need assistance? The detention, he added, was owing to delay in getting intelligence of the Prince's arrival to His Majesty, who had been closely engaged, arranging for certain ceremonies which were to occur in the evening. Perhaps His Majesty had appointed the audience imagining the ceremonies might prove entertaining to the Prince. These civilities, and others, were properly responded to, and presently the cortege was in motion.

The lower terrace was a garden of singular perfection.

On the second terrace, the party came to the ruined Church where, during a halt, the officer told of the fire. His Majesty had registered a vow, he said, at the end of the story, to rebuild the edifice in a style superior to any former restoration.

The Prince, while listening, observed the place. Excepting the Church, it was as of old. There the grove of cypresses, very ancient, and tall and dark. There, too, the Chapel of purplish stone, and at one side of it the sentry box and bench, and what seemed the identical detail of Varangians on duty. There the enclosed space between the edifices, and the road across the pavement to the next terrace only a little deeper worn. There the arched gateway of massive masonry through which the road conducted, the carving about it handsome as ever; and there, finally, from the base of the Chapel, the brook, undiminished in volume and song, ran off out of sight into the grove, an old acquaintance of the Prince's.

Moving on through the arched way, the guide led up to the third and last terrace. Near the top there was a cut, and on its right embankment a party of workmen spreading and securing a canopy of red cloth.

"Observe, O Prince," the officer said. "From this position, if I mistake not, you will witness the ceremony I mentioned as in preparation."

The guest had time to express his gratification, when the Palace of Blacherne, the Very High Residence, burst upon him in long extended view, a marvel of imperial prodigality and Byzantine genius.

CHAPTER II
THE AUDIENCE

The sedan was set down before a marble gate on the third terrace.

"My duty is hardly complete. Suffer me to conduct you farther," the officer said, politely, as the Prince stepped from the box.

"And my servants?"

"They will await you."

The speakers were near the left corner of a building which projected considerably from the general front line of the Palace. The wall, the gateway, and the building were of white marble smoothly dressed.

After a few words with Syama, the Prince followed his guide into a narrow enclosure on the right of which there was a flight of steps, and on the left a guard house. Ascending the steps, the two traversed a passage until they came to a door.

"The waiting-room. Enter," said the conductor.

Four heavily curtained windows lighted the apartment. In the centre there were a massive table, and, slightly removed from it, a burnished copper brazier. Bright-hued rugs covered the floor, and here and there stools carven and upholstered were drawn against the painted walls. The officer, having seen his charge comfortably seated, excused himself and disappeared.

Hardly was he gone when two servants handsomely attired came in with refreshments—fruits in natural state, fruits candied, sweetened bread, sherbet, wine and water. A chief followed them, and, with much humility of manner, led the Prince to a seat at the table, and invited him to help himself. The guest was then left alone; and while he ate and drank he wondered at the stillness prevalent; the very house seemed in awe.

Ere long another official entered, and after apologizing for introducing himself, said: "I am Dean of the Court. In the absence of my lord Phranza, it has fallen to me to discharge, well as I can, the duties of Grand Chamberlain."

The Prince, observant of the scrutinizing glance the Dean gave his person, acknowledged the honor done him, and the pleasure he derived from the acquaintance. The Dean ought to be happy; he had great fame in the city and abroad as a most courteous, intelligent, and faithful servant; there was no doubt he deserved preeminently the confidence his royal master reposed in him.

"I am come, O Prince," the old functionary said, after thanks for the friendly words, "to ascertain if you are refreshed, and ready for the audience."

"I am ready."

"Let us to His Majesty then. If I precede you, I pray pardon."

Drawing the portiere aside, the Dean held it for the other's passage.

They entered an extensive inner court, surrounded on three sides by a gallery resting on pillars. On the fourth side, a magnificent staircase ascended to a main landing, whence, parting right and left, it terminated in the gallery. Floor, stairs, balustrading, pillars, everything here was red marble flooded with light from a circular aperture in the roof open to the sky.

Along the stairs, at intervals, officers armed and in armor were stationed, and keeping their positions faced inwardly, they seemed like statues. Other armed men were in the galleries. The silence was impressive. Coming presently to an arched door, the Prince glanced into a deep chamber, and at the further end of it beheld the Emperor seated in a chair of state on a dais curtained and canopied with purple velvet.

"Take heed now, O Prince," said the Dean, in a low voice. "Yonder is His Majesty. Do thou imitate me in all things. Come."

With this kindly caution the Dean led into the chamber of public audience. Just within the door, he halter, crossed hands upon his breast, and dropped to his knees, his eyes downcast; rising, he kept on about halfway to the dais, and again knelt; when near his person's length from the dais, he knelt and fully prostrated himself. The Prince punctiliously executed every motion, except that at the instant of halting the last time he threw both hands up after the manner of Orientals. A velvet carpet of the accepted imperial color stretched from door to dais greatly facilitated the observances.

A statuesque soldier, with lance and shield, stood at the left of the dais, a guard against treachery; by the chair, bare-headed, bare-legged, otherwise a figure in a yellow tunic lightly breastplated, appeared the sword-bearer, his slippers stayed with bands of gold, a blade clasped to his body by the left forearm, the hilt above his shoulder; and spacious as the chamber was, a row of dignitaries civil, military, and ecclesiastical lined the walls each in prescribed regalia. The hush already noticed was observable here, indicative of rigid decorum and awful reverence. "Rise, Prince of India," the Emperor said, without movement.

The visitor obeyed.

The last of the Palaeologae was in Basilean costume; a golden circlet on his head brilliantly jewelled and holding a purple velvet cap in place; an overgown of the material of the cap but darker in tint, and belted at the waist; a mantle stiff with embroidery of pearls hanging by narrow bands so as to drop from the shoulder over the breast and back, leaving the neck bare; an ample lap-robe of dark purple cloth sparkling with precious stones covering his nether limbs. The chair was square in form without back or arms; its front posts twined and intricately inlaid with ivory and silver, and topped each with a golden cone for hand-rest. The bareness of the neck was relieved by four strings of pearls dropped from the circlet two on a side, and drawn from behind the ears forward so as to lightly tip the upper edge of the mantle. The right hand rested at the moment on the right cone of the chair; the left was free. The attitude of the figure thus presented was easy and unconstrained, the countenance high and noble, and altogether the guest admitted to himself that he had seldom been introduced to royalty more really imposing.

There was hardly an instant allowed for these observations. To set his guest at ease, Constantine continued: "The way to our door is devious and upward. I hope it has not too severely tried you."

"Your Majesty, were the road many times more trying I would willingly brave it to be the recipient of honors and attentions which have made the Emperor of Constantinople famous in many far countries, and not least in mine."

The courtierly turn of the reply did not escape the Emperor. It had been strange if he had not put the character of his guest to question; indeed, an investigation had proceeded by his order, with the invitation to audience as a result; and now the self-possession of the stranger, together with his answer, swept the last doubt from, the imperial mind. An attendant, responding to a sign, came forward.

"Bring me wine," and as the servant disappeared with the order, Constantine again addressed his visitor. "You maybe a Brahman or an Islamite," he said, with a pleasant look to cover any possible mistake: "in either case, O Prince, I take it for granted that the offer of a draught of Chian will not be resented."

"I am neither a Mohammedan, nor a devotee of the gentle son of Maya. I am not even a Hindoo in religion. My faith leads me to be thankful for all God's gifts to his creatures. I will take the cup Your Majesty deigns to propose."

The words were spoken with childlike simplicity of manner; yet nowhere in these pages have we had a finer example of the subtlety which, characteristic of the speaker, seemed inspiration rather than study. He knew from general report how religion dominated his host, and on the spur of the moment, thought to pique curiosity with respect to his own faith; seeing, as he fancied, a clear path to another audience, with ampler opportunity to submit and discuss the idea of Universal Brotherhood in God.

The glance with which he accompanied assent to the cup was taken as a mere accentuation of gratitude; it was, however, for discovery. Had the Emperor noticed the declaration of what he was not? Did his intelligence suggest how unusual it was for an Indian to be neither a Mohammedan, nor a Brahman, nor even a Buddhist in religion? He saw a sudden lifting of the brows, generally the preliminary of a question; he even made an answer ready; but the other's impulse seemed to spend itself in an inquiring look, which, lingering slightly, might mean much or nothing. The Prince resolved to wait.

Constantine, as will be seen presently, did observe the negations, and was moved to make them the subject of remark at the moment; but inordinately sensitive respecting his own religious convictions, he imagined others like himself in that respect, and upon the scruple, for which the reader will not fail to duly credit him, deferred inquiry until the visitor was somewhat better understood.

Just then the cupbearer appeared with the wine; a girlish lad he was, with long blond curls. Kneeling before the dais, he rested a silver platter and the liquor sparkling on it in a crystal decanter upon his right knee, waiting the imperial pleasure.

Taking the sign given him, the Dean stepped forward and filled the two cups of chased gold also on the platter, and delivered them. Then the Emperor held his cup up while he said in a voice sufficiently raised for general hearing:

"Prince of India, I desired your presence to-day the rather to discharge myself of obligations for important assistance rendered my kinswoman, the Princess Irene of Therapia, during her detention at the White Castle; a circumstance of such late occurrence it must be still fresh in your memory. By her account the Governor was most courteous and hospitable, and exerted himself to make her stay in his stronghold agreeable as possible. Something truly extraordinary, considering the forbidding exterior of the house, and the limited means of entertainment it must have to offer, she declared he succeeded in converting what threatened to be a serious situation into an adventure replete with pleasant surprises. A delegate is now at the Castle assuring the Governor of my appreciation of his friendly conduct. By her account, also, I am bounden to you, Prince, scarcely less than to him."

The gravity of the visitor at hearing this was severely attacked. Great as was his self-control, he smiled at thought of the dilemma the Governor was in, listening to a speech of royal thanks and receiving rich presents in lieu of his young master Mahommed. When the envoy returned and reported, if perchance he should describe the Turk whom he found in actual keeping of the Castle, the discrepancy between his picture of the man and that of the Princess would be both mysterious and remarkable.

"Your Majesty," the Prince returned, with a deprecating gesture, "the storm menaced me quite as much as the Princess, and calls for confession of my inability to see wherein I rendered her service free of regard for myself. Indeed, it is my duty to inform Your Majesty, all these noble witnesses hearing me, that I am more beholden to your noble kinswoman for help and deliverance in the affair than she can be to me. But for the courage and address, not to mention the dignity and force with which she availed herself of her royal relationship, resolving what was at first a simple invitation to refuge into a high treaty between the heads of two great powers, I and my daughter"—

"Daughter, said you?"

"Yes, Your Majesty—Heaven has so favored me—I, my daughter, and my frightened boatmen would have been committed to the river near the Castle, without recourse except in prayer to Heaven. Nay, Your Majesty, have I permission to say on, Charity had never a sweeter flowering than when the Princess remembered to take the stranger under her protection. I am past the age of enthusiasm and extravagance—my beard and dimming eyes prove the admission—yet I declare, weighing each word, she has the wit, the spirit, the goodness, the loveliness to be the noblest of queens to the best of kings; and fails she such choice, it will be because destiny has been struck by some unaccountable forgetfulness."

By this time the courtiers, drawn in from the walls, composed a very brilliant circle around the throne, each one curious to hear the stranger as he had been to see him; and they were quick to point his last sentence; for most of them had been with the Emperor in the voyage to Therapia, which was still a theme of wager and wrangle scarcely less interesting than in its first hour. By one impulse they ventured a glance at the royal face, seeking a revelation; but the countenance was steady as a mask.

"The encomium is well bestowed, and approves thy experience, Prince, as a reader of women," Constantine said, with just enough fervor. "Henceforth

I shall know the degree of trust to repose in thy judgment, other problems as difficult being in controversy. Nevertheless, is the lady to be believed, then, O Prince, I repeat my acknowledgment of indebtedness. It pleases me to greatly estimate thy influence and good judgment happily exerted. Mayst thou live long, Prince of India, and always find thyself as now among friends who charge themselves to be watchful for opportunities to befriend thee."

He raised the cup.

"It is Your Majesty's pleasure," the guest replied, and they drank together.

"A seat for the Prince of India," the Emperor next directed.

The chair, when brought, was declined.

"In my palace—for at home I exercise the functions of a king—it often falls to me to give audiences; if public, we call them *durbars;* and then an inferior may not sit in my presence. The rule, like all governing the session, is of my own enactment. I see plainly how greatly Your Majesty designs to heap me with honors; and if I dare decline this one, it is not from disposition to do a teacher's part, but from habit which has the sanction of heredity, and the argument self addressed: Shall I despise my own ordinances? God forbid!"

A murmur from the concourse was distinctly audible, which the Dean interpreted by repeated affirmative nods. In other words, by this stroke the able visitor won the court as he had already won its head; insomuch that the most doubting of the doubters would not have refused to certify him on belief the very Prince of India he claimed to be. The Emperor, on his part, could not but defer to scruples so cogently and solemnly put; at the same time, out of his very certainty respecting the guest, he passed to a question which in probability the reader has been for some time entertaining.

"The makers of a law should be first to observe it; for having done so, they then have God's license to exert themselves in its enforcement; and when one is found observant of a principle which has root so perceptibly in conscience, to deny him his pleasure were inexcusable. Have thy will, Prince."

The applause which greeted the decision of His Majesty was hardly out of ear when he proceeded:

"Again I pray you, Sir Guest—I greatly misapprehend the travellers who tell of India, if the people of that venerable country are not given to ceremonials religious as well as secular. Many of our own observances of a sacred nature are traceable to study and discernment of the good effects of form in worship, and since some of them are unquestionably borrowed from temples of the Pagan gods, yet others may be of Hindoo origin. Who shall say? Wherefore, speaking generally, I should fear to ask you to any of our Church mysteries which I did not know were purely Greek. One such we have this evening. We call it *Pannychides*. Its principal feature is a procession of monastic brethren from the holy houses of the city and Islands—all within the jurisdiction of our Eastern Church, which, please God, is of broader lines than our State. The fathers have been assembling for the celebration several days. They will form in the city at set of sun, throwing the march into the night. Here, within our grounds, more particularly at the door of the Chapel of our Holy Virgin of Blacherne, I will meet them. They will pass the night in prayer, an army on bended knees, sorrowing for the pains of our Saviour in Gethsemane. I was uncertain what faith you profess; yet, Prince, I thought—forgive me, if it was an error—a sight of the spirit of our Churchmen as it will be manifested on this occasion might prove interesting to you; so I have taken the liberty of ordering a stand erected for your accommodation at a position favorable to witnessing the procession in movement up the terraces. No one has seen the spectacle without realizing as never before the firmness of the hold Christ has taken upon the souls of men." The last words startled the Prince. Christ's hold upon the souls of men! The very thing he wanted to learn, and, if possible, measure. A cloud of thoughts fell about him; yet he kept clear head, and answered quietly:

"Your Majesty has done me great kindness. I am already interested in the Mystery. Since we cannot hope ever to behold God with these mortal eyes, the nearest amend for the deprivation is the privilege of seeing men in multitudes demonstrating their love of Him."

Constantine's eyes lingered on the Prince's face. The utterances attracted him. The manner was so artfully reverential as not to leave a suspicion of the guile behind it. Going down great galleries, every one has had his attention suddenly arrested; he pauses, looks, and looks again, then wakes to find the attraction was not a picture, but only a flash within his own mind. So, with the guest before him, the Emperor was thinking of the man rather than seeing him—thinking of him with curiosity fully awakened, and a desire to know him better. And had he followed up the desire, he would have found its source in the idea that India was a region in which reflection and psychological experiment had been exhausted—where if one appeared with a thought it turned old ere it could be explained—where wisdom had fructified until there was no knowledge more—where the teaching capacity was all there was remaining. That is to say, in the day of the last Byzantine Emperor, centuries ago, humanity in India was, as now, a clock stopped, but stopped in the act of striking, leaving a glory in the air imaginable like the continuing sound of hushed cathedral bells.

"Prince," he at length said, "you will remain here until the procession is announced at the Grand Gate. I will then give you a guide and a guard. Our steward has orders to look after your comfort." Turning then to the acting Chamberlain, he added: "Good Dean, have we not a little time in which to hear our guest further?"

"Your Majesty, an hour at least."

"You hear, O Prince? Provided always that it be not to your displeasure, tell me what I am to understand by the disclaimer which, broadly interpreted, leaves you either a Jew or a Christian?"

CHAPTER III
THE NEW FAITH PROCLAIMED

The question came earlier than the Prince expected, and in different form. Those in position to observe his face saw it turn a trifle pale, and he hesitated, and glanced around uneasily, as though not altogether assured of his footing. This might have been by-play; if so, it was successful; every countenance not sympathetic was serious.

"Your Majesty's inquiry must be for information. I am too humble for an unfriendly design on the part of one so exalted as the Emperor of Constantinople. It might be otherwise if I represented a church, a denomination, or a recognized religion; as it is, my faith is my own."

"But bethink thee, Prince, thou mayst have the truth—the very God's truth," Constantine interposed, with kindly intent. "We all know thy country hath been the cradle of divine ideas. So, speak, and fear not."

The glance the Emperor received was winsomely grateful.

"Indeed, Your Majesty, indeed I have need of good countenance. The question put me has lured more men to bloody graves than fire, sword and wave together. And then why I believe as I believe demands time in excess of what we have; and I am the bolder in this because in limiting me Your Majesty limits yourself. So I will now no more than define my Faith. But first, it does not follow from my disclaimer that I can only be a Jew or a Christian; for as air is a vehicle for a multitude of subtleties in light, faith in like manner accommodates a multitude of opinions."

While speaking, the Prince's voice gradually gained strength; his color returned, and his eyes enlarged and shone with strange light. Now his right hand arose, the fingers all closed except the first one, and it was long and thin, and he waved it overhead, like a conjuring wand. If the concourse had been unwilling to hear him, they could not have turned away.

"I am not a Hindoo, my Lord; because I cannot believe men can make their own gods."

The Father Confessor to the Emperor, at the left of the dais in a stole of gold and crimson cloth, smiled broadly.

"I am not a Buddhist," the Prince continued; "because I cannot believe the soul goes to nothingness after death."

The Father Confessor clapped his hands.

"I am not a Confucian; because I cannot reduce religion to philosophy or elevate philosophy into religion."

The blood of the audience began to warm.

"I am not a Jew; because I believe God loves all peoples alike, or if he makes distinctions, it is for righteousness' sake."

Here the chamber rang with clapping.

"I am not an Islamite; because when I raise my eyes to Heaven, I cannot tolerate sight of a man standing between me and God—no, my Lord, not though he be a Prophet."

The hit was palpable, and from hate of the old enemy, the whole assemblage broke into an uproar of acclamation. Only the Emperor kept his gravity. Leaning heavily on the golden cone at the right of his chair, his chin depressed, his eyes staring, scarcely breathing, he waited, knowing, that having gone so far, there was before the speaker an unavoidable climax; and seeing it in his face, and coming, he presently aroused, and motioned for silence.

"I am not"—

The Prince stopped, but when the hush was deepest went on—"I am not a Christian; because—because I believe—God is God."

The Father Confessor's hands were ready to clap, but they stayed so; the same spell took hold of the bystanders, except that they looked at the Emperor, and he alone seemed to comprehend the concluding phrase. He settled back easily in his seat, saying, "Thy Faith then is—"

"God!"

The monosyllable was the Prince's.

And with clear sight of the many things reprobated—Images, Saints, the Canonized, even the worship of Christ and the Holy Mother—with clear sight also of the wisdom which in that presence bade the guest stop with the mighty name—at the same time more curious than ever to hear in full discourse the man who could reduce religion to a single word and leave it comprehensible, Constantine drew a breath of relief, and said, smiling, "Of a surety, O Prince, there was never a Faith which, with such appearance of simplicity in definition, is capable of such infinity of meaning. I am full of questions; and these listening, my lords of the court, are doubtless in a similar mood. What sayest thou, O my most orthodox Confessor?" The Father bowed until the hem of his blazing stole overlaid the floor.

"Your Majesty, we too are believers in God; but we also believe in much beside; so, if but for comparison of creeds, which is never unprofitable while in good nature, I should like to hear the noble and fair speaking guest further."

"And you, my Lords?"

The throng around answered, "Yes, yes!"

"We will have it so then. Look, good Logothete, for the nearest day unoccupied."

A handsome man of middle age approached the dais, and opening a broad-backed book, evidently the record of the royal appointments, turned a number of leaves, and replied: "Your Majesty, two weeks from tomorrow."

"Note the same set aside for the Prince of India.-Dost hear, Prince?"

The latter lowered his face the better to conceal his pleasure.

"All days are alike to me," he answered.

"In this our palace, then—two weeks from to-morrow at the hour of noon. And now"—the rustle and general movement of the courtiers was instantly stayed—"and now, Prince, didst thou not speak of exercising the functions of a king at home? Thy capital must be in India, but where, pray? And how callest thou thyself? And why is this city so fortunate as to have attracted thy wandering feet? It is not every king so his own master as to turn traveller, and go about making study of the world; although, I admit, it would be better could every king do so."

These questions were rapidly put, but as the Prince was prepared for them, he responded pleasantly:

"In answering the questions Your Majesty now honors me with. I am aware how serious the mistake would be did I think of your curiosity alone. A most excellent quality in a great man is patience. Alas, that it should be one of the most abused! ... Among the oldest of Hindoo titles is *Rajah*. It means King rather than Prince, and I was born to it. Your Majesty may have heard of Oodeypoor, the bosom jewel of Rajpootana, the white rose just bloomed of Indian cities. At the foot of a spur of the Arawalli mountains, a river rises, and on its right bank reposes the city; from which, southeast a little way, a lake lies outspread, like a mirror fallen face upward. And around the lake are hills, tall and broken as these of the Bosphorus; and seen from the water the hills are masses of ivy and emerald woods thickly sprinkled with old fortresses and temples, and seven-roofed red pagodas, each the home of a great gold-decked Buddha, with lesser Buddhas in family. And in the lake are islands all palaces springing from the water line in open arches, and sculptured walls, and towered gates; and of still days their wondrous cunning in the air is renewed afresh in the waveless depths below them. If they are glorious then, what are they when reconstructed for festal nights in shining lamps? For be it said, my Lord, if a stranger in the walls of this centre of empire may speak a word which has the faintest savor of criticism, the Indian genius analyzed beauty before there was a West, and taking suggestions from spark and dewdrop, applied them to architecture. Smile not, I pray, for you may see the one in the lamp multiplied for outline traceries, and the other in the fountain, the cascade, and the limpid margin at the base of walls. Or if still you think me exaggerating, is not the offence one to be lightly forgiven where the offender is telling of his birthplace? In one of the palaces of that Lake of Palaces I was born, the oldest son of the Rajah of Meywar, Oodeypoor his capital. In these words, which I hope may be kindly judged, Your Majesty will find answers to one, if not two of the questions you were pleased to ask me—Why I am here? And why making study of the world? Will Your Majesty pardon my boldness, if I suggest that a reply to those inquiries would be better at the audience set for me next? I fear it is too long for telling now."

"Be it so," said Constantine, "yet a hint of it may not be amiss. It may set us to thinking; and, Prince, a mind prepared for an idea is like ground broken and harrowed for seed."

The Prince hesitated.

"Your Majesty—my Lord"—he then said firmly, "the most sorrowful of men are those with conceptions too great for them, and which they must carry about with nothing better to sustain their sinking spirits than a poor hope of having them one day adopted; for until that day they are like a porter overladen and going from house to house unknowing the name of the owner of his burden or where to look for him. I am such an unfortunate.... Oodeypoor, you must understand, is more than comely to the eye of a native; it is a city where all religions are tolerated. The Taing, the Brahman, the Hindoo, the Mohammedan, the Buddhist live together there, protected and in peace, with their worship and houses of worship; nor is there any shutting of mouths, because controversy long since attained finality amongst them; or perhaps it were better saying, because opinions there have now their recognized grooves, and run in them from generation to generation—opinions to which men are born as to their property, only without right of change or modification; neither can they break away from them. There is no excuse if an intelligent man in such a situation does not comprehend all the religions thus in daily practice; or if one does comprehend them he should not flatter himself possessed of any superior intellect.... The Rajah, my father, died, and I mounted his silver throne, and for ten years administered justice in the Hall of Durbars to which he had been used, he and his father's father, Children of the Sun, most pure of blood. By that time I was of mature mind, and having given myself up to study, came to believe there is but one doctrine—principle—call it what you will, my Lord—but one of heavenly origin—one primarily comprehensible by all—too simple indeed to satisfy the egotism of men; wherefore, without rejecting, they converted it into a foundation, and built upon it each according to his vanity, until, in course of ages, the foundation was overlaid with systems of belief, childish, unnatural, ridiculous, indecent, or else too complicated for common understanding"—

"This principle—what is it, Prince?" Constantine asked nervously.

"Your Majesty, I have already once named it."

"Mean you God?"

"And now, my Lord, thou hast pronounced it."

The stillness in the chamber was very deep. Every man seemed to be asking, what next?

"One day, Your Majesty—it was in my tenth year of government—a function was held in a tent erected for the purpose—a *shamiana* vastly larger than any hall. I went up to it in state, passing through lines of elephants, an hundred on either hand, covered with cloth of gold and with houdahs of yellow silk roofed with the glory of peacocks. Behind the mighty brutes soldiery blotted out the landscape, and the air between them and the sky was a tawny cloud of flaunting yak-tails; nor had one use for ears, so was he deafened by beat of drums and blowing of brazen horns twice a tall man's height. I sat on a throne of silver and gold, all my ministers present. My brother entered, he the next entitled. Halfway down the aisle of chiefs I met him, and then led him to my seat, and saluted him Rajah of Meywar. Your Majesty, so I parted with crown and title—laid them down voluntarily to search the world for men in power in love with God enough to accept him as their sum of faith. Behold why I travel making the earth a study! Behold why I am in Constantinople!"

Constantine was impressed.

"Where hast thou been?" he at length asked—"where before coming here?"

"It were easier did Your Majesty ask where I have not been. For then I could answer, Everywhere, except Rome."

"Dost thou impugn our devotion to God?"

"Not so, not so, my Lord! I am seeking to know the degree of your love of Him."

"How, Prince?"

"By a test."

"What test?"

No man listening could have said what mood the Emperor was in; yet the guest replied with an appearance of rising courage: "A trial, to find all the other things entering into Faith which Your Majesty and Your Majesty's lords and subjects are willing to lay down for God's sake."

With a peremptory gesture Constantine silenced the stir and rustle in the chamber. "It is right boldly put," he said.

"But none the less respectfully. My Lord, I am striving to be understood."

"You speak of a trial. To what end?"

"One Article of Faith, the all-essential of Universal Brotherhood in Religion."

"A magnificent conception! But is it practicable?"

Fortunately or unfortunately for the Prince, an officer that moment made way through the courtiers, and whispered to the Dean, who at once addressed himself to the Emperor.

"I pray pardon, but it pleased Your Majesty to bid me notify you when it is time to make ready for the Mystery to-night. The hour is come; besides which a messenger from Scholarius waits for an interview."

Constantine arose.

"Thanks, worthy Dean," he said; "we will not detain the messenger. The audience is dismissed."

Then descending from the dais, he gave his hand to the Prince. "I see the idea you have in mind, and it is worthy the bravest effort. I shall look forward to the next audience with concern. Forget not that the guestship continues. My steward will take you in charge. Farewell."

The Prince, sinking to his knees, kissed the offered hand, whereupon the Emperor said as if just reminded: "Was not your daughter with my kinswoman in the White Castle?"

"Your Majesty, the Princess on that occasion most graciously consented to accept my daughter as her attendant."

"Were she to continue in the same attendance, Prince, we might hope to have her at court some day."

"I lay many thanks at Your Majesty's feet. She is most honored by the suggestion." Constantine in lead of his officers then passed out, while, in care of the steward, the Prince was conducted to the reception room, and served with refreshments. Afterwhile through the windows he beheld the day expiring, and the first audience finished, and the second appointed, he was free to think of the approaching Mystery.

Be it said now he was easy in feeling—satisfied with the management of his cause—satisfied with the impression he had made on the Emperor and the court as well. Had not the latter applauded and voted to hear him again? When taken with the care habitually observed by leading personages in audiences formal as that just passed, how broadly sympathetic the expressions of the monarch had been.

In great cheerfulness the Prince ate and drank, and even occupied the wine-colored leisure conning an argument for the occasion in prospect—noon, next day two weeks! And more clearly than ever his scheme seemed good. Could he carry it through—could he succeed—the good would be recognized—never a doubt of that. If men were sometimes blind, God was always just.

In thought he sped forward of the coming appointment, and saw himself not only the apostle of the reform, but the chosen agent, the accredited go-between of Constantine and the young Mahommed. He remembered the points of negotiation between them. He would not require the Turk to yield the prophetic character of Mahomet; neither should the Byzantine's faith in Christ suffer curtailment; he would ask them, however, to agree to a new relation between Mahomet and Christ on the one side and God on the other—that, namely, long conceded, as having existed between God and Elijah. And then, an article of the utmost materiality, the very soul of the recast religion, he would insist that they obligate themselves to worship God alone, worship being His exclusive prerogative, and that this condition of exclusive worship be prescribed the only test of fraternity in religion; all other worship to be punishable as heresy. Nor stopped he with Mahommed and Constantine; he doubted not bringing the Rabbis to such a treaty. How almost identical it was with the Judaism of Moses. The Bishop of Rome might protest. What matter? Romanism segregated must die. And so the isms of the Brahman and the Hindoo, so the Buddhist, the Confucian, the Mencian—they would all perish under the hammering of the union. Then, too, Time would make the work perfect, and gradually wear Christ and Mahomet out of mind—he and Time together. What if the task did take ages? He had an advantage over other reformers—he could keep his reform in motion—he could guide and direct it—he could promise himself life to see it in full acceptance. In the exuberance of triumphant feeling, he actually rejoiced in his doom, and for the moment imagined it more than a divine mercy.

CHAPTER IV
THE PANNYCHIDES

An invitation from the Emperor to remain and view the procession marching up the heights of Blacherne had been of itself a compliment; but the erection of a stand for the Prince turned the compliment into a personal honor. To say truth, however, he really desired to see the Pannychides, or in plain parlance, the Vigils. He had often heard of them as of prodigious effect upon the participants. Latterly they had fallen into neglect; and knowing how difficult it is to revive a dying custom, he imagined the spectacle would be poor and soon over. While reflecting on it, he looked out of the window and was surprised to see the night falling. He yielded then to restlessness, until suddenly an idea arose and absorbed him.

Suppose the Emperor won to his scheme; was its success assured? So used was he to thinking of the power of kings and emperors as the sole essential to the things he proposed that in this instance he had failed to concede importance to the Church; and probably he would have gone on in the delusion but for the Mysteries which were now to pass before him. They forced him to think of the power religious organizations exercise over men.

And this Church—this old Byzantine Church! Ay, truly! The Byzantine conscience was under its direction; it was the Father Confessor of the Empire; its voice in the common ear was the voice of God. To cast Christ out of its system would be like wrenching a man's heart out of his body. It was here and there—everywhere in fact—in signs, trophies, monuments—in crosses and images—in monasteries, convents, houses to the Saints, houses to the Mother. What could the Emperor do, if it were obstinate and defiant? The night beheld through the window crept into the Wanderer's heart, and threatened to put out the light kindled there by the new-born hope with which he had come from the audience.

"The Church, the Church! It is the enemy I have to fear," he kept muttering in dismal repetition, realizing, for the first time, the magnitude of the campaign before him. With a wisdom in wickedness which none of his successors in design have shown, he saw the Christian idea in the bosom of the Church unassailable except a substitute satisfactory to its professors could be found. Was God a sufficient substitute? Perhaps—and he turned cold with the reflection—the Pannychides were bringing him an answer. It was an ecclesiastical affair, literally a meeting of Churchmen *en masse*. Where—when—how could the Church present itself to any man more an actuality in the flesh? Perhaps—and a chill set his very crown to crawling—

perhaps the opportunity to study the spectacle was more a mercy of God than a favor of Constantine.

To his great relief, at length the officer who had escorted him from the Grand Gate came into the room.

"I am to have the honor," he said, cheerfully, "of conducting you to the stand His Majesty has prepared that you may at ease behold the Mysteries appointed for the night. The head of the procession is reported appearing. If it please you, Prince of India, we will set out."

"I am ready."

The position chosen for the Prince was on the right bank of a cut through which the road passed on its ascent from the arched gateway by the Chapel to the third terrace, and he was borne thither in his sedan.

Upon alighting, he found himself on a platform covered by a canopy, carpeted and furnished with one chair comfortably cushioned. At the right of the chair there was a pyramid of coals glowing in a brazier, and lest that might not be a sufficient provision against the damps of the hours, a great cloak was near at hand. In front of the platform he observed a pole securely planted and bearing a basket of inflammables ready for conversion into a torch. In short, everything needful to his well-being, including wine and water on a small tripod, was within reach.

Before finally seating himself the Prince stepped out to the brow of the terrace, whence he noticed the Chapel below him in the denser darkness of the trees about it like a pool. The gleam of armor on the area by the Grand Gate struck him with sinister effect. Flowers saluted him with perfume, albeit he could not see them. Not less welcome was the low music with which the brook cheered itself while dancing down to the harbor. Besides a cresset burning on the landing outside the Port entrance, two other lights were visible; one on the Pharos, the other on the great Galata tower, looking in the distance like large stars. With these exceptions, the valley and the hill opposite Blacherne, and the wide-reaching Metropolis beyond them, were to appearances a blacker cloud dropped from the clouded sky. A curious sound now came to him from the direction of the city. Was it a rising wind? Or a muffled roll from the sea? While wondering, some one behind him said:

"They are coming."

The voice was sepulchral and harsh, and the Prince turned quickly to the speaker.

"Ah, Father Theophilus!"

"They are coming," the Father repeated.

The Prince shivered slightly. The noise beyond the valley arose more distinctly.

"Are they singing?" he asked.

"Chanting," the other answered.

"Why do they chant?"

"Knowest thou our Scriptures?"

The Wanderer quieted a disdainful impulse, and answered:

"I have read them."

The Father continued:

"Presently thou wilt hear the words of Job: 'Oh, that thou wouldst hide me in the grave, that thou wouldst keep me in secret, until thy wrath be past, that thou wouldst appoint me a set time and remember me.'"

The Prince was startled. Why was one in speech so like a ghost selected his companion? And that verse, of all to him most afflicting, and which in hours of despair he had repeated until his very spirit had become colored with its reproachful plaint—who put it in the man's mouth?

The chant came nearer. Of melody it had nothing; nor did those engaged in it appear in the slightest attentive to time. Yet it brought relief to the Prince, willing as he was to admit he had never heard anything similar— anything so sorrowful, so like the wail of the damned in multitude. And rueful as the strain was, it helped him assign the pageant a near distance, a middle distance, and then interminability.

"There appear to be a great many of them," he remarked to the Father.

"More than ever before in the observance," was the reply.

"Is there a reason for it?"

"Our dissensions."

The Father did not see the pleased expression of his auditor's face, but proceeded: "Yes, our dissensions. They multiply. At first the jar was between the Church and the throne; now it is the Church against the Church—a Roman party and a Greek party. One man among us has concentrated in himself the learning and devotion of the Christian East. You will see him directly, George Scholarius. By visions, like those in which the old prophets received the counsel of God, he was instructed to revive the *Pannychides*. His messengers have gone hither and thither, to the monasteries, the convents, and the eremitic colonies wherever accessible. The greater the presence, he says, the greater the influence."

"Scholarius is a wise man," the Prince said, diplomatically.

"His is the wisdom of the Prophets," the Father answered.

"Is he the Patriarch?"

"No, the Patriarch is of the Roman party—Scholarius of the Greek."

"And Constantine?"

"A good king, truly, but, alas; he is cumbered with care of the State."

"Yes, yes," said the Prince. "And the care leads to neglect of his soul. Kings are sometimes to be pitied. But there is then a special object in the Vigils?"

"The Vigils to-night are for the restoration of the unities once more, that the Church may find peace and the State its power and glory again. God is in the habit of taking care of His own."

"Thank you, Father, I see the difference. Scholarius would intrust the State to the Holy Virgin; but Constantine, with a worldlier inspiration, adheres to the craft held by Kings immemorially. The object of the Vigils is to bring the Emperor to abandon his policy and defer to Scholarius?"

"The Emperor assists in the Mystery," the Father answered, vaguely.

The procession meantime came on, and when its head appeared in front of the Grand Gate three trumpeters blew a flourish which called the guards into line. A monk advanced and held parley with an officer; after which he was given a lighted torch, and passed under the portal in lead of the multitude. The trumpeters continued plying their horns, marking the slow ascent.

"Were this an army," said Father Theophilus, "it would not be so laborious; but, alas! the going of youth is nowhere so rapid as in a cloister; nor is age anywhere so feeble. Ten years kneeling on a stony floor in a damp cell brings the anchorite to forget he ever walked with ease."

The Prince scarcely heard him; he was interested in the little to be seen crossing the area below—a column four abreast, broken into unequal divisions, each division with a leader, who, at the gate, received a torch. Occasionally a square banner on a cross-stick appeared—occasionally a section in light-colored garments; more frequently a succession of heads without covering of any kind; otherwise the train was monotonously rueful, and in its slow movement out of the darkness reminded the spectator on the height of a serpent crawling endlessly from an underground den. Afterwhile the dim white of the pavement was obscured by masses stationary on the right and left of the column; these were the people stopping there because for them there was no further pursuit of the spectral parade.

The horns gave sonorous notice of the progress during the ascent. Now they were passing along the first terrace; still the divisions were incessant down by the gate—still the chanting continued, a dismal dissonance in the distance, a horrible discord near by. If it be true that the human voice is music's aptest instrument, it is also true that nothing vocalized in nature can excel it in the expression of diabolism.

Suddenly the first torch gleamed on the second terrace scarce an hundred yards from the Chapel.

"See him now there, behind the trumpeters—Scholarius!" said Father Theophilus, with a semblance of animation.

"He with the torch?"

"Ay!—And he might throw the torch away, and still be the light of the Church."

The remark did not escape the Prince. The man who could so impress himself upon a member of the court must be a power with his brethren of the gown generally. Reflecting thus, the discerning visitor watched the figure stalking on under the torch. There are men who are causes in great events, sometimes by superiority of nature, sometimes by circumstances. What if this were one of them? And forthwith the observer ceased fancying the mystical looking monk drawing the interminable train after him by the invisible bonds of a will mightier than theirs in combination—the fancy became a fact. "The procession will not stop at the Chapel," the Father said; "but keep on to the palace, where the Emperor will join it. If my Lord cares to see the passage distinctly, I will fire the basket here."

"Do so," the Prince replied.

The flambeau was fired.

It shed light over the lower terraces right and left, and brought the palace in the upper space into view from the base of the forward building to the Tower of Isaac; and here, close by, the Chapel with all its appurtenances, paved enclosure, speeding brook, solemn cypresses, and the wall and arched gateway at the hither side stood out in almost daytime clearness. The road in the cut underfoot must bring the frocked host near enough to expose its spirit.

The bellowing of the horns frightened the birds at roost in the melancholy grove, and taking wing, they flew blindly about.

Then ensued the invasion of the enclosure in front of the Chapel—Scholarius next the musicians. The Prince saw him plainly; a tall man, stoop-shouldered, angular as a skeleton; his hood thrown back; head tonsured; the whiteness of the scalp conspicuous on account of the band of black hair at the base; the features high and thin, cheeks hollow, temples pinched. The dark brown cassock, leaving an attenuated neck completely exposed, hung from his frame apparently much too large for it. His feet disdained sandals. At the brook he halted, and letting the crucifix fall from his right hand, he stooped and dipped the member thus freed into the water, and rising flung the drops in air. Resuming the crucifix, he marched on.

It cannot be said there was admiration in the steady gaze with which the Prince kept the monk in eye; the attraction was stronger—he was looking for a sign from him. He saw the tall, nervous figure cross the brook with a faltering, uncertain step, pass the remainder of the pavement, the torch in one hand, the holy symbol in the other; then it disappeared under the arch of the gate; and when it had come through, the sharp espial was beforehand with it, and waiting. It commenced ascending the acute grade—now it was in the cut—and now, just below the Prince, it had but to look up, and its face would be on a level with his feet. At exactly the right moment, Scholarius did look up, and—stop.

The interchange of glances between the men was brief, and can be likened to nothing so aptly as sword blades crossing in a red light.

Possibly the monk, trudging on, his mind intent upon something which was part of a scene elsewhere, or on the objects and results of the solemnities in celebration, as yet purely speculative, might have been disagreeably surprised at discovering himself the subject of study by a stranger whose dress proclaimed him a foreigner; possibly the Prince's stare, which we have already seen was at times powerfully magnetic, filled him with aversion and resentment; certain it is he raised his head, showing a face full of abhorrence, and at the same time waved the crucifix as if in exorcism.

The Prince had time to see the image thus presented was of silver on a cross of ivory wrought to wonderful realism. The face was dying, not dead; there were the spikes in the hands and feet, the rent in the side, the crown of thorns, and overhead the initials of the inscription: This is the King of the Jews. There was the worn, buffeted, bloodspent body, and the lips were parted so it was easy to think the sufferer in mid-utterance of one of the exclamations which have placed his Divinity forever beyond successful denial. The swift reversion of memory excited in the beholder might have been succeeded by remorse, but for the cry:

"Thou enemy of Jesus Christ—avaunt!"

It was the voice of Scholarius, shrill and high; and before the Prince could recover from the shock, before he could make answer, or think of answering, the visionary was moving on; nor did he again look back.

"What ails thee, Prince?"

The sepulchral tone of Father Theophilus was powerful over the benumbed faculties of His Majesty's guest; and he answered with a question:

"Is not thy friend Scholarius a great preacher?"

"On his lips the truth is most unctuous."

"It must be so—it must be so! For"—the Prince's manner was as if he were settling a grave altercation in his own mind—"for never did a man offer me the Presence so vitalized in an image. I am not yet sure but he gave me to see the Holy Son of the Immaculate Mother in flesh and blood exactly as when they put Him so cruelly to death. Or can it be, Father, that the effect upon me was in greater measure due to the night, the celebration, the cloud of ministrants, the serious objects of the Vigils?"

The answer made Father Theophilus happy as a man of his turn could be—he was furnished additional evidence of the spiritual force of Scholarius, his ideal.

"No," he answered, "it was God in the man."

All this time the chanting had been coming nearer, and now the grove rang with it. A moment, and the head of the first division must present itself in front of the Chapel. Could the Wanderer have elected then whether to depart or stay, the *Pannychides* would have had no further assistance from him—so badly had the rencounter with Scholarius shaken him. Not that he was afraid in the vulgar sense of the term. Before a man can habitually pray for death, he must be long lost to fear. If we can imagine conscience gone, pride of achievement, without which there can be no mortification or shame in defeat, may yet remain with him, a source of dread and weakness. The chill which shook Brutus in his tent the evening before Philippi was not in the least akin to terror. So with the Prince at this juncture. There to measure the hold of the Christian idea upon the Church, it seemed Scholarius had brought him an answer which finished his interest in the passing Vigils. In brief, the Reformer's interest in the Mystery was past, and he wished with his whole soul to retreat to the sedan, but a fascination held him fast.

"I think it would be pleasanter sitting," he said, and returned to the platform.

"If I presume to take the chair, Father," he added, "it is because I am older than thou."

Hardly was he thus at ease when a precentor, fat, and clad in a long gown, stepped out of the grove to the clear lighted pavement in front of the Chapel. His shaven head was thrown back, his mouth open to its fullest stretch, and tossing a white stick energetically up and down in the air, he intoned with awful distinctness: "The waters wear the stones. Thou washest away the things which grow out of the dust of the earth, and Thou destroyest the hopes of man."

The Prince covered his ears with his hands.

"Thou likest not the singing?" Father Theophilus asked, and continued: "I admit the graces have little to do with musical practice in the holy houses of the Fathers." But he for whom the comfort was meant made no reply. He was repeating to himself: "Thou prevailest forever against him, and he passeth."

And to these words the head of the first division strode forward into the light. The Prince dropped his hands in time to hear the last verse: "But his flesh upon him shall have pain, and his soul within him shall mourn."

For whom was this? Did the singers know the significancy of the text to him? The answer was from God, and they were merely messengers bringing it. He rose to his feet; in his rebellious passion the world seemed to melt and swim about him. He felt a longing to burn, break, destroy—to strike out and kill. When he came to himself, Father Theophilus, who thought him merely wonder struck by the mass of monks in march, was saying in his most rueful tone: "Good order required a careful arrangement of the procession; for though the participants are pledged to godly life, yet they sometimes put their vows aside temporarily. The holiest of them have pride in their establishments, and are often too ready to resort to arms of the flesh to assert their privileges. The Fathers of the Islands have long been jealous of the Fathers of the city, and to put them together would be a signal for riot. Accordingly there are three grand divisions here—the monks of Constantinople, those of the Islands, the shores of the Bosphorus and the three seas, and finally the recluses and hermits from whatever quarter. Lo! first the Fathers of the Studium—saintly men as thou wilt see anywhere."

The speech was unusually long for the Father; a fortunate circumstance of which the Prince availed himself to recover his self-possession. By the time the brethren eulogized were moving up the rift at his feet, he was able to observe them calmly. They were in long gowns of heavy gray woollen stuff, with sleeves widening from the shoulders; their cowls, besides covering head and visage, fell down like capes. Cleanly, decent-looking men, they marched slowly and in order, their hands united palm to palm below their chins. The precentor failed to inspire them with his fury of song.

"These now coming," Father Theophilus said of the second fraternity, "are conventuals of Petrion, who have their house looking out on the harbor here. And these," he said of the third, "are of the Monastery of Anargyres—a very ancient society. The Emperor Michael, surnamed the Paphlegonian, died in one of their cells in 1041. Brotherhood with them is equivalent to saintship."

Afterwhile a somewhat tumultuous flock appeared in white skirts and loose yellow cloaks, their hair and beard uncut and flying. The historian apologized.

"Bear with them," he said; "they are mendicants from the retreats of Periblepte, in the quarter of Psammatica. You may see them on the street corners and quays, and in all public places, sick, blind, lame and covered with sores. They have St. Lazarus for patron. At night an angel visits them with healing. They refuse to believe the age of miracles is past."

The city monastics were a great host carrying banners with the name of their Brotherhoods inscribed in golden letters; and in every instance the Hegumen, or Abbot, preceded his fraternity torch in hand.

A company in unrelieved black marched across the brook, and their chanting was lugubrious as their garb.

"Petra sends us these Fathers," said Theophilus—"Petra over on the south side. They sleep all day and watch at night. The second coming they say will happen in the night, because they think that time most favorable for the trumpeting herald and the splendor of the manifestations."

Half an hour of marching—men in gray and black and yellow, a few in white—men cowled—men shorn and unshorn—barefooted men and men in sandals—a river of men in all moods, except jovial and happy, toiling by the observing stand, seldom an upturned face, spectral, morose, laden body and mind—young and old looking as if just awakened after ages of entombment;—a half hour of dismal chanting the one chapter from the book of the man in the land of Uz, of all utterances the most dismal;—a half hour of waiting by the Prince for one kindly sign, without discovering it—a half hour, in which, if the comparison be not too strong, he was like a soul keeping watch over its own abandoned body. Then Father Theophilus said:

"From the cloisters of St. James of Manganese! The richest of the monasteries of Constantinople, and the most powerful. It furnishes Sancta

Sophia with renowned preachers. Its brethren cultivate learning. Their library is unexcelled, and they boast that in the hundreds of years of their society life, they had never an heretic. Before their altars the candles are kept burning and trimmed forever. Their numbers are recruited from the noblest families. Young men to whom the army is open prefer God-service in the elegant retirement of St. James of Manganese. They will interest you, Prince; and after them we will have the second grand division."

"Brethren of the Islands?"

"Yes, of the Islands and the sea-shores."

Upon the pavement then appeared a precentor attired like a Greek priest of the present day; a rimless hat black and high, and turned slightly outward at the top; a veil of the same hue; the hair gathered into a roll behind, and secured under the hat; a woollen gown very dark, glossy, and dropping in ample folds unconfined from neck to shoe. The Hegumen followed next, and because of his age and infirmities a young man carried the torch for him. The chanting was sweet, pure, and in perfect time. All these evidences of refinement and respectability were noticed by the Prince, and looking at the torch-bearer again, he recognized the young monk, his room-mate in the White Castle.

"Knowest thou the youth yonder?" he asked, pointing to Sergius.

"A Russian recently arrived," the Father replied. "Day before yesterday he was brought to the palace and presented to the Emperor by the Princess Irene. He made a great impression."

The two kept their eyes on the young man until he disappeared ascending the hill.

"He will be heard from;" and with the prediction the Prince gave attention to the body of the Brotherhood.

"These men have the bearing of soldiers," he said presently.

"Their vows respecting war are liberal. If the *panagia* were carried to the walls, they would accompany it in armor."

The Prince smiled. He had not the faith in the Virgin of Blacherne which the Father's answer implied.

The St. James' were long in passing. The Prince kept them in sight to the last four. They were the aristocracy of the Church, prim, proud; as their opportunities were more frequent, doubtless they were more wicked than their associates of the humbler fraternities; yet he could not promise himself favor from their superior liberality. On the contrary, having a great name for piety to defend, if a test offered, they were the more certain to be hard and vindictive—to send a heretic to the stake, and turn a trifling variation from the creed into heresy.

"Who is this?" the Prince exclaimed, as a noble-looking man in full canonicals stepped out of the cypress shadows, first of the next division.

"Master of Ceremonies for the Church," Father Theophilus replied. "He is the wall between the Islanders and the Metropolitans."

"And he who walks with him singing?"

"The *Protopsolete*—leader of the Patriarch's Choir."

Behind this singer the monks of the Isles of the Princes! In movement, order, dress, like their predecessors in the march—Hegumen with their followers in gray, black and white—hands palm to palm prayerfully— chanting sometimes better, sometimes worse—never a look upward but always down, as if Heaven were a hollow in the earth, an abyss at their feet, and they about to step into it.

The Prince was beginning to tire. Suddenly he thought of the meeting of pilgrims at El Zaribah. How unlike was the action there and here! That had been a rush, an inundation, as it were, by the sea, fierce, mad, a passion of Faith fostered by freedom; this, slow, solemn, sombre, oppressive—what was it like? Death in Life, and burial by programme so rigid there must not be a groan more or a tear less. He saw Law in it all—or was it imposition, force, choice smothered by custom, fashion masquerading in the guise of Faith? The hold of Christ upon the Church began to look possible of measurement.

"Roti first!" said the Father. "Rocky and bare, scarce a bush for a bird or grass for a cricket. Ah, verily he shall love God dearly or hate the world mortally who of free will chooses a cloister for life at Roti!"

The brethren of the three convents of the Island marched past clad in short brown frocks, bareheaded, barefooted. The comments of the historian were few and brief.

"Poor they look," he said of the first one, "and poor they are, yet Michael Rhangabe and Romain Lacapene were glad to live and die with them." Of the second: "When Romain Diogenes built the house these inhabit, he little dreamed it would shelter him, a refugee from the throne." Of the third: "Dardanes was a great general. In his fortunate days he built a tower on Roti with one cell in it; in an evil hour he aspired to the throne—failed— lost his eyes, retired to his lonesome tower—by his sanctity there drew a fraternity to him, and died. That was hundreds of years ago. The brethren still pray for his soul. Be it that evil comes of good; not less does good come of evil—and so God keeps the balances."

In the same manner he descanted on the several contingents from Antigone as they strode by; then of those from God's houses at Halki, the pearl of the Marmora; amongst them the monastery of John the Precursor, and the Convents of St. George, Hagia Trias, and lastly the Very Holy House of the All Holy Mother of God, founded by John VIII. Palaeologus. After them, in turn, the consecrated from Prinkipo, especially those from the Kamares of the Basilissa, Irene, and the Convent of the Transfiguration.

The faithful few from the solitary Convent on the Island of Oxia, and the drab-gowned abstinents of the monastery of Plati, miserables given to the abnormity of mixing prayer and penance with the cultivation of snails for the market in Constantinople, were the last of the Islanders.

Then in a kind of orderly disorganization the claustral inculpables from holy houses on Olympus down by the Dardanelles, the Bosphorus, and the Bithynian shore behind the Isles of the Princes, and some from retreats in the Egean and along the Peloponnesus, their walls now dust, their names forgotten.

"Where is the procession going?" the Prince now asked.

"Look behind you—up along the front of the palace."

And casting his eyes thither, the questioner beheld the ground covered with a mass of men not there before.

"What are they doing?"

"Awaiting the Emperor. Only the third grand division is wanting now; when it is up His Majesty will appear."

"And descend to the Chapel?"

"Yes."

For a time a noise more like the continuous, steady monotone of falling water than a chant had been approaching from the valley, making its darkness vocal. It threatened the gates awhile; now it was at the gates. The Prince's wonder was great, and to appease it Father Theophilus explained:

"The last division is at hand."

In the dim red light over the area by the gate below, the visitor beheld figures hurriedly issuing from the night—figures in the distance so wild and fantastic they did not at first seem human. They left no doubt, however, whence the sound proceeded. The white sand of the road up the terraces was beaten to dust under the friction and pressure of the thousands of feet gone before; this third division raised it into an attending cloud, and the cloud and the noise were incessant.

Once more the Prince went out to the brink of the terrace. The monotony of the pageant was broken; something new was announcing itself. Spectres—devils—gnomes and jinn of the Islamitic Solomon—rakshakas and hanumen of the Eastern Iliads—surely this miscellany was a composition of them all. They danced along the way and swung themselves and each other, howling like dervishes in frenzy. Again the birds took wing and flew blindly above the cypresses, and the end of things seemed about to burst when a yell articulate yet unintelligible shook the guarded door of the venerable Chapel.

Then the demoniacs—the Prince could not make else of them—leaping the brook, crowding the pent enclosure, hasting to the arched exit, were plainly in view. Men almost naked, burned to hue of brick-dust; men in untanned sheepskin coats and mantles; men with every kind of headgear, turbans, handkerchiefs, cowls; men with hair and beard matted and flying; now one helped himself to a louder yell by tossing in air the dirty garment he had torn from his body, hirsute as a goat's; now one leaped up agile as a panther; now one turned topsy-turvy; now groups of them swirled together like whimsical eddies in a pool. Some went slowly, their arms outspread in silent ecstasy; some stalked on with parted lips and staring eyes, trance-like or in dead drunkenness of soul; nevertheless the great majority of them, too weary and far spent for violent exertion, marched with their faces raised, and clapping their hands or beating their breasts, now barking short and sharp, like old hounds dreaming, then finishing with long-drawn cries not unlike the ending of a sorrowful chorus. Through the gate they crowded, and at sight of their faces full of joy unto madness, the Prince quit pitying them, and, reminded of the Wahabbees at El Zaribah, turned to Father Theophilus.

"In God's name," he said, "who are these?"

"A son of India thou, and not know them at sight?"

There was surprise in the question, and a degree of unwarranted familiarity, yet the Father immediately corrected himself, by solemnly adding: "Look there at that one whirling his mantle of unshorn skin over his head. He has a cave on Mt. Olympus furnished with a stool, a crucifix, and a copy of the Holy Scriptures; he sleeps on the stone; the mantle is his bedding by night, his clothing by day. He raises vegetables, and they and snow-water seeping through a crevice in his cavern subsist him.... And the next him—the large man with the great coat of camel's hair which keeps him scratched as with thorns—he is from the Monastery of St. Auxentius, the abode of a powerful fraternity of ascetics. A large proportion of this wing of the celebrants is of the same austere house. You will know them by the penitential, dun-colored garment—they wear no other.... Yonder is a brother carrying his right arm at a direct angle above his shoulder, stiff and straight as a stick of seasoned oak. He is of a colony of Stylites settled on this shore of the upper Bosphorus overlooking the Black Sea. He could not lower the arm if he wished to; but since it is his certificate of devoutness, the treasures of the earth laid at his feet in a heap would be insufficient to induce him to drop it though for an instant. His colony is one of many like it. Spare him thy pity. He believes the clinch of that hand holds fast the latch of Heaven.... The shouters who have just entered the arch in a body have hermitaries in close grouping around the one failing monastery on Plati, and live on lentils and snails; aside from which they commit themselves to Christ, and so abound in faith that the Basileus in his purple would be very happy were he true master of a tithe of their happiness.... Hast thou not enough, O Prince? Those crossing the brook now?—Ah, yes! They are anchorites from Anderovithos, the island. Pitiable creatures looked at from the curtained windows of a palace—pitiable, and abandoned by men and angels! Be not sure. Everything is as we happen to see it—a bit of philosophy, which, as they despise the best things secularly considered of this life, steels them to indifference for what you and I, and others not of their caste, may think. They have arrived at a summit above the corrupting atmosphere of the earth, where every one of them has already the mansion promised him by our Blessed Lord, and where the angels abide and delight to serve him.... For the rest, O Prince, call them indifferently recluses, hermits, anticenobites, mystics, martyrs, these from Europe, those from isolations deep somewhere in Asia. Who feeds them? Did not ravens feed Elijah? Offer them white bread and robes of silk, yesterday's wear of a king. 'What!' they will ask. 'Shall any man fare better than John the Forerunner?' Speak to them of comfortable habitations, and they will answer with the famous saying, 'Foxes have holes, and the birds of the air have nests; but the Son of Man hath not where to lay His head.' What more is there to be said? Thou seest them, thou knowest them."

Yes, the Prince knew them. Like the horde which stood by the Black Stone envious of Mirza's dying, these were just as ready to die for Christ. He smiled grimly, and thought of Mahommed, and how easy the Church had made the conquest of which he was dreaming.

It was with a sense of relief he beheld the tail of the division follow its body up to the palace.

Then, last of all, came the dignitaries of the Church, the Cartulaire, least in rank, with many intermediates, up to the Cyncelle, who, next to the absent Patriarch, represented him. If what had preceded in the procession was poor and unpretentious, this part was splendid to excess. They were not more than eighteen or twenty in number, but they walked singly with considerable intervals between them; while on the right and left of each, a liveried servant carried a torch which gave him to be distinctly seen. And the flashing of gold on their persons was wonderful to the spectator. Why not? This rare and anointed body was the Church going in solemnity to assist the Basileus in a high ceremony.

Afterwhile the Emperor appeared descending to the Chapel.

To the Prince's amazement, he was in a plain, priestly black frock, without crown, sword, sceptre or guard; and so did his guise compare with the magnificence of the ecclesiastics surrounding him, he actually seemed in their midst a prisoner or a penitent. He passed his visitor like one going from the world forgetting and forgot.

"An explanation, Father," said the Prince. "The Church is in its robes, but my august friend, the Emperor, looks as if he had suffered dethronement."

"Thou wilt presently see His Majesty enter the Chapel alone. The legend supposes him there in presence directly of God; if so, what merit would there be in regalia? Would his sword or sceptre make his supplication more impressive?"

The Prince bowed.

And while he watched, the gold-clad escort halted before the Holy House, the door opened, and Constantine went in unattended. Then, the door being shut behind him, the clergy knelt, and remained kneeling. The light from the torches was plenteous there, making the scene beautiful.

And yet further, while he stood watching, the trumpeting and chanting on the level in front of the palace behind him ceased, and a few minutes afterwards, he was aware of the noise of many feet rushing in a scramble from all directions to the Chapel. Here and there flambeaux streamed out, with hundreds of dark-gowned excited figures speeding after them as best they could.

The bank the Prince occupied was overrun, like other contiguous spaces. The object of the invaders was to secure a position near the revered building as possible; for immediately on attaining it they dropped to their knees, and began counting their rosaries and mumbling prayers. At length it befell that the terraces far and near were densely crowded by monks in low recitation.

"My Lord," said Father Theophilus, in a tone of reserved depth, "the Mystery is begun. There is no more to be seen. Good-night!" And without ado, he too knelt where he stood, beads in hand, eyes fixed upon the one point of devotional interest.

When the sedan was brought, the Prince gave one last glance at the scene, feeling it was to be thenceforward and forever a burden on his memory. He took in and put away the weather-stained Chapel, centre of so much travail; the narrow court in front of it brilliantly lighted and covered with priests high and low in glittering vestments; the cypresses looming skyward, stately and stiff, like conical monuments: the torches scattered over the grounds, revealing patches of men kneeling, their faces turned toward the Chapel: the mumbling and muttering from parts unlighted telling of other thousands in like engagement. He had seen battle-fields fresh in their horrors; decks of ships still bloody; shores strewn with wreckage and drowned sailors, and the storm not spent; populous cities shaken down by earthquakes, the helpless under the ruins pleading for help; but withal never had he seen anything which affected him as did that royal park at mid of night, given up to that spectral multitude!

It seemed he could not get away from the spectacle soon enough; for after issuing from the Grand Gate, he kept calling to his carriers, impatiently: "Faster, my men, faster!"

CHAPTER V
A PLAGUE OF CRIME

Sergius' life in Constantinople had been almost void of incident. His introduction to the Patriarch by the Princess Irene started him well with that reverend official, whose confidence and love she commanded to a singular degree. His personal qualities, however, were very helpful. The gentleness of his nature, his youth, his simplicity, respectfulness, intelligence and obvious piety were all in his favor; at the same time the strongest attraction he possessed with the strangers amongst whom he found himself was his likeness according to the received Byzantine ideal to Christ. He had a habit, moreover, of walking slowly, and with a quiet tread, his head lowered, his hands clasped before him. Coming in this mood suddenly upon persons, he often startled them; at such times, indeed, the disturbed parties were constrained to both observe and forgive him—he reminded them so strikingly of the Nazarene as He must have looked while in solitary walks by the sea or along the highways of Galilee. Whatever the cause, it is very certain His Serenity, the Patriarch, from mere attention to the young Russian, passed speedily to interest in him, and manifested it in modes pleasant and noticeable. By his advice, Sergius attached himself to the Brotherhood of the Monastery of St. James of Manganese. This was the first incident in his city life out of the usual. The second was his presentation at court, where he was not less successful with the Emperor than he had been with the Patriarch. Yet Sergius was not happy. His was the old case of a spirit willing, even anxious, to do, but held in restraint. He saw about him such strong need of saving action; and the Christian plan, as he understood it, was so simple and efficacious. There was no difference in the value of souls. Taking Christ's own words, everything was from the Father, and He held the gates of Heaven open for the beggar and the emperor alike. Why not return to the plan devised, practised, and exemplified by the Saviour Himself? The idea bore heavily upon his mind, and accounted for the bent head and slow step fast becoming habitudes. At times the insurgent impulses seemed beyond control. This was particularly when he walked in crowded places; for then the people appeared an audience summoned and ready to hear him; he had only to go into their midst, call to them, and begin speaking; but often as he beheld the calm, patient, pleading face of the Princess Irene, and heard her say ever so gently: "Wait, wait! I know the situation—you do not. Our object is the most good. God will send the opportunity. Then martyrdom, if it come, is going to Heaven. Wait—I will give you the signal. You are to speak for me as well as yourself. You are to be my voice"—so often he grew reconciled.

There was another trouble more difficult of comprehension and description. Under its influence the sky did not look so blue as formerly; the breeze was less refreshing; the sun where it scattered its golden largesse over the sea failed to relieve it of dulness; and in all things, himself included, there was something wanting—exactly what he could not tell. However, as he had been indulging comparisons of life in Constantinople with life in Bielo-Osero, and longing for the holy quiet of the latter, he concluded he was homesick, and was ashamed. It was childishness! The Great Example had no home! And with that thought he struggled manfully to be a man forever done with such weaknesses.

It became his wont of afternoons when the weather was tolerable to seek the city wall opposite the old Chalcedonian point. In going thither, he sometimes passed through the Hippodrome and Sta. Sophia, both in such contact to the collection of palaces known as the Bucoleon that each might have been fairly considered an appurtenance of the other. The exercises in the spacious palaestrae had small interest for him; there was always such evident rancor between the factions Blue and Green. The dome of the great Church he regarded man's best effort at construction, beyond which there was nothing more attainable; but how it dwindled and faded when from the wall he looked at the sky, the sea, and the land, the handiworks of God!

On the wall, at a point marked by a shallow angle, there was a cracked stone bench, offering seawardly a view of the Isles of the Princes, and the Asian domain beyond Broussa to the Olympian heights; westwardly, the Bucoleon and its terraced gardens were near by, and above them in the distance the Tower of Isaac Angelus arose over Blacherne, like a sentinel on guard against the opposing summits of Galata and Pera. From the bench, the walk, besides being wide and smooth, extended, with a slight curvature northward to the Acropolis, now Point Serail, and on the south to the Port of Julian. The airy promenade thus formed was reached by several stairs intermediate the landmarks mentioned; yet the main ascent was near the Imperial stables, and it consisted of a flight of stone steps built against the inner face of the wall, like a broad buttress. This latter was for the public, and of sunny days it was used incessantly. Everybody in the category of invalids affected it in especial, since litters and sedans were not inhibited there. In short, the popularity of this mural saunter can be easily imagined.

The afternoon of the day the Prince of India was in audience by the Emperor's invitation, Sergius was the sole occupant of the stone bench. The hour was pleasant; the distant effects were perfect; birds and boats enlivened the air and water; and in listening to the swish of waves amongst the rocks and pebbles below, so like whisperings, he forgot where he was, and his impatience and melancholy, and the people strolling negligently past. One of his arms lay along the edge of the bulwark before him, and he was not thinking so much as simply enjoying existence. To such as noticed him he appeared a man in the drowsy stage next to sleep.

Afterwhile a voice aroused him, and, without moving, he became aware of two men stopped and talking. He could not avoid hearing them.

"She is coming," said one.

"How do you know?" the other asked.

"Have I not told you I keep a spy on the old Prince's house? A messenger from him has just reported the chair arrived for her; and this being her favorite stroll, she will be here presently."

"Have you considered the risks of your project?"

"Risks? Pah!"

The exclamation was with a contemptuous laugh.

"But they have grown since last night," the other persisted. "The Indian is now at the Palace, His Majesty's guest."

"Yes, I had report of that also; but I have studied the game, and if you fear to join me, I will see it through alone. As an offence against law, it is abduction, not murder; and the penalty, imprisonment, can be easily changed to banishment, which with me means at the utmost a short absence to give friends an opportunity to prepare for my return. Consider, moreover, the subject of the offence will be a woman. Can you name an instance in which the kidnapper of a woman has been punished?—I mean in our time?"

"True, women are the cheapest commodity in the market; therefore"—

"I understand," the first speaker interposed, a little impatiently, "but Princes of India are not common in Constantinople, while their daughters are less so. See the temptation! Besides, in the decadence of our Byzantine empire, the criminal laws fail worse and worse of execution. Only last night my father, delivering a lecture, said neglect in this respect was one of the reasons of the Empire's going. Only the poor and degraded suffer penalties now. And I—pah! What have I to fear? Or thou? And from whom? When the girl's loss is discovered—you observe I am viewing the affair in its most malignant aspect—I know the course the Prince will take. He will run to the palace; there he will fall at the Emperor's feet, tell his tale of woe, and"—

"And if thou art denounced?"

The conspirator laughed again. "The worse for the Prince," he at length replied. "The Hegumen, my honored father, will follow him to the palace, and—but let the details go! The relations between the Basileus and the Church are strained to breaking; and the condition is not sanable while the quarrel between the Patriarch and Scholarius waxes hotter."

"The Patriarch and Scholarius quarrelling? I had not heard of that."

"Openly, openly! His Majesty and the Patriarch are tenderly sympathetic. What more is wanting to set the Prophet scolding? The Patriarch, it is now known, will not be at the *Pannychides* to-night. His health began failing when, over his objection, it was decided to hold the Mystery, and last week he betook himself to the Holy Mountain. This morning the Prophet"—

"Thou meanest Scholarius?"

"Scholarius denounced him as an *azymite*, which is bad, if true; as unfaithful to God and the Church, which is worse; and as trying to convert the Emperor into an adherent of the Bishop of Rome, which, considering the Bishop is Satan unchained, will not admit of a further descent in sin. The Mystery tonight is Scholarius' scheme in contravention of His Serenity's efforts. Oh, it is a quarrel, and a big one, involving Church and State, and the infallibility of our newly risen Jeremiah. Thus full-handed, thinkest thou in a suit the Prince of India against the venerable Hegumen of all the St. James', His Majesty will hesitate? Is thy opinion of him as a politician so uncomplimentary? Think again, I say—think again!"

"Thy father's Brotherhood are His Majesty's friends!"

"Ah, the very point! They despise Scholarius now, and what an ado, what a political display, to drive them into his arms! The Princes of India, though they were numerous as the spectre caravan, could not carry influence that far."

Here there was a rest in the conversation.

"Well, since thou wilt not be persuaded to let the enterprise go," the protesting friend next said, "at least agree with me that it is indiscreet to speak of it in a place public as this."

The laugh of the conspirator was heartier than before.

"Ah, hadst thou warned me not to speak of it to the"—

"Enough of that! The Prince of India is nothing to me—thou art my friend."

"Agree with me then that thou hast ears, while the public"—

"Have not, thou wouldst say. Still there are things which may not be whispered in a desert without being overheard."

"The Pagans who went before us had a god of wisdom, and they called him Hermes. I should say thou hast been to school to him. 'Twas he, doubtless, who taught outlaws to seek safety in crowded cities. By the same philosophy, where can one talk treason more securely than on this wall? Afraid of discovery! Not I, unless thou mumblest in thy sleep. We go about our good intents—the improvement of our fortune for instance—with awful care, and step by step, fortifying. The practice is applicable to wickedness. I am no bungler. I will tell thee a tale.... Thou knowest the Brotherhood of the Monastery of St. James of Manganese is very ancient, and that the house in which it is quartered is about as old as the Brotherhood. Their archives are the richest in the empire. They have a special chamber and a librarian. Were he of the mind, he might write a history of Constantinople by original data without leaving his library. Fortunately the mere keepers of books seldom write books.... My father's office is in the Monastery, and I frequently find myself in his company there. He never fails to improve the opportunity to lecture me, for he is a good man. One day, by invitation, I accompanied the librarian to his place of keeping, and saw it, and wondered how he could be willing to give his days—he is now an old man—to such a mass of rot and smells. I spare you mention of the many things he showed me; for there was but one of real ado with what we are considering, an old document illuminated with an untarnished chrysobula. 'Here,' said he, 'is something curious.' The text was short—writers in those days knew the tricks of condensation, and they practised them virtuously. I asked him to give it to me—he refused—he would sooner have given me the last lock on his head, which is a great deal, seeing that hair grows precious exactly as it grows scantier. So I made him hold the lamp while I read.... The document was dated about A.D. 1300—a century and a half gone, and proved to be a formal report by the Patriarch to a council of Bishops and Hegumen.... Thou knowest, I am sure, the great cistern; not the Philoxenus, but the larger one, with an entrance west of Sta. Sophia, sometimes called the Imperial, because built by the first Constantine and enlarged by Justinian."

"I know it."

"Well, there was a great ceremony there one day; the same with which the report was concerned. The clergy attended in force and panoply led by His Serenity in person—monks, nuns, deacons and deaconesses—in a word, the Church was present. The cistern had been profaned. A son of Satan, moved by a most diabolical ingenuity, had converted it into a den of wickedness surpassing sinful belief; and the procession and awful conclave were to assist His Serenity in restoring the water to wholesomeness, impossible, in the belief of consumers, except by solemn exorcism.... Heed now, my friend—I am about to tap the heart of my story. A plague struck the city—a plague of crime. A woman disappeared. There was search for her, but without success. The affair would have been dismissed within the three days usually allotted wonders of the kind, had not another like it occurred—and then another. The victims, it was noticed, were young and beautiful, and as the last one was of noble family the sensation was universal. The whole capital organized for rescue. While the hunt was at its height, a fourth unfortunate went the way of the others. Sympathy and curiosity had been succeeded by anxiety; now the public was aroused to anger, and the parents of handsome girls were sore with fear. Schemes for discovery multiplied; ingenuity was exhausted; the government took part in the chase—all in vain. And there being then a remission in the disappearance, the theory of suicide was generally accepted. Quiet and confidence were returning, when, lo! the plague broke out afresh! Five times in five weeks Sta. Sophia was given to funeral services. The ugly women, and the halt, and those long hopeless of husbands shared the common terror. The theory of suicide was discarded. It was the doing of the Turks, everybody said. The Turks were systematically foraging Constantinople to supply their harems with Christian beauty; or if the Turks were innocent, the devil was the guilty party. On the latter presumption, the Church authorities invented a prayer of special application. Could anything better signify the despair of the community? A year passed—two years—three—and though every one resolved himself into a watchman and hunter; though heralds cried rewards in the Emperor's name three times each day on the street corners, and in every place of common resort; though the fame of the havoc, rapine, spoliation, or whatsoever it may please thee to call the visitation, was carried abroad until everybody here and there knew every particular come to light concerning it, with the pursuit, and the dragging and fishing in the sea, never a clew was found. One—two—three years, during which at intervals, some long, some short, the ancient Christian centre kept on sealing its doors, and praying. Finally the disappearances were about to be accepted as incidents liable to happen at any time to any young and pretty woman. They were placed in the category with death. There was mourning by friends—that was about all. How much longer the mystery would have continued may not be said.... Now accidents may not have brought the world about, yet the world could not get along without accidents. To illustrate. A woman one day, wanting water for her household, let a bucket down one of the wells of the cistern, and drew up a sandal slippery and decaying. A sliver buckle adhered to it. Upon inspecting the prize, a name was observed graven on its underside. The curious came to see—there was discussion—at length an examiner blessed with a good memory coupled the inscription with one of the lost women. It was indeed her name! A clew to the great mystery was at last obtained. The city was thrown into tumult, and an exploration of the cistern demanded. The authorities at first laughed. 'What!' they said. 'The Royal reservoir turned into a den of murder and crime unutterable by Christians!' But they yielded. A boat was launched on the darkened waters—But hold!"

The voice of the speaker changed. Something was occurring to stop the story. Sergius had succumbed to interest in it; he was listening with excited sense, yet kept his semblance of sleep.

"Hold!" the narrator repeated, in an emphatic undertone. "See what there is in knowing to choose faithful allies! My watchman was right. She comes—she is here!"

"Who is here?"

"She—the daughter of the old Indian. In the sedan to my left—look!"

Sergius, catching the reply, longed to take the direction to himself, and look, for he was comprehending vaguely. A blindfolded man can understand quite well, if he is first informed of the business in progress, or if it be something with which he is familiar; imagination seems then to take the place of eyes. A detective, having overheard the conversation between the two men, had not required sight of them; but the young monk was too recently from the cloisters of Bielo-Osero to be quick in the discernment of villanies. He knew the world abounded in crime, but he had never dealt with it personally; as yet it was a destroying wolf howling in the distance. He yearned to see if what he dimly surmised were true—if the object at the moment so attractive to his dangerous neighbors were indeed the daughter of the strange Indian he had met at the White Castle. His recollection of her was wonderfully distinct. Her face and demeanor when he assisted her from the boat had often reverted to his thought. They spoke to him so plainly of simplicity and dependence, and she seemed so pure and beautiful! And making the acknowledgment to himself, his heart took to beating quick and drum-like. He heard the shuffle and slide of the chairmen going; when they ceased a new and strange feeling came and possessed itself of his spirit, and led it out after her. Still he managed to keep his head upon his arm.

"By the saintly patron of thy father's Brotherhood, she is more than lovely! I am almost persuaded."

"Ah, I am not so mad as I was!" the conspirator replied, laughing; then he changed to seriousness, and added, like one speaking between clinched teeth—"I am resolved to go on. I will have her—come what may, I will have her! I am neither a coward nor a bungler. Thou mayst stay behind, but

I have gone too far to retreat. Let us follow, and see her again—my pretty Princess!"

"Stay—a moment."

Perception was breaking in on Sergius. He scarcely breathed.

"Well?" was the answer.

"You were saying that a boat was launched in the cistern. Then what?"

"Of discovery? Oh, yes—the very point of my argument! A raft was found moored between four of the great pillars in the cistern, and there was a structure on it with furnished rooms. A small boat was used for going and coming."

"Wonderful!"

"Come—or we will lose the sight of her."

"But what else?"

"Hooks, such as fishermen use in hunting lobsters were brought, and by dragging and fishing the missing women were brought to light—that is, their bones were brought to light. More I will tell as we go. I will not stay longer."

Sergius heard them depart, and presently he raised his head. His blood was cold with horror. He was having the awful revelation which sooner or later bursts upon every man who pursues a walk far in life.

CHAPTER VI
A BYZANTINE GENTLEMAN OF THE PERIOD

Sergius kept his seat on the bench; but the charm of the glorious prospect spread out before it was gone.

Two points were swimming in his consciousness, like motes in a mist: first, there was a conspiracy afoot; next, the conspiracy was against the daughter of the Prince of India.

When at the door of the old Lavra upon the snow-bound shore of the White Lake, he bade Father Hilarion farewell and received his blessing, and the commission of an Evangel, the idea furthest from him was to signalize his arrival in Constantinople by dropping first thing into love. And to be just, the idea was now as distant from him as ever; yet he had a vision of the child-faced girl he met on the landing at the White Castle in the hands of enemies, and to almost any other person the shrinking it occasioned would have been strange, if not suspicious. His most definite feeling was that something ought to be done in her behalf.

Besides this the young monk had another incentive to action. In the colloquy overheard by him the chief speaker described himself a son of the Hegumen of the St. James'. The St. James'! His own Brotherhood! His own Hegumen! Could a wicked son have been born to that excellent man? Much easier to disbelieve the conspirator; still there were traditions of the appearance of monsters permitted for reasons clear at least to Providence. This might be an instance of the kind. Doubtless the creature carried on its countenance or person evidences of a miracle of evil. In any event there could be no harm in looking at him.

Sergius accordingly arose, and set out in pursuit of the conspirators. Could he overtake the sedan, they were quite certain to be in the vicinity, and he doubted not discovering them.

The steps of the sedan-carriers, peculiarly quick and sliding, seemed in passing the bench to have been going northwardly toward Point Demetrius. Thither he first betook himself.

In the distance, over the heads of persons going and coming, he shortly beheld the top of a chair in motion, and he followed it rapidly, fearing its occupant might quit the wall by the stairs near the stables of the Bucoleon.

But when it was borne past that descent he went more leisurely, knowing it must meet him on the return.

Without making the Point, however, the chair was put about toward him. Unable to discover any one so much as suggestive of the plotters, and fearing a mistake, he peered into the front window of the painted box. A woman past the noon of life gave him back in no amiable mood the stare with which he saluted her.

There was but one explanation: he should have gone down the wall southwardly. What was to be done? Give up the chase? No, that would be to desert his little friend. And besides he had not put himself within hearing of the design against her—it was a doing of Providence. He started back on his trace.

The error but deepened his solicitude. What if the victim was then being hurried away?

At the head of the stairway by the stables he paused; as it was deserted, he continued on almost running—on past the cracked bench—past the Cleft Gate. Now, in front, he beheld the towers of the imperial residence bearing the name Julian, and he was upbraiding himself for indecision, and loading his conscience with whatever grief might happen the poor girl, when he beheld a sedan coming toward him. It was very ornate, and in the distance shone with burnishments—it was the chair—hers. By it, on the right hand, strode the gigantic negro who had so astonished him at the White Castle. He drew a long breath, and stopped. They would be bold who in daylight assailed that king of men!

And he was taking note of the fellow's barbaric finery, the solemn stateliness of his air, and the superb indifference he manifested to the stare of passers-by, when a man approached the chair on the opposite side. The curtain of the front window was raised, and through it, Sergius observed the inmate draw hastily away from the stranger, and drop a veil over her face.

Here was one of the parties for whom he was looking. Where was the other? Then the man by the left window looked back over his shoulder as if speaking, and out of the train of persons following the sedan, one stepped briskly forward, joined the intruder, and walked with him long enough to be spoken to, and reply briefly; after which he fell back and disappeared. This answered the inquiry.

Assured now of one of the conspirators in sight, the monk resolved to await the coming up. Through the front window of the carriage, which was truly a marvel of polish and glitter, the girl might recognize him; perhaps she would speak; or possibly the negro might recall him; in either event he would have an excuse for intervention.

Meantime, calmly as he could—for he was young, and warm blooded, and in all respects a good instrument to be carried away by righteous indignation—he took careful note of the stranger, who kept his place as if by warrant, occasionally addressing the shrinking maiden.

Sergius was now more curious than angry; and he cared less to know who the conspirator was than how he looked. His surprise may be imagined when, the subject of investigation having approached near enough to be perfectly observed, instead of a monster marked, like Cain, he appeared a graceful, though undersized person, with an agreeable countenance. The most unfavorable criticism he provoked was the loudness—if the word can be excused—of his dress.

A bright red cloak, hanging in ample folds from an exaggerated buckle of purple enamel on his left shoulder, draped his left side; falling open on the right, it was caught by another buckle just outside the right knee. The arrangement loosed the right arm, but was a serious hamper to walking, and made it inconvenient to get out the rapier, the handle of which was protrusively suggested through the cloak. A tunic of bright orange color, short in sleeve and skirt, covered his body. Where undraped, tight-fitting hose terminating in red shoes, flashed their elongated black and yellow stripes with stunning effect. A red cap, pointed at top, and rolled up behind, but with a long visor-like peak shading the eyes, and a white heron feather slanted in the band, brought the head into negligent harmony with the rest of the costume. The throat and left arm were bare, the latter from halfway above the elbow.

This was the monk's first view of a Byzantine gentleman of the period abroad in full dress to dazzle such of the gentler sex as he might chance to meet.

If Sergius' anticipation had been fulfilled; if, in place of the elegant, rakish-looking chevalier in florid garb, he had been confronted by an individual awry in body or hideous in feature, he would not have been confused, or stood repeating to himself, "My God, can this be a son of the Hegumen?"

That one so holy could have offspring so vicious stupefied him. The young man's sins would find him out—thus it was written—and then, what humiliation, what shame, what misery for the poor father!

Speeding his sympathy thus in advance, Sergius waited until the foremost of the sedan carriers gave him the customary cry of warning. As he stepped aside, two things occurred. The occupant of the box lifted her veil and held out a hand to him. He had barely time to observe the gesture and the countenance more childlike because of the distress it was showing, when the negro appeared on the left side of the carriage. Staying a moment to swing the javelin with which he was armed across the top of the buckler at his back, he leaped forward with the cry of an animal, and caught the gallant, one hand at the shoulder, the other at the knee. The cry and the seizure were parts of the same act. Resistance had been useless had there been no surprise. The Greek had the briefest instant to see the assailant— an instant to look up into the face blacker of the transport of rage back of it, and to cry for help. The mighty hands raised him bodily, and bore him swiftly toward the sea-front of the wall.

There were spectators near by; amongst them some men; but they were held fast by terror. No one moved but Sergius. Having seen the provocation, he alone comprehended the punishment intended.

The few steps to the wall were taken almost on the run. There, in keeping with his savage nature, the negro wished to see his victim fall, but a puff of wind blew the red cloak over his eyes, and he stopped to shake it aside. The Greek in the interval seeing the jagged rocks below, and the waves rolling in and churning themselves into foam, caught at his enemy's head, and the teeth of the gold-gilt iron crown cut his palms, bringing the blood. He writhed, and into Nilo's ears—pitiless if they had not been dead—poured screams for mercy. Then Sergius reached out, and caught him.

Nilo made no resistance. When he could free his eyes from the cloak he looked at the rescuer, who, unaware of his infirmity, was imploring him:

"As thou lovest God, and hopest mercy for thyself, do no murder!"

Now, if not so powerful as Nilo, Sergius was quite as tall; and while they stood looking at each other, their faces a little apart, the contrast between them was many sided. And one might have seen the ferocity of the black visage change first with pleased wonder; then brighten with recognition.

The Byzantine gained his feet quickly, and in his turn taken with a murderous impulse, drew his sword. Nilo, however, was quickest; the point of his javelin was magically promotive of Sergius' renewed efforts to terminate the affair. A great many persons were now present. To bring a multitude in hot assemblage, strife is generally more potent than peace, assume what voice the latter may. These rallied to Sergius' assistance; one brought the defeated youth his hat, fallen in the struggle; others helped him rearrange his dress; and congratulating him that he was alive, they took him in their midst, and carried him away. To have drawn upon such a giant! What a brave spirit the lad must possess!

It pleased Sergius to think he had saved the Byzantine. His next duty was to go to the relief of the little Princess. A dull fancy would have taught how trying the situation must have been to her; but with him the case was of a quick understanding quickened by solicitude. Taking Nilo with him, he made haste to the sedan.

If we pause here, venturing on the briefest break in the narrative, it is for the reader's sake exclusively. He will be sure to see how fair the conditions are for a romantic passage between Lael and Sergius, and we fear lest he fly his imagination too high. It is true the period was still roseate with knighterrantry; men wore armor, and did battle behind shields; women were objects of devotion; conversation between lovers was in the style of high-flown courtesy, chary on one side, energized on the other by calls on the Saints to witness vows and declarations which no Saint, however dubious his reputation, could have listened to, much less excused; yet it were not well to overlook one or two qualifications. The usages referred to were by no means prevalent amongst Christians in the East; in Constantinople they had no footing at all. The two Comneni, Isaac and Alexis, approached more nearly the Western ideal of Chivalry than any of the Byzantine warriors; if not the only genuine Knights of Byzantium, they were certainly the last of them; yet even they stood aghast at the fantastic manners of the Frankish armigerents who camped before their gates en route to the Holy Land. As a consequence, the language of ordinary address and intercourse amongst natives in the Orient was simple and less discolored by what may be called pious profanity. Their discourse was often dull and prolix, but never a composite of sacrilege and exaggeration. Only in their writings were they pedantic. From this the reader can anticipate somewhat of the meeting between Sergius and Lael. It is to be borne in mind additionally that they were both young; she a child in years; he a child in lack of worldly experience. Children cannot be other than natural.

Approaching the sedan anxiously, he found the occupant pale and faint. Nilo being close at his side, she saw them both in the same glance, and reached her hand impulsively through the window. It was a question to which the member was offered. Sergius hesitated. Then she brought her face up unveiled.

"I know you, I know you," she said, to Sergius. "Oh, I am so glad you are come! I was so scared—so scared—I will never go from home again. You will stay with me—say you will—it will be so kind of you.... I did not want Nilo to kill the man. I only wanted him driven off and made let me alone. He has followed and persecuted me day after day, often as I came out. I could not set foot in the street without his appearing. My father would have me bring Nilo along. He did not kill him, did he?"

The hand remained held out during the speech, as if asking to be taken. Meanwhile the words flowed like a torrent. The eyes were full of beseechment, and irresistibly lovely. If her speech was innocent, so was her appearance; and just as innocently, he took the hand, and held it while answering:

"He was not hurt. Friends have taken him away. Do not be afraid."

"You saved him. I saw you—my heart was standing still in my throat. Oh, I am glad he is safe! I am no longer afraid. My father will be grateful; and he is generous—he loves me nearly as much as I love him. I will go home now. Is not that best for me?"

Sergius had grown the tall man he was without having been so entreated—nay, without an adventure in the least akin to this. The hand lay in his folded lightly. He remembered once a dove flew into his cell. The window was so small it no doubt suggested to the poor creature a door to a nesting place. He remembered how he thought it a messenger from the Heaven which he never gave over thinking of and longing for, and he wanted to keep it, for afterwhile he was sure it would find a way to tell him wherewith it was charged. And he took the gentle stray in his hand, and nursed it with exceeding tenderness. There are times when it seems such a blessing that memories lie shallow and easy to stir; and now he recalled how the winged nuncio felt like the hand he was holding—it was almost as soft, and had the same magnetism of life—ay, and the same scarce perceptible tremble. To be sure it was merely for the bird's sake he kept hold of the hand, while he answered:

"Yes, I think it best, and I will go with you to your father's door."

To the carriers he said: "You will quit the wall at the grand stairs. The Princess wishes to be taken home."

The sensation of manliness incident to caring for the weak was refreshingly delightful. While the chair was passing he took place at the window. The fingers of the little hand still rested on the silken lining, like pinkish pearls. He beheld them longingly, but a restraint fell upon him. The pinkish pearls became sacred. He would have had them covered from the dust which the whisking breezes now blew up. The breezes were insolent. The sun, sinking in gold over the Marmora, ought to temper the rays it let fall on them. Long as the orb had shone, how curious that it never acquired art enough to know the things which too much of its splendor might spoil. Then too he desired to speak with Lael—to ask if she was any longer afraid—he could not. Where had his courage gone? When he caught the young Greek from Nilo, the shortest while ago, he was wholly unconscious of timidity. The change was wonderful. Nor was the awkwardness beginning to hamper his hands and feet less incomprehensible. And why the embarrassment when people paused to observe him?

Thus the party pursued on until the descent from the wall; he on the right side of the chair, and Nilo on the left. Down in the garden where they were following a walk across the terrace toward Sta. Sophia, Lael put her face to the window, and spoke to him. His eagerness lest a word were lost was remarkable. He did not mind the stooping—and from his height that was a great deal—nor care much if it subjected him to remark.

"Have you seen the Princess lately—she who lives at Therapia?" Lael asked.

"Oh, yes," he answered. "She is my little mother. I go up there often. She advises me in everything."

"It must be sweet to have such a mother," Lael said, with a smile.

"It is sweet," he returned.

"And how lovely she is, and brave and assuring," Lael added. "Why, I forgot when with her to be afraid. I forgot we were in the hands of those dreadful Turks. I kept thinking of her, and not of myself."

Sergius waited for what more she had to say.

"This afternoon a messenger came from her to my father, asking him to let me visit her."

The heart of the monk gave a jump of pleasure.

"And you will go?"

A little older and wiser, and she would have detected a certain urgency there was in the tone with which he directed the inquiry.

"I cannot say yet. I have not seen my father since the invitation was received; he has been with the Emperor; but I know how greatly he admires the Princess. I think he will consent; if so, I will go up to Therapia to-morrow."

Sergius, silently resolving to betake himself thither early next morning, replied with enthusiasm: "Have you seen the garden behind her palace?"

"No."

"Well, of course I do not know what Paradise is, but if it be according to my fancy, I should believe that garden is a piece of it."

"Oh, I know I shall be pleased with the Princess, her garden—with everything hers."

Thereupon Lael settled back in her chair, and nothing more was said till the sedan halted in front of the Prince's door. Appearing at the window there, she extended a hand to her escort. The pinkish pearls did not seem so far away as before, and they were now offered directly. He could not resist taking them.

"I want you to know how very, very grateful I am to you," she said, allowing the hand to stay in his. "My father will speak to you about the day's adventure. He will make the opportunity and early.—But—but"—

She hesitated, and a blush overspread her face.

"But what?" he said, encouragingly.

"I do not know your name, or where you reside."

"Sergius is my name."

"Sergius?"

"Yes. And being a monk, I have a cell in the Monastery of St. James of Manganese. I belong to that Brotherhood, and humbly pray God to keep me in good standing. Now having told you who I am, may I ask"—

He failed to finish the sentence. Happily she divined his wish.

"Oh," she said, "I am called Gul-Bahar by those who love me dearest, though my real name is Lael."

"By which am I to call you?"

"Good-by," she continued, passing his question, and the look of doubt which accompanied it. "Good-by—the Princess will send for me to-morrow."

When the chair was borne into the house, it seemed to Sergius the sun had rushed suddenly down, leaving a twilight over the sky. He turned homeward with more worldly matter to think of than ever before. For the first time in his life the cloister whither he was wending seemed lonesome and uncomfortable. He was accustomed to imagine it lighted and warmed by a presence out of Heaven—that presence was in danger of supersession. Occasionally, however, the girlish Princess whom he was thus taking home with him gave place to wonder if the Greek he had saved from Nilo could be a son of the saintly Hegumen; and the reflection often as it returned brought a misgiving with it; for he saw to what intrigues he might be subjected, if the claim were true, and the claimant malicious in disposition. When at last he fell asleep on his pillow of straw the vision which tarried with him was of walking with Gul-Bahar in the garden behind the Homeric palace at Therapia, and it was exceedingly pleasant.

CHAPTER VII
A BYZANTINE HERETIC

While the venerable Chapel on the way up the heights of Blacherne was surrounded by the host of kneeling monastics, and the murmur of their prayers swept it round about like the sound of moaning breezes, a messenger found the Hegumen of the St. James' with the compliments of the Basileus, and a request that he come forward to a place in front of the door of the holy house. The good man obeyed; so the night long, maugre his age and infirmities, he stayed there stooped and bent, invoking blessings upon the Emperor and Empire; for he loved them both; and by his side Sergius lingered dutifully torch in hand. Twelve hours before he had engaged in the service worshipfully as his superior, nor would his thoughts have once flown from the Mystery enacting; but now—alas, for the inconstancy of youth!—now there were intervals when his mind wandered. The round white face of the Princess came again and again looking at him plainly as when in the window of the sedan on the promenade between the Bucoleon and the sea. He tried to shut it out; but often as he opened the book of prayers which he carried in common with his brethren, trying to read them away; often as he shook the torch thinking to hide them in the resinous smoke, the pretty, melting, importunate eyes reappeared, their fascination renewed and unavoidable. They seemed actually to take his efforts to get away for encouragement to return. Never on any holy occasion had he been so negligent—never had negligence on his part been so obstinate and nearly like sin.

Fortunately the night came to an end. A timid thing when first it peeped over the hills of Scutari, the day emboldened, and at length filled the East, and left of the torches alive on the opposing face of Blacherne only the sticks, the cups, and the streaming smoke. Then the great host stirred, arose, and in a time incredibly brief, silently gave itself back to the city; while the Basileus issued from his solitary vigils in the Chapel, and, in a chastened spirit doubtless, sought his couch in one of the gilded interiors up somewhere under the Tower of Isaac.

The Hegumen of the St. James', overcome by the unwonted draughts upon his scanty store of strength, not to mention the exhaustion of spirit he had undergone, was carried home in a chair. Sergius was faithful throughout. At the gate of the monastery he asked the elder's blessing.

"Depart not, my son; stay with me a little longer. Thy presence is comforting to me."

The adjuration prevailed. Truth was, Sergius wished to set out for Therapia; but banishing the face of the little Princess once more, he helped the holy man out of the chair, through the dark-stained gate, down along the passages, to his apartment, bare and penitential as that of the humblest neophyte of the Brotherhood. Having divested the superior of his robes, and, gently as he could, assisted him to lay his spent body on the narrow cot serving for couch, he then received the blessing.

"Thou art a good son, Sergius," the Hegumen said, with some cheer. "Thou dost strengthen me. I feel thou art wholly given up to the Master and His religion—nay, so dost thou look like the Master that when thou art by I fancy it is He caring for me. Thou art at liberty now. I give thee the blessing."

Sergius knelt, received the trembling hands on his bowed head, and kissed them with undissembled veneration.

"Father," he said, "I beg permission to be gone a few days."

"Whither?"

"Thou knowest I regard the Princess Irene as my little mother. I wish to go and see her."

"At Therapia?"

"Yes, Father."

The Hegumen averted his eyes, and by the twitching of the fingers clasped upon his breast exposed a trouble at work in the depths of his mind.

"My son," he at length said, "I knew the father of the Princess Irene, and was his sympathizer. I led the whole Brotherhood in the final demand for his liberation from prison. When he was delivered, I rejoiced with a satisfied soul, and took credit for a large part of the good done him and his. It is not to magnify myself, or unduly publish my influence that the occurrence is recalled, but to show you how unnatural it would be were I unfriendly to his only child. So if now I say anything in the least doubtful of her, set it down to conscience, and a sense of duty to you whom I have received into the fraternity as one sent me specially by God.... The life the Princess leads and her manners are outside the sanctions of society. There is no positive wrong in a woman of her degree going about in public places unveiled, and it must be admitted she does it most modestly; yet the example is pernicious in its effect upon women who are without the high qualities which distinguish her; at the same time the habit, even as she illustrates it, wears an appearance of defiant boldness, making her a subject of indelicate remark—making her, in brief, a topic for discussion. The objection, I grant, is light, being at worst an offence against taste and custom; much more serious is her persistence in keeping up the establishment at Therapia. A husband might furnish her an excuse; but the Turk is too near a neighbor—or rather she, a single woman widely renowned for beauty, is too tempting to the brutalized unbelievers infesting the other shore of the Bosphorus. Feminine timidity is always becoming; especially is it so when honor is more concerned than life or liberty. Unmarried and unprotected, her place is in a holy house on the Islands, or here in the city, where, aside from personal safety, she can have the benefit of holy offices. Now rumor is free to accuse her of this and that, which charity in multitude and without stint is an insufficient mantle to save her from. They say she prefers guilty freedom to marriage; but no one, himself of account, believes it—the constitution of her household forbids the taint. They say she avails herself of seclusion to indulge uncanonized worship. In plain terms, my son, it is said she is a heretic."

Sergius started and threw up his hands. Not that he was surprised at the charge, for the Princess herself had repeatedly admitted it was in the air against her; but coming from the venerated chief of his Brotherhood, the statement, though a hearsay, sounded so dreadfully he was altogether unprepared for it. Knowing the consequences of heresy, he was also alarmed for her, and came near betraying himself. How interesting it would be to learn precisely and from the excellent authority before him, in what the heresy of the Princess consisted. If there was criminality in her faith, what was to be said of his own?

"Father," he remarked, calmly as possible, "I mind not the other sayings, the reports which go to the Princess' honor—they are the tarnishments which malice is always blowing on things white because they are white—but if it be not too trying to your strength, tell me more. Wherein is she a heretic?"

Again, the gaunt fingers of the Hegumen worked nervously, while his eyes averted themselves.

"How can I satisfy your laudable question, my son, and be brief?" and with the words he brought his look back, resting it on the young man's face. "Give attention, however, and I will try.... I take it you know the Creed is the test of orthodoxy, and"—he paused and searched the eyes above his wistfully—"and that it has your unfaltering belief. You know its history, I am sure—at least you know it had issue from the Council of Nicaea over which Constantine, the greatest of ail Emperors, condescended to preside in person. Never was proceeding more perfect; its perfection proved the Divine Mind in its composition; yet, sad to say, the centuries since the august Council have been fruitful of disputes more or less related to those blessed canons, and sadder still, some of the disputes continue to this day. Would to God there was no more to be said of them!"

The good man covered his face with his hands, like one who would shut out a disagreeable sight. "But it is well to inform you, my son, of the questions whose agitation has at last brought the Church down till only Heaven can save it from rupture and ruin. Oh, that I should live to make the acknowledgment—I who in my youth thought it founded on a rock eternal as Nature itself!... A plain presentation of the subject in contention may help you to a more lively understanding of the gravity and untimeliness of the Princess' departure.... First, let me ask if you know our parties by name. Verily I came near calling them *factions*, and that I would not willingly, since it is an opprobrious term, resort to which would be denunciatory of myself—I being one of them."

"I have heard of a Roman party and of a Greek party; but further, I am so recently come to Constantinople, it would be safer did I take information of you."

"A prudent answer, by our most excellent and holy patron!" exclaimed the Hegumen, his countenance relaxing into the semblance of a smile. "Be always as wise, and the St. James' will bless themselves that thou wert brought to us.... Attend now. The parties are Greek and Roman; though most frequently its enemies speak of the latter as *azymites*, which you will understand is but a nickname. I am a Romanist; the Brotherhood is all Roman; and we mind not when Scholarius, and his arch-supporter, Duke Notaras, howl *azymite* at us. A disputant never takes to contemptuous speeches except when he is worsted in the argument."

The moderation of the Hegumen had been thus far singularly becoming and impressive; now a fierce light gleamed in his eyes, and he cried, with a spasmodic clutch of the hands: "We are not of the forsworn! The curse of the perjured is not on our souls!"

The intensity of his superior astonished Sergius; yet he was shrewd enough to see and appreciate the disclosures of the outburst; and from that moment he was possessed of a feeling that the quarrel between the parties was hopelessly past settlement. If the man before him, worn with years, and actually laboring for the breath of life, could be so moved by contempt for the enemy, what of his co-partisans? Age is ordinarily a tamer of the passions. Here was an instance in which much contention long continued had counteracted the benign effect. As a teacher and example, how unlike this Hegumen was to Hilarion. The young man's heart warmed with a sudden yearning for the exile of the dear old Lavra whose unfailing sweetness of soul could keep the frigid wilderness upon the White Lake in summer purple the year round. Never did love of man for man look so lovely; never did it seem so comprehensive and all sufficient! The nearest passion opposition could excite in that pure and chastened nature was pity. But here! Quick as the reflection came, it was shut out. There was more to be learned. God help the heretic in the hands of this judge at this time! And with the mental exclamation Sergius waited, his interest in the definition of heresy sharpened by personal concern.

"There are five questions dividing the two parties," the Hegumen continued, when the paroxysm of hate was passed. "Listen and I will give them to you in naked form, trusting time for an opportunity to deal with them at large.... First then the Procession of the Holy Ghost. That is, does the Holy Ghost proceed from the Son, or from the Father and the Son? The Greeks say from the Son; the Romans say the Father and the Son being One, the Procession must needs be from both of them conjunctively.... Next the Nicene Creed, as originally published, did undoubtedly make the Holy Ghost proceed from the Father alone. The intent was to defend the unity of the Godhead. Subsequently the Latins, designing to cast the assertion of the identity of the Spirit of the Father and the Spirit of the Son in a form which they thought more explicit, planted in the body of the Creed the word *filioque*, meaning *from the Son*. This the Greeks declare an unwarranted addition. The Latins, on their part, deny it an addition in any proper sense; they say it is but an explanation of the principle proclaimed, and in justification trace the usage from the Fathers, Greek and Latin, and from Councils subsequent to the Nicene.... When we consider to what depths of wrangle the two themes have carried the children of God who should be brethren united in love, knowing rivalry only in zeal for the welfare of the Church, that other subjects should creep in to help widen the already dangerous breach has an appearance like a judgment of God; yet it would be dealing unfairly with you, my son, to deny the pendency of three others in particular. Of these we have first, Shall the bread in the Eucharist be leavened or unleavened? About six hundred years ago the Latins began the use of unleavened bread. The Greeks protested against the innovation, and through the centuries arguments have been bandied to and fro in good-natured freedom; but lately, within fifty years, the debate has degenerated into quarrel, and now—ah, in what terms suitable to a God-fearing servant can I speak of the temper signalizing the discussion now? Let it pass, let it pass!... We have next a schism respecting Purgatory. The Greeks deny the existence of such a state, saying there are but two places awaiting the soul after death— Heaven and Hell."

Again the Hegumen paused, arrested, as it were, by a return of vindictive passion.

"Oh, the schismatics!" he exclaimed. "Not to see in the Latin idea of a third place a mercy of God unto them especially! If only the righteous are admitted to the All Holy Father immediately upon the final separation of body and spirit; if there is no intermediate state for the purgation of such of the baptized as die sodden in their sins, what shall become of them?"

Sergius shuddered, but held his peace.

"Yet another point," the superior continued, ere the ruffle in his voice subsided—"another of which the wranglers have made the most; for as you know, my son, the Greeks, thinking themselves teachers of all things intellectual, philosophy, science, poetry, art, and especially religion, and that at a period when the Latins were in the nakedness of barbarism, are filled with pride, like empty bottles with air; and because in the light of history their pride is not unreasonable, they drop the more readily into the designs of the conspirators against the Unity of the Church—I speak now of the Primacy. As if power and final judgment were things for distribution amongst a number of equals! As if one body were better of a hundred heads! Who does not know that two wills equally authorized mean the absence of all will! Of the foundations of God Chaos alone is unorganized; and to such likeness Scholarius would reduce Christendom! God forbid! Say so, my son—let me hear you repeat it after me—God forbid:"

With an unction scarcely less fervid than his chief's, Sergius echoed the exclamation; whereupon the elder looked at him, and said, with a flush on his face, "I fear I have given rein too freely to disgust and abhorrence. Passion is never becoming in old men. Lest you misjudge me, my son, I shall take one further step in explanation; it will be for you to then justify or condemn the feeling you have witnessed in me. A deeper wound to conscience, a grosser provocation to the divine vengeance, a perfidy more impious and inexcusable you shall never overtake in this life, though you walk in it thrice the years of Noah.... There have been repeated attempts to settle the doctrinal differences to which I have referred. A little more than a hundred years ago—it was in the reign of Andronicus III.—one Barlaam, a Hegumen, like myself, was sent to Italy by the Emperor with a proposal of union; but Benedict the Pope resolutely refused to entertain the proposition, for the reason that it did not contemplate a final arrangement of the question at issue between the Churches. Was he not right?"

Sergius assented.

"In 1369, John V. Palaeologus, under heavy pressure of the Turks, renewed overtures of reconciliation, and to effectuate his purpose, he even became a Catholic. Then John VI., the late Emperor, more necessitous than his predecessor, submitted such a presentation to the Papal court that Nicolos of Cusa was despatched to Constantinople to study and report upon the possibilities of a doctrinal settlement and union. In November, 1437, the Emperor, accompanied by Joseph, the Patriarch, Besserion, Archbishop of Nicaea, and deputies empowered to represent the other Patriarchs, together with a train of learned assistants and secretaries, seven hundred in all, set out for Italy in response to the invitation of Eugenius IV, the Pope. Landing at Venice, the Basileus was escorted to Ferrara, where Eugenius received him with suitable pomp. The Council of Basle, having been adjourned to Ferrara for the better accommodation of the imperial guest, was opened there in April, 1438. But the plague broke out, and the sessions were transferred to Florence where the Council sat for three years. Dost thou follow me, my son?"

"With all my mind, Father, and thankful for thy painstaking."

"Nay, good Sergius, thy attention more than repays me.... Observe now the essentials of all the dogmatic questions I named to you as to-day serving the conspiracy against the Unity of our beloved Church were settled and accepted at the Council of Florence. The primacy of the Roman Bishop was the last to be disposed of, because distinguishable from the other differences by a certain political permeation; finally it too was reconciled in these words—bear them in memory, I pray, that you may comprehend their full import—'The Holy Apostolic See and Roman Pontiff hold the Primacy over all the world; the Roman Pontiff is the successor of Peter, Prince of Apostles, and he is the true Vicar of Christ, the head of the whole Church, the Father and Teacher of all Christians.' [Footnote: Addis and Arnold's Catholic Die. 349.] In Italy, 1439—mark you, son Sergius, but a trifle over eleven years ago—the members of the Council from the East and West, the Greeks with the Latins—Emperor, Patriarchs, Metropolitans, Deacons, and lesser dignitaries of whatever title—signed a Decree of Union which we call the *Hepnoticon*, and into which the above acceptances had been incorporated. I said all signed the decree—there were two who did not, Mark of Ephesus and the Bishop Stauropolis. The Patriarch of Constantinople, Joseph, died during the Council; yet the signatures of his colleagues collectively and of the Emperor perfected the Decree as to Constantinople. What sayest thou, my son? As a student of holy canons, what sayest thou?"

"I am but a student," Sergius replied; "still to my imperfect perception the Unity of the Church was certainly accomplished."

"In law, yes," said the Hegumen, with difficulty rising to a sitting posture— "yes, but it remained to make the accomplishment binding on the consciences of the signatories. Hear now what was done. A form of oath was draughted invoking the most awful maledictions on the parties who should violate the decree, and it was sworn to."

"Sworn to?"

"Ay, son Sergius—sworn to by each and all of those attendant upon the Council—from Basileus down to the humblest catechumen inclusive, they took the oath, and by the taking bound their consciences under penalty of the eternal wrath of God. I spoke of certain ones forsworn, did I not?"

Sergius bowed.

"And worse—I spoke of some whose souls were enduring the curse of the perjured. That was extreme—it was passion—I saw thee shudder at it, and I did not blame thee. Hear me now, and thou wilt not blame me.... They came home, the Basileus and his seven hundred followers. Scarcely were they disembarked before they were called to account. The city, assembled on the quay, demanded of them: 'What have you done with us? What of our Faith? Have you brought us the victory?' The Emperor hurried to his palace; the prelates hung their heads, and trembling and in fear answered: 'We have sold our Faith—we have betrayed the pure sacrifice—we have become Azymites.' [Footnote: *Hist. de l'eglise* (L'Abbe Rohrbacher), 3d ed. Vol. 22. 30. MICHEL DUCAS.] Thus spake Bessarion; thus Balsamon, Archdeacon and Guardian of the Archives; thus Gemiste of Lacedaemon; thus Antoine of Heraclius; thus spake they all, the high and the low alike, even George Scholarius, whom thou didst see marching last night first penitent of the Vigils. 'Why did you sign the Decree?' And they answered, 'We were afraid of the Franks.' Perjury to impiety—cowardice to perjury!... And now, son Sergius, it is said—all said—with one exception. Some of the Metropolitans, when they were summoned to sign the Decree, demurred, 'Without you pay us to our satisfaction we shall not sign.' The silver was counted down to them. Nay, son, look not so incredulous—I was there—I speak of what I saw. What could be expected other than that the venals would repudiate everything? And so they did, all save Metrophanes, the Syncelle, and Gregory, by grace of God the present Patriarch. If I speak with heat, dost thou blame me? If I called the recusants forsworn and perjured, thinkest thou the pure in Heaven charged my soul with a sin? Answer as thou lovest the right?"

"My Father," Sergius replied, "the denunciation of impiety cannot be sinful, else I have to unlearn all I have ever been taught; and being the chief Shepherd of an honorable Brotherhood, is it not thy duty to cry out at every appearance of wrong? That His Serenity, the Patriarch, receives thy acquittal and is notably an exception to a recusancy so universal, is comforting to me; to have to cast him out of my admiration would be grievous. But pardon me, if from fear thou wilt overlook it, I again ask thee to speak further of the heresy of the Princess Irene."

Sergius, besides standing with his back to the door of the cell, was listening to the Hegumen with an absorption of sense so entire that he was unaware of the quiet entrance of a third party, who halted after a step or two but within easy hearing.

"The request is timely—most timely," the Hegumen replied, without regarding the presence of the newcomer. "I had indeed almost forgotten the Princess.... With controversies such as I have recounted raging in the Church, like wolves in a sheepfold, comes one with new doctrines to increase the bewilderment of the flock, how is he to be met? This is what the Princess has done, and is doing."

"Still, Father, you leave me in the dark."

The Hegumen faltered, but finally said: "Apart from her religious views and novel habits, the Princess Irene is the noblest nature in Byzantium. Were we overtaken by some great calamity, I should look for her to rise by personal sacrifice into heroism. In acknowledgment of my fatherly interest in her, she has often entertained me at her palace, and spoken her mind with fearless freedom, leaving me to think her pursued by presentiments of a fatality which is to try her with terrible demands, and that she is already prepared to submit to them."

"Yes," said Sergius, with an emphatic gesture, "there are who live martyrs all their days, reserving nothing for death but to bring them their crowns."

The manner of the utterance, and the thought compelled the Hegumen's notice.

"My son," he said, presently, "thou hast a preacher's power. I wish I foreknew thy future. But I must haste or"—

"Nay, Father, permit me to help you recline again."

And with the words, Sergius helped the feeble body down.

"Thanks, my son," he received, in return, "I know thy soul is gentle."

After a rest the speech was resumed.

"Of the Princess—she is given to the Scriptures; in the reading, which else would be a praiseworthy usage, she refuses light except it proceed from her own understanding. We are accustomed when in doubt—thou knowest it to be so—to take the interpretations of the Fathers; but she insists the Son of God knew what He meant better than any whose good intentions are lacking in the inspirations of the Holy Ghost."

A gleam of pleasure flitted over the listener's countenance.

"So," the Hegumen continued, "she hath gone the length of fabricating a creed for herself, and substituting it for that which is the foundation of the Church—I mean the Creed transmitted to us from the Council of Nicaea."

"Is the substitute in writing, Father?"

"I have read it."

"Then thou canst tell me whence she drew it."

"From the Gospels word and word.... There now—I am too weak to enter into discussion—I can only allude to effects."

"Forgive another request"—Sergius spoke hastily—"Have I thy permission, to look at what she hath written?"

"Thou mayst try her with a request; but remember, my son"—the Hegumen accompanied the warning with a menacious glance—"remember proselyting is the tangible overt act in heresy which the Church cannot overlook.... To proceed. The Princess' doctrines are damnatory of the Nicene; if allowed, they would convert the Church into a stumbling-block in the way of salvation. They cannot be tolerated.... I can no more—the night was too much for me. Go, I pray, and order wine and food. To-morrow—or when thou comest again—and delay not, for I love thee greatly—we will return to the subject."

Sergius saw the dew gathering on the Hegumen's pallid forehead, and observed his failing voice. He stooped, took the wan hand from the laboring breast, and kissed it; then turning about quickly to go for the needed restoration, he found himself face to face with the young Greek whom he rescued from Nilo in the encounter on the wall.

CHAPTER VIII
THE ACADEMY OF EPICURUS

"I would have a word with you," the Greek said, in a low tone, as Sergius was proceeding to the door.

"But thy father is suffering, and I must make haste."

"I will accompany thee."

Sergius stopped while the young man went to the cot, removed his hat and knelt, saying, "Thy blessing, father."

The Hegumen laid a hand on the petitioner's head.

"My son, I have not seen thee for many days," he said; "yet in hope that thou hast heard me, and abandoned the associates who have been endangering thy soul and my good name, and because I love thee—God knows how well—and remember thy mother, who lived illustrating every beatitude, and died in grace, praying for thee, take thou my blessing."

With tears starting in his own eyes, Sergius doubted not the effect of the reproof upon the son; and he pitied him, and even regretted remaining to witness the outburst of penitence and grief he imagined forthcoming. The object of his sympathy took down the hand, kissed it in a matter-of-fact way, arose, and said, carelessly: "This lamentation should cease. Why can I not get you to understand, father, that there is a new Byzantium? That even in the Hippodrome nothing is as it used to be except the colors? How often have I explained to you the latest social discovery admitted now by everybody outside the religious orders, and by many within them—I mean the curative element in sin."

"Curative element in sin!" exclaimed the father.

"Ay—Pleasure."

"O God!" sighed the old man, turning his face hopelessly to the wall, "Whither are we drifting?"

He hardly heard the prodigal's farewell.

"If you wish to speak with me, stay here until I return."

This Sergius said when the two passed out of the cell. Going down the darkened passage, he glanced behind him, and saw the Greek outside the door; and when he came back with the Hegumen's breakfast, and reentered the apartment, he brushed by him still on the outside. At the cot, Sergius offered the refreshment on his knees, and in that posture waited while his superior partook of it; for he discerned how the aged heart was doubly stricken—once for the Church, deserted by so many of its children, and again for himself, forsaken by his own son.

"What happiness to me, O Sergius, wert thou of my flesh and blood!"

The expression covered every feeling evoked by the situation. Afterwhile another of the Brotherhood appeared, permitting Sergius to retire.

"I am ready to hear you now," he said, to the Greek at the door.

"Let us to your cell then."

In the cell, Sergius drew forth the one stool permitted him by the rules of the Brotherhood.

"Be seated," he said.

"No," the visitor returned, "I shall be brief. You do not know my father. The St. James' should relieve him of active duty. His years are sadly enfeebling him."

"But that would be ungrateful in them."

"Heaven knows," the prodigal continued, complainingly, "how I have labored to bring him up abreast of the time; he lives entirely in the past. But pardon me; if I heard aright, my father called you Sergius."

"That is my monastic name."

"You are not a Greek?"

"The Great Prince is my political sovereign."

"Well, I am Demedes. My father christened me Metrophanes, after the late Patriarch; but it did not please me, and I have entitled myself. And now we know each other, let us be friends."

Sergius' veil had fallen over his face, and while replacing it under the hat, he replied, "I shall strive, Demedes, to love you as I love myself."

The Greek, it should be remembered, was good featured, and of a pleasant manner; so much so, indeed, as to partially recompense him for his failure in stature; wherefore the overture was by no means repulsive.

"You may wonder at my plucking you from my father's side; you may wonder still more at my presumption in seeking to attach myself to you; but I think my reasons good.... In the first place, it is my duty to acknowledge that but for your interference yesterday the gigantic energumen by whom I was unexpectedly beset would have slain me. In fact, I had given myself up for lost. The rocks at the foot of the wall seemed springing out of the water to catch me, and break every bone in my body. You will accept my thanks, will you not?"

"The saving two fellow beings, one from murder, the other from being murdered, is not, in my opinion, an act for thanks; still, to ease you of a sense of obligation, I consent to the acknowledgment."

"It does relieve me," Demedes said, with a taking air; "and I am encouraged to go on."

He paused, and surveyed Sergius deliberately from head to foot, and the admiration he permitted to be seen, taken as a second to his continuing words, could not have been improved by a professed actor.

"Are not flesh and blood of the same significance in all of us? With youth and health superadded to a glorious physical structure, may we not always conclude a man rich in spirit and lusty impulses? Is it possible a gown and priestly hat can entirely suppress his human nature? I have heard of Anthony the Anchorite."

The idea excited his humor, and he laughed.

"I mean no irreverence," he resumed; "but you know, dear Sergius, it is with laughter as with tears, we cannot always control it.... Anthony resolved to be a Saint, but was troubled by visions of beautiful women. To escape them, he followed some children of Islam into the desert. Alas! the visions went with him. He burrowed then in a tomb—still the visions. He hid next in the cellar of an old castle—in vain—the visions found him out. He flagellated himself for eighty and nine years, every day and night of which was a battle with the visions. He left two sheepskins to as many bishops, and one haircloth shirt to two favorite disciples—they had been his armor against the visions. Finally, lest the seductive goblins should assail him in death, he bade the disciples lose him by burial in an unknown place. Sergius, my good friend"—here the Greek drew nearer, and laid a hand lightly on the monk's flowing sleeve—"I heard some of your replies to my father, and respect your genius too much to do more than ask why you should waste your youth"—

"Forbear! Go not further—no, not a word!" Sergius exclaimed. "Dost thou account the crown the Saint at last won nothing?"

Demedes did not seem in the least put out by the demonstration; possibly he expected it, and was satisfied with the hearing continued him.

"I yield to you," he said, with a smile, "and willingly since you convince me I was not mistaken in your perception.... My father is a good man. His goodness, however, but serves to make him more sensitive to opposition.

The divisions of the Church give him downright suffering. I have heard him go on about them hours at a time. Probably his proneness to lamentation should be endured with respectful patience; but there is a peculiarity in it—he is blind to everything save the loss of power and influence the schisms are fated to entail upon the Church. He fights valorously in season and out for the old orthodoxies, believing that with the lapse of religion as at present organized the respectability and dominion of the holy orders will also lapse. Nay, Sergius, to say it plainly, he and the Brotherhood are fast keying themselves up to a point in fanaticism when dissent appears blackest heresy. To you, a straightforward seeker after information, it has never occurred, I suspect, to inquire how far—or rather how close—beyond that attainment lie punishments of summary infliction and most terrible in kind? Torture—the stake—holocausts in the Hippodrome—spectacles in the Cynegion—what are they to the enthused Churchmen but righteous judgments mercifully executed on wayward heretics? I tell you, monk—and as thou lovest her, heed me—I tell you the Princess Irene is in danger."

This was unexpected, and forcibly put; and thinking of the Princess, Sergius lost the calmness he had up to this time successfully kept.

"The Princess—tortured—God forbid!"

"Recollect," the Greek continued—"for you will reflect upon this—recollect I overheard the close of your interview with my father. To-morrow, or upon your return from Therapia, be it when it may, he will interrogate you with respect to whatever she may confide to you in the least relative to the Creed, which, as he states, she has prepared for herself. You stand warned. Consider also that now I have in part acquitted myself of the obligation I am under to you for my life."

The simple-mindedness of the monk, to whom the book of the world was just beginning to open, was an immense advantage to the Greek. It should not be surprising, therefore, if the former relaxed his air, and leaned a little forward to hear what was further submitted to him.

"Have you breakfasted?" the prodigal asked, in his easy manner.

"I have not."

"Ah! In concern for my father, you have neglected yourself. Well, I must not be inconsiderate. A hungry man is seldom a patient listener. Shall I break off now?"

"You have interested me, and I may be gone several days."

"Very well. I will make haste. It is but justice to the belligerents in the spiritual war to admit the zeal they have shown; Gregory the Patriarch, and his Latins, on the one side, and Scholarius and his Greeks on the other. They have occupied the pulpits alternately, each refusing presence to the other. They decline association in the Sacramental rites. In Sta. Sophia, it is the Papal mass to-day; to-morrow, it will be the Greek mass. It requires a sharp sense to detect the opposition in smell between the incense with which the parties respectively fumigate the altars of the ancient house. I suppose there is a difference. Yesterday the parabaloni came to blows over a body they were out burying, and in the struggle the bier was knocked down, and the dead spilled out. The Greeks, being the most numerous, captured the labarum of the Latins, and washed it in the mud; yet the monogram on it was identical with that on their own. Still I suppose there was a difference."

Demedes laughed.

"But seriously, Sergius, there is much more of the world outside of the Church—or Churches, as you prefer—than on the inside. In the tearing each other to pieces, the militants have lost sight of the major part, and, as normally bound, it has engaged in thinking for itself. That is, the shepherd is asleep, the dogs are fighting, and the sheep, left to their individual conduct, are scattered in a hunt for fresher water and greener pasturage. Have you heard of the Academy of Epicurus?"

"No."

"I will tell you about it. But do you take the seat there. It is not within my purpose to exhaust you in this first conference."

"I am not tired."

"Well"—and the Greek smiled pleasantly—"I was regardful of myself somewhat in the suggestion. My neck is the worse of having to look up so constantly.... The youth of Byzantium, you must know, are not complaining of neglect; far from it—they esteem it a great privilege to be permitted to think in freedom. Let me give you of their conclusions. There is no God, they say, since a self-respecting God would not tolerate the strife and babble carried on in his name to the discredit of his laws. Religion, if not a deceit, is but the tinkling of brazen cymbals. A priest is a professor eking out an allowance of fine clothes and bread and wine; with respect to the multitude, he is a belled donkey leading a string of submissive camels. Of what account are Creeds except to set fools by the ears? Which—not what—*which* is the true Christian Faith? The Patriarch tells us, 'Verily it is this,' and Scholarius replies, 'Verily the Patriarch is a liar and a traitor to God for his false teaching'—he then tells us it is that other thing just as unintelligible. Left thus to ourselves—I acknowledge myself one of the wandering flock—flung on our own resources—we resorted to counselling each other, and agreed that a substitute for religion was a social necessity. Our first thought was to revive Paganism; worshipping many gods, we might peradventure stumble upon one really existent: whether good or bad ought not to trouble us, provided he took intelligent concern in the drift of things. To quarrel about his qualities would be a useless repetition of the folly of our elders—the folly of swimming awhile in a roaring swirl. Some one suggested how much easier and more satisfactory it is to believe in one God than in many; besides which Paganism is a fixed system intolerant of freedom. Who, it was argued, would voluntarily forego making his own gods? The privilege was too delightful. Then it was proposed that we resolve ourselves each into a God unto himself. The idea was plausible; it would at least put an end to wrangling, by giving us all an agreeable object to worship, while for mental demands and social purposes generally we could fall back on Philosophy. Had not our fathers tried Philosophy? When had society a better well being than in the halcyon ages of Plato and Pythagoras? Yet there was a term of indecision with us—or rather incubation. To what school should we attach ourselves? A copy of the Enchiridion of Epictetus fell into our hands, and after studying it faithfully, we rejected Stoicism. The Cynics were proposed; we rejected them—there was nothing admirable in Diogenes as a patron. We next passed upon Socratus. *Sons of Sophroniscus* had a lofty sound; still his system of moral philosophy was not acceptable, and as he believed in a creative God, his doctrine was too like a religion. Though the Delphian oracle pronounced him the wisest of mankind, we concluded to look further, and in so doing, came to Epicurus. There we stopped. His promulgations, we determined, had no application except to this life; and as they offered choice between the gratification of the senses and the practice of virtue, leaving us free to adopt either as a rule of conduct, we formally enrolled ourselves Epicureans. Then, for protection against the Church, we organized. The departure might send us to the stake, or to Tamerlane, King of the Cynegion, or, infinitely worse, to the cloisters, if we were few; but what if we took in the youths of Byzantium as an entirety? The policy was clear. We founded an Academy—the Academy of Epicurus—and lodged it handsomely in a temple; and three times every week we have a session and lectures. Our membership is already up in the thousands, selected from the best blood of the Empire; for we do not confine our proselyting to the city."

Here Sergius lifted his hand. He had heard the prodigal in silence, and it had been difficult the while to say which dominated his feeling—disgust, amazement, or pity. He was scarcely in condition to think; yet he comprehended the despairing cry of the Hegumen, Oh, my God! whither are we drifting? The possibilities of the scheme flew about him darkly, like birds in a ghastly twilight. He had studied the oppositions to religion enough to appreciate the attractive power there was for youth in the pursuit of pleasure. He knew also something of the race Epicureanism had run in the old competitions of philosophy—that it had been embraced by more of the cultivated Pagan world than the other contemporary systems together. It had been amongst the last, if not in fact the very last, of the conquests of Christianity. But here it was again; nor that merely—here it was once more a subject of organized effort. Who was responsible for the resurrection? The Church? How wicked its divisions seemed to him! Bishop fighting Bishop—the clergy distracted—altars discredited—sacred ceremonies neglected—what did it all mean, if not an interregnum of the Word? Men cannot fight Satan and each other at the same time. With such self-collection as he could command, he asked: "What have you in substitution of God and Christ?"

"A Principle," was the reply.

"What Principle?"

"Pleasure, the Purpose of this Life, and its Pursuit, an ennobled occupation."

"Pleasure to one is not pleasure to another—it is of kinds."

"Well said, O Sergius! Our kind is gratification of the senses. Few of us think of the practice of virtue, which would be dreaming in the midst of action."

"And you make the pursuit an occupation?"

"In our regard the heroic qualities of human nature are patience, courage and judgment; hence our motto—Patience, Courage, Judgment. The pursuit calls them all into exercise, ennobling the occupation."

The Greek was evidently serious. Sergius ran him over from the pointed shoes to the red feather in the conical red hat, and said in accents of pity:

"Oh, alas! Thou didst wrong in re-entitling thyself. Depravity had been better than Demedes."

The Greek lifted his brows, and shrugged his shoulders.

"In the Academy we are used to taking as well as giving," he said, wholly unembarrassed. "But, my dear Sergius, it remains for me to discharge an agreeable commission. Last night, in full session, I told of the affair on the wall. Could you have heard my description of your intervention, and the eulogium with which I accompanied it, you would not have accused me of ingratitude. The brethren were carried away; there was a tempest of applause; they voted you a hero; and, without a dissent, they directed me to inform you that the doors of the Academy were open"—

"Stop," said Sergius, with both hands up as if to avert a blow. After looking at the commissioner a moment, his eyes fiercely bright, he walked the floor of the cell twice.

"Demedes," he said, halting in front of the Greek, a reactionary pallor on his countenance, "the effort thou art making to get away from God proves how greatly He is a terror to thee. The Academy is only a multitude thou hast called together to help hide thee from Christ. Thou art an organizer of Sin—a disciple of Satan"—he was speaking not loud or threateningly, but with a force before which the other shrank visibly—"I cannot say I thank thee for the invitation on thy tongue unfinished, but I am better of not hearing it. Get thee behind me."

He turned abruptly, and started for the door.

The Greek sprang after him, and took hold of his gown.

"Sergius, dear Sergius," he said, "I did not intend to offend you. There is another thing I have to speak about. Stay!"

"Is it something different?" Sergius asked.

"Ay—as light and darkness are different."

"Be quick then."

Sergius was standing under the lintel of the door. Demedes slipped past him, and on the outside stopped.

"You are going to Therapia?" he asked.

"Yes."

"The Princess of India will be there. She has already set out."

"How knowest thou?"

"She is always under my eyes."

The mockery in the answer reminded Sergius of the Academy. The prodigal was designing to impress him with an illustration of the Principle it had adopted in lieu of God. The motto, he was having it thus early understood, was not an empty formula, but an inspiring symbol, like the Cross on the flag. This votary, the advertisement as much as said, was in pursuit of the little Princess—he had chosen her for his next offering to the Principle which, like another God, was insatiable of gifts, sacrifices, and honors. Such the thoughts of the monk.

"You know her?" Demedes asked.

"Yes."

"You believe her the daughter of the Prince of India?"

"Yes."

"Then you do not know her."

The Greek laughed insolently.

"The best of us, and the oldest can be at times as much obliged by information as by a present of bezants. The Academy sends you its compliments. The girl is the daughter of a booth-keeper in the bazaar—a Jew, who has no princely blood to spare a descendant—a dog of a Jew, who makes profit by lending his child to an impostor."

"Whence hadst thou this—this—"

The Greek paid no attention to the interruption.

"The Princess Irene gives a fete this afternoon. The fishermen of the Bosphorus will be there in a body. I will be there. A pleasant time to you, and a quick awakening, O Sergius!"

Demedes proceeded up the passage, but turned about, and said: "Patience, Courage, Judgment. When thou art witness to all there is in the motto. O Sergius, it may be thou wilt be more placable. I shall see to it that the doors of the Academy are kept open for thee."

The monk stood awhile under the lintel bewildered; for the introduction to wickedness is always stunning—a circumstance proving goodness to be the natural order.

CHAPTER IX
A FISHERMAN'S FETE

The breakfast to which Sergius addressed himself was in strict observance of the Rules of the Brotherhood; and being plain, it was quickly despatched. Returning to his cell, he let his hair loose, and combed it with care; then rolling it into a glistening mass, he tucked it under his hat. Selecting a fresher veil next, he arranged that to fall down his back and over the left shoulder. He also swept the dark gown free of dust, and cleansing the crucifix and large black horn beads of his rosary, lingered a moment while contemplating the five sublime mysteries allotted to the third chaplet, beginning with the Resurrection of Christ and ending with the Coronation of the Blessed Virgin. In a calmness of spirit such as follows absolution, he finally sallied from the Monastery, and ere long arrived at the landing outside the Fish Market Gate on the Golden Horn. The detentions had been long; so for speed he selected a two-oared boat.

"To Therapia—by noon," he said to the rower, and, dropping into the passenger's box, surrendered himself to reflection.

The waterway by which the monk proceeded is not unfamiliar to the reader, a general idea of it having been given in the chapter devoted to the adventures of the Prince of India in his outing up the Bosphorus to the Sweet Waters of Asia. The impression there sought to be conveyed—how feebly is again regretfully admitted—was of a panorama remarkable as a composition of all the elements of scenic beauty blent together in incomparable perfection. Now, however, it failed the tribute customary from such as had happily to traverse it.

The restfulness of the swift going; the shrinking of the flood under the beating of the oars; the sky and the wooded heights, and the stretches of shore, town and palace lined; the tearing through the blue veil hanging over the retiring distances; the birds, the breezes, the ships hither coming and yonder going, and the sparkles shooting up in myriad recurrence on the breaking waves—all these pleasures of the most delicate of the receiving senses were tyrannically forbidden him.

The box in which he sat half reclining was wide enough for another passenger side by side with him, and it seemed he imagined the vacant place occupied now by Demedes, and now by Lael, and that he was speaking to them; when to the former, it was with dislike, and a disposition to avoid the touch of his red cloak, though on the sleeve ever so lightly; when to the latter, his voice would lower, his eyes soften, and the angry spots on his brow and cheeks go out—not more completely could they have disappeared had she actually exorcised them with some of the sweet confessions lovers keep for emergencies, and a touch of finger besides.

"So," he would say, Demedes for the time on the seat, "thou deniest God, and hast a plot against Christ. Shameful in the son of a good father!... What is thy Academy but defiance of the Eternal Majesty? As well curse the Holy Ghost at once, for why should he who of preference seeketh a bed with the damned he disappointed? Or is thy audacity a blasphemous trial of the endurance of forgiveness?".... Exit Demedes, enter Lael.... "The child—she is a child! By such proof as there is in innocence, and in the loveliness of blushing cheeks, and eyes which answer the Heavenly light they let in by light as Heavenly let out, she is a child! What does evil see in her to set it hungering after her? Or is there in virtue a signal to its enemies—Lo, here! A light to be blown out, lest it disperse our darkness!".... Reenter Demedes.... "Abduct her!—How?—When? To that end is it thou keepest her always under eye? The Princess Irene gives a Fisherman's Fete—the child will be there—thou wilt be there. Is this the day of the attempt? Bravos as fishermen, to seize her—boats to carry her off—the Bosphorus wide and deep, and the hills beyond a hiding-place, and in the sky over them the awful name Turk. The crime and the opportunity hand in hand! Let them prosper now, and I who have from the cradle's side despatched my soul faith in hand to lay it at Heaven's gate may never again deny a merit in the invocation of Sin virtuous as prayer".... To Lael in the seat.... "But be not afraid. I will be there also. I"... A sudden fear fell upon him. If the abduction were indeed arranged for the afternoon, to what might he not be led by an open attempt to defeat it? Bloodshed—violence! He whose every dream had been of a life in which his fellow-men might find encouragement to endure their burdens, and of walking before them an example of love and forbearance, submissive and meek that he might with the more unanswerable grace preach obedience and fraternity to them— Merciful Heaven! And he shuddered and drew the veil hastily over his face, as if, in a bloody tumult, the ideal life, so the ultimate happiness, were vanishing before his eyes. Taking the confessions of such as have been greatly tried, few men, few even of those renowned for courage and fine achievement, ever pass their critical moments of decision unassailed by alternative suggestions due to fear. Sergius heard them now. "Return to thy cell, and to thy beads, and prayer," they seemed to say. "What canst thou, a stranger in a strange land, if once the Academy of which thou wert this morning informed, becomes thy enemy? Ay, return to thy cell! Who is she for whom thou art putting thyself in the way of temptation? The daughter of a booth-keeper in the bazaar—a Jew, who hath no princely blood to spare a descendant—a dog of a Jew, who maketh profit by lending his child to an impostor."

The suggestion was powerful. In the heat of the debate, however, an almost forgotten voice reached him, reciting one of the consolations of Father Hilarion: "Temptations are for all of us; nor shall any man be free of them. The most we can hope is to be delivered from them. What vanity to think we can travel threescore and ten years from our cradles, if so long we live, without an overture of some kind from the common enemy! On the other side, what a triumph to put his blandishments by! The Great Exemplar did not fly from Satan; he stayed, and overcame him."

"Be not afraid," Sergius said, as if to Lael, and firmly, like one resolved of fear and hesitation. "I will be there also."

Then looking about him, at his left hand he beheld the village of Emirghian, bent round a mountain's base, in places actually invading the water. In face of such a view a susceptible nature must needs be very sick of soul to go blindly on. The brightly painted houses cast tremulous reflections to a vast depth in the limpid flood, and where they ceased, down immeasurably, the vivid green of the verdure on the mountain's breast suggested the beginning of the next of the seven Mohammedan earths. Above this borrowed glory he seemed afloat; and to help the impression, the sound of many voices singing joyously was borne to him. He waved his hand, and the rowers, resting from their labor, joined him in listening.

The little gulf of Stenia lies there landlocked, and out of it a boat appeared, skimming around the intervening promontory. In a mass of flowers, in a shade of garlands hanging from a low mast, its arms and shrouds wreathed with roses, the singers sat timing their song with their oars. The refrain was supported by zitheras, flutes and horns. The vessel turned northwardly when fairly out in the strait; and then another boat came round the point— and another—and another—and many others, all decorated, and filled with men, women and children making music.

Sergius' boatmen recognized the craft, deep in the water, black and long, and with graceful upturned ends.

"Fishermen!" they said.

And he rejoined: "Yes. The Princess Irene gives them a fete. Make haste. I will go with them. Fall in behind."

"Yes, yes—a good woman! Of such are the Saints!" they said, signing the cross on breast arid brow.

The singing and the gala air of the party put Sergius in his wonted spirits; and as here and there other boats fell into the line, similarly decorated, their occupants adding to the volume of the singing, by the time Therapia was sighted the good-natured, happy fishermen had given him of their floral abundance, and adopted him.

What a scene the Therapian bay presented! Boats, boats, boats—hundreds of them in motion, hundreds lining the shore, the water faithfully repeating every detail of ornature, and apparently a-quiver with pleasure. The town was gay with colors; while on the summit and sides of the opposite promontory every available point answered flaunt with flaunt. And there were song and shouting, gladsome cries of children, responses of mothers, and merriment of youth and maiden. Byzantium might be in decadence, her provinces falling away, her glory wasting; the follies of the court and emperors, the best manhood of the empire lost in cloisters and hermitages, the preference of the nobility for intrigue and diplomacy might be all working their deplorable results—nay, the results might be at hand! Still the passion of the people for fetes and holidays remained. Tastes are things of heredity. In nothing is a Byzantine of this day so nearly a classic Greek as in his delicacy and appreciation where permitted to indulge in the beautiful.

The boatmen passed through the gay entanglement of the bay slowly and skilfully, and finally discharged their passengers on the marble quay a little below the regular landing in front of the red pavilion over the entrance to the Princess' grounds. The people went in and out of the gate without hindrance; nor was there guard or policeman visible. Their amiability attested their happiness.

The men were mostly black-bearded, sunburned, large-handed, brawny fellows in breeches black and amply bagged, with red sashes and light blue jackets heavily embroidered. The legs below the knees were exposed, and the feet in sandals. White cloths covered their heads. Their eyes were bright, their movements agile, their air animated. Many of them sported amulets of shell or silver suspended by ribbons or silken cords around their bare necks. The women wore little veils secured by combs, but rather as a headdress, and for appearances. They also affected the sleeveless short jacket over a snowy chemise; and what with bright skirts bordered with worsted chenille, and sandal straps carried artfully above the ankles, they were not wanting in picturesqueness. Some of the very young amongst them justified the loveliness traditionally ascribed to the nymphs of Hellas and the fair Cycladean Isles. Much the greater number, however, were in outward seeming prematurely old, and by their looks, their voices ungovernably shrill, and the haste and energy with which they flung themselves into the amusement of the hour unconsciously affirmed that fishermen's wives are the same everywhere. One need not go far to find the frontiers of society—too frequently they are close under the favorite balcony of the king.

Something on the right cheek of the gate under the pavilion furnished an attraction to the visitors. When Sergius came up, he was detained by a press of men and women in eager discussion; and following their eyes and the pointing of their fingers, he observed a brazen plate overhead curiously inscribed. The writing was unintelligible to him as to his neighbors. It looked Turkish—or it might have been Arabic—or it might not have been writing at all. He stayed awhile listening to the conjectures advanced. Presently a gypsy approached leading a bear, which, in its turn, was drawing a lot of noisy boys. He stopped, careless of the unfriendly glances with which he was received, and at sight of the plate saluted it with a low salaam several times unctuously repeated.

"Look at the hamari there. He can tell what the thing means."

"Then ask him."

"I will. See here, thou without a religion, consort of brutes! Canst thou tell what this"—pointing to the plate—"is for? Come and look at it!"

"It is not needful for me to go nearer. I see it well enough. Neither am I without a religion. I do not merely profess belief in God—I believe in Him," the bear-keeper replied.

The fisherman took the retort and the laugh it occasioned good-humoredly, and answered: "Very well, we are even; and now perhaps thou canst tell me what I asked."

"Willingly, since thou canst be decent to a stranger.... The young Mahommed, son of Amurath, Sultan of Sultans"—the gypsy paused to salute the title—"the young Mahommed, I say, is my friend." The bystanders laughed derisively, but the man proceeded. "He has resided this long time at Magnesia, the capital of a prosperous province assigned to his governorship. There never was one of such station so civil to his people, and much learning has had a good effect upon his judgment; it has taught him that the real virtue of amusement lies in its variety. Did he listen exclusively to his doctors discoursing of philosophy, or to his professor of mathematics, or to his poets and historians, he would go mad even as they are mad; wherefore, along with his studies, he hunts with hawk and hound; he tilts and tourneys; he plays the wandering minstrel; and not seldom Joqard and I—hey, fellow, is it not so?" he gave the bear a tremendous jerk—"Joqard and I have been to audience with him in his palace."

"A wonderful prince no doubt; but I asked not of him. The plate, man—what of this plate? If nothing, then give way to Joqard."

"There are fools and fools—that is, there are plain fools and wise fools. The wise fool answering the plain fool, is always more particular with his premises than his argument."

The laugh was with the hamari again; after which he continued: "So, having done with explanation, now to satisfy you."

From the breast of his gown, he brought forth a piece of bronze considerably less than the plate on the gate, but in every other respect its counterpart.

"See you this?" he said, holding the bronze up to view.

There was quick turning from plate to plate, and the conclusion was as quick.

"They are the same, but what of it?"

"This—Joqard and I went up one day and danced for the Prince, and at the end he dismissed us, giving me a red silk purse fat with gold pieces, and to Joqard this passport. Mark you now. The evil minded used to beat us with cudgels and stones—I mean among the Turk—but coming to a town now, I tie this to Joqard's collar, and we have welcome. We eat and drink, and are given good quarters, and sped from morning to morning without charge."

"There is some magic in the plate, then?"

"No," said the hamari, "unless there is magic in the love of a people for the Prince to be their ruler. It certifies Joqard and I are of Prince Mahommed's friends, and that is enough for Turks; and the same yonder. By the sign, I know this gate, these grounds, and the owner of them are in his protection. But," said the bear-keeper, changing his tone, "seeing one civil answer deserves another, when was Prince Mahommed here?"

"In person? Never."

"Oh, he must have been."

"Why do you say so?"

"Because of the brass plate yonder."

"What does it prove?"

"Ah, yes!" the man answered laughingly. "Joqard and I pick up many odd things, and meet a world of people—don't we, fellow?" Another furious jerk of the leading strap brought a whine from the bear, "But it is good for us. We teach school as we go; and you know, my friend, for every *solidus* its equivalent in *noumia* is somewhere."

"I will give you a *noumia*, if you will give me an answer."

"A bargain—a bargain, with witnesses!"

Then after a glance into the faces around, as if summoning attention to the offer, the hamari proceeded.

"Listen. I say the brass up there proves Prince Mahommed was here in person. Wishing to notify his people that he had taken in his care everything belonging to this property, the owner included, the Prince put his signature to the proclamation."

"Proclamation?"

"Yes—you may call it plain brass, if you prefer; none the less the writing on it is *Mahommed*: and because such favors must bear his name on them, they are reserved for his giving. No other man, except the great Sultan, his father, would bestow one of them. Joqard had his from the Prince's hand directly; wherefore—I hope, friend, you have the *noumia* ready—the brass on this post must have been fixed there by the Prince with his own hand."

The fishermen were satisfied; and it was wonderful how interesting the safeguard then became to them. By report they knew Mahommed the prospective successor of the terrible Amurath; they knew him a soldier conspicuous in many battles; and from the familiar principle by which we admire or dread those possessed of qualities unlike and superior to our own, their ideas and speculations concerning him were wild and generally harsh. Making no doubt now that he had really been to the gate, they asked themselves, What could have been his object? To look at the plate was next thing to looking at the man. Even Sergius partook of the feeling. To get a better view, he shifted his position, and was beset by inquietudes not in the understanding of the fishermen.

The Princess Irene, her property and dependents, were subjects of protection by the Moslem; that much was clear; but did she know the fact? Had she seen the Prince? Then the Hegumen's criticism upon the persistence with which she kept her residence here, a temptation to the brutalized unbeliever on the other shore, derived a point altogether new.

Sergius turned away, and passed into the well-tended grounds. While too loyal to the little mother, as he tenderly called the Princess, to admit a suspicion against her, with painful clearness, he perceived the opportunity the affair offered her enemies for the most extreme accusations; and he resolved to speak to her, and, if necessary, to remonstrate.

Traversing the shelled roadway up to the portico of the palace, he looked back through the red pavilion, and caught a glimpse of Joqard performing before a merry group of boys and elders male and female.

CHAPTER X
THE HAMARI

The love of all things living which was so positively a trait of character with the Princess Irene was never stinted in her dealings with her own country folk. On this occasion her whole establishment at Therapia was accorded her guests; yet, while they wandered at will merry-making through the gardens, and flashed their gay colors along the side and from the summit of the promontory, they seemed to have united in holding the palace in respectful reserve. None of them, without a special request, presumed to pass the first of the steps leading up into the building.

When Sergius, approaching from the outer gate, drew nigh the front of the palace, he was brought to a stop by a throng of men and women packed around a platform the purpose of which was declared by its use. It was low, but of generous length and breadth, and covered with fresh sail-cloth; at each corner a mast had been raised, with yard-arms well squared, and dressed profusely in roses, ferns, and acacia fronds. On a gallery swung to the base of the over-pending portico, a troupe of musicians were making the most of flute, cithara, horn, and kettle-drum, and not vainly, to judge from the flying feet of the dancers in possession of the boards.

Lifting his eyes above the joyous exhibition, he beheld the carven capitals of the columns, tied together with festoonery of evergreens, and relieved by garlands of shining flowers, and above the musicians, under a canopy shading her from the meridian sun, the Princess Irene herself. A bright carpet hanging down the wall enriched the position chosen by her, and in the pleasant shade, surrounded by young women, she sat with uncovered head and face, delighted with the music and the dancing—delighted that it was in her power to bring together so many souls to forget, though so briefly, the fretting of hard conditions daily harder growing. None knew better than she the rapidity of the national decadence.

It was not long until the young hostess noticed Sergius, taller of his high hat and long black gown; and careless as usual of the conventionalities, she arose, and beckoned to him with her fan; and the people, seeing whom she thus honored, opened right and left, and with good-will made way for him. Upon his coming her attendants drew aside—all but one, to whom for the moment he gave but a passing look.

The Princess received him seated. The youthful loveliness of her countenance seemed refined by the happiness she was deriving from the spectacle before her. He took the hand she extended him, kissed it respectfully, with only a glance at the simple but perfected Greek of her costume, and immediately the doubts, and fears, and questions, and lectures in outline he had brought with him from the city dropped out of mind. Suspicion could not look at her and live.

"Welcome, Sergius," she said, with dignity. "I was afraid you would not come to-day."

"Why not? If my little mother's lightest suggestions are laws with me, what are her invitations?"

For the first time he had addressed her by the affectionate term, and the sound was startling. The faintest flush spread over her cheek, admonishing him that the familiarity had not escaped attention. Greatly to his relief, she quietly passed the matter.

"You were at the *Pannychides?*" she asked.

"Yes, till daybreak."

"I thought so, and concluded you would be too weary to see us to-day. The Mystery is tedious."

"It might become so if too frequently celebrated. As it was, I shall not forget the hillside, and the multitude of frocked and cowled figures kneeling in the dim red light of the torches. The scene was awful."

"Did you see the Emperor?"

She put the question in a low tone.

"No," he returned. "His Majesty sent for our Hegumen to come to the Chapel. The good man took me with him, his book and torch bearer; but when we arrived, the Emperor had passed in and closed the door, and I could only imagine him on his knees alone in the room, except as the relics about him were company."

"How unspeakably dismal!" she said with a shudder, adding in sorrowful reflection, "I wish I could help him, for he is a prince with a tender conscience; but there is no way—at least Heaven does not permit me to see anything for him in my gift but prayer."

Sergius followed her sympathetically, and was surprised when she continued, the violet gray of her eyes changing into subtle fire. "A sky all cloud; the air void of hope; enemies mustering everywhere on land; the city, the court, the Church rent by contending factions—behold how a Christian king, the first one in generations, is plagued! Ah, who can interpret for Providence? And what a miracle is prophecy!"

Thereupon the Princess bethought herself, and cast a hurried glance out over the garden.

"No, no! If these poor souls can forget their condition and be happy, why not we? Tell me good news, Sergius, if you have any—only the good. But see! Who is he making way through the throng yonder? And what is it he is leading?"

The transition of feeling, though sudden and somewhat forced, was successful; the Princess' countenance again brightened; and turning to follow her direction, Sergius observed Lael, who had not fallen back with the other attendants. The girl had been a modest listener; now there was a timid half smile on her face, and a glistening welcome in her eyes. His gaze stopped short of the object which had inspired his hostess with such interest, and dropped to the figured carpet at the guest's feet; for the feeling the recognition awakened was clouded with the taunt Demedes had flung at him in the hall of the monastery, and he questioned the rightfulness of this appearance. If she were not the daughter of the Prince of India, she was an—impostor was the word in his mind.

"I was expecting you," she said to him, artlessly.

Sergius raised his face, and was about to speak, when the Princess started from her seat, and moved to the low balustrade of the portico.

"Come," she called, "come, and tell me what this is."

Sergius left a friendly glance with Lael.

Where the roadway from the gate led up to the platform an opening had been made in the close wall of spectators attracted by the music and dancing. In the opening, the hamari was slowly coming forward, his turban awry, his brown face overrun and shining with perspiration, his sharp gypsy eyes full of merriment. With the leading strap over a shoulder, he tugged at Joqard. Sergius laughed to see the surprise of the men and women, and at the peculiar yells and screams with which they struggled to escape. But everybody appearing in good nature, he said to the Princess: "Do not be concerned. A Turk or Persian with a trained bear. I passed him at the gate."

He saw the opportunity of speaking about the brass plate on the post, and while debating whether to avail himself of it, the hamari caught sight of the party at the edge of the portico, stopped, surveyed them, then prostrated himself in the abjectest Eastern manner. The homage was of course to the Princess—so at least the assemblage concluded; and jumping to the idea that the bear-keeper had been employed by her for their divertisement, each man in the company resolved himself into an ally and proceeded to assist him. The musicians were induced to suspend their performance, and the dancers to vacate the platform; then, any number of hands helping them up, Joqard and his master were promoted to the boards, sole claimants of attention and favor.

The fellow was not in the least embarrassed. He took position on the platform in front of the Princess, and again saluted her Orientally, and with the greatest deliberation, omitting no point of the prostration. Bringing the bear to a sitting posture with folded paws, he bowed right and left to the spectators, and made a speech in laudation of Joqard. His grimaces and gesticulation kept the crowd in a roar; when addressing the Princess, his manner was respectful, even courtierly. Joqard and he had travelled the world over; they had been through the Far East, and through the lands of the Frank and Gaul; they had crossed Europe from Paris to the Black Sea, and up to the Crimea; they had appeared before the great everywhere— Indian Rajahs, Tartar Khans, Persian Shahs, Turkish Sultans; there was no language they did not understand. The bear, he insisted, was the wisest of animals, the most susceptible of education, the most capable and willing in service. This the ancients understood better than the moderns, for in recognition of his superiority they had twice exalted him to the Heavens, and in both instances near the star that knew no deviation. The hamari was a master of amplification, and his anecdotes never failed their purpose.

"Now," he said, "I do not care what the subject of discourse may be; one thing is true—my audience is always composed of believers and unbelievers; and as between them"—here he addressed himself to the Princess—"as between them, O Most Illustrious of women, my difficulty has been to determine which class is most to be feared. Every philosopher must admit there is quite as much danger in the man who withholds his faith when it ought to be given, as in his opposite who hurries to yield it without reason. My rule as an auditor is to wait for demonstration. So"— turning to the assemblage—"if here any man or woman doubts that the bear is the wisest of animals, and Joqard the most learned and accomplished of bears, I will prove it." Then Joqard was called on.

"For attend, O Illustrious Princess!—and look ye, O men and women, pliers of net and boat!—look ye all! Now shall Joqard himself speak for Joqard."

The hamari began talking to the bear in a jargon utterly unintelligible to his hearers, though they fell to listening with might and main, and were silent that they might hear. Nothing could have been more earnest than his communications, whatever they were; at times he put an arm about the brute's neck; at times he whispered in its ear; and in return it bowed and grunted assent, or growled and shook its head in refusal, always in the most knowing manner. In this style, to appearance, he was telling what he wanted done. Then retaining the leading strap, the master stepped aside, and Joqard, left to himself, proceeded to prove his intelligence and training by facing the palace, bringing his arms overhead, and falling forward. Everybody understood the honor intended for the Princess; the bystanders shouted; the attendants on the portico clapped their hands, for indeed never in their remembrance had the prostration been more profoundly executed. Arising nimbly the performer wheeled about, reared on his hind feet, clasped his paws on his head, and acknowledged the favor of the commonalty by resolving himself into a great fur ball, and rolling a somersault. The acclamation became tumultuous. One admirer ran off and returned with an armful of wreaths and garlands, and presently Joqard was wearing them royally.

With excellent judgment the hamari proceeded next to hurry the exhibition, passing from one trick to another almost without pause until the wrestling match was reached. This has been immemorially the reliable point in performances of the kind he was giving, but he introduced it in a manner of his own.

Standing by the edge of the platform, as the friend and herald of Joqard, he first loudly challenged the men before him, every one ambitious of honor and renown, to come up and try a fall; and upon their hanging back, he berated them. Wherever a tall man stood observable above the level of heads, he singled him out. Failing to secure a champion, he finally undertook the contest himself.

"Ho, Joqard," he cried, while tying the leading strap around the brute's neck, "thou fearest nothing. Thy dam up in the old Caucasian cave was great of heart, and, like her, thou wouldst not quail before Hercules, were he living. But thou shalt not lick thy paws and laugh, thinking Hercules hath no descendant."

Retiring a few steps he tightened the belt about his waist, and drew his leathern jacket closer.

"Get ready!" he cried.

Joqard answered promptly and intelligently by standing up and facing him, and in sign of satisfaction with the prospect of an encounter so to his taste, he lolled the long red tongue out of his jaws. Was he licking his chops in anticipation of a feast or merely laughing? The beholders became quiet; and Sergius for the first time observed how very low in stature the hamari seemed.

"Look out, look out! O thou with the north star in the tip of thy tail! I am coming—for the honor of mankind, I am coming."

They danced around each other watching for an opening. "Aha! Now thou thinkest to get the advantage. Thou art proud of thy fame, and cunning, but I am a man. I have been in many schools. Look out!"

The hamari leaped in and with both hands caught the strap looped around Joqard's neck; at the same time he was himself caught in Joqard's ready arms. The growl with which the latter received the attack was angry, and lent the struggle much more than a mere semblance of danger. Round and about they were borne; now forward, then back; sometimes they were likely to tumble from the boards. The hamari's effort was to choke Joqard into submission; Joqard's was to squeeze the breath out of the hamari's body; and they both did their parts well.

After some minutes the man's exertions became intermittent. A little further on the certainty of triumph inspired Joqard to fierce utterances; his growls were really terrible, and he hugged so mercilessly his opponent grew livid in the face. The women and children began to cry and scream, and many of the men shouted in genuine alarm: "See, see! The poor fellow is choking to death!" The excitement and fear extended to the portico; some of the attendants there, unable to endure the sight, fled from it. Lael implored Sergius to save the hamari. Even the Princess was undecided whether the acting was real or affected.

Finally the crisis came. The man could hold out no longer; he let go his grip on the strap, and, struggling feebly to loose his body from the great black arms, shouted hoarsely: "Help, help!" As if he had not strength to continue the cry, he threw his hands up, and his head back gasping.

The Princess Irene covered her eyes. Sergius stepped over the balustrade; but before he could get further, a number of men were on the stage making to the rescue. And seeing them come, the hamari laid one hand on the strap, and with the other caught the tongue protruding from Joqard's open jaws; as a further point in the offensive so suddenly resumed, he planted a foot heavily on one of his antagonist's. Immediately the son of the proud Caucasian dam was flat on the boards simulating death.

Then everybody understood the play, and the merriment was heightened by the speech the hamari found opportunity to make his rescuers before they could recover from their astonishment and break up the tableau they formed. The Princess, laughing through her tears, flung the victor some gold pieces, and Lael tossed her fan to him. The prostrations with which he acknowledged the favors were marvels to behold.

By and by, quiet being restored, Joqard was roused from his trance, and the hamari, calling the musicians to strike up, concluded the performance with a dance.

Milton Keynes UK
Ingram Content Group UK Ltd.
UKHW030622061024
449204UK00004B/408

9 789362 096746